AF572100

Photographing Baby and Child

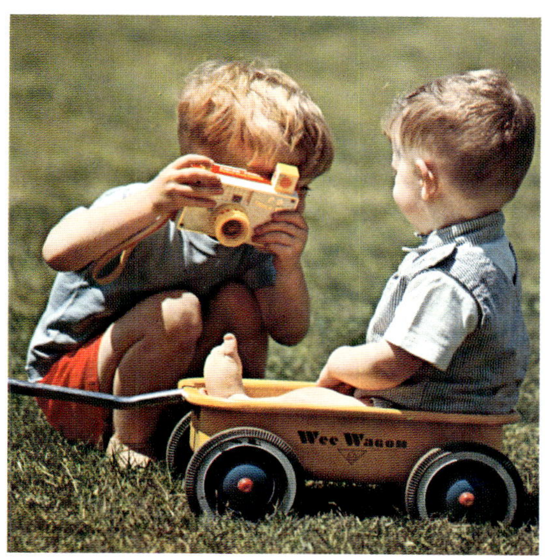

Ronald Bloomquist

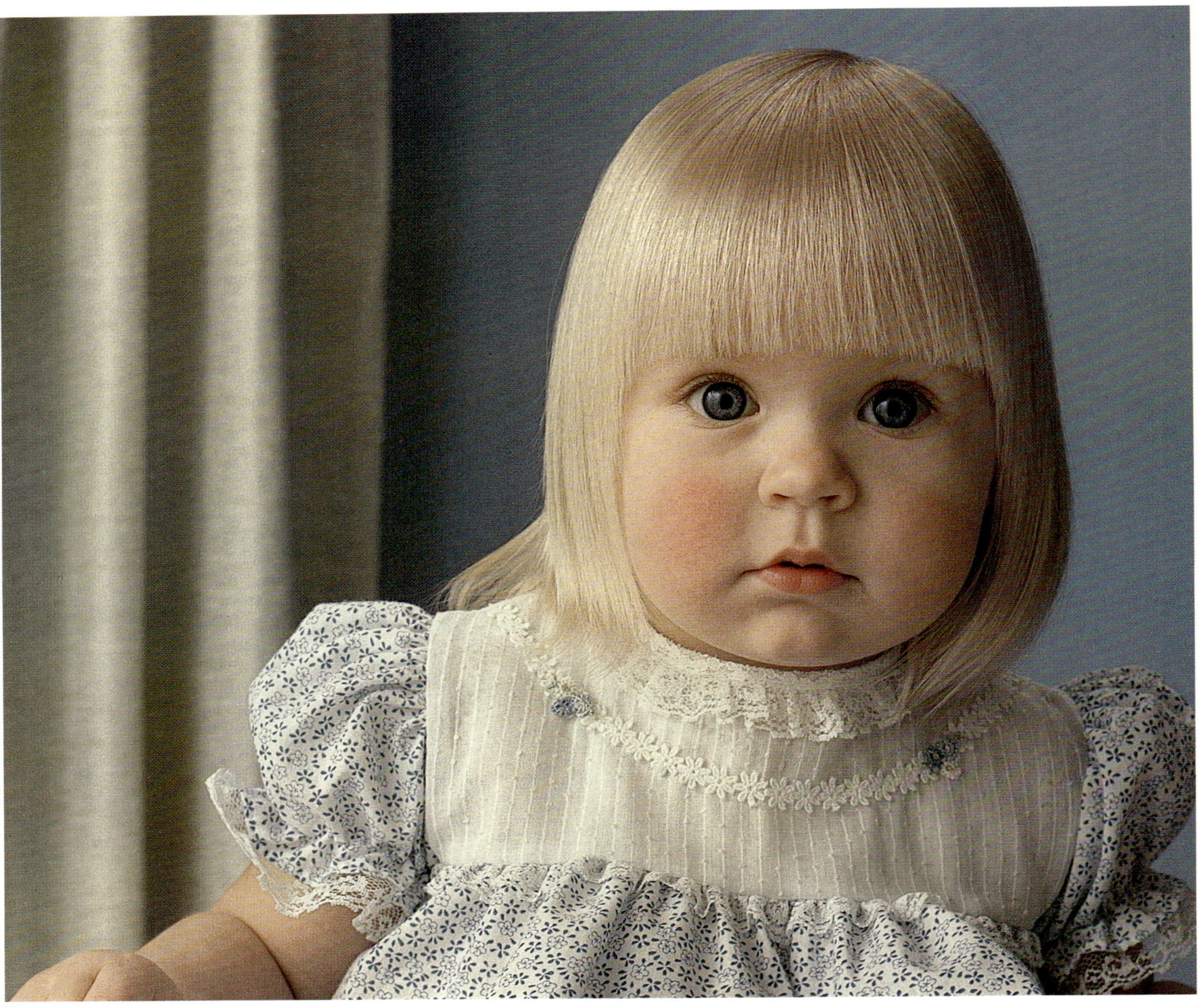
Norm Kerr

Somebody's Child

Just a picture of Somebody's child,—
Sweet face set in golden hair,
Violet eyes, and cheeks of rose,
Rounded chin, with a dimple there.

Tender eyes where the shadows sleep,
Lit from within by a secret ray,—
Tender eyes that will shine like stars
When love and womanhood come this way:

Scarlet lips with a story to tell,—
Blessed be he who shall find it out,
Who shall learn the eyes' deep secret well,
And read the heart with never a doubt.

LOUISE CHANDLER MOULTON

PHOTOGRAPHING
Baby and Child

Edited by George Hornby and the Editors of
EASTMAN KODAK COMPANY

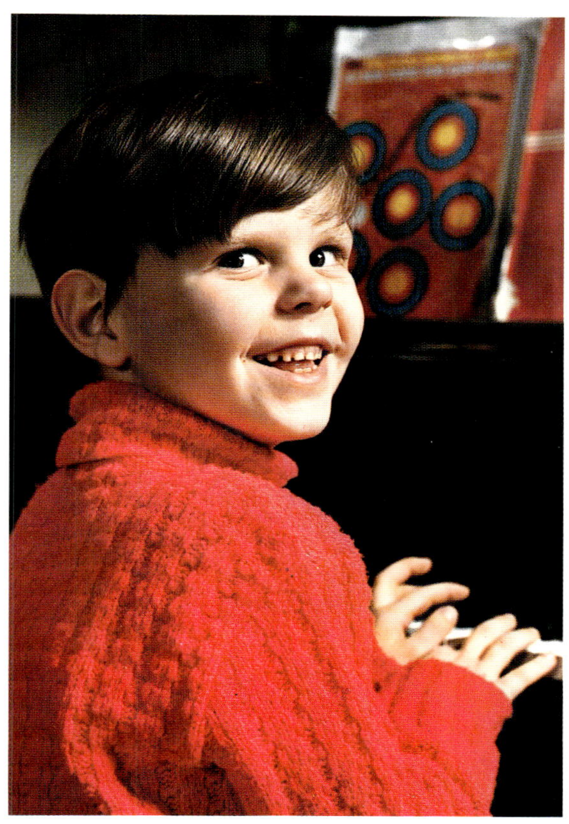

CROWN PUBLISHERS, INC. : NEW YORK

Gary Vaughn

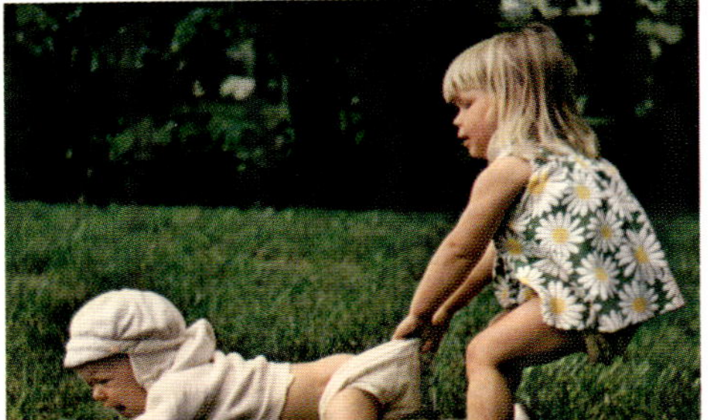

Published simultaneously in Canada by General Publishing Company Limited
Designed by George Hornby
Printed in the United States of America

Library of Congress Cataloging in Publication Data

Main Entry under title:

Photographing Baby and Child.

Includes index.
1. Photography of children. I. Hornby, George. II. Eastman Kodak Company.

TR575.P63 778.9'25 77-6476
ISBN 0-517-53016-3

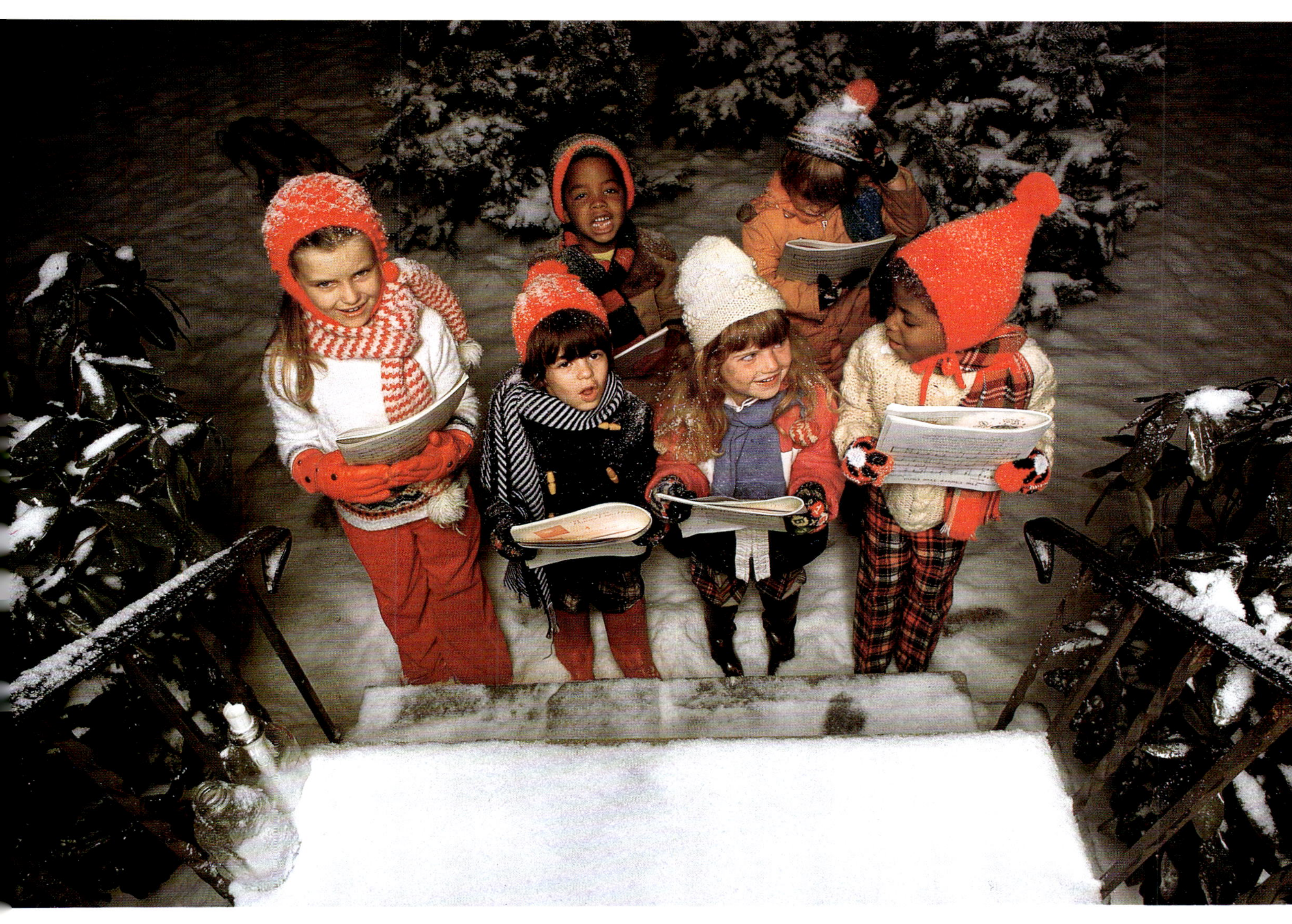

Christmastime and children—an ideal combination for providing plenty of picture opportunities. *See Special Occasions, pages 110-117.*

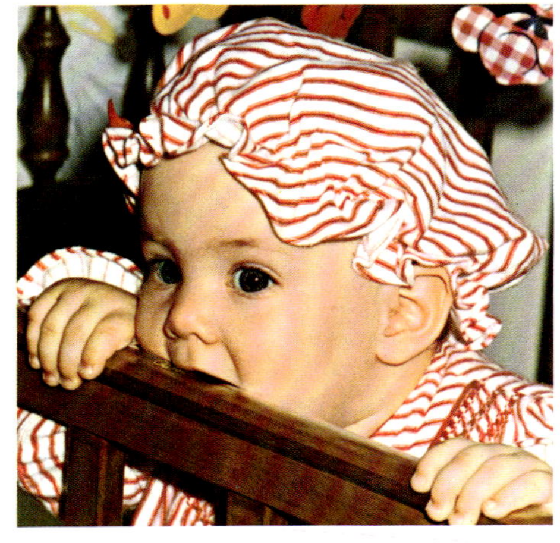

Table of Contents

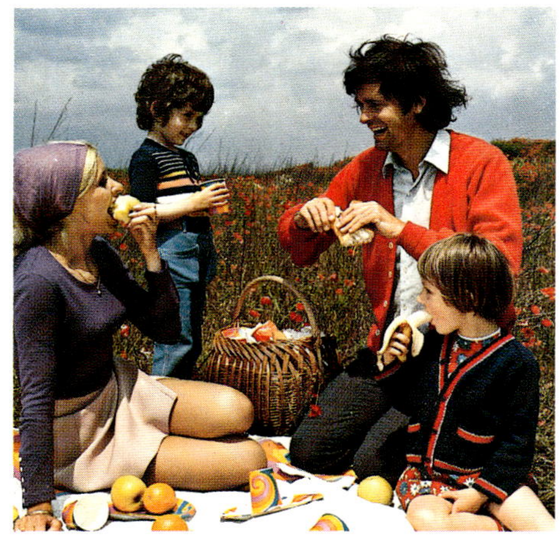

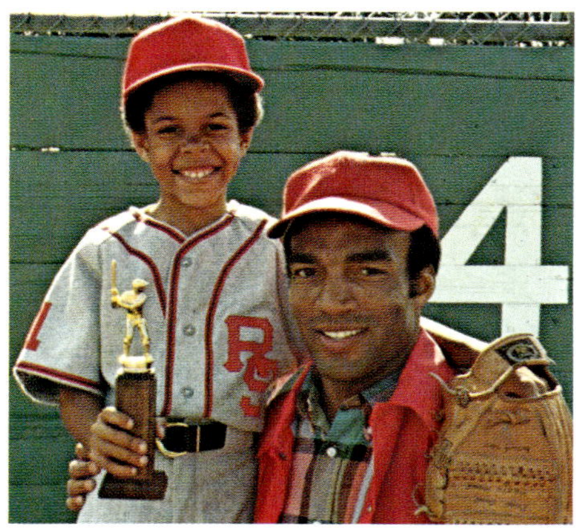

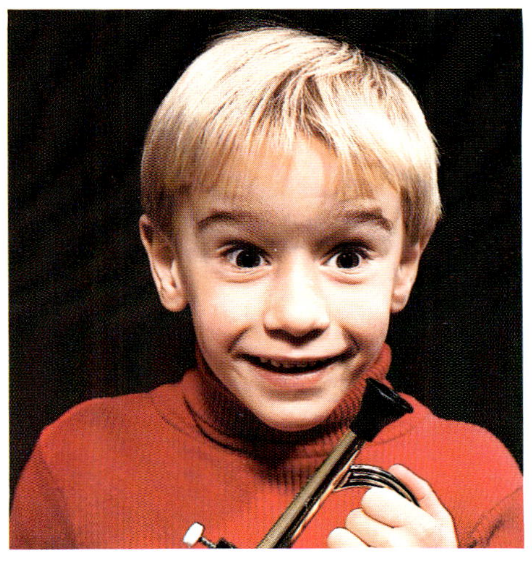

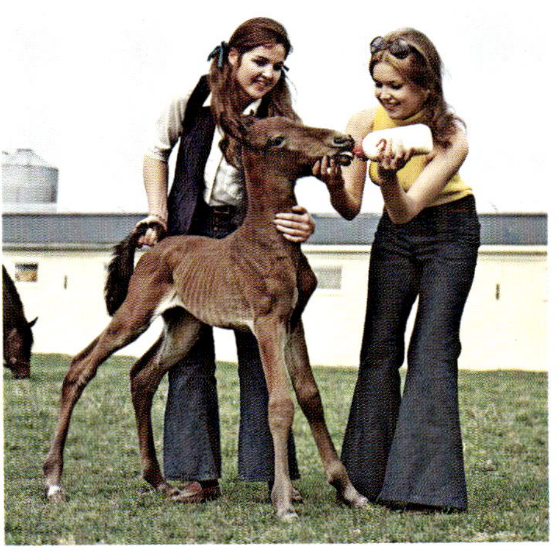

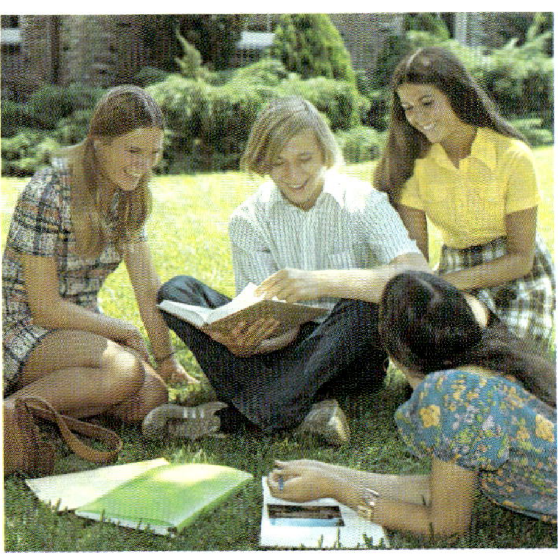

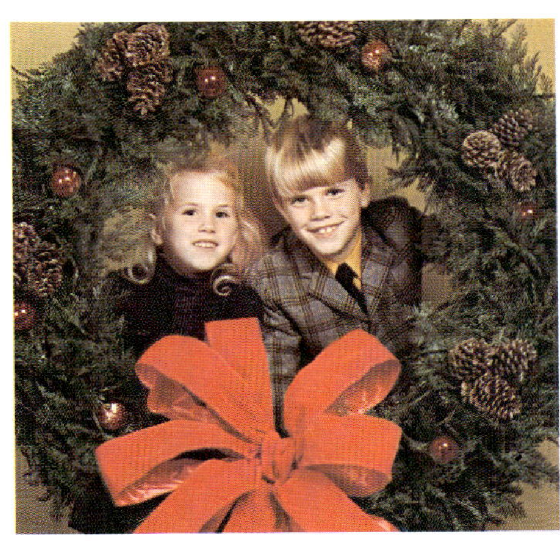

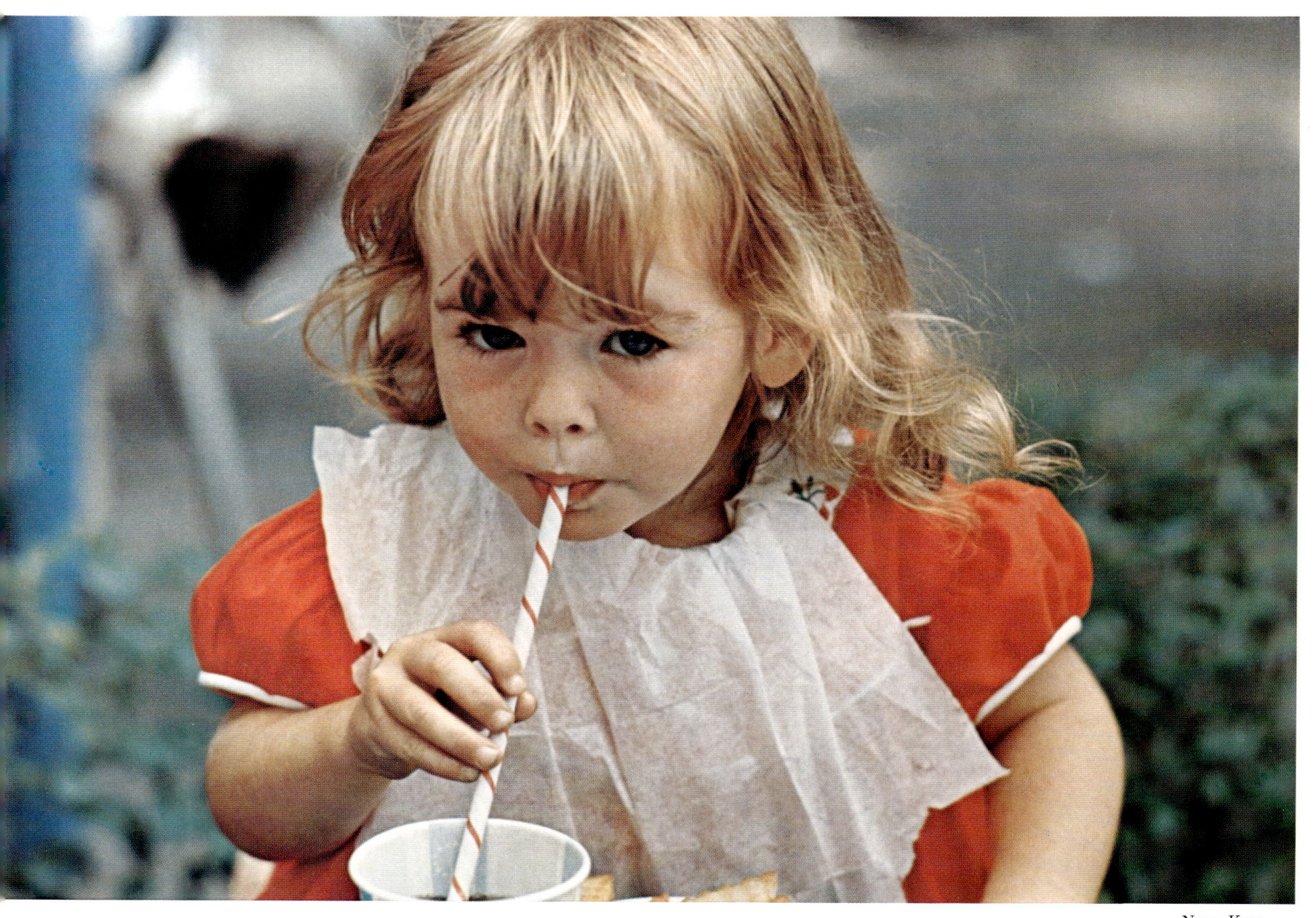

Norm Kerr

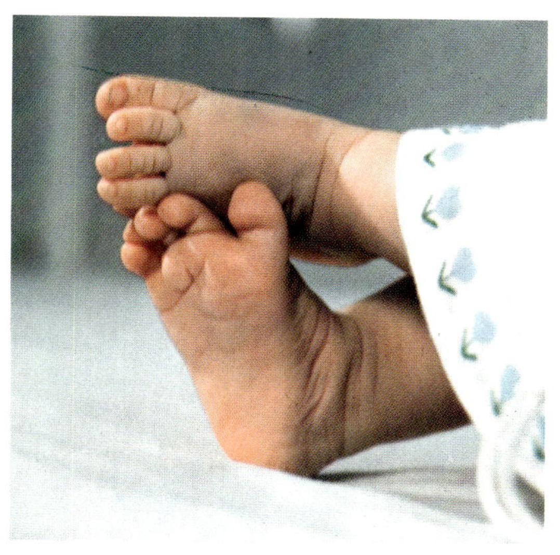

A Time for Taking Pictures

In the pages that follow, we've presented—in pictures and words—inspiration, ideas, and technical advice to help you achieve the finest pictures of your sprouting offspring. Whether your camera is simple or complex and whether your photographic interests tend toward making you the casual, family historian or the serious photo hobbyist, you're sure to find plenty of illustrations and tips to help motivate and guide you toward making better pictures of your children.

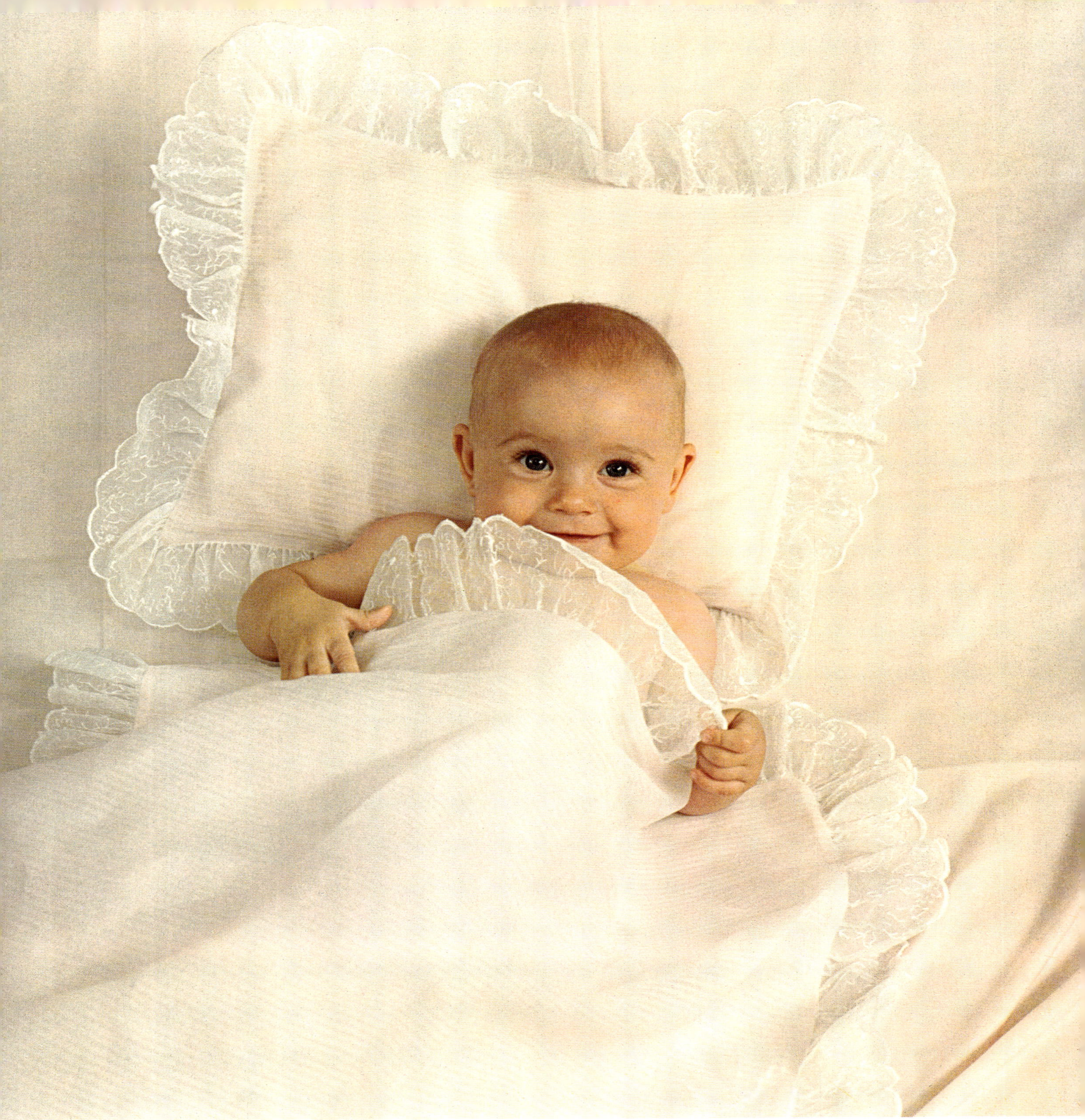

H. Halma

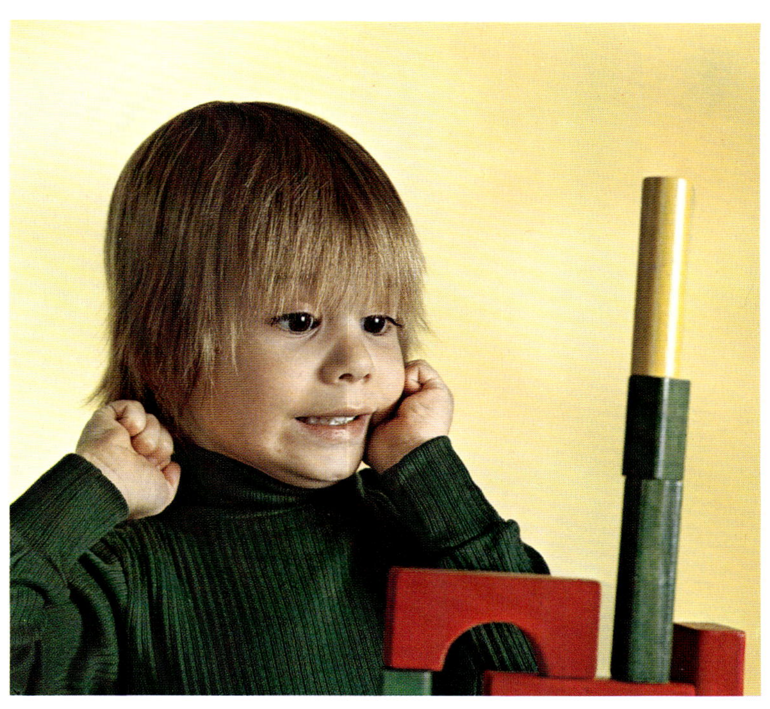

Part One: Baby and Child

We think we remember the growth of our children, and we do remember the high spots. The triumphs and minor tragedies. But how much we miss with the camera of our memory. For the life of a child is a kaleidoscope of changing moods, aptitudes, activities, and developing personality and physical growth. Photographs help us capture these facets to enjoy ourselves and to pass on to our children and our children's children. But we must realize that the pictures we can chortle or sigh over tomorrow we have to take today.

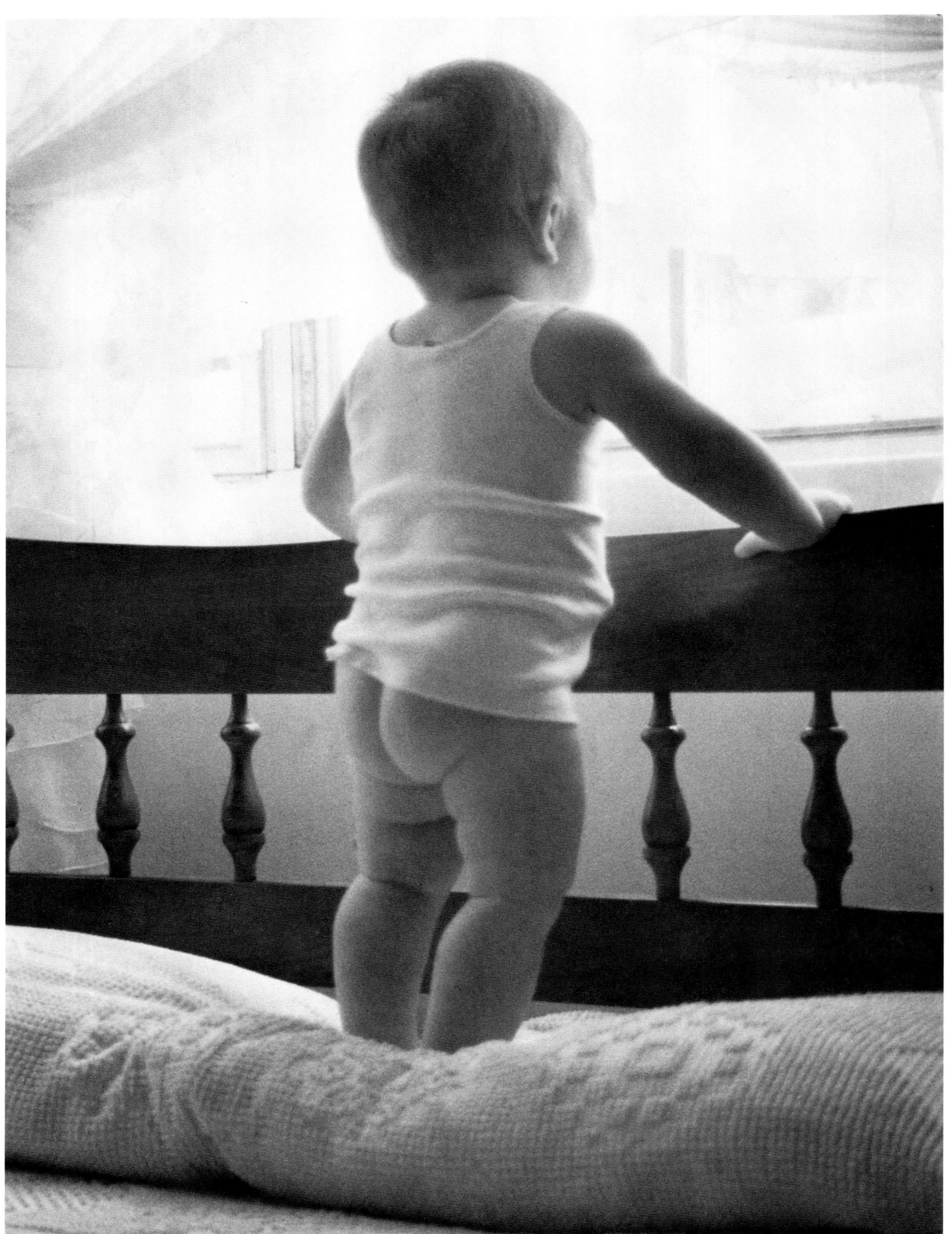

April Petrone

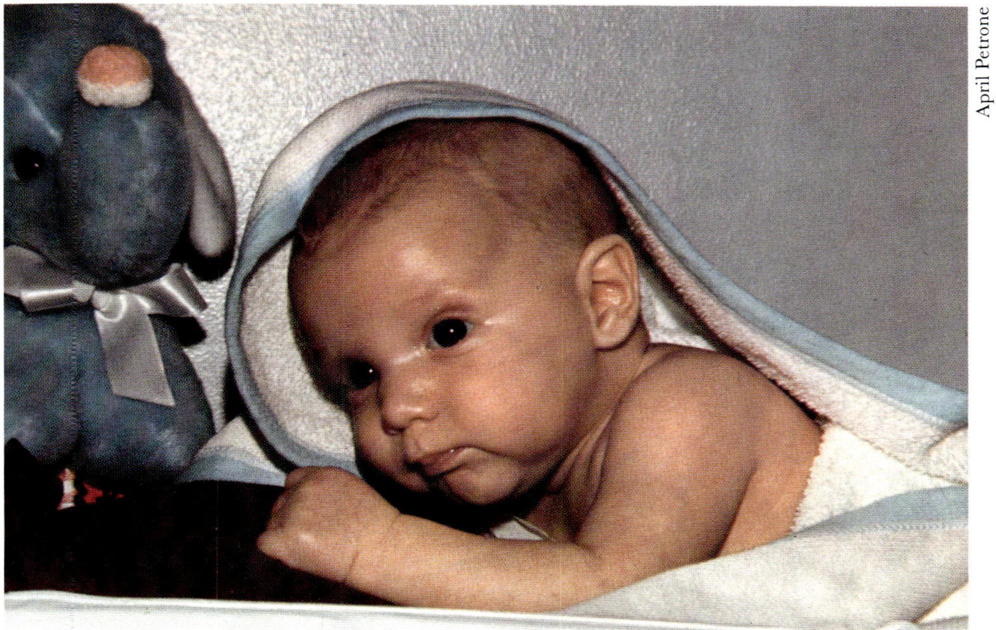

April Petrone

Flash and KODACOLOR II Film were used here to capture this effective close-up.

The New Baby

Let's begin our discussion on photographing children at the logical point—the birth of a baby. If you are about to be proud parents, there's little or no need to remind you to have your camera ready for the big event. You have both looked forward to this exciting time for months and most likely have built up an enthusiasm which is now being shared by your close friends and relatives. To reinforce the news of the baby's arrival, pictures are a must.

You can start making pictures of your latest arrival right in the hospital. There's a miraculous newness to every baby, and your hospital pictures will provide a good comparison with later ones.

Many hospital nurseries are lighted brightly enough to permit picture-taking without flash if you have an automatic or adjustable camera with an *f*/1.9 or *f*/2.8 lens. Be careful not to include any bright outside windows in your picture. The light from the window will cause the camera exposure meter to give an incorrect reading resulting in an underexposed picture with subjects in front of the window appearing as silhouettes.

Although we'll be talking about flash techniques in detail in PART TWO, there's one important point to consider when taking flash pictures of the baby in the hospital nursery area. Nurseries are protected from the outside world by large glass windows. Unfortunately for photography, the baby often must remain on one side while the camera-carrying parent—with nose pressed to the glass—views from the other side. Although the glass is transparent, it does have a nasty habit of reflecting light from the flash. You can avoid harsh flash reflections by taking your pictures at an oblique angle to the glass, rather than head-on.

To get a close-up photo of the baby at this point, you'll need the assistance of the nurse. Ask the nurse to either hold the newborn up so that

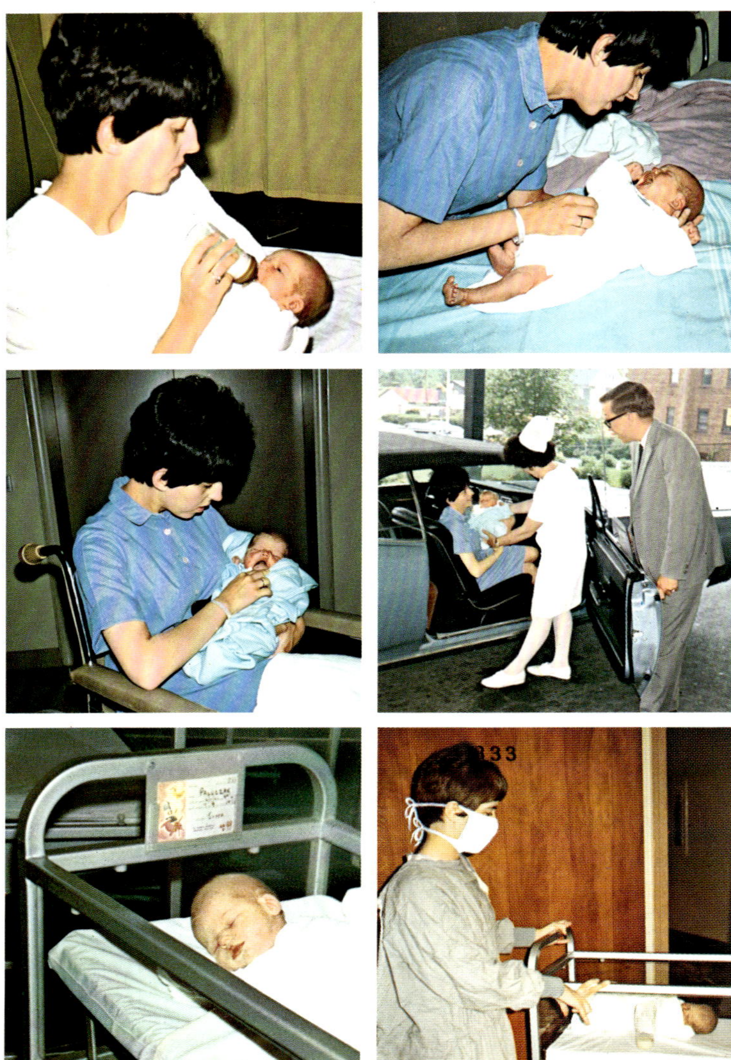

Start making pictures of your infant right at the hospital. Include a photo of the entire family in your story by asking a roommate or hospital aide to snap a picture of Mom, Dad, and Baby together.

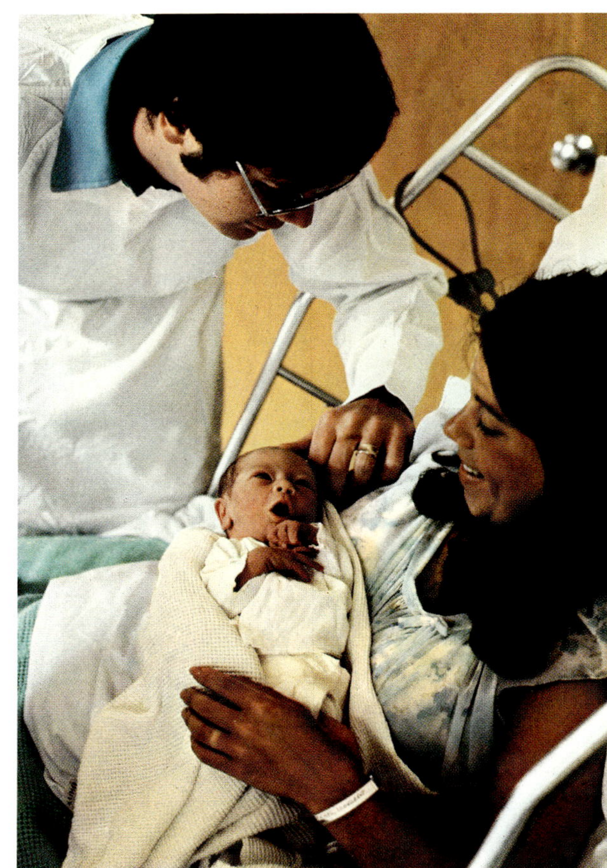

Tom McCarthy

you can take pictures or move the bassinet to some convenient location near the nursery window. Move in as close as you can to the window.

You might like to consider using an instant camera for recording the newborn. Instant pictures can keep this important day in your life fresh in your mind from just moments after you press the shutter release on the camera. Take instant prints of the baby to show your friends and relatives and children at home. An instant print of the brand-new family addition, along with a birth announcement tucked into an envelope, can be sent to a relative who is unable to be with you at this exciting time.

Regardless of the type of camera, be sure that it stays with Mom in the hospital so that she can take pictures whenever there's a good opportunity. She might want to ask a hospital aide or a roommate to take a picture while she's holding the baby.

Your baby book could tell a picture story of the hospital stay. In addition to the photo situations we've already mentioned, the story could include a picture of Mom's first opportunity to dress the baby. If you have a friend along on the going-home day, this person could take a picture for you so that the whole family will be in the scene.

Tom McCarthy

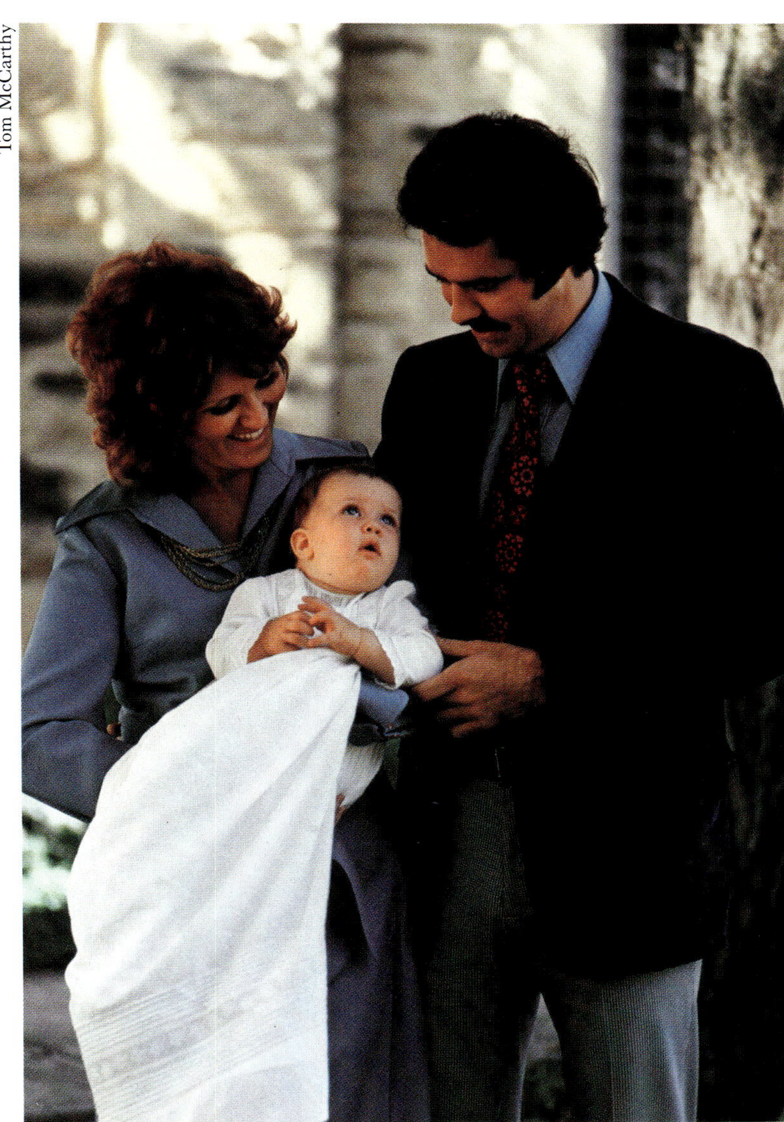

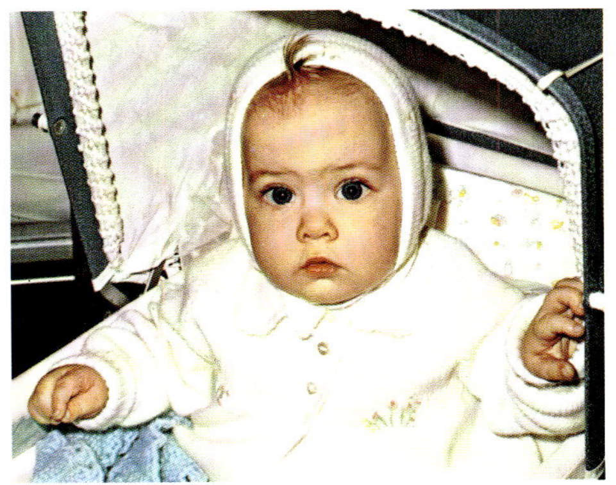

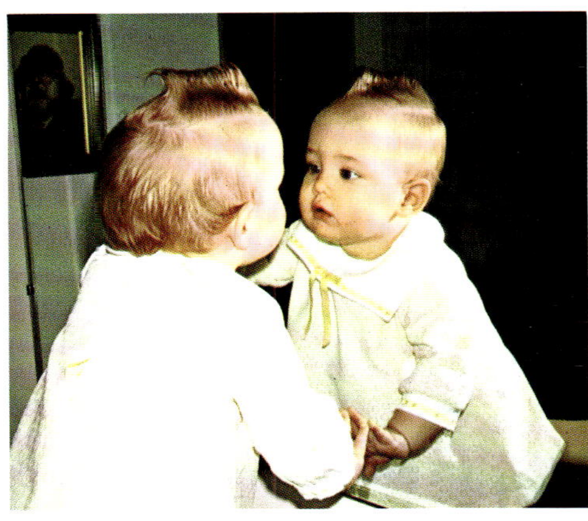

Be ready to record each of your baby's discoveries for your picture album by keeping a camera and some extra film always close at hand.

The first few weeks and months will be filled with lots of firsts for the new parents as well as for the baby! No photographic chronicle of babyhood should ignore these activities. Keep the camera handy to snap pictures of Grampa and Gramma holding the baby; the struggle with soap, water, and slippery infant at bath time; and the little one tucked into bed for the night.

Take pictures of the baby's regular routine. They'll bring back happy memories in the years ahead. For the easiest and best nap-time picture, roll the crib or bassinet near a window that is flooded with bright daylight. You'll be able to snap away just as though you were outdoors.

Nearly all baby photos should be taken close-up, so move in as close as your camera will allow. Even most inexpensive cameras will allow you to be as close as 4 feet away from your child—a good distance to record the happy smiles, funny mannerisms, and waving arms and legs.

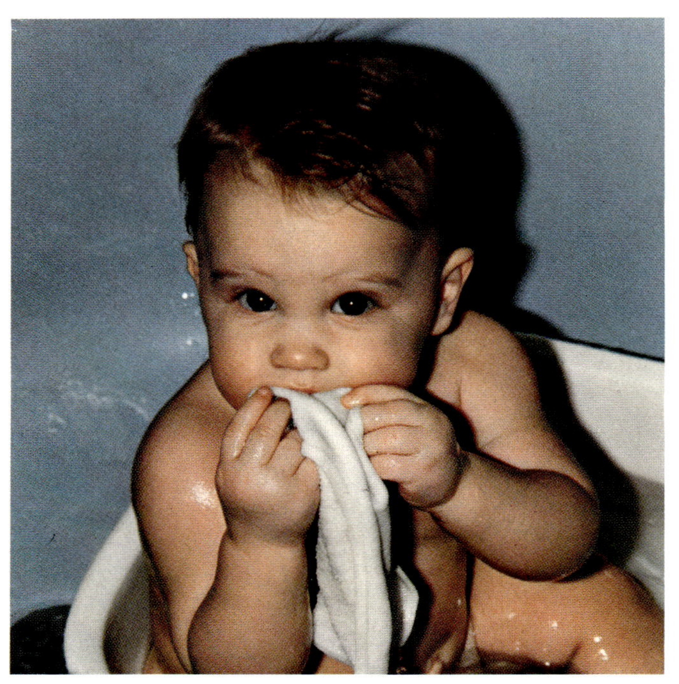

April Petrone

At ages from 3 to 6 months, babies become capable of really doing things. Although perhaps not ready to solo in a high-chair or baby seat, they manage quite well when propped up by a pillow or two. Put a rattle, stuffed toy, or soft blanket into the hands of a baby, and you'll have all the snapshot material your camera can handle. Whenever you have control over the location of the picture subject, as you do here, choose a spot that provides a plain, uncluttered background. Backgrounds with lots of distracting detail can make your picture look disorganized and draw attention away from the little one.

If the baby loses interest in the toy before you've finished taking pictures, provide some entertainment by making a noise with a toy or a song.

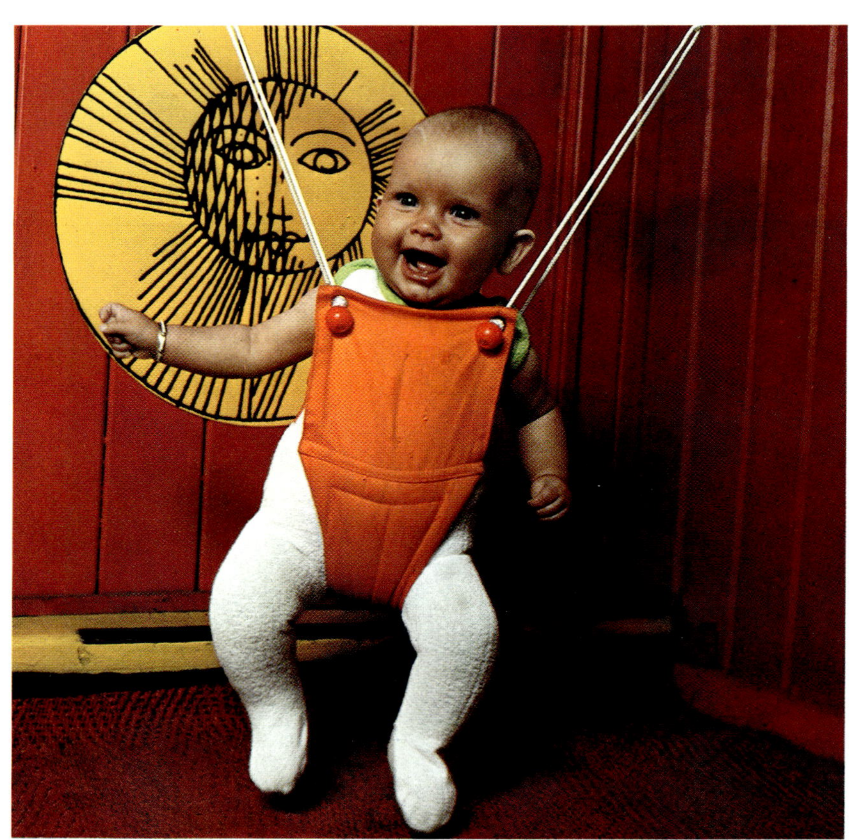

Norm Kerr

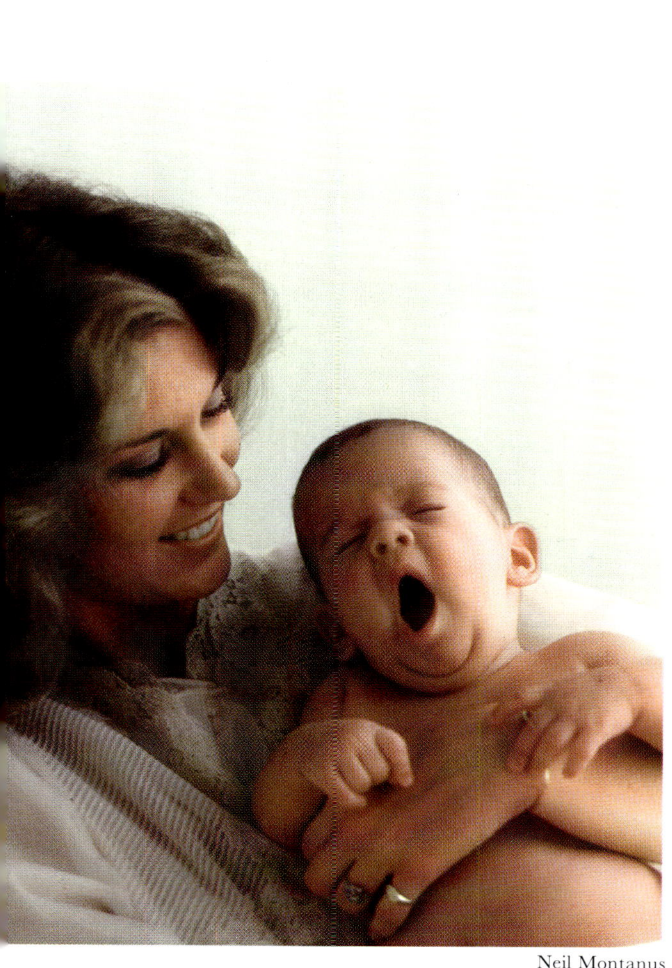

Neil Montanus

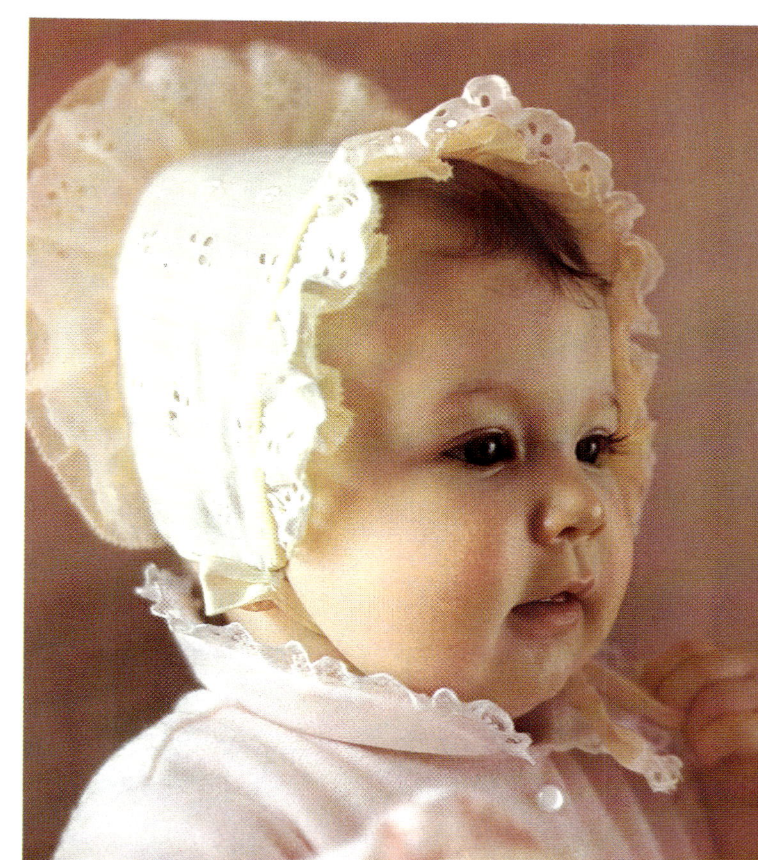

Emiel Blaakman

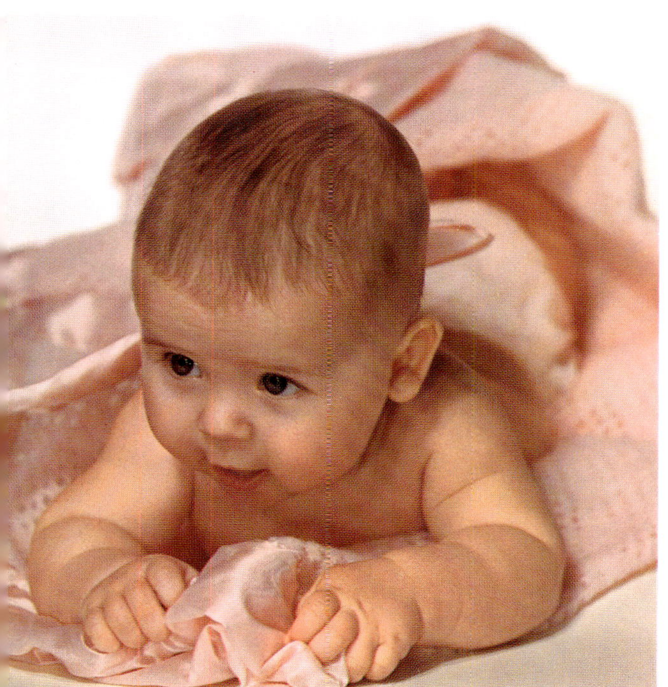

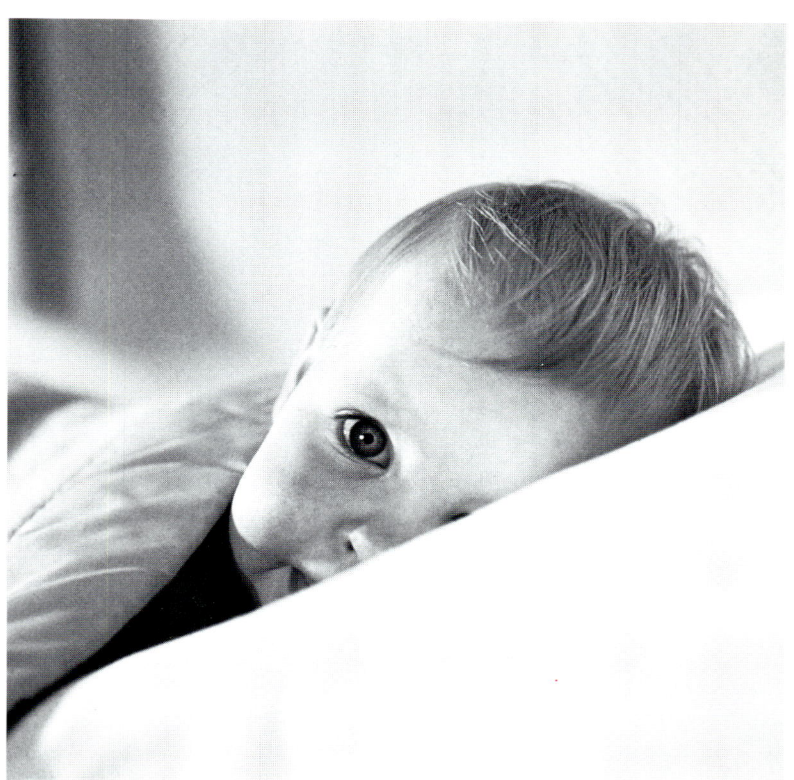

For photos with impact, move in with your camera as close as you can to your tiny tot.

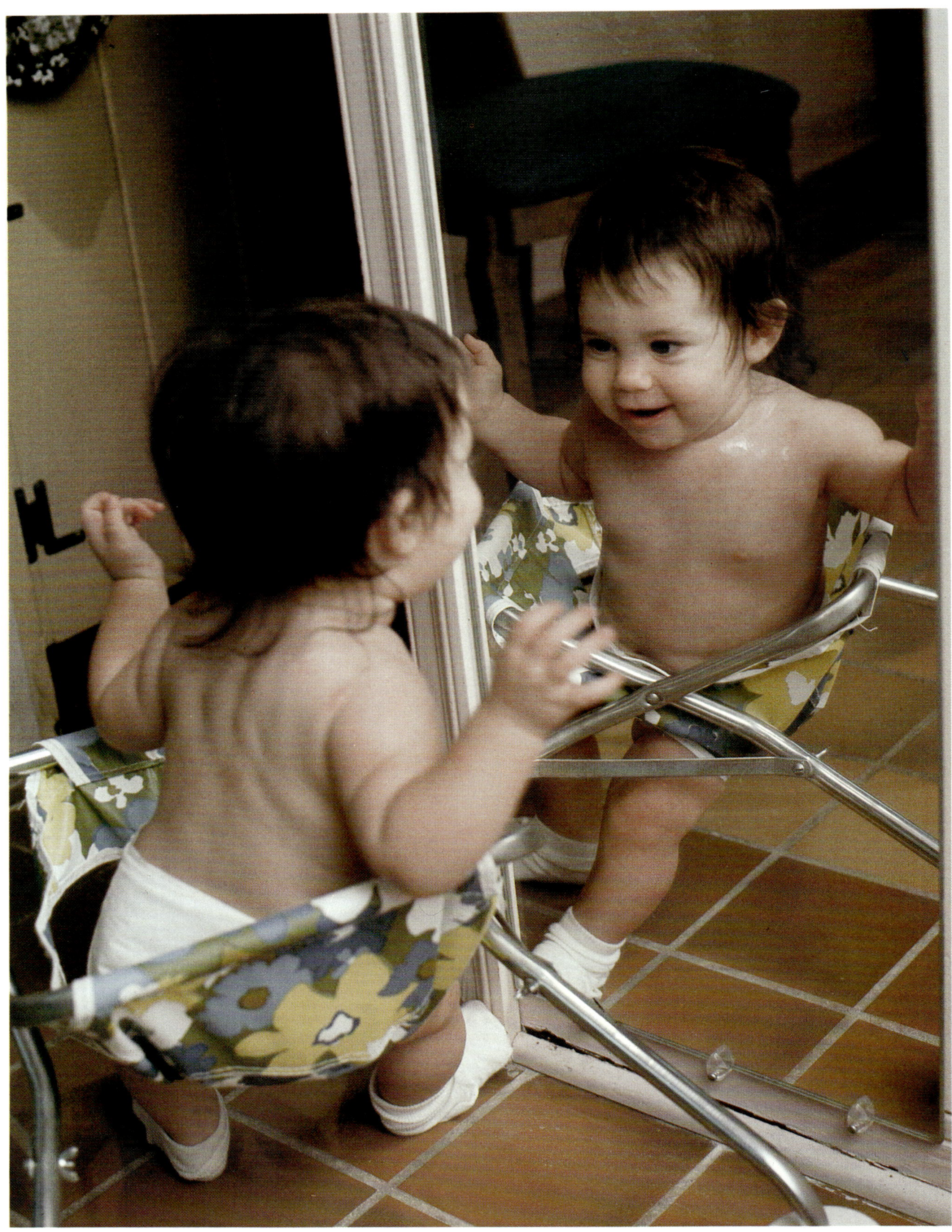

Tom McCarthy

Goodness! To think you've lived here 6 whole months and just now discovered there's a kid your age right next door.

The right combination of expression, props, clothes, and color can add a prizewinning essence to pictures of toddlers.

Mrs. Robert Dale Hoepner

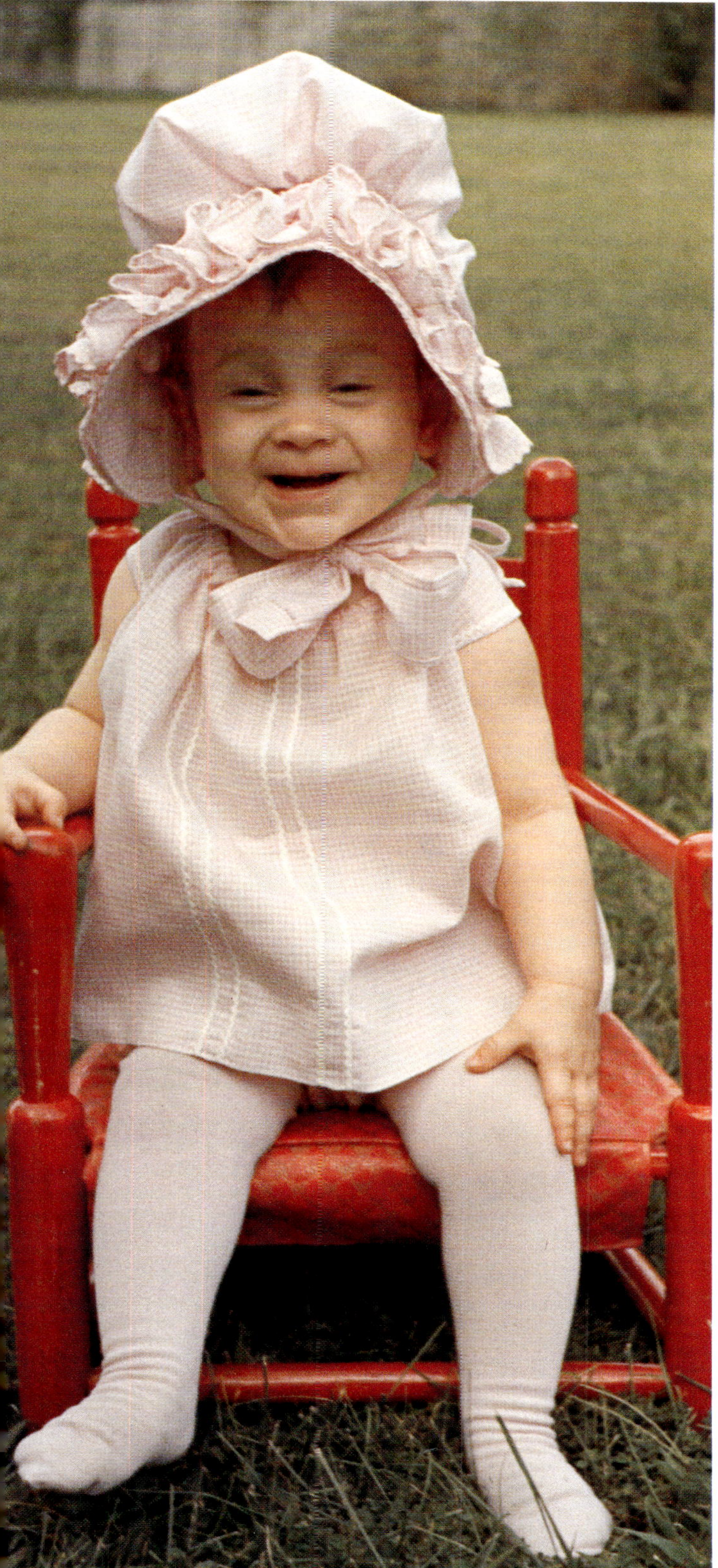

Arthur Whitty

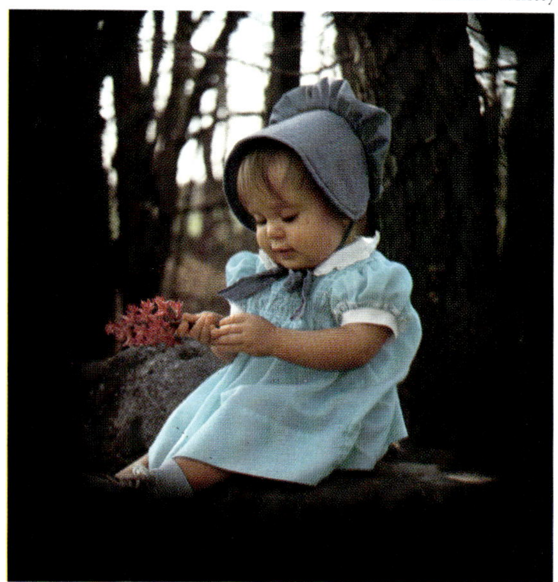

The Toddling Stage

Now deeply entrenched in the age of discovery, a child can provide a nearly constant parade of excellent picture-taking situations for you. Be ready to capture the moment when this little person comes face to face with a puppy for the first time or lays hands onto his or her first lollipop.

Attempts at being self-sufficient at the dinner table can provide you with some of your funniest subject material. To document those moments when the baby puts the food everywhere but into the mouth, take your pictures during the first few weeks that he or she tries to do it alone. Try to arrange the high-chair where the background won't be distracting, and take pictures during the whole meal. Add some color by dressing the baby in bright clothing. Maybe you can even arrange for colorful food—such as pink pudding or strawberry jelly.

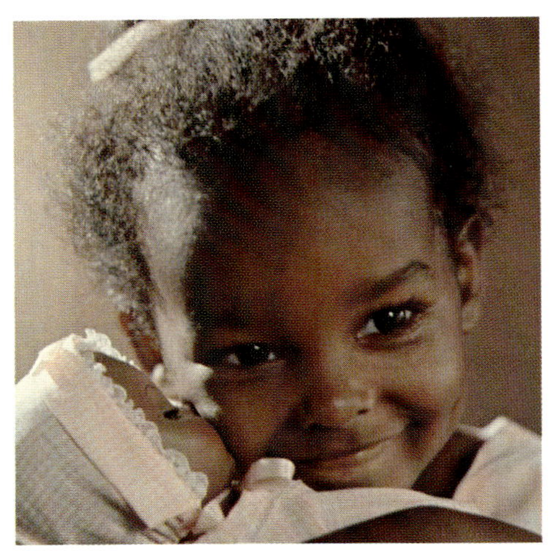
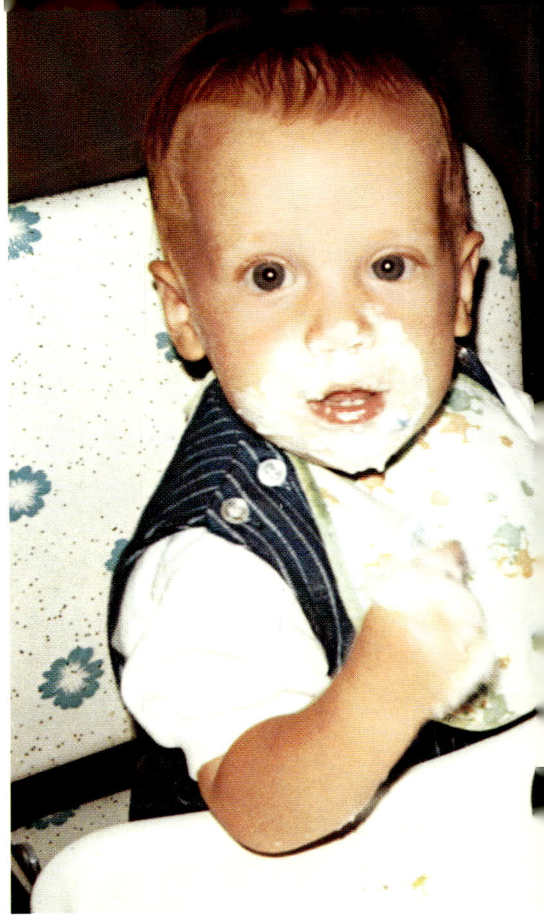
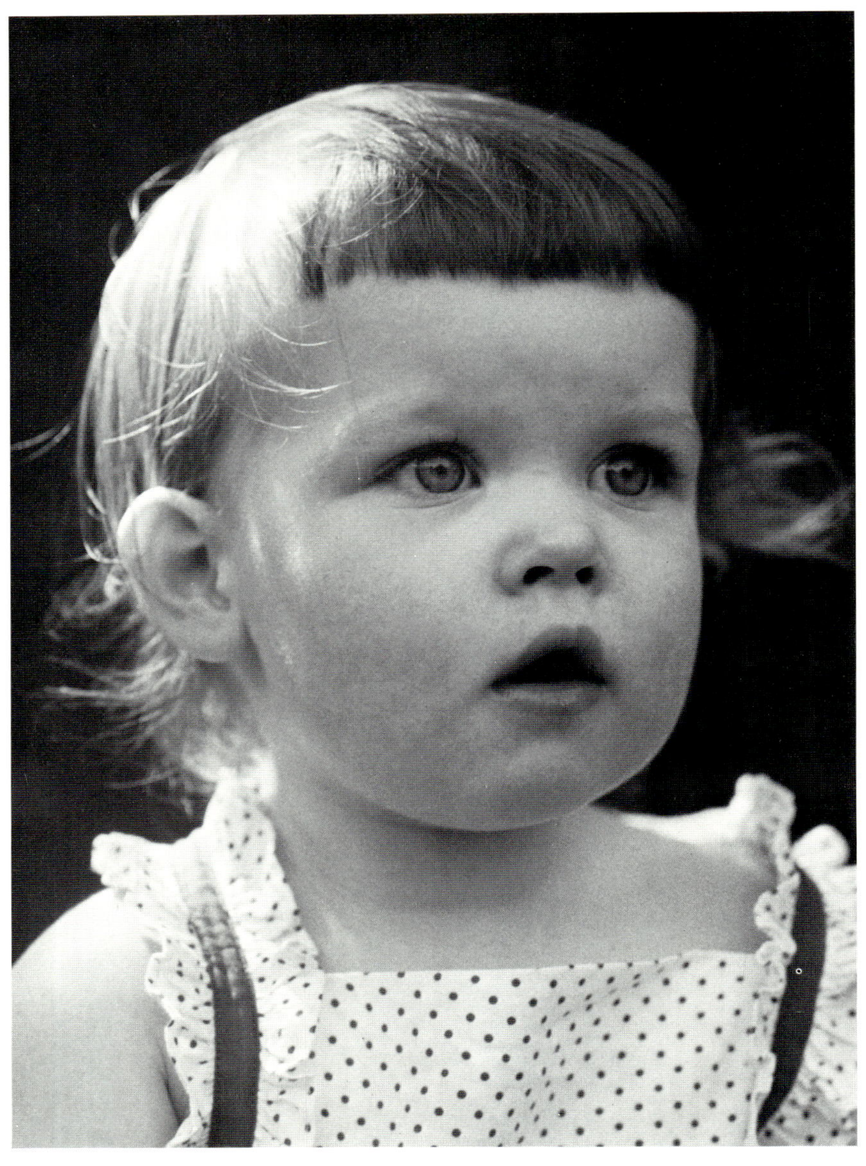
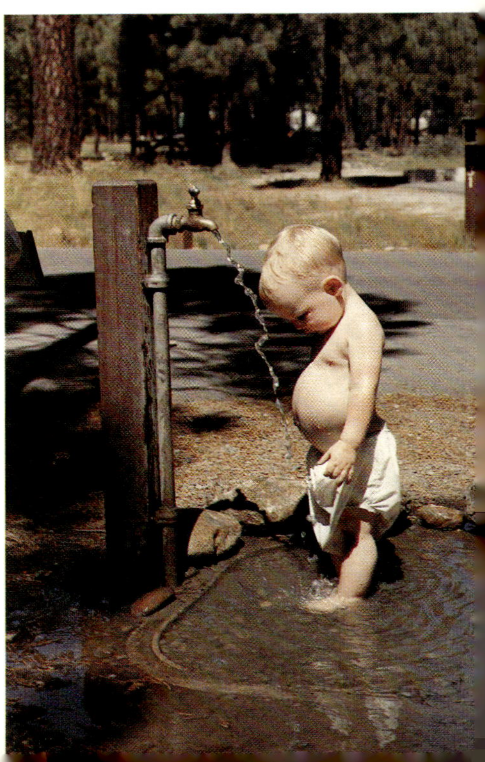

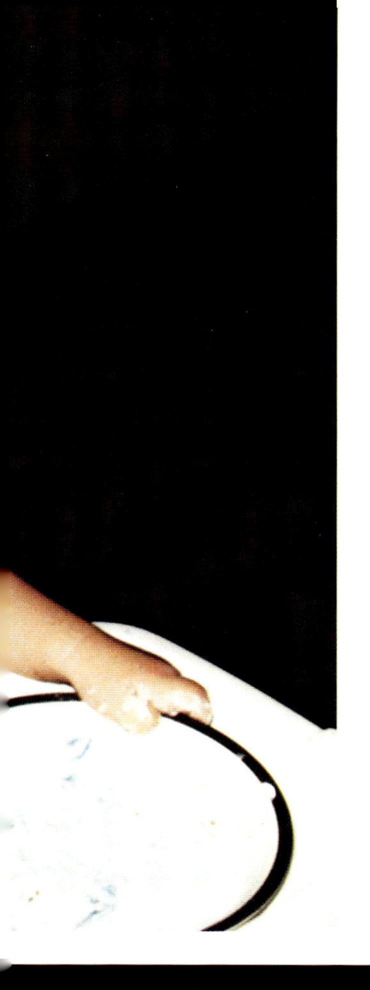

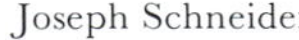

Joseph Schneider

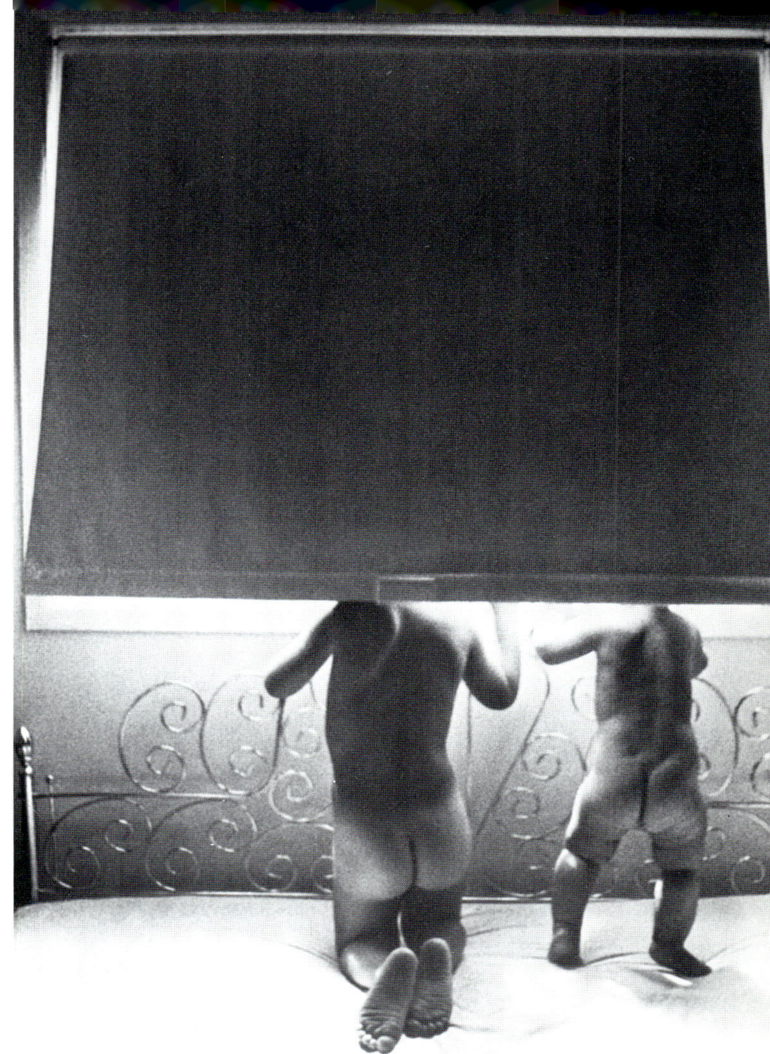

Bennet Greenberg

Toddlers, being profoundly interested in just about everything around them, often strike a natural pose that's too good to pass up. Follow your little one around for an hour or so, watching for these moments. Watch the light, too. Daylight coming through windows often provides enough illumination for photography, particularly if you have an adjustable camera loaded with a high-speed film. If you have a simple, fixed-lens camera and a color film of medium sensitivity, such as KODACOLOR II Film, use flash for indoor close-ups.

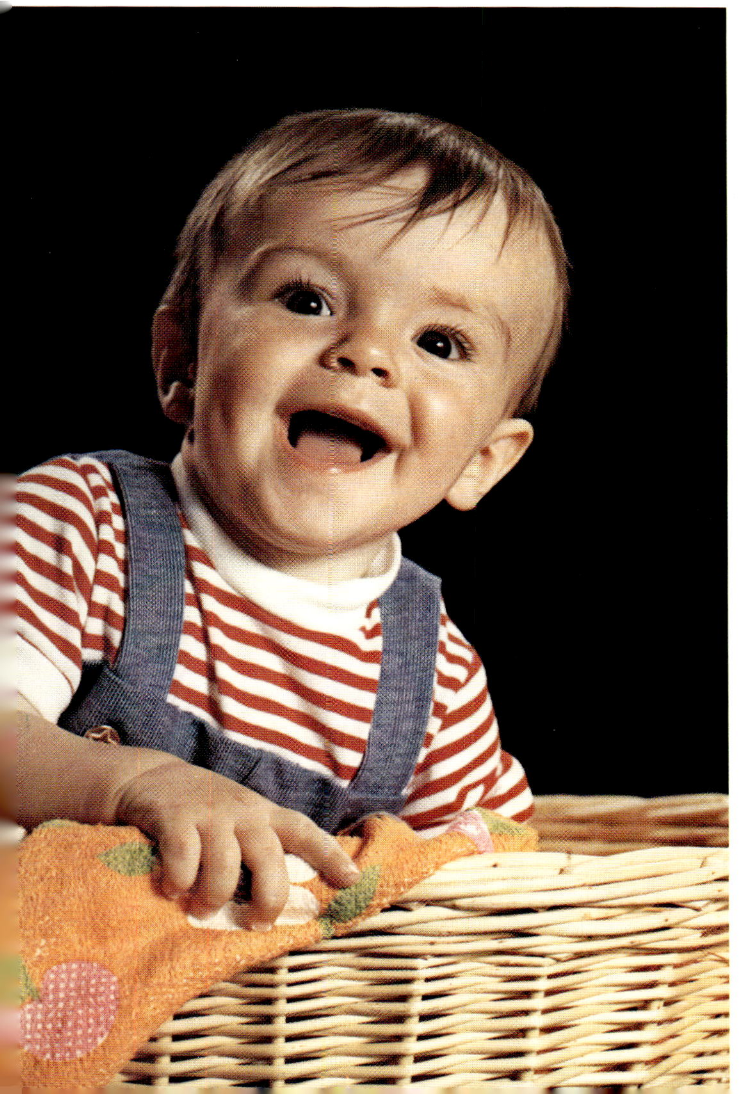

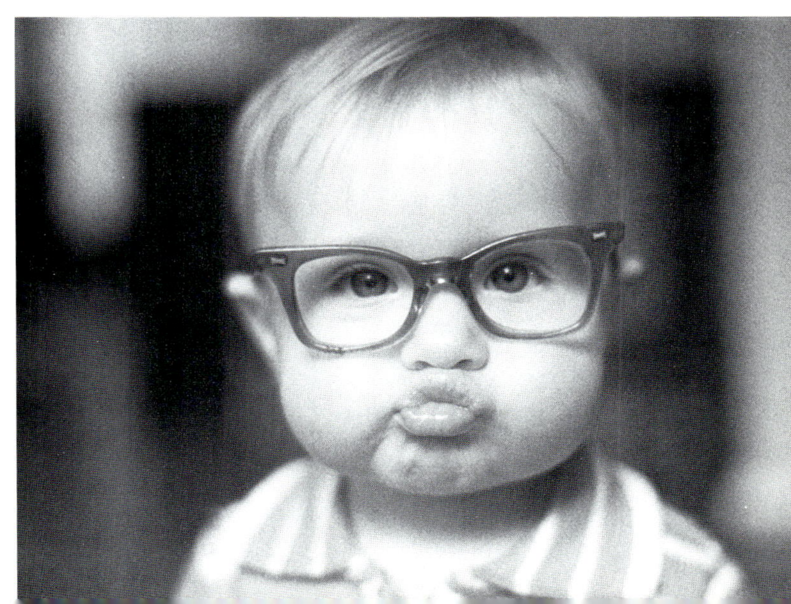

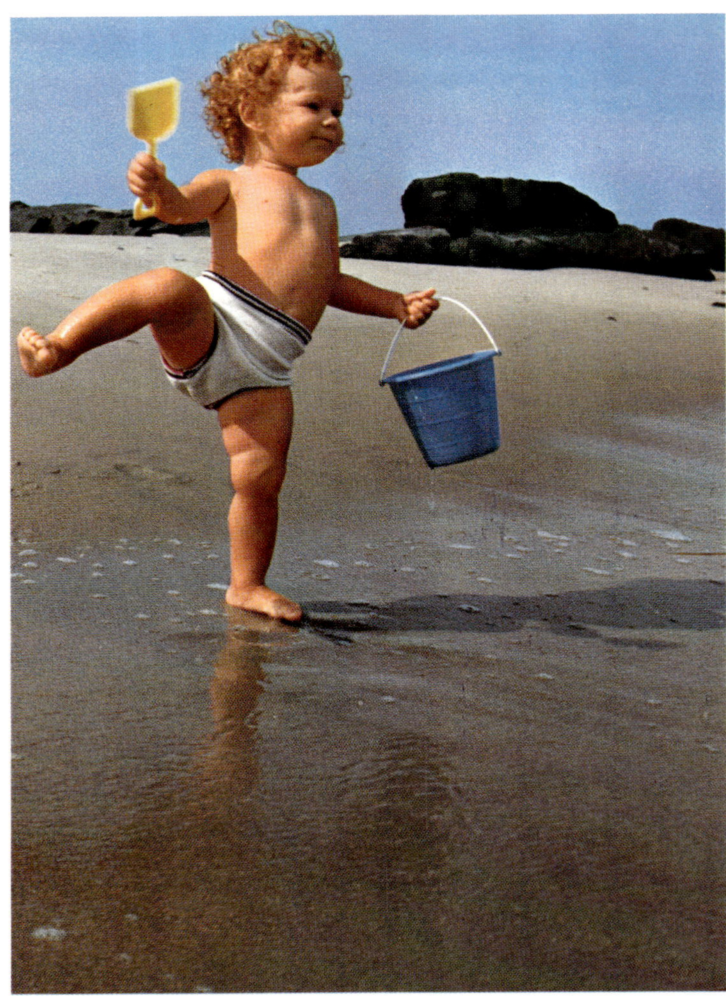

William J. Jones

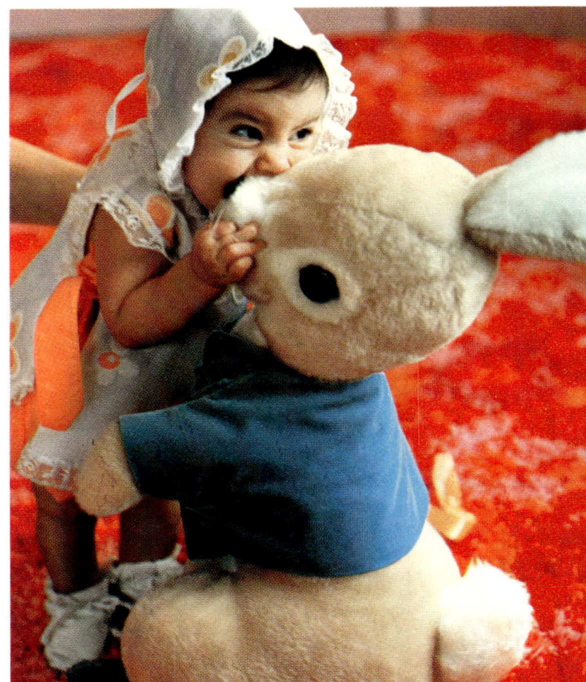

Tom McCarthy

Jeffrey Pierce

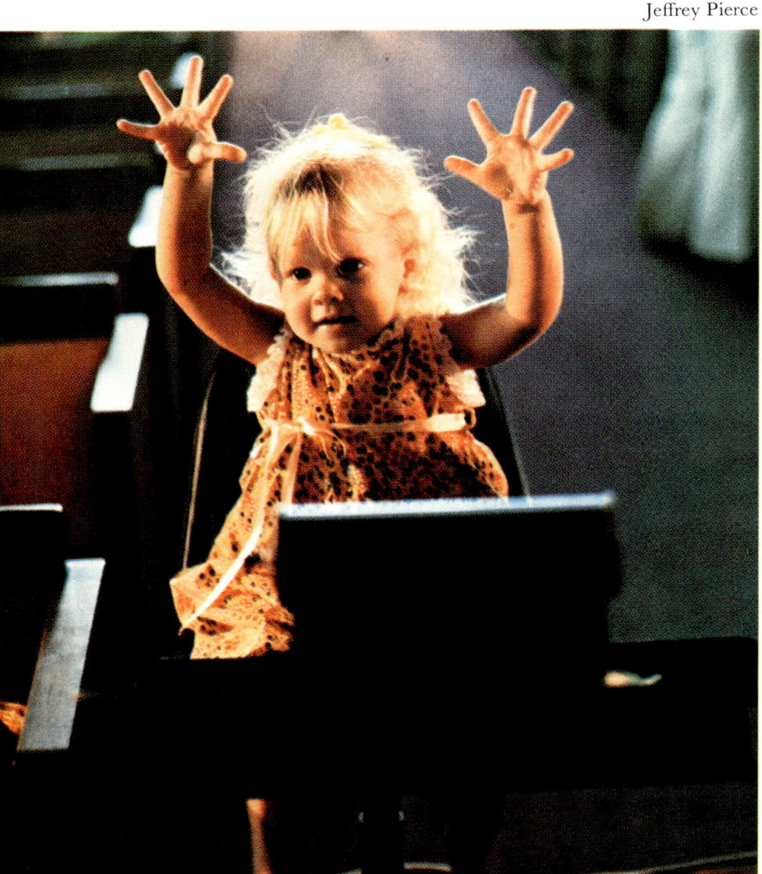

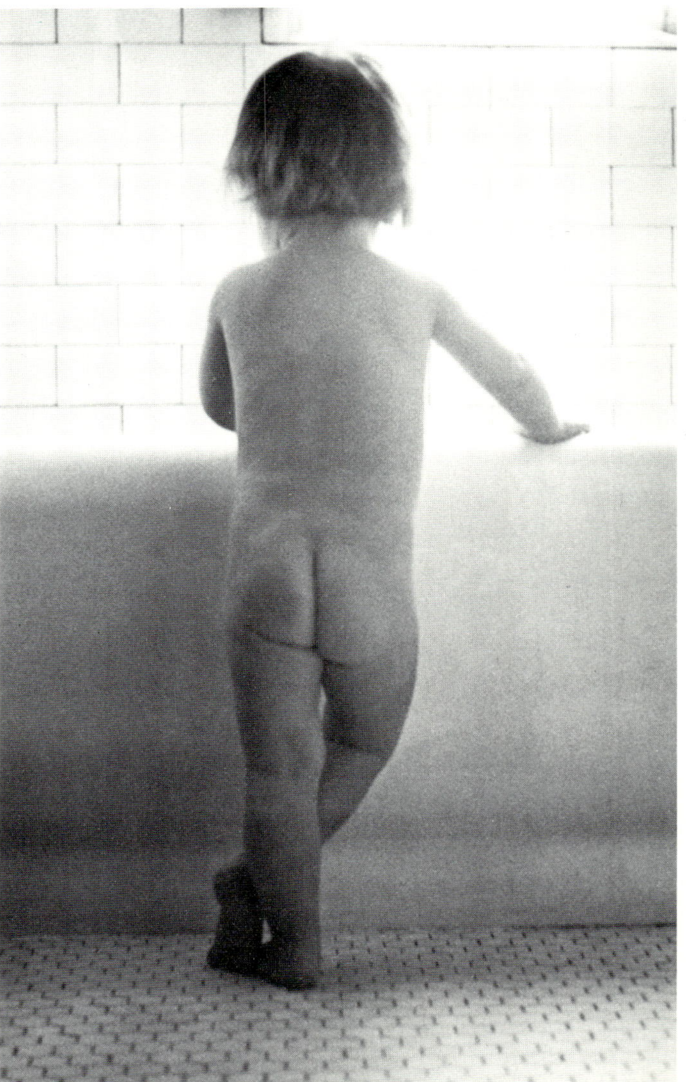

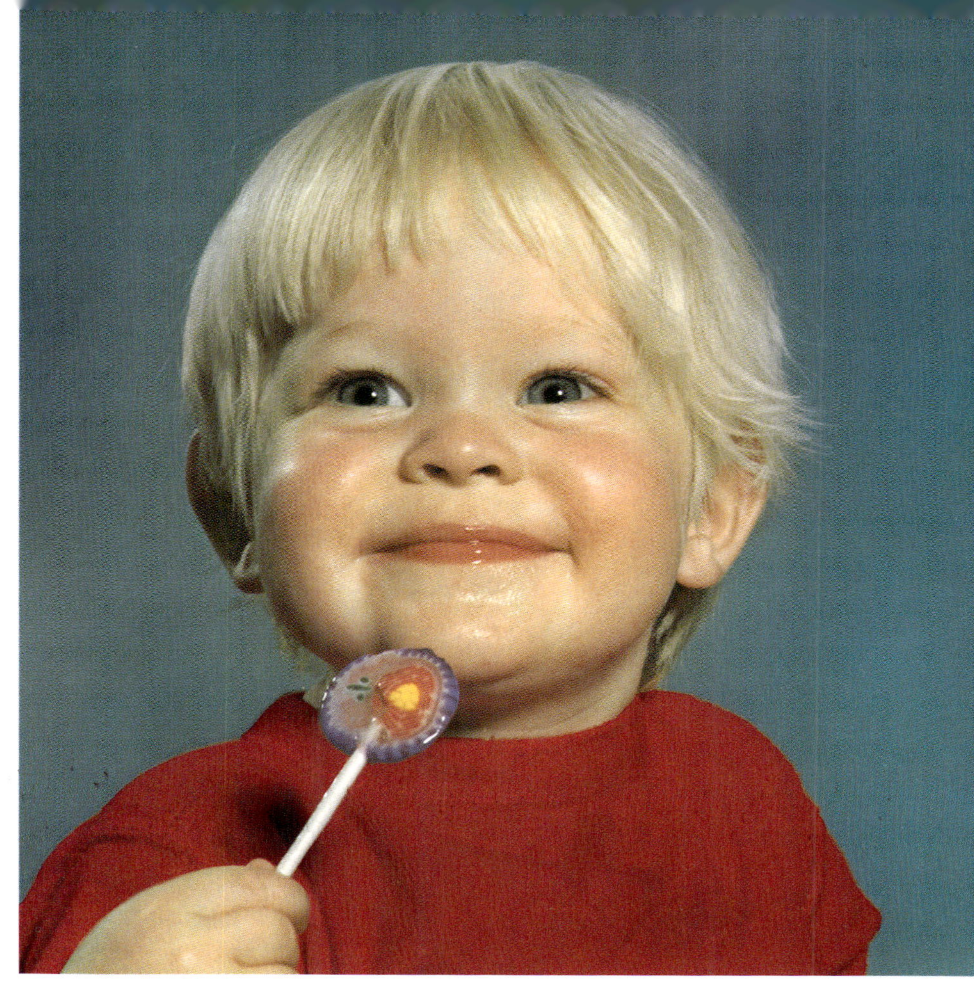

A solid-colored background kept this close-up straightforward and simple. For more information on using backgrounds, *see pages 66-69.*

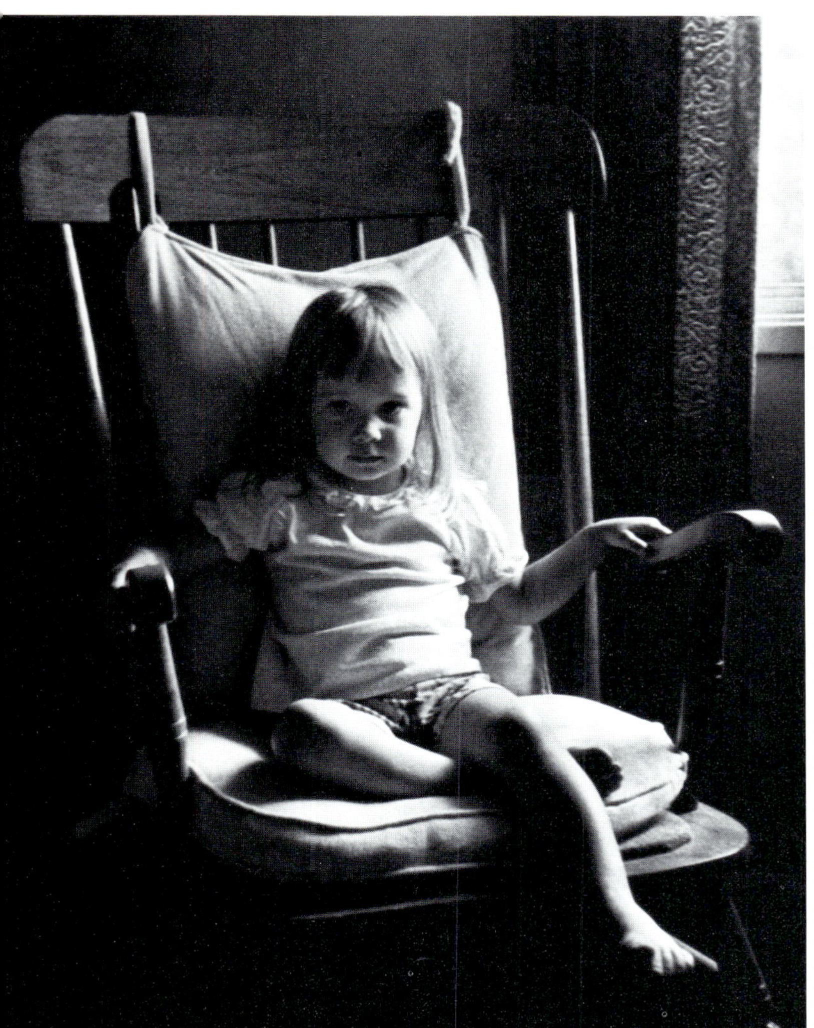

This striking, informal portrait was made with only daylight illumination entering the room from a large window. The photographer knelt for an eye-level camera angle to help create a direct, personal photointerpretation.

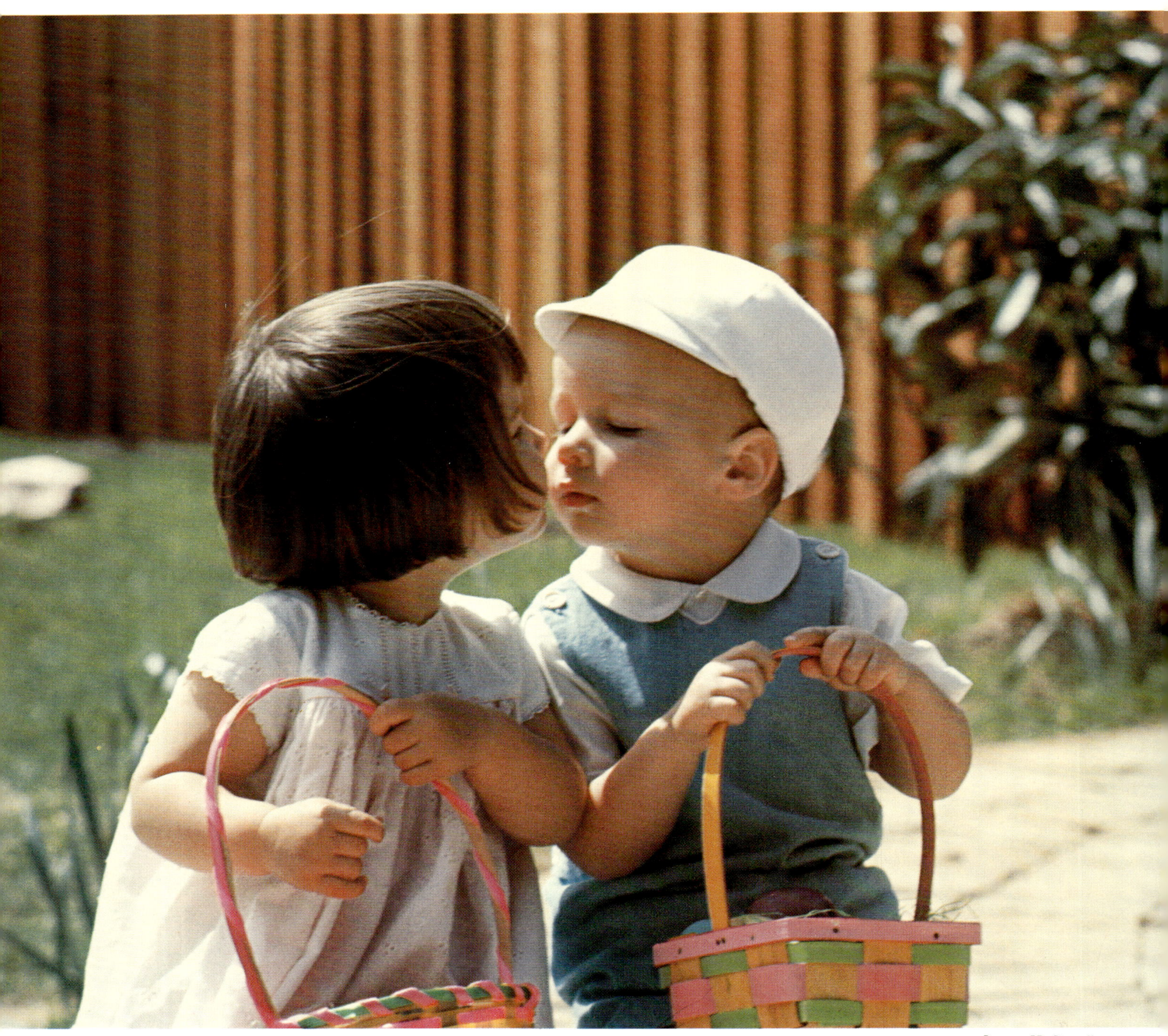

Lamar H. Carroll

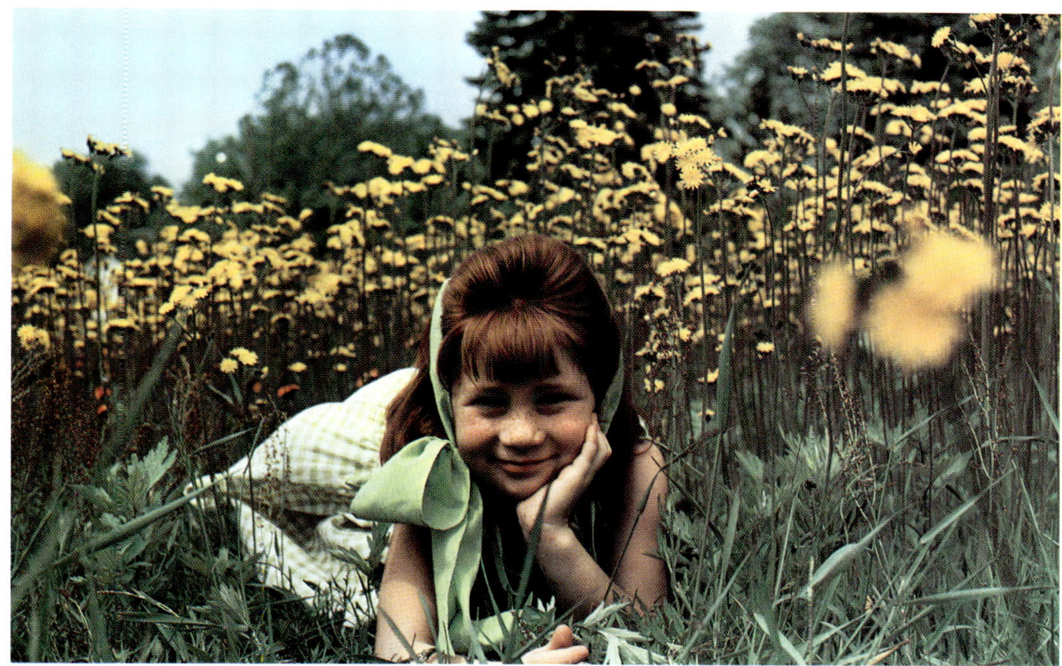

Doris Barker

Growing Up

The toddler grows and grows, and all of a sudden it seems you're faced with an independent, inquisitive, and always active youngster who is off playing with companions, away at school, or perhaps busy with a Scout meeting. During these growing-up years, the opportunities to be family historian with a camera are many, but they often require the photographer to do a little running to keep up with all this activity.

Children usually have far more important (to them) things to do than to hold still for a picture. To help you get the pictures you want during their busy schedules, keep in mind these simple tips:

- Know where to find your camera! Usually, your best picture opportunities occur when you're least expecting them—such as when your youngster suddenly appears dressed in a ridiculous outfit, or when he or she is deeply engrossed in the construction of an interstate expressway right in the middle of the sandbox. These moments won't wait while you dash away, hunting for that roll of film you're not quite sure you even have on hand. Keep the camera in a convenient location and always loaded with film.

- Since the chances are probably better than 50-50 that your subject will be indoors for that great and unexpected picture-taking event, have extra flash on hand. If your camera requires batteries to power the flash, be sure that they are fresh and the flash contacts are clean. Check with your camera instruction manual for the proper flash maintenance procedures appropriate for your particular equipment.

W. B. Pope

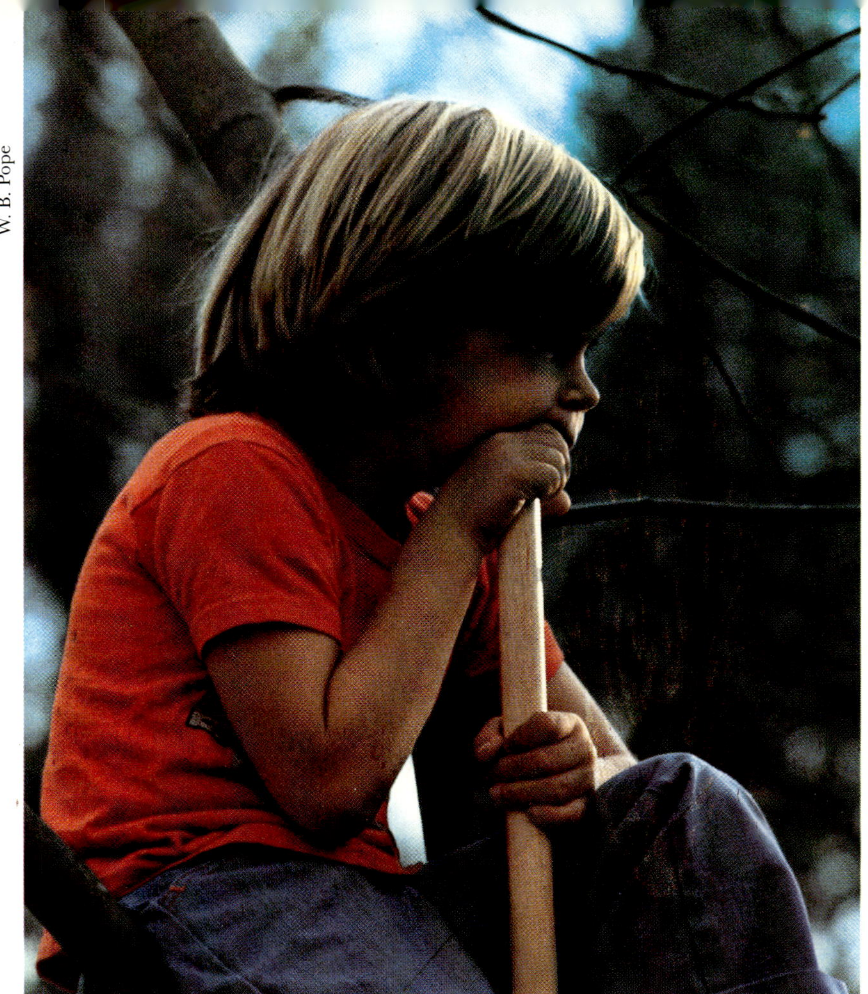

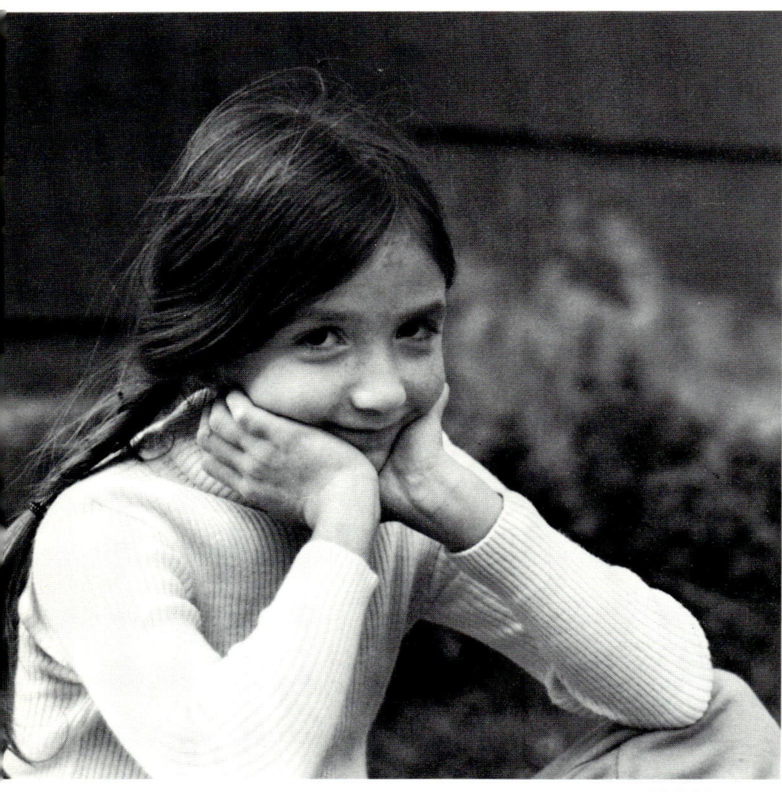

Neil Montanus

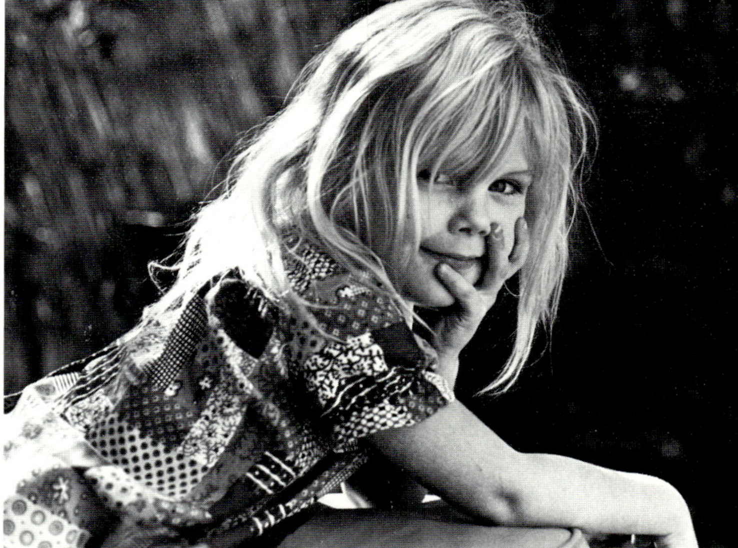

Carol Opotter

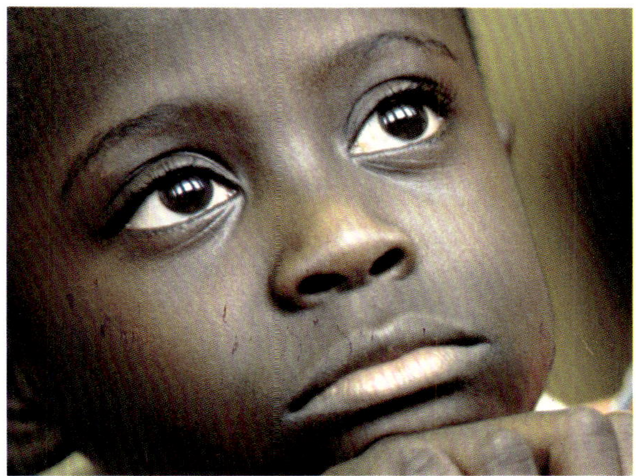
O. J. Roth

Andrew DeLucia

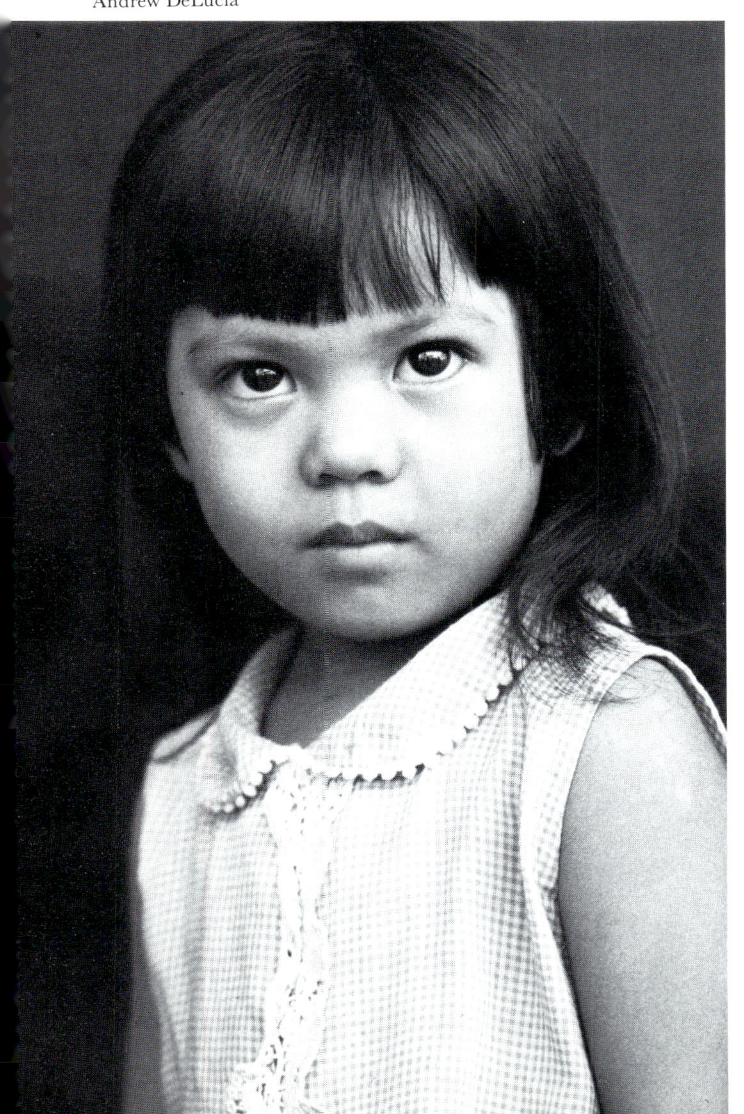

Jeff Taylor

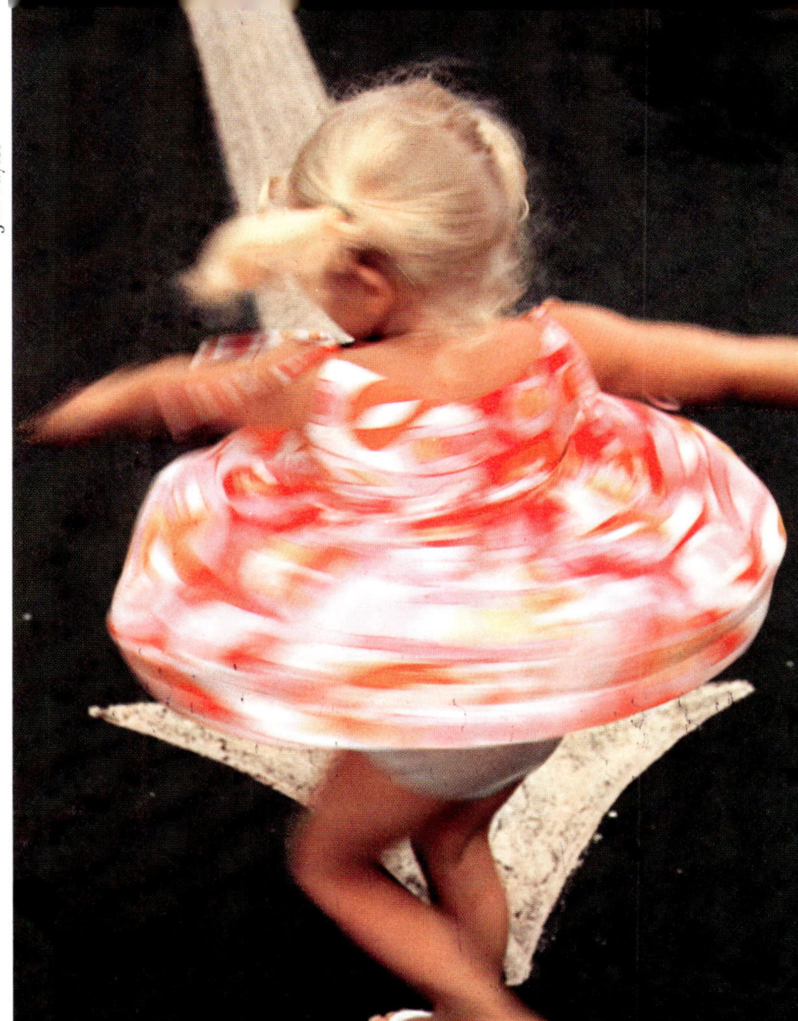

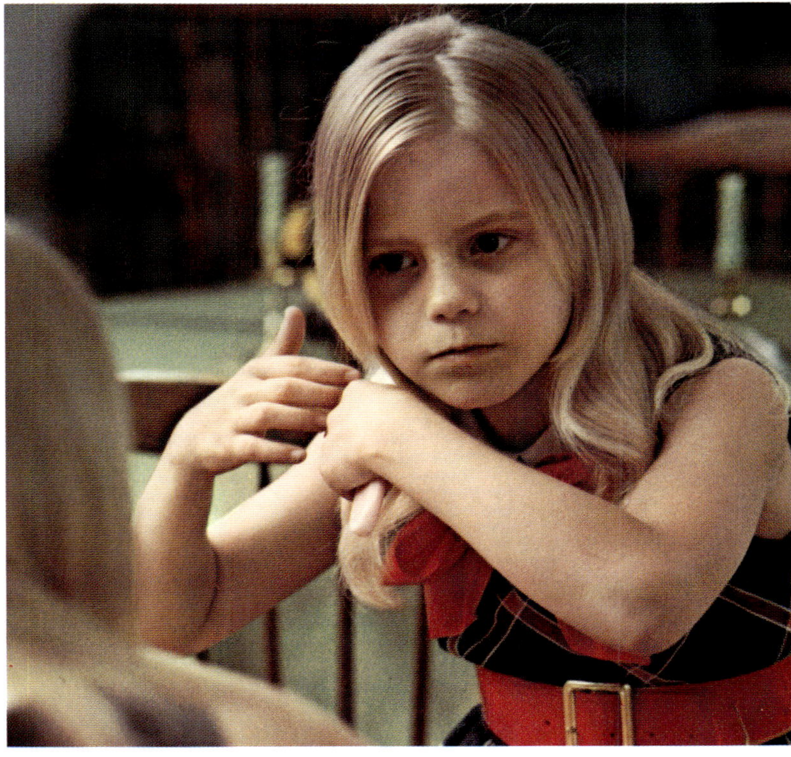

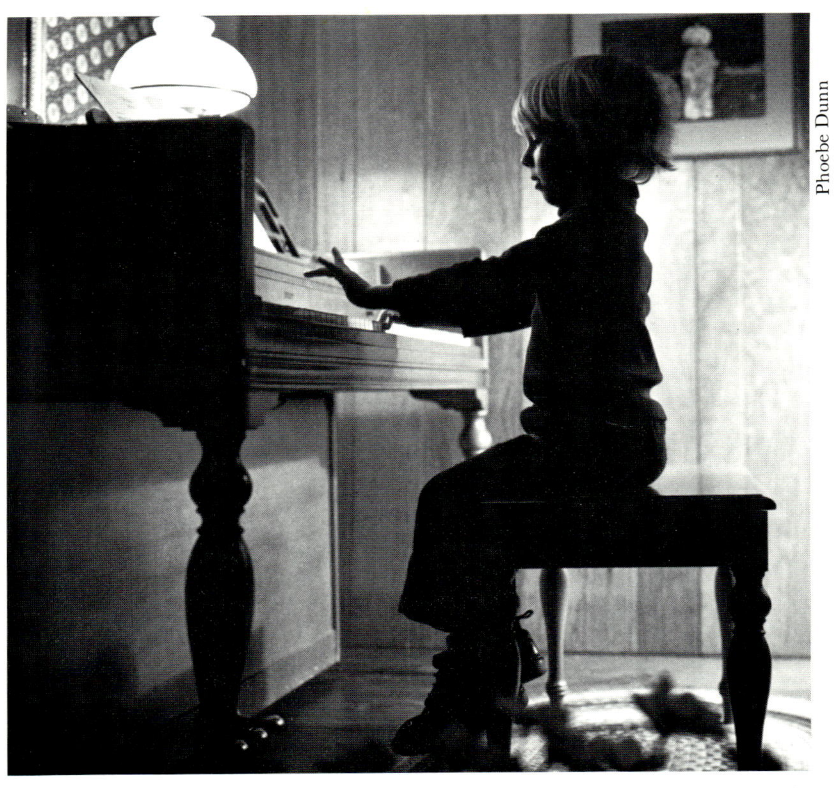
Phoebe Dunn

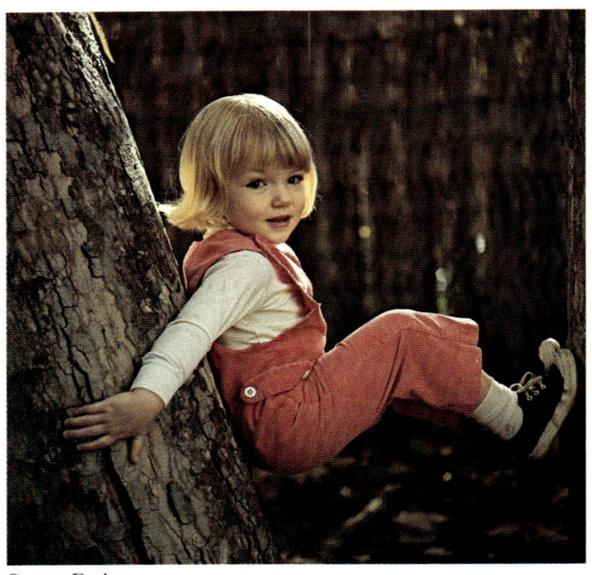
George Dodge

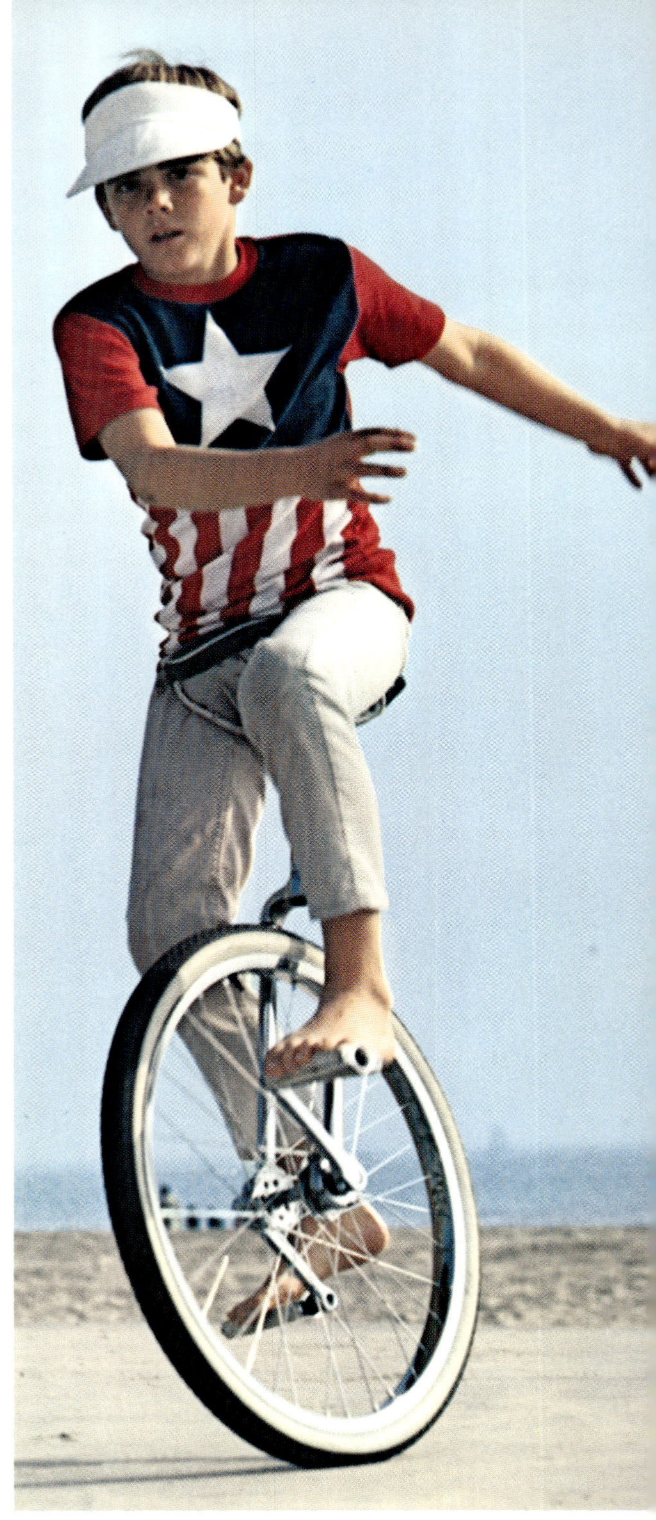

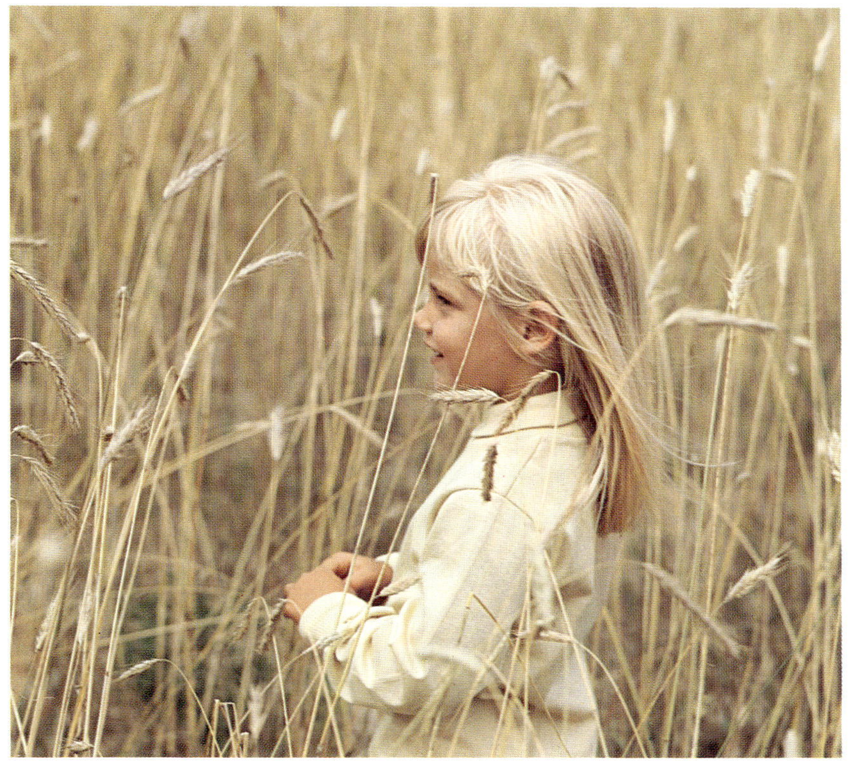

Phoebe Dunn

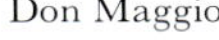

Don Maggio

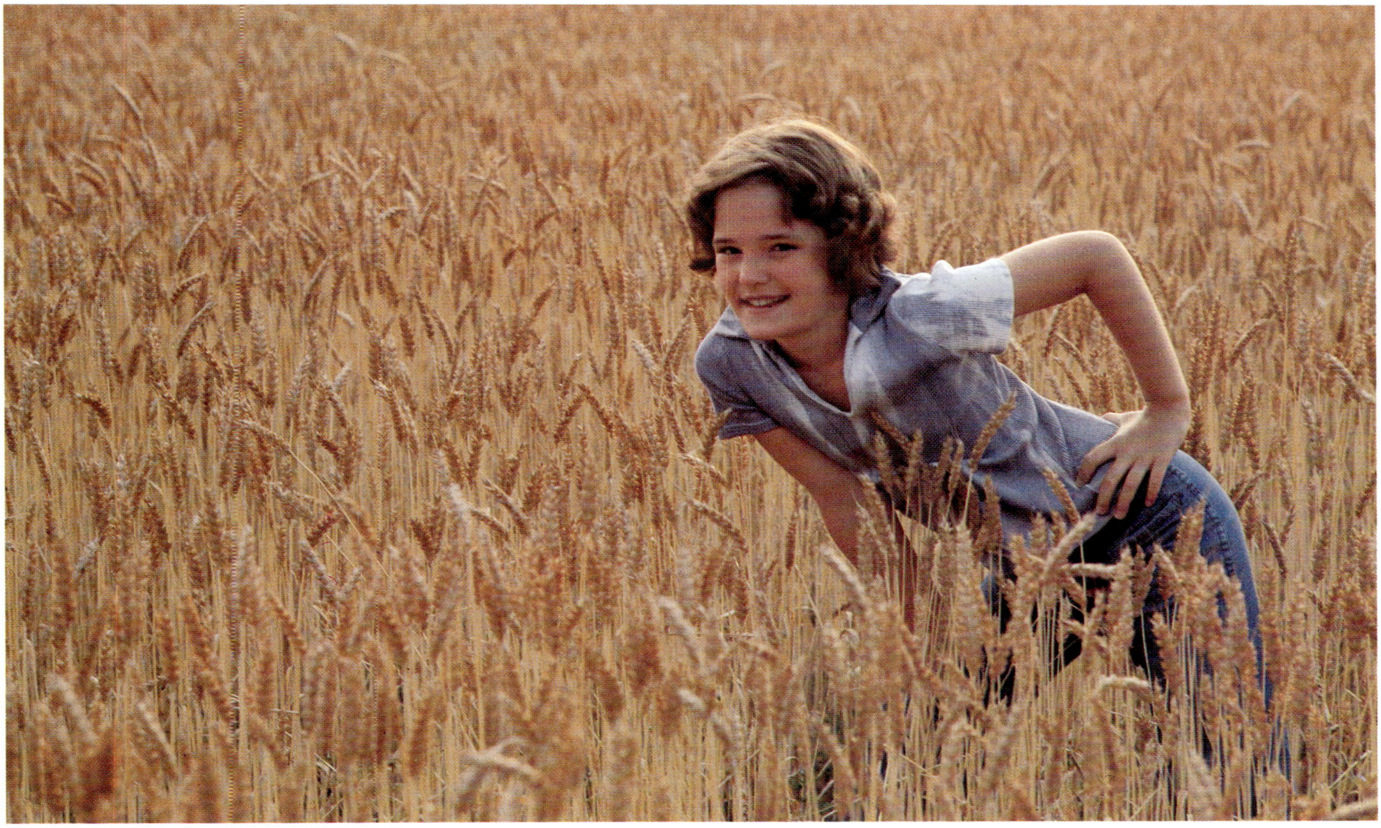

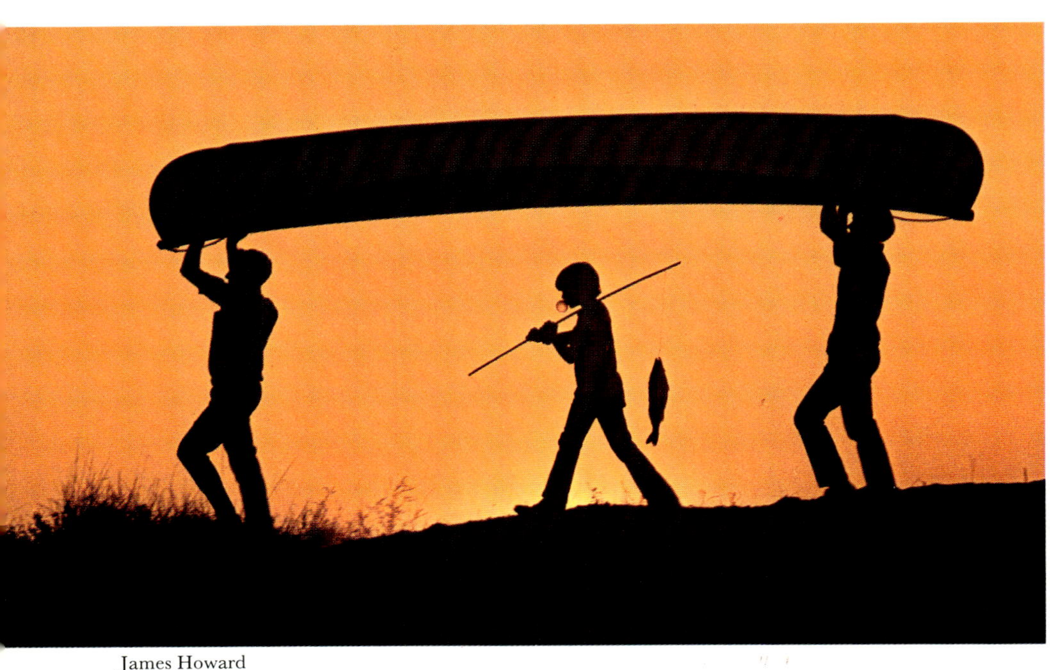

James Howard

Peter Gales

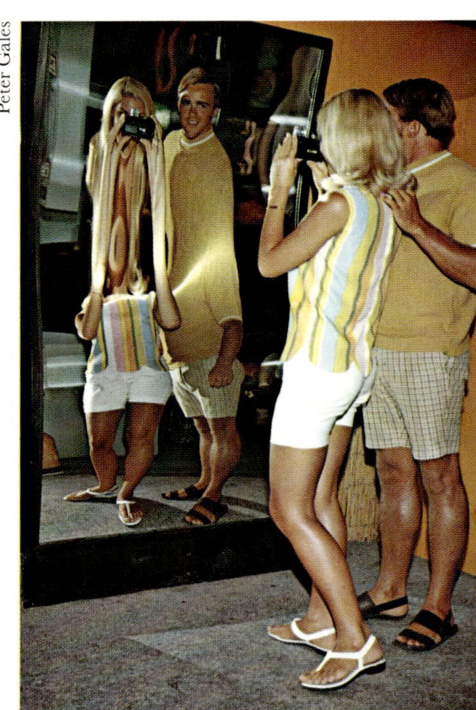

Don Maggio

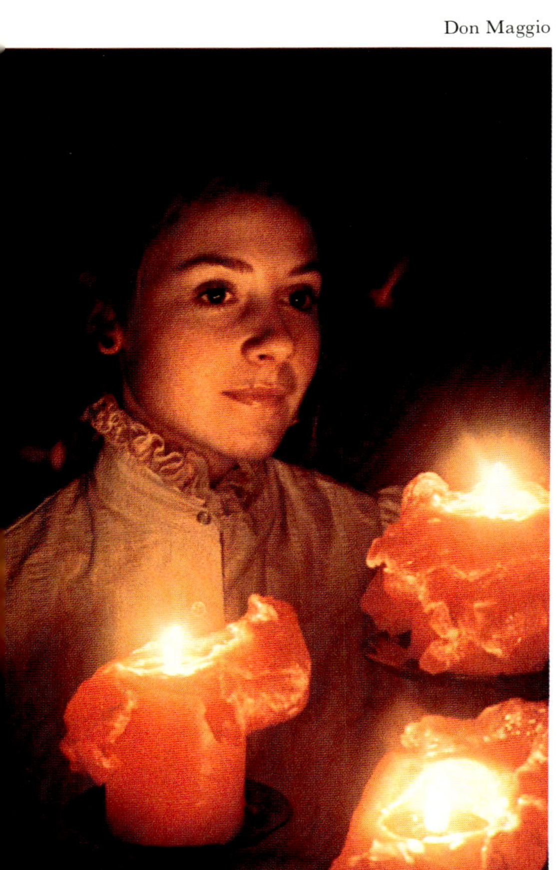

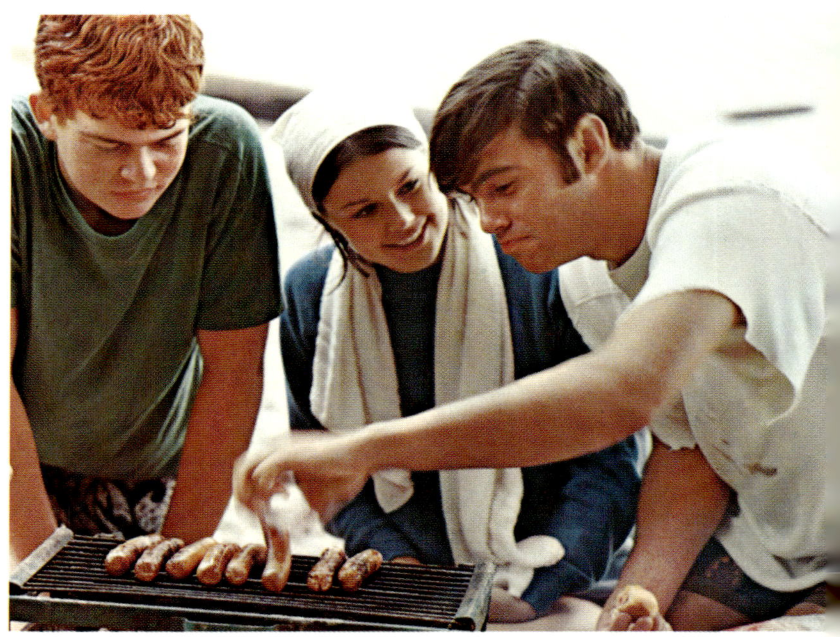

Peter Gales

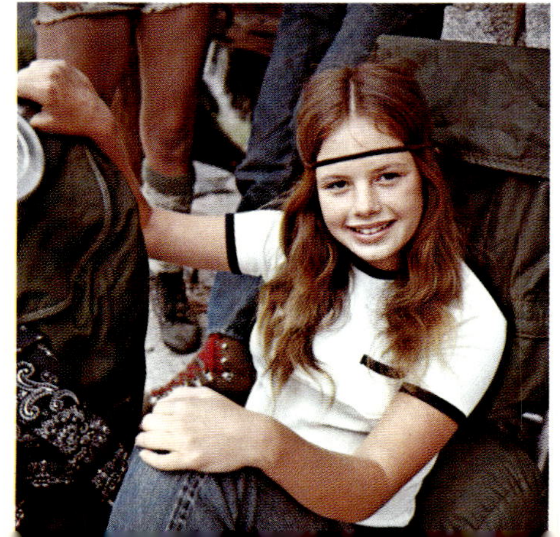

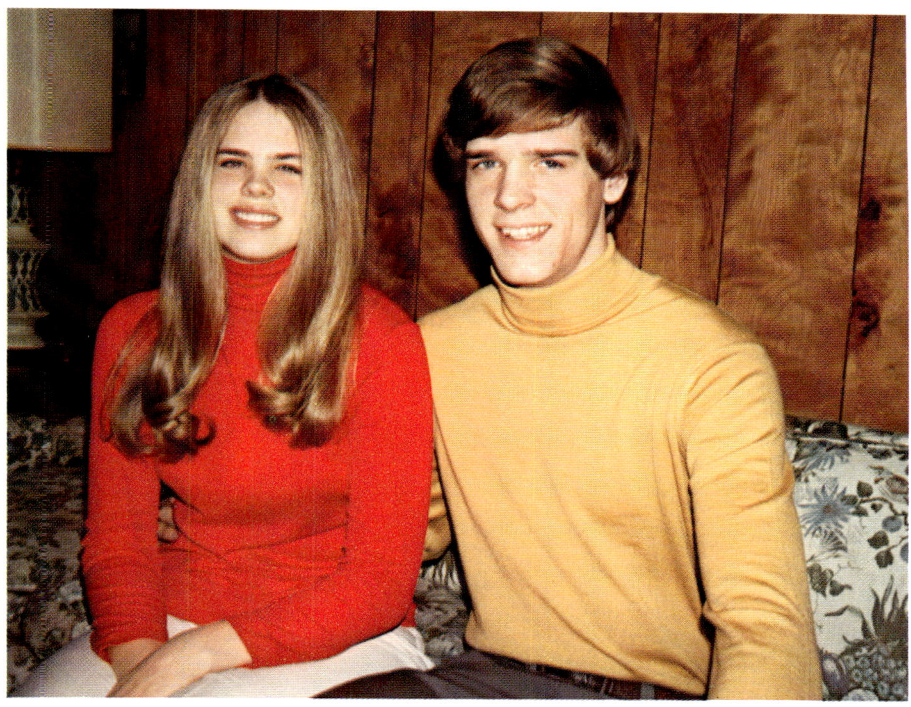

The Teenager

On the desk of a person we know stands a framed color enlargement of two teenage family members, adorned in down parkas. Shiny skis are bound to their huge, bright colored boots. Behind them is a deep blue sky and a mountainful of snow. They look happy and tanned. It's a picture that says something very personal and warm to all who see it. The photograph is an honest interpretation of two healthy young people involved in one of their favorite leisure-time activities.

A picture like this one has a special place in the family album, in a frame, or however it's placed on display. It's a natural look at a slice of life, having the successful ingredients of human interest, impact, and storytelling message.

In our next two chapters we'll be going into various ways to achieve these and other elements that help make effective, informal portraits of children. But for now, let's concern ourselves with images of teenage life. How do you record teenagers onto film? Well, for one thing, you have to *be* there, eager to join in their activities, to share their enthusiasm, to respect their sensitivities. At this age, the obvious presence of a camera—constantly pointed in their direction—can often be an intrusion, possibly inhibiting the natural expressions you're after. Keep your photo coverage low-key. Have the camera adjusted for proper exposure, and focus ahead of time whenever possible so when the opportune moment arrives, you can make the picture smoothly and quickly without more than a few seconds' (if that) break in the normal actions of your subject.

Pocket cameras are particularly convenient for capturing the active life-styles of teenagers. Because pocket cameras are small and extremely lightweight, they can go with you nearly everywhere (even to the ski slopes) without constantly

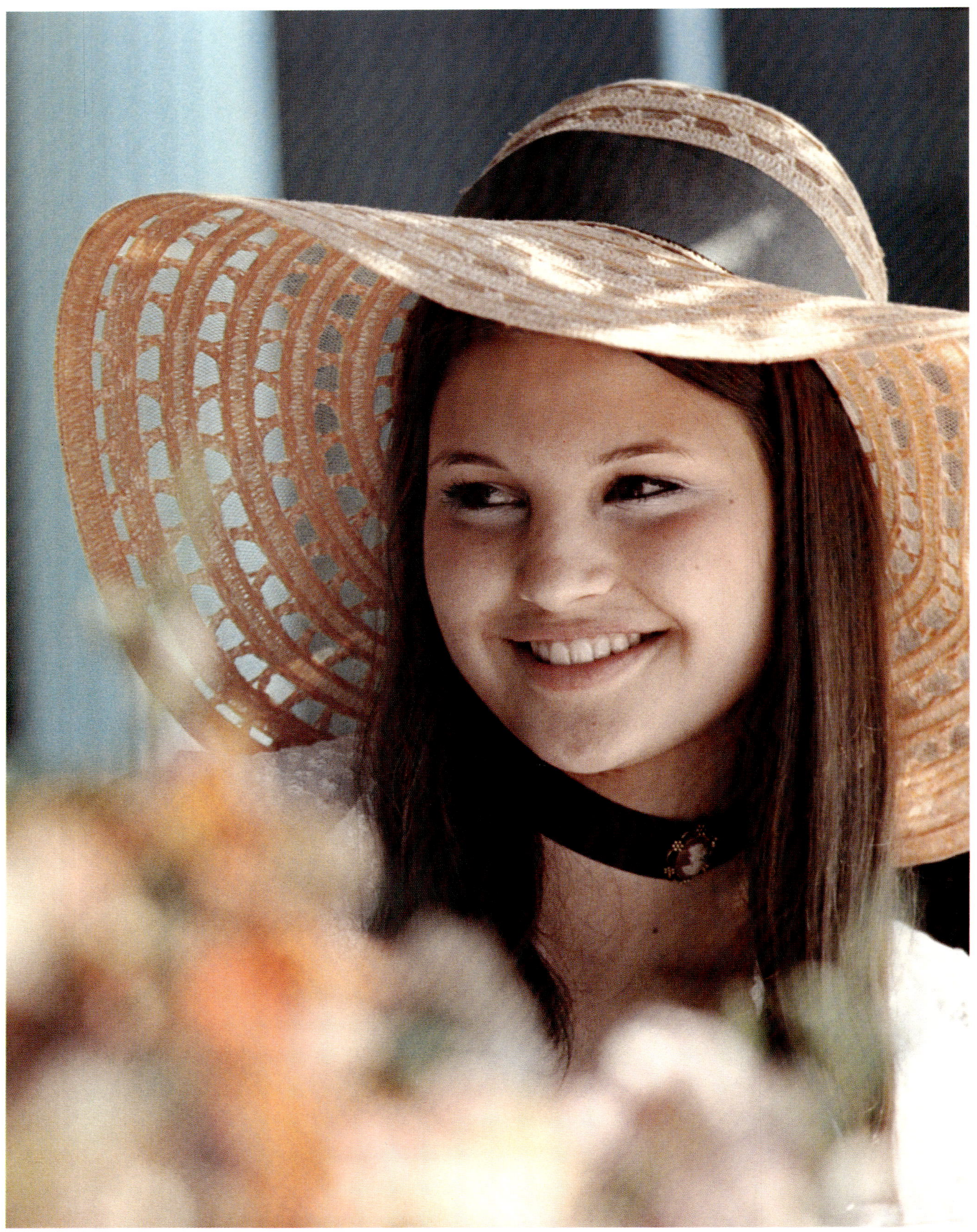

Don Maggio

You can isolate your subject from a cluttered background or foreground by carefully focusing an adjustable camera on the subject. At a wide lens aperture (f/2.8 or f/4, for example), both foreground and background will appear blurred.

reminding you of their presence. Extra film cartridges can be stowed in a pocket, and the camera can be completely forgotten about until those times when you or someone with you says "Hey—that would make a good picture." A simple reach for the camera, a glimpse through the viewfinder, a press on the shutter release, and the picture is yours.

Most teenagers enjoy seeing themselves in pictures—particularly in color prints that they can carry around with them and show to others. It's a thoughtful practice to share your pictures with your young subjects. In fact, it's a courteous act to let them review with you all pictures taken of the event to give them the opportunity to edit any of themselves they don't care for before you show the batch to others. Teenagers, like adults, can be sensitive about appearance. Respect your models and their desires, and you'll get even more cooperation from them the next time you set out to take their pictures.

One way to gain plenty of interest and cooperation when snapping your teen subjects is to use an instant camera. Modern products such as KODAK Instant Cameras and KODAK Instant Print Film PR10 can provide you with a color print only a few minutes after you've taken the picture. The print develops outside the camera in normal room light and requires no extra coating or drying steps. There's a certain thrill involved in watching one's image appear in the print. Within minutes, the plain white, laminated sheet ejected from the camera develops into a beautiful color print, right before the eyes of you and your subjects. Take full advantage of the situation when your subjects discover that you're using an instant camera and ask to see the picture. If others handle the prints before they are completely developed (about 8 minutes), make sure they hold them by the edges only. Heat and pressure from fingers touching the picture area, as well as bending or flexing during the first few minutes of development, could cause uneven development in spots where contact or stress occurs.

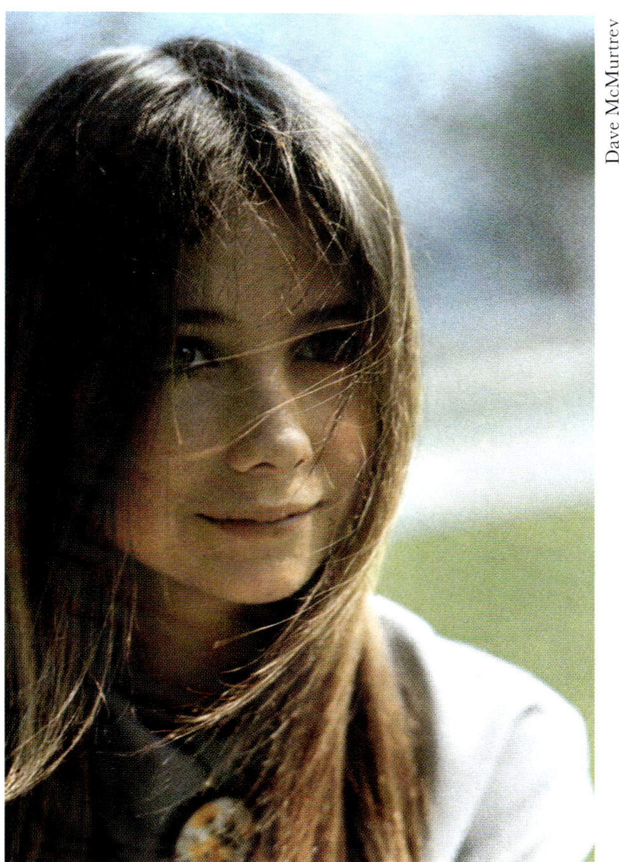

Dave McMurtrey

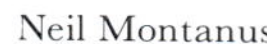

Neil Montanus

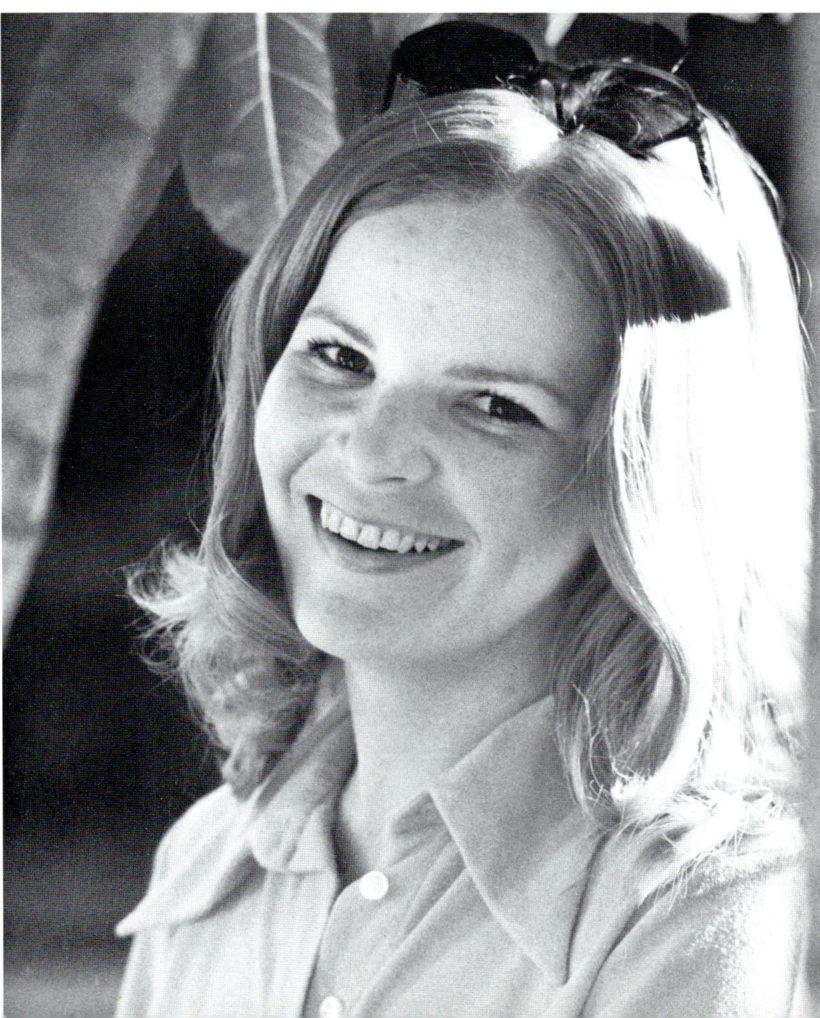

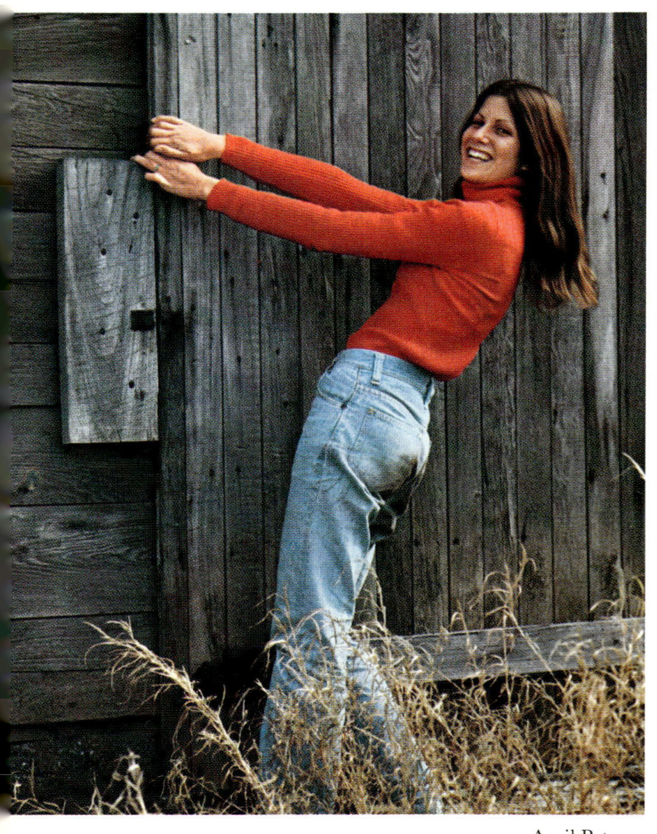
April Petrone

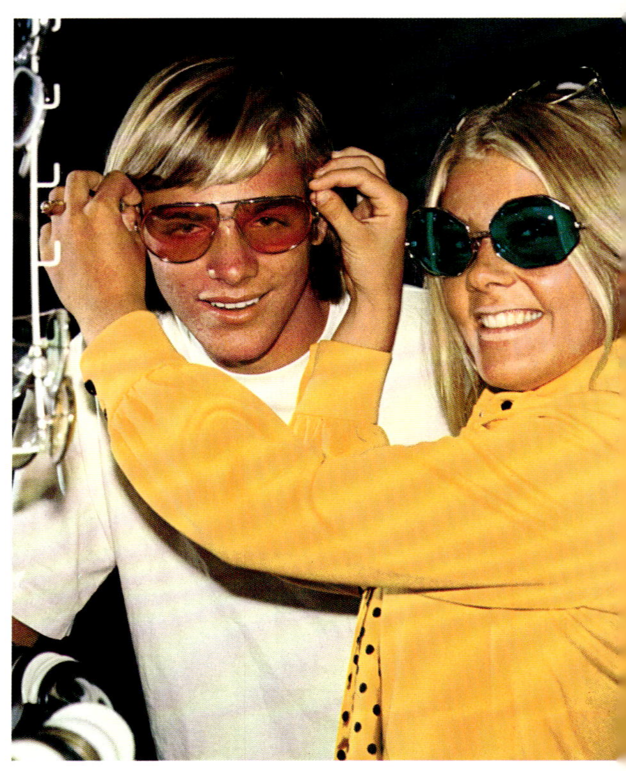

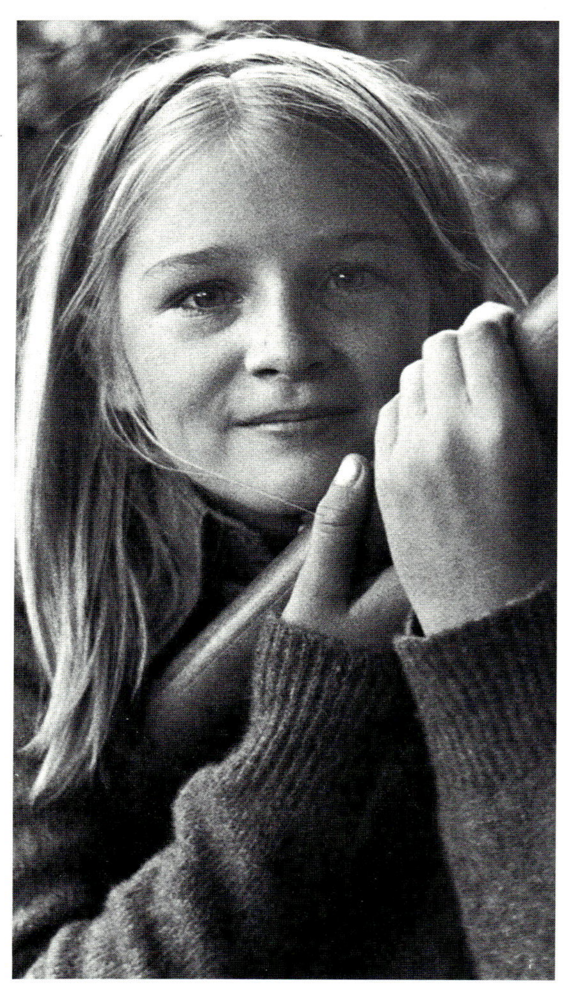
Everett Watson

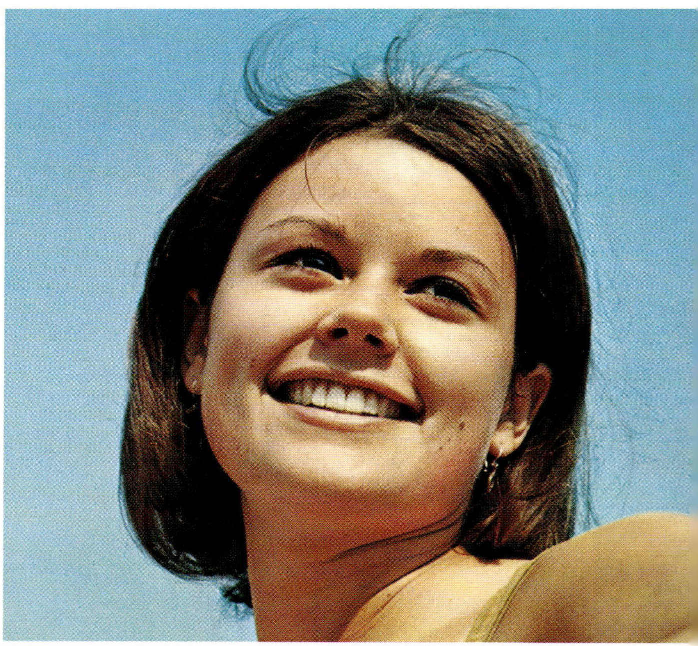
Norm Kerr

Peter Gales
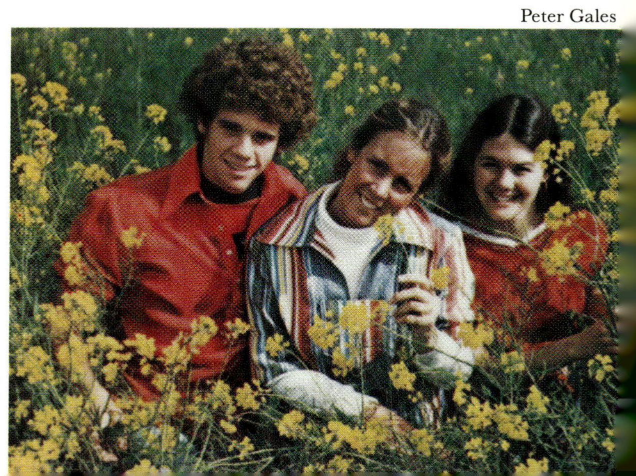

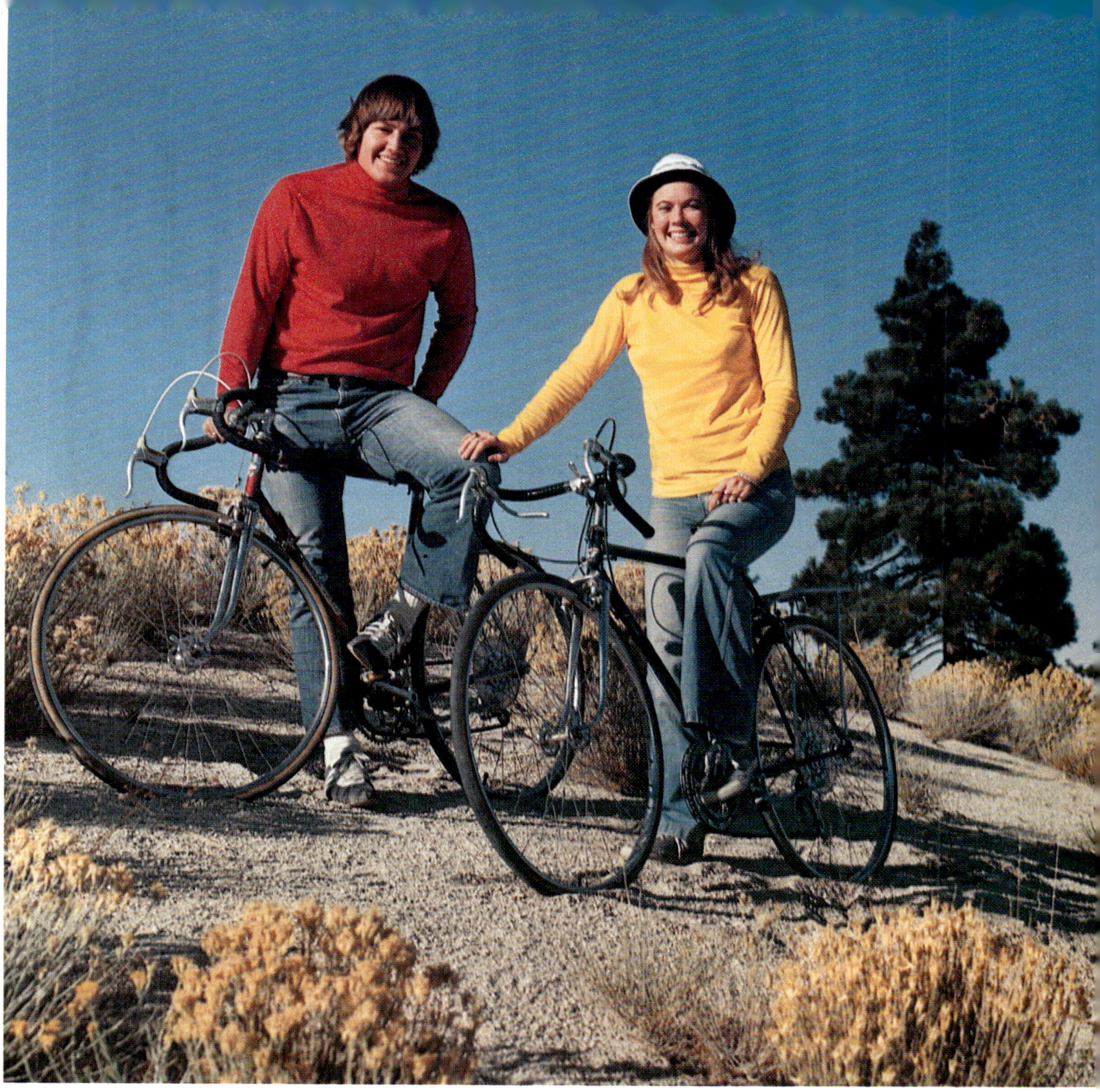

Peter Gales

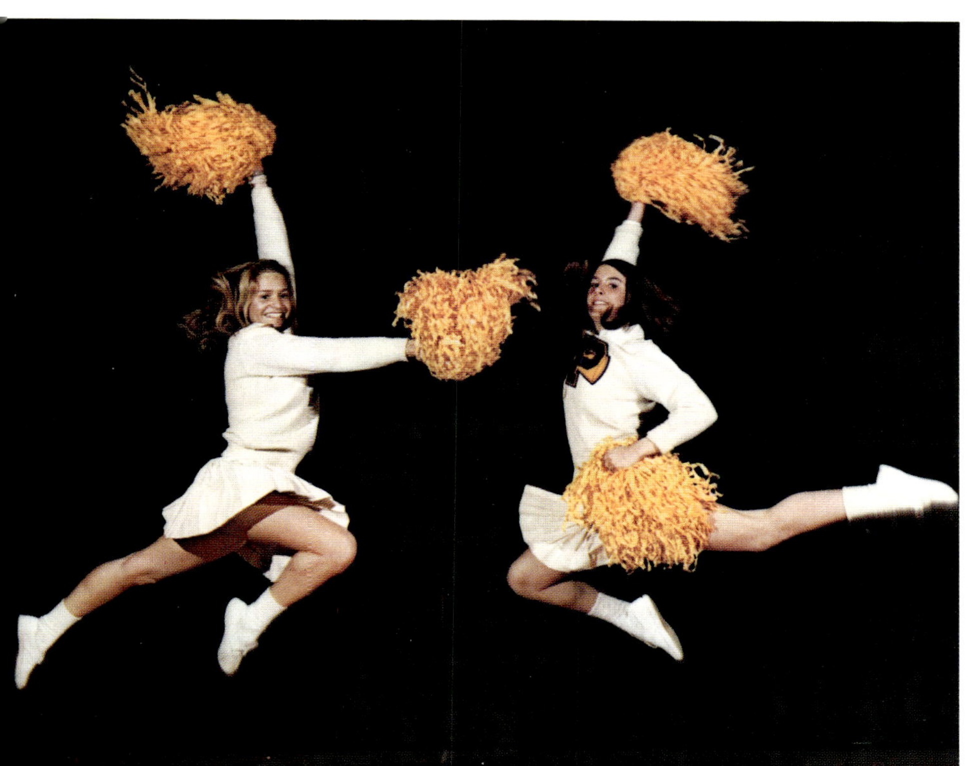

To help get plenty of cooperation from your teenage subjects the next time you set out to take their pictures:

- *Snap them at their best. Don't force a picture-taking session onto someone who may not feel like posing at the moment. You'll be rewarded with better pictures if you wait for a positive attitude.*
- *Choose an activity, props, and a location in which your subjects will feel relaxed and comfortable.*
- *Offer to share your photo results with your subjects. They probably would all like to see* and have *pictures of themselves.*

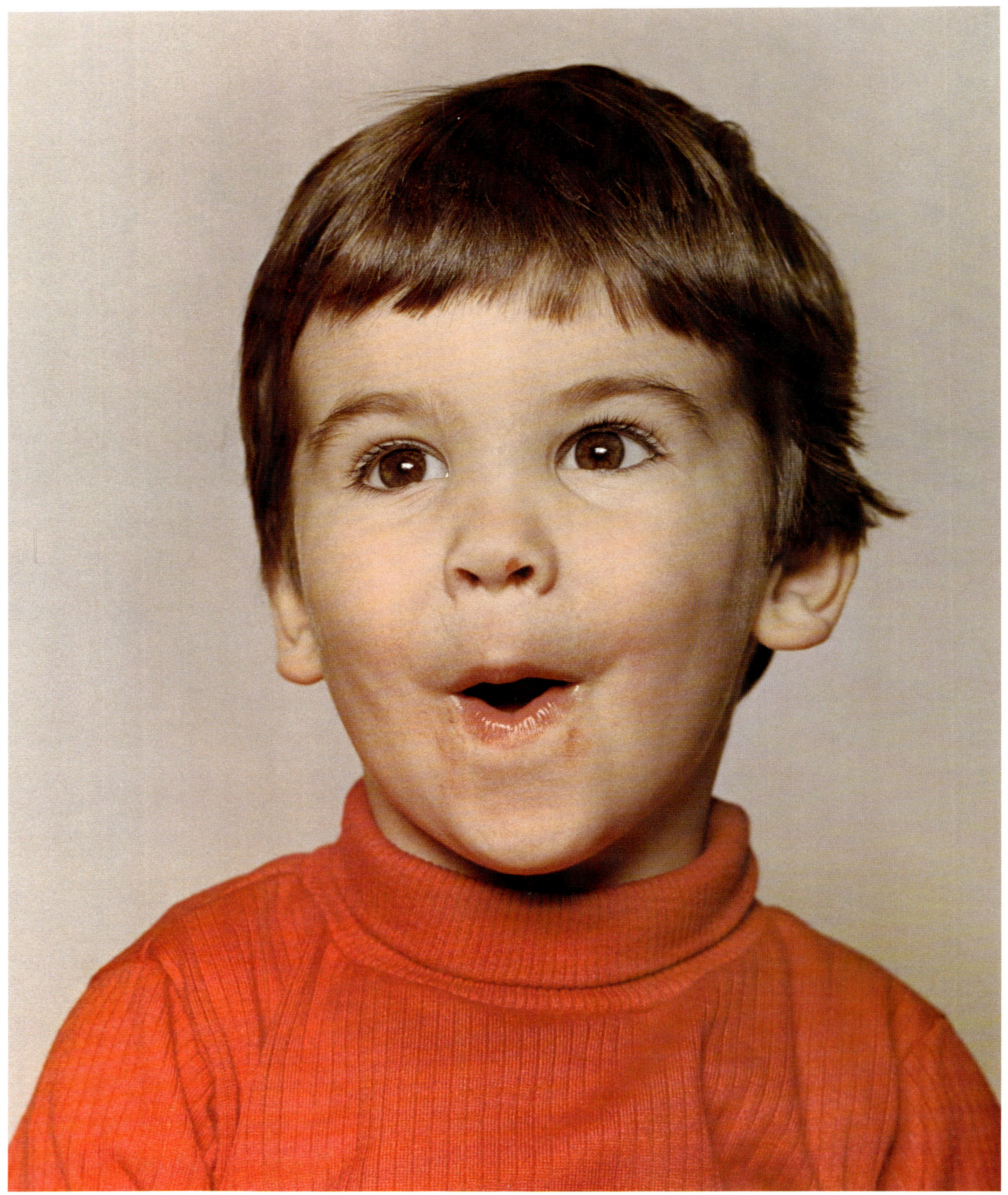

Keith Boas

This picture was made with umbrella flash—an electronic flash unit aimed into an umbrella having a highly reflective surface. For more information on this bounce-light technique, see the description and diagram on page 59.

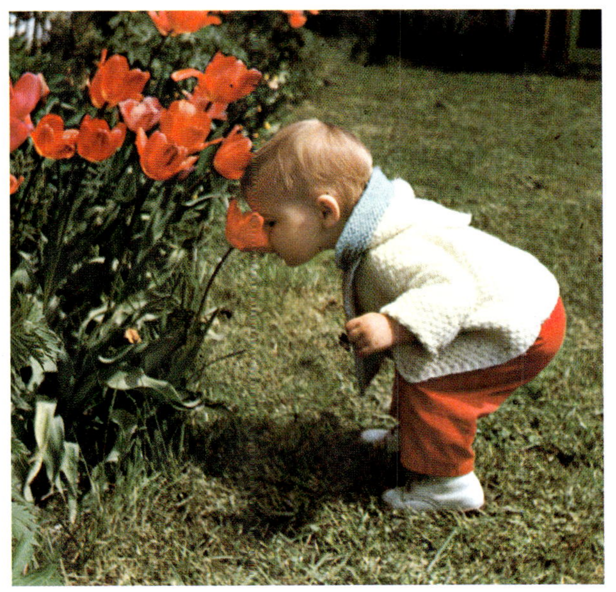

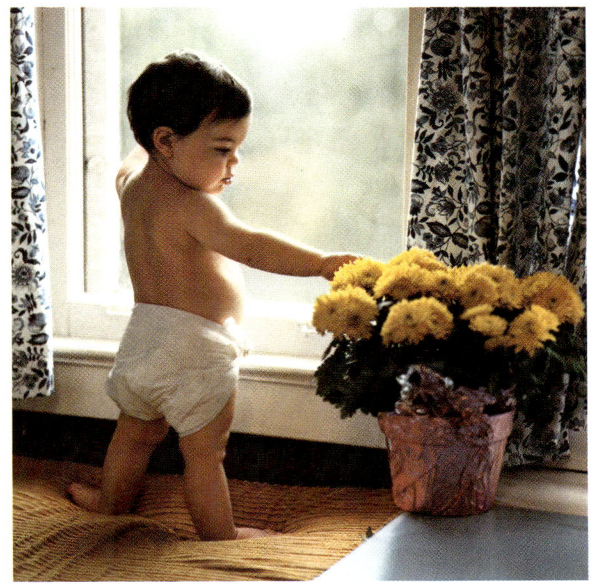

Don Maggio

Part Two: Photographing Children Naturally

Can you remember having your picture taken when you were a child? Someone—your mother, father, or perhaps another relative—would bring out the family camera and begin directing you with comments such as "Hold still," or "Get the hair out of your eyes," or "Stop squinting," or the inevitable "S-m-i-l-e!"

Millions of family snapshots are taken pretty much this way each year. And, for the most part, they are enjoyable to look at and save. There's only one problem with this approach to photographing children—the pictures all tend to look the same after awhile. In this chapter we're going to suggest many ways that you can improve your picture-taking techniques to make more personal photos of children and, at the same time, add variety to your collection of child pictures. We'll be talking about how you can take outstanding child photographs almost as easily as you can a casual snapshot by combining a knowledge of child psychology with an understanding of a few good camera-handling techniques.

Neil Montanus

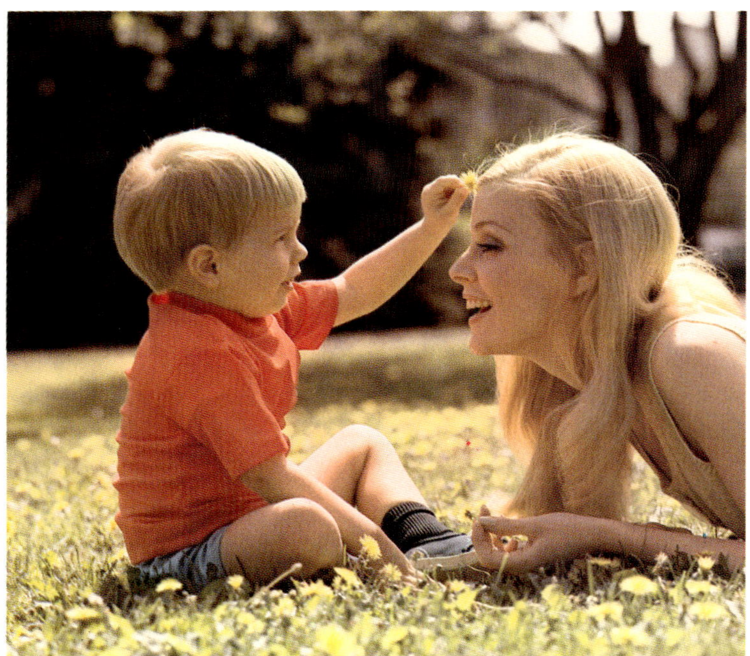

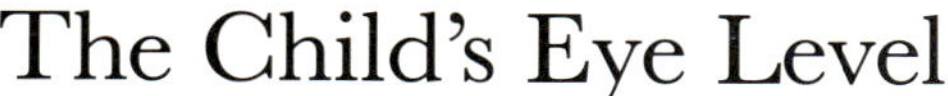

For a personalized, you-are-there feeling, take pictures at the child's eye level.

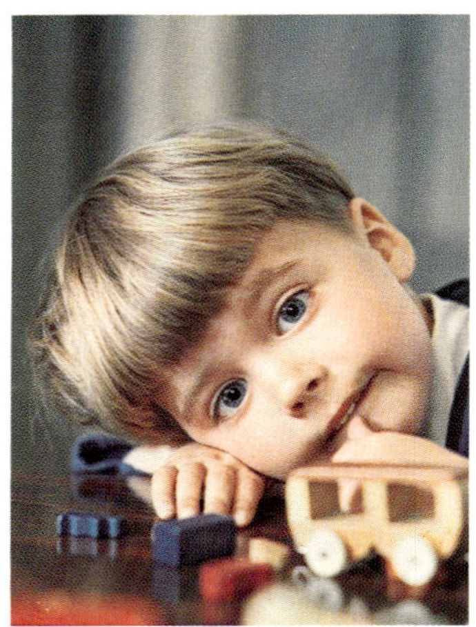

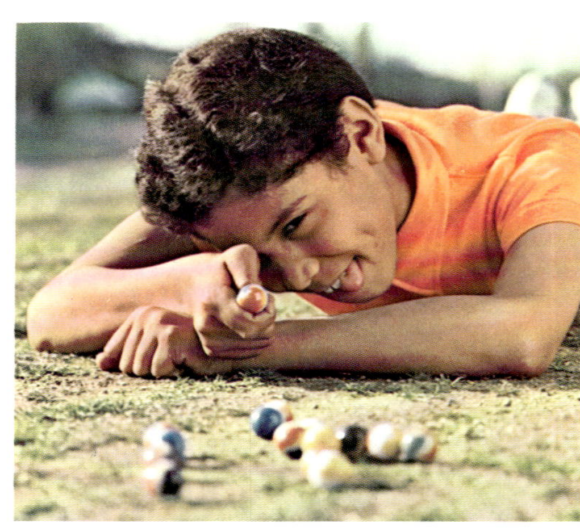

The Child's Eye Level

An easy and natural way to establish a good rapport with a child is to talk with him or her at eye level. This might involve kneeling, sitting with the child, or possibly lifting the child into your arms. Whatever the position, the resulting angle provides you with the best view of the child's face and the opportunity for personal, one-to-one eye contact. Pictures taken at eye level also help personalize the moment. Your viewers can better see the child's features and expression. Pictures taken from a high point of view—while standing over a child who is playing on the ground or floor, for example—will generally be less appealing. The next time that perfect picture opportunity presents itself, put *yourself* and your camera at the child's eye level, even if it means lying on the floor or lawn. Your picture result will reward you for your effort.

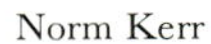

Norm Kerr

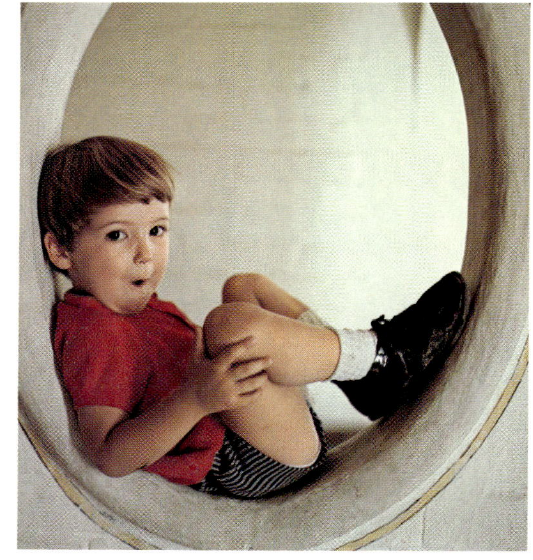

Indoors or outdoors, clear, sharp close-ups call for focusing the camera with care and gently squeezing the shutter release.

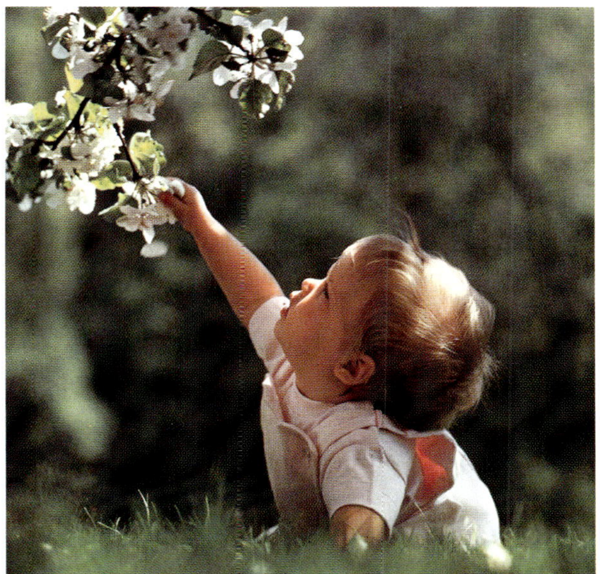

Phoebe Dunn

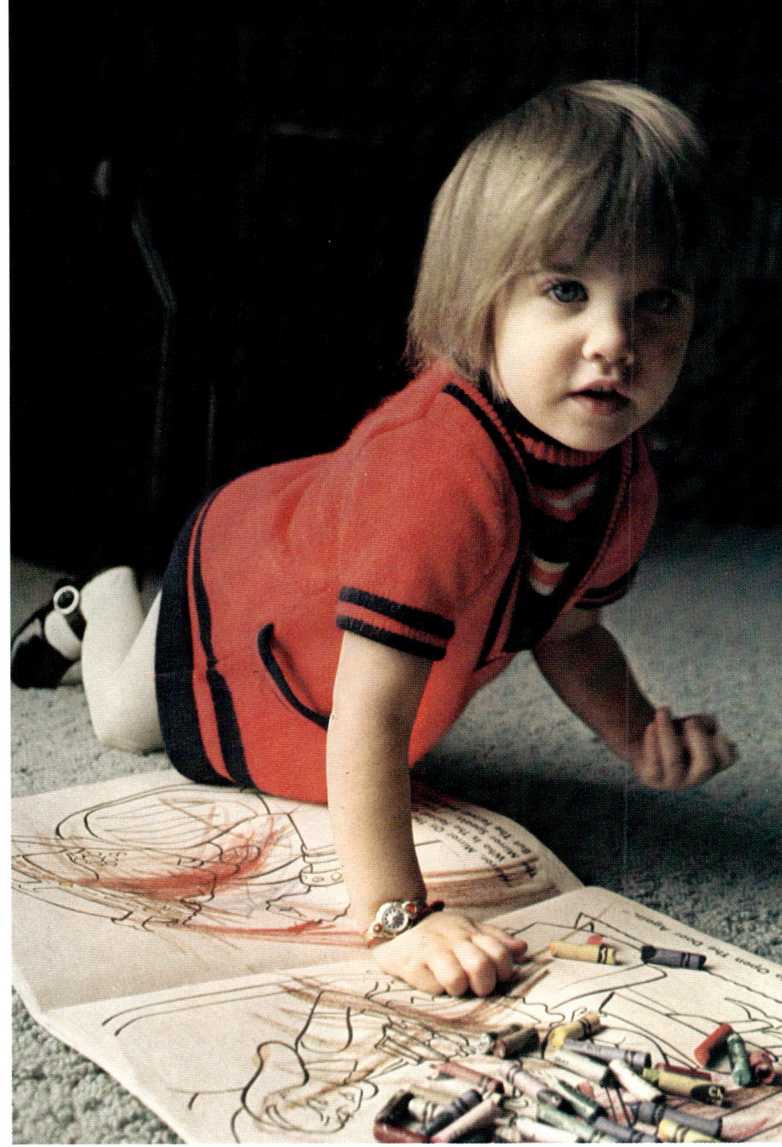

Neil Montanus

Bob Clemens

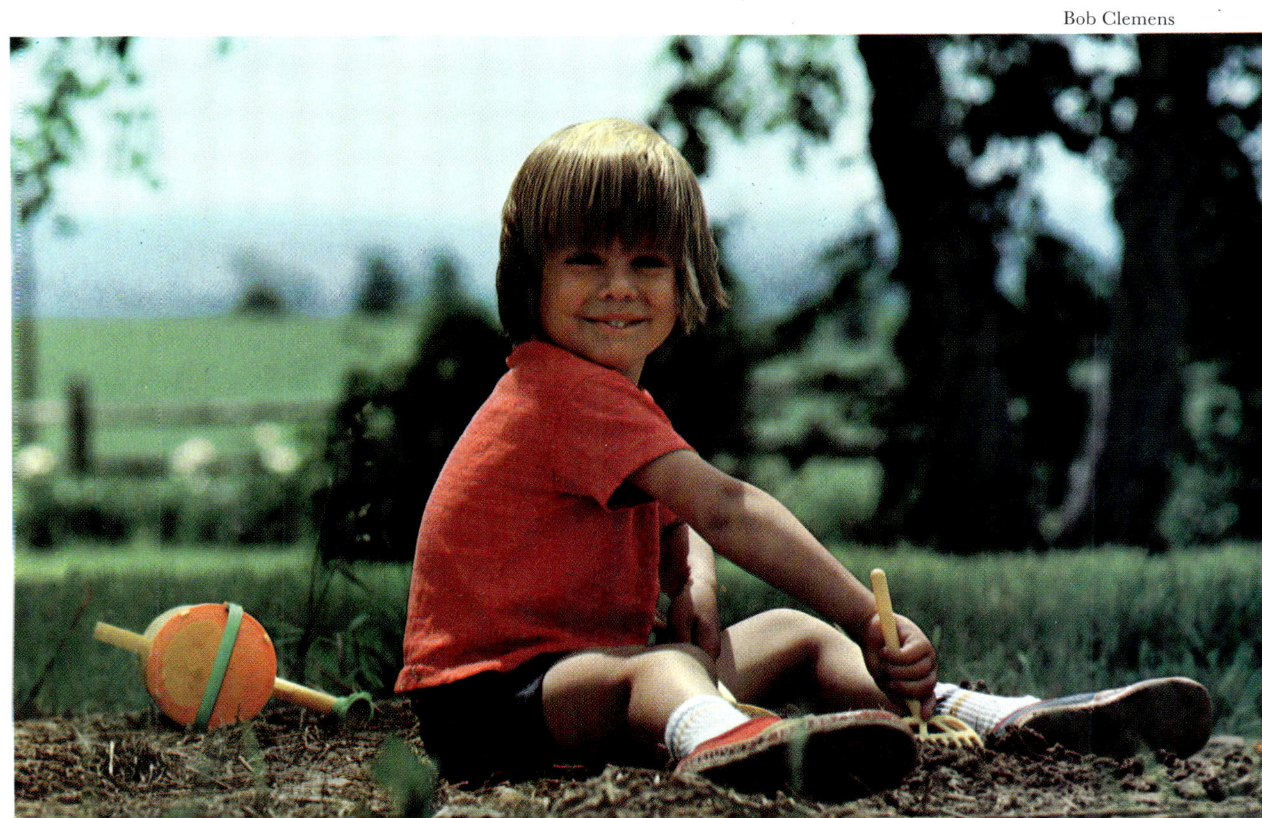

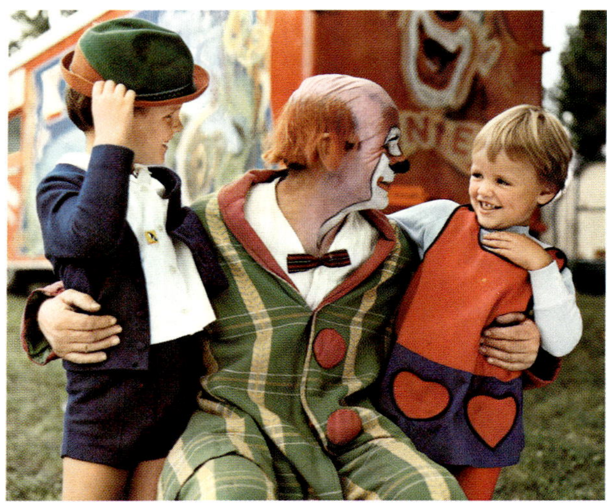

Norm Kerr

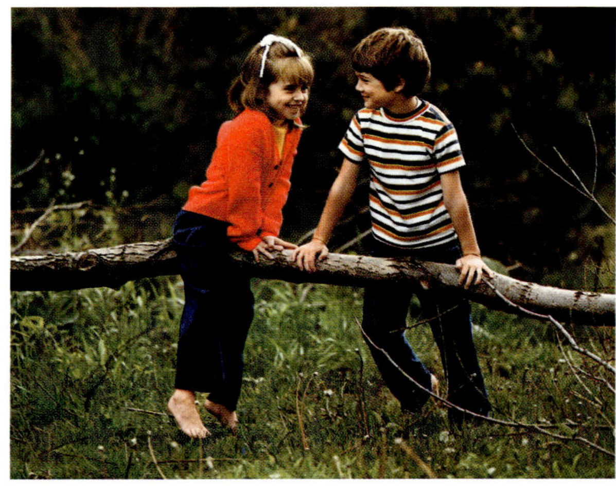

Don Maggio

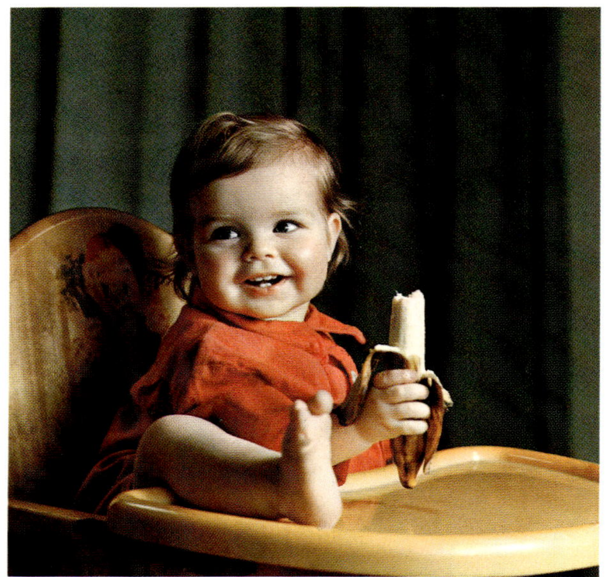

Joseph Schneider

Have you ever noticed how many different facial expressions there are? If you're conscious of a child's moods, you can make several excellent pictures capturing a variety of personality traits.

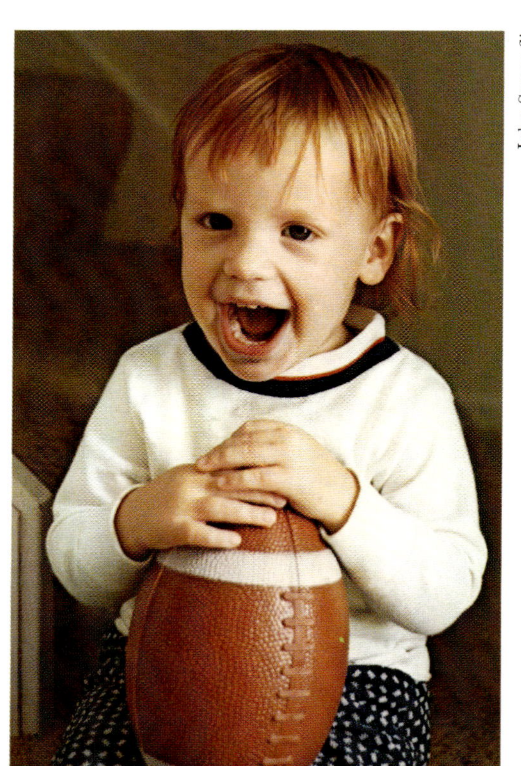

John Stampfli

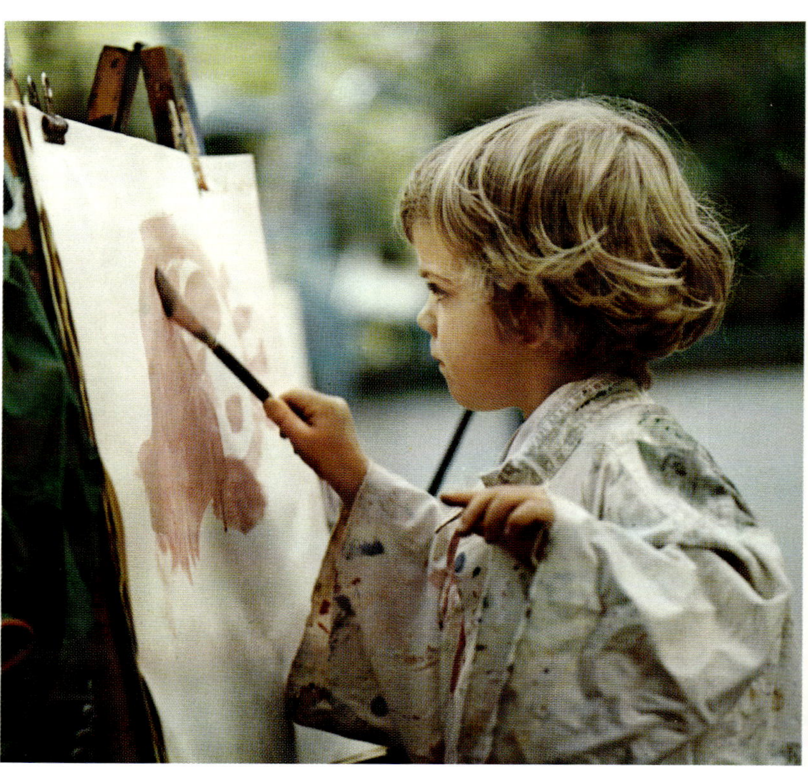

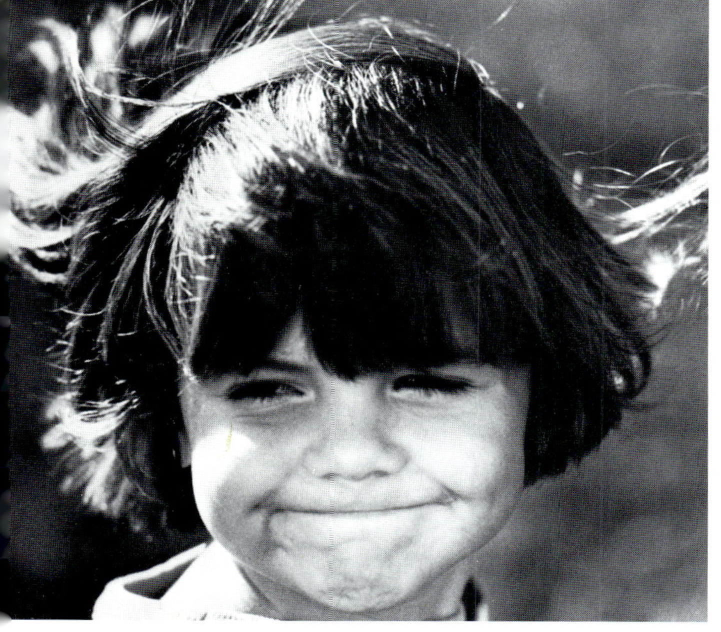

Ruben Ramireza

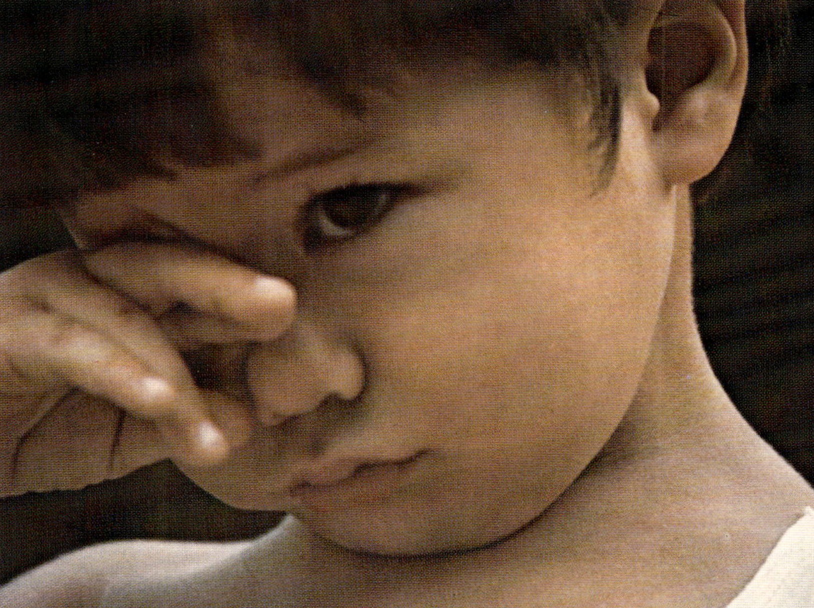

Terri Spillett

Capturing Natural Expressions

Setting out to make a successful picture of a child involves little more than capturing his or her spirit on film. Nearly all photos of babies have this natural quality—they're unaware of the camera. But as children grow they become very much aware of the presence of the camera. They usually try too hard to pose and forced expressions and poses replace their normal, youthful mannerisms. The child's naturalness usually won't return until after you've taken the picture and put the camera away.

Children sometimes don't respond too well to posing directions. As soon as you ask your young models to act or stand in a certain way, they become self-conscious and lose all or most of the naturalness you hoped to achieve. Most little children are extremely eager, often overacting in their attempts to please. Other children may approach the entire situation with a complete lack of interest and, as a result, provide little cooperation. If you try to correct these attitudes, you'll probably get a less than satisfactory response.

But if the youngster is happily wrapped up in an activity of his or her own choosing, you can easily document this natural enthusiasm without the need for any specific posing directions. Take several pictures in a short time as soon as you notice the beginnings of what possibly may emerge into an interesting situation. For example, be ready with your camera when the child is about to discover the presence of an intriguing subject such as a puppy, clown, Santa Claus, or a shiny new toy. During these first few moments of discovery, the child will almost certainly provide you and your camera with a generous variety of happy, excited, natural expressions.

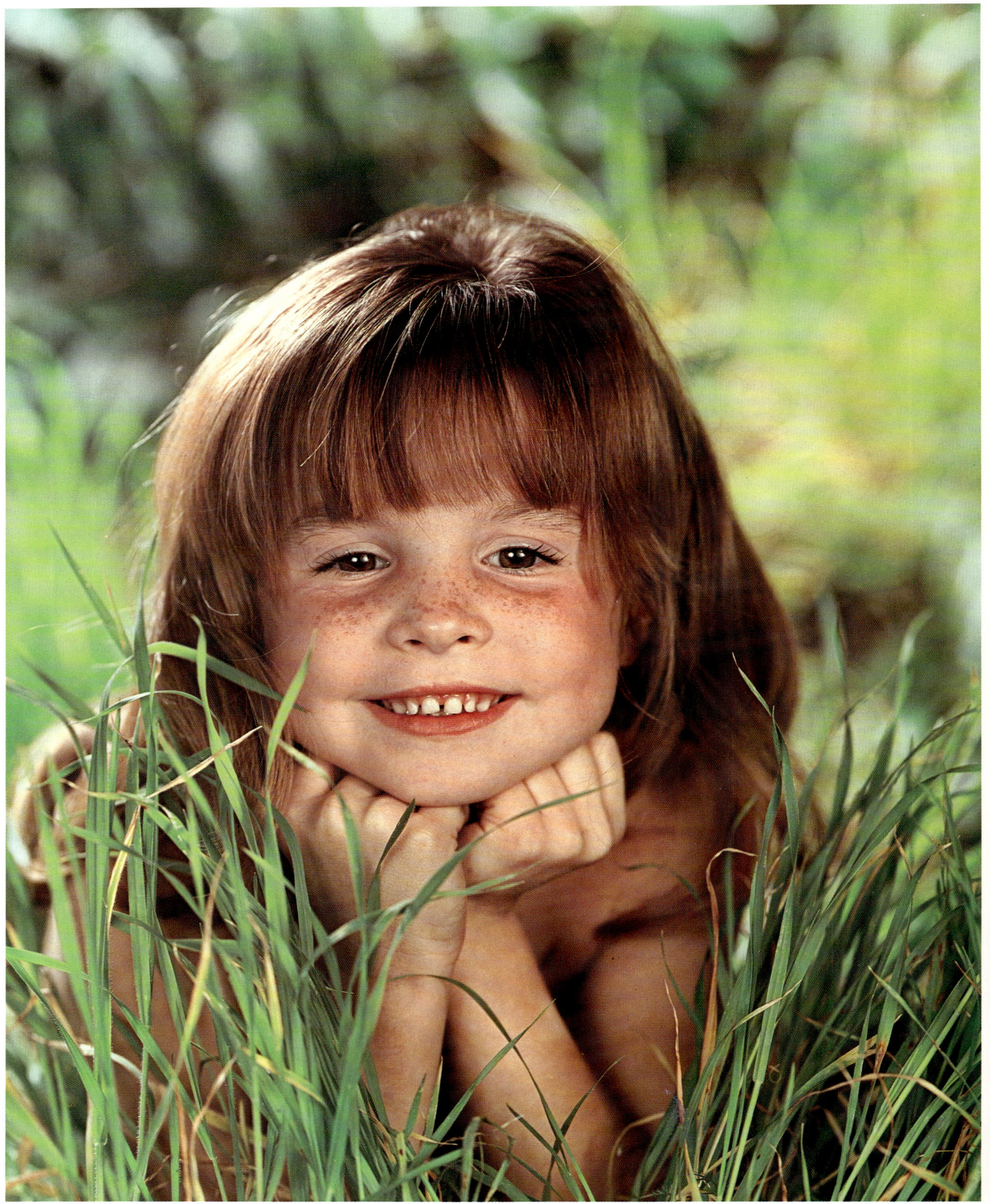

Move in close! Here a frame of summer greenery provided an artistic setting and an element of contrast with the child's red hair.

John Mechling

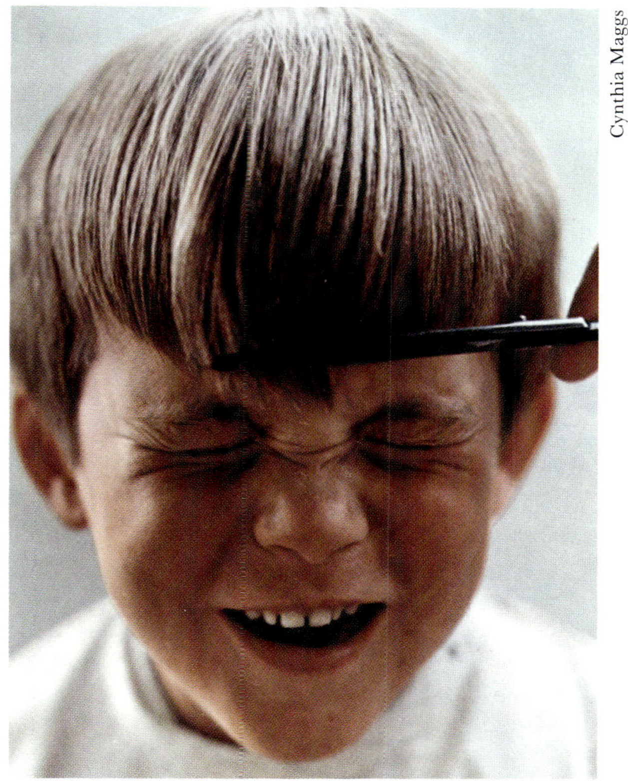

Cynthia Maggs

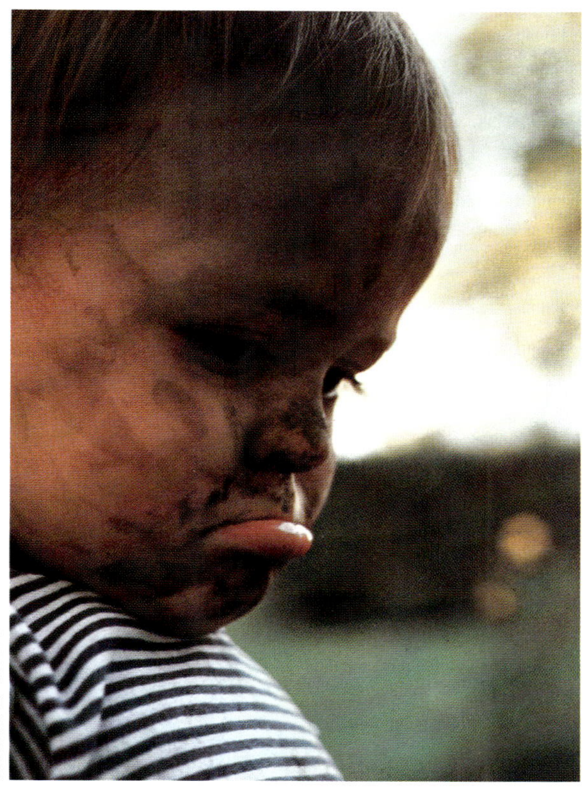

Ronald L. Gearhart

Close-Ups for Impact

Moving in close to your subject is one of the easiest ways to make your pictures better. Close-up pictures of children are better and more interesting because you can clearly see their expressions. Most cameras (even those with fixed-focus lenses) can get as close as 4 feet (1.2 meters), an ideal distance for good close-ups of people and most pets.

If you have a camera with adjustable focusing, shutter speeds, and interchangeable lens capability, you might like to consider using a lens of longer than normal focal length for picturing children. A 100 mm lens on a 35 mm camera, for instance, permits your subject to appear twice as close as it would with the normal (50 mm) lens. This image magnification feature can give you an intimate close-up of a child's face from a distance of several feet away. Longer than normal focal-length (telephoto) lenses are ideal for separating the camera from a child's immediate attention. With the camera farther away, the child will nearly always be more relaxed.

A side benefit from using a telephoto lens is the absence of facial distortion. When you move in close to a subject, as you might with a wide angle or normal lens, nearby objects look unusually large, and distant objects in the same picture look small and far away. This is because the distance between the near and far points is great compared with the distance from the camera to the rear point. A close-up picture—taken about 3 feet (.9 meter) or closer—of a person's face made with a normal or wide-angle lens gives features a distorted appearance. The nose, since it is closer to the camera, looks large, while more distant ears look smaller than normal. With a telephoto lens, you can be several feet away from your subject and still get a nice-size head-and-shoulder image on the film. This means that the nose-to-ears distance is very small in relation to the total subject distance, so the exaggerated perspective mentioned earlier doesn't exist.

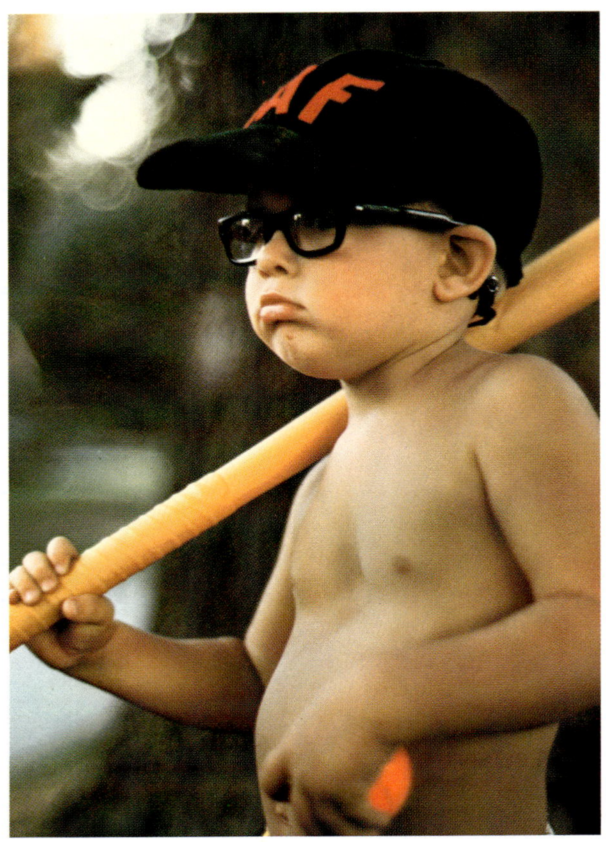

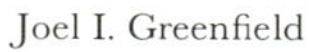
Joel I. Greenfield

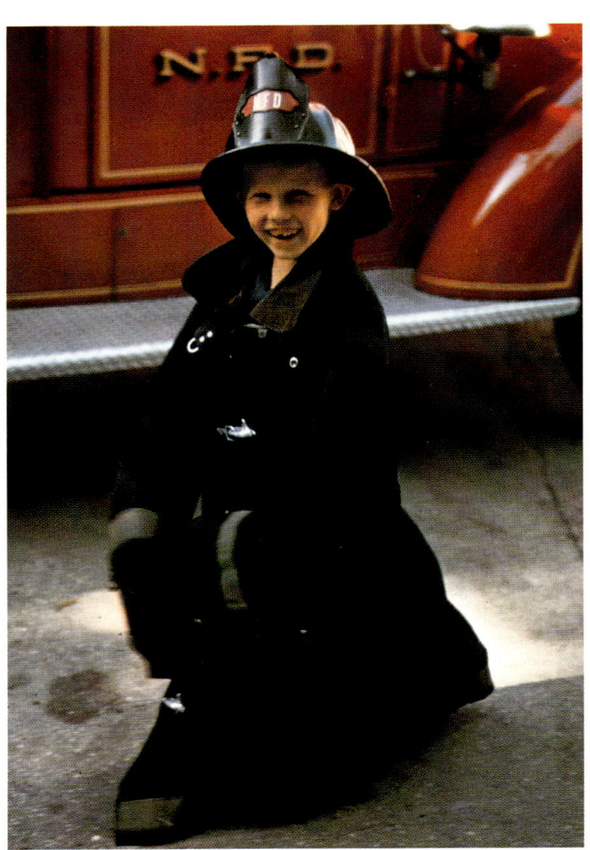

Tom McCarthy

To aid you in taking pictures of children being themselves, select props that appeal to their interests or curiosity.

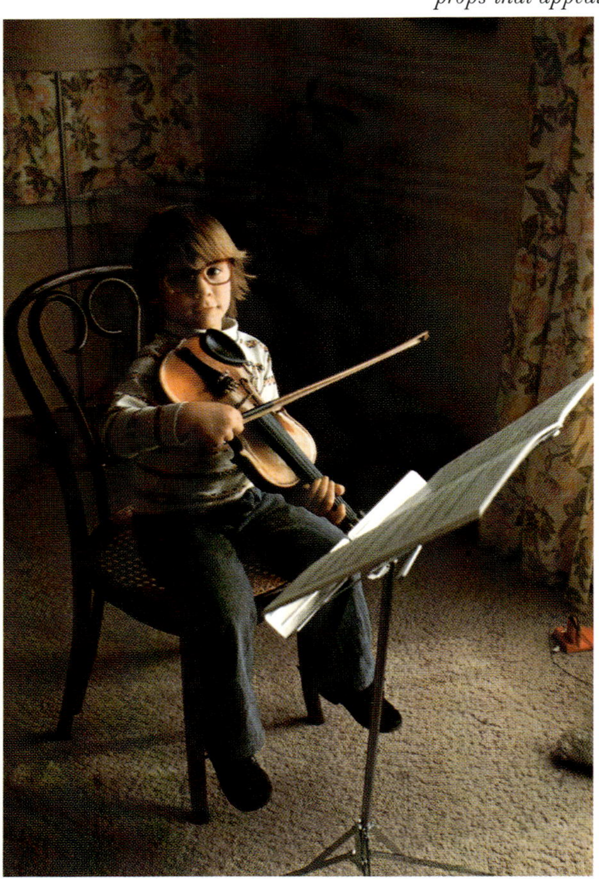

Tom McCarthy

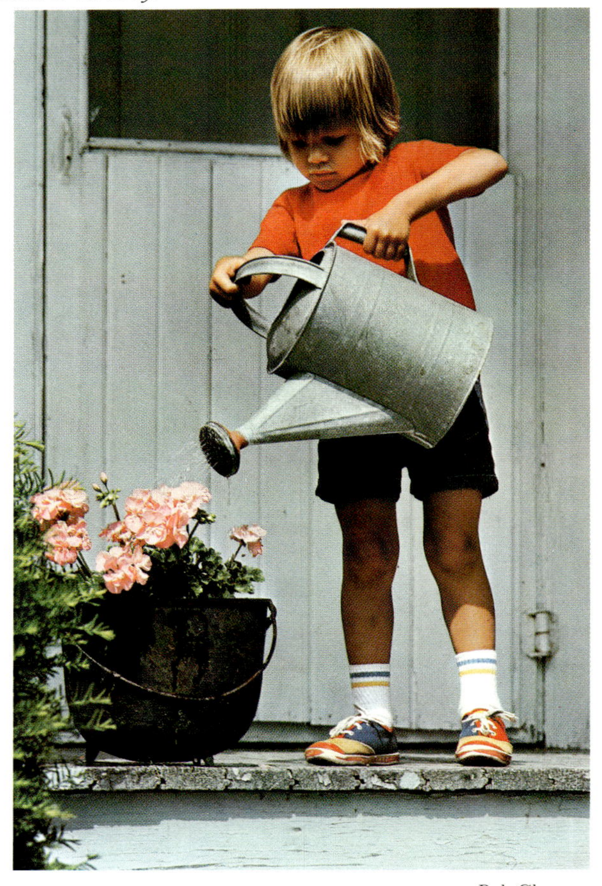

Bob Clemens

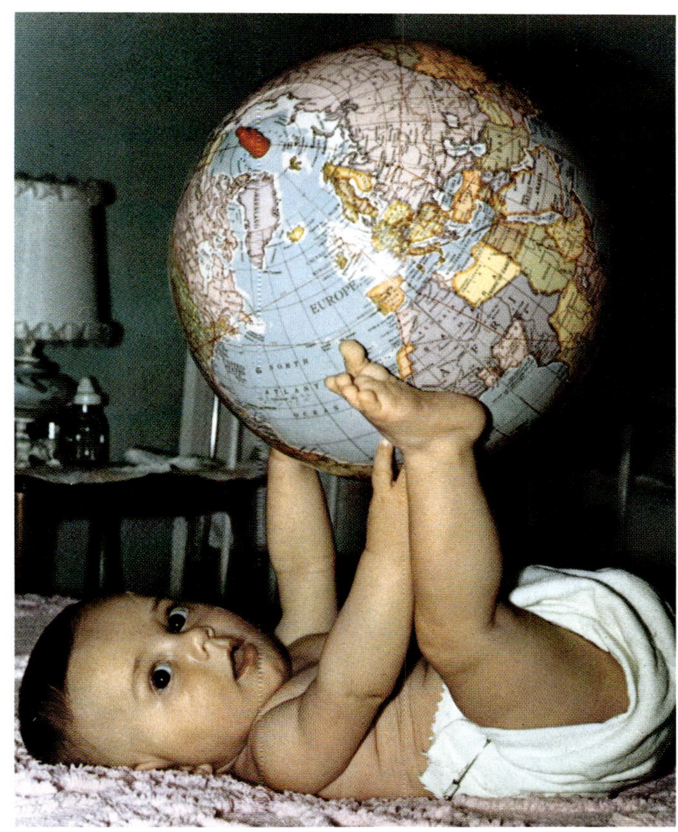

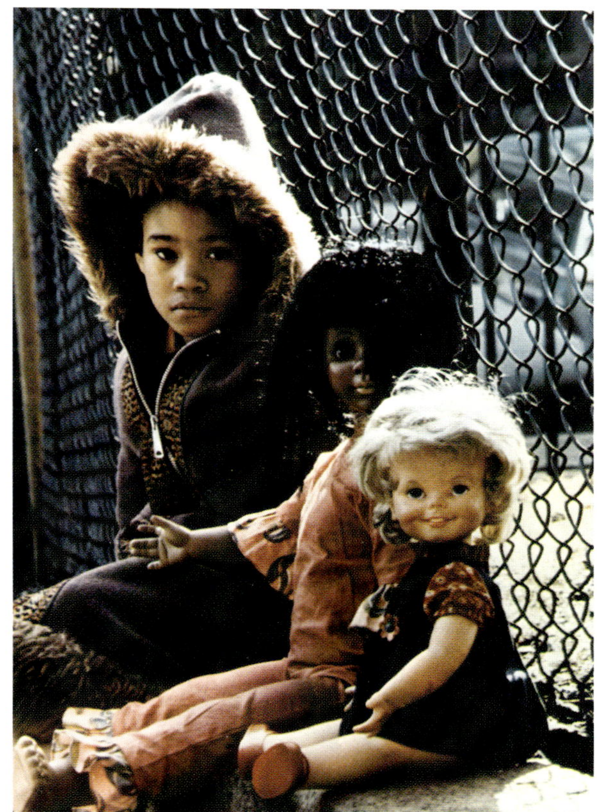

Raymond McAlpin

Props

While it may not always be successful to ask the child to assume a particular pose, you can control the situation to a great extent by giving the child something interesting to do. This will create a distraction and help keep the child in one place. With babies, a stuffed animal or noisy toy are usually all you need to inspire plenty of cute expressions. While the props or suggested activities will be different with older children, the principle remains the same. Appeal to the child's curiosity. Know what interests the youngster and what attracts and holds attention. The child's age usually has a very direct relationship on the kinds of props best for attracting attention and helping you achieve natural-looking pictures. The list of props is endless, including all kinds of colors, sounds, toys, games, balloons, and even food. When your model begins to lose interest in playing with or investigating a particular item, have another prop or two nearby to add new interest—and some additional photographic opportunities.

Children love the adventure that new and different places have to offer. Take your camera with you to the beach, pool, playground, park, zoo, farm—anywhere children love to play. Interesting props for children abound in these areas, and if the child is new to the environment, you'll be provided with plenty of good picture material. Sand and water at the beach, for example, offer lots of entertainment to keep children busy while you snap the pictures. When you take pictures of them playing in the sand, don't forget to get down to their level and move in close. At playgrounds, children love to climb, swing, and slide. These areas give you the opportunity to take pictures of children being themselves.

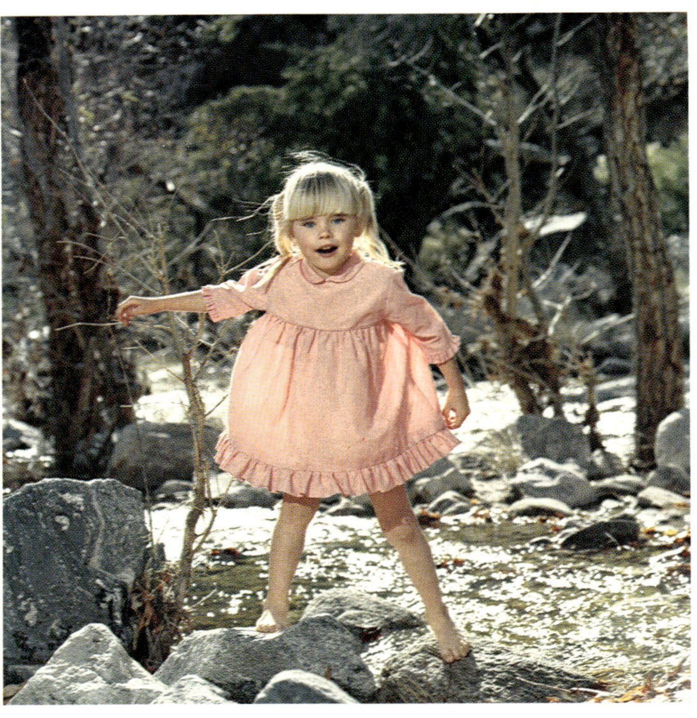

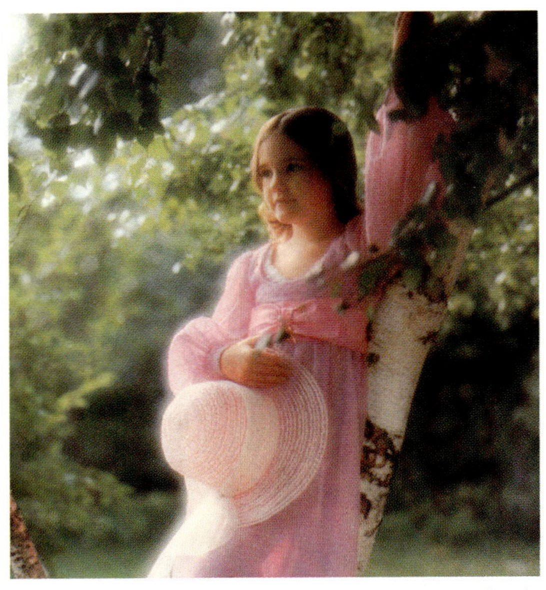

Don Maggio

Clothing

So far we've covered several easy-to-handle techniques and methods of subject control for helping you get successful pictures of children. The choice of clothing is another area that you should consider. Don't overdress your subject. When you have control over what the child is to wear for the picture-taking session, choose colorful, well-fitting, comfortable clothing. Remember—you're after a natural-looking photograph. The proper choice of clothes can make the picture look pleasing and believable. It can also help your model look and feel relaxed and happy. Solid-colored clothing generally contributes toward keeping the picture simple. Clothes overpowered with stripes, plaids, or flower patterns will tend to create clutter in the picture, which can easily compete with the child for attention.

It's a good idea to also avoid loose-fitting clothes unless you are attempting to produce a special effect. Snug but comfortable clothing will do wonders in making the child appear neat, well-groomed, and healthy.

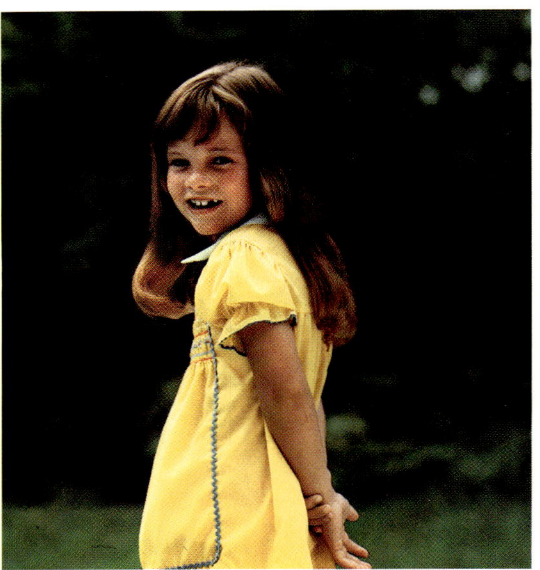

Don Maggio

Lee Howick

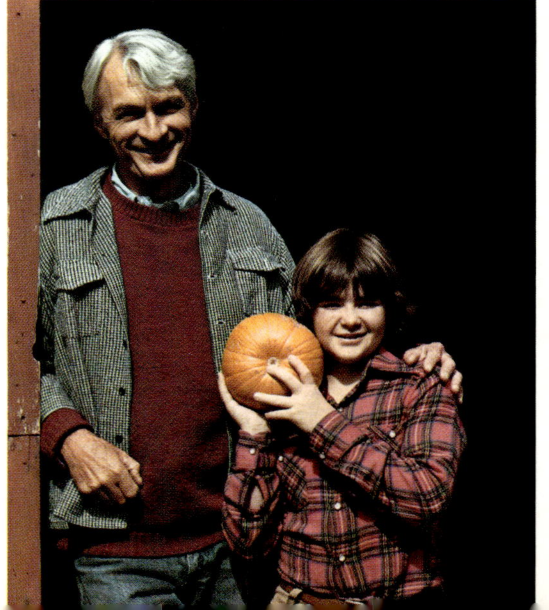

Keep your picture simple and natural-looking by having your subjects wear well-fitting clothes that are not overpowered by bold stripes and designs.

On sunny days, take advantage of natural reflectors such as water, a white tablecloth, or light-colored ground to fill in the shadows on your subject's face. If no natural reflector is available, use fill-in flash or a large sheet of white cardboard.

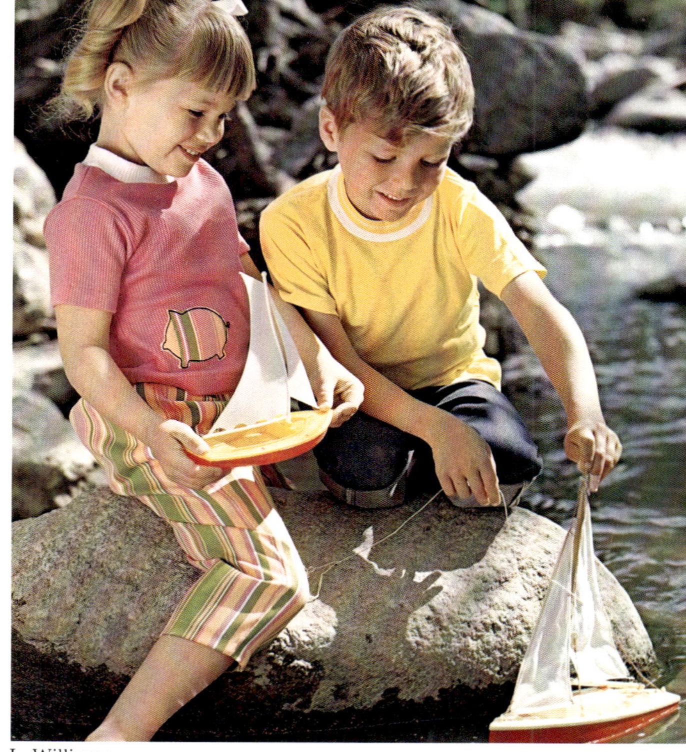

L. Willinger

Lighting: Outdoors

Outdoor lighting is quite variable. The weather, time of day, and your particular location outdoors all play major roles in determining both light quality and quantity. Sometimes there might be brilliant sunlight shining on the front, side, or back of the child. At other times it may be the shadowless light of an overcast day or the dim light of a deep forest. Knowing how to make the most of the various outdoor lighting situations will mean better pictures for you and also present you with extra picture opportunities.

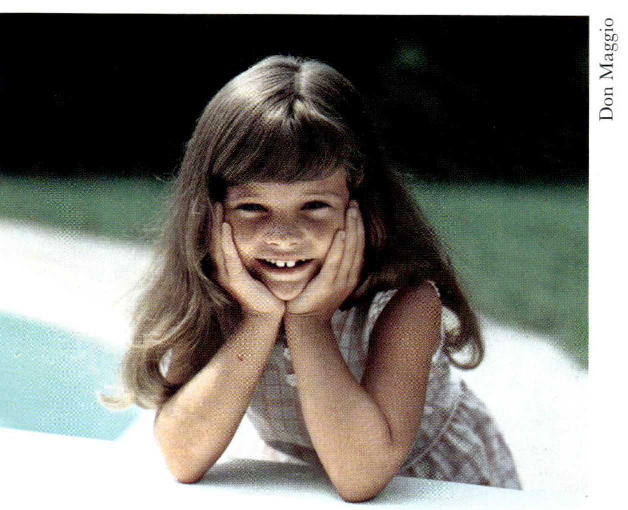

Don Maggio

Bright Sunlight

Most outdoor pictures of people are made in bright sunlight. It offers the advantage of making colors look their brightest. Exposure calculation is also easy in bright sunlight because you can use the same exposure settings most of the time. As long as your subjects have full sunlight on their faces, your settings will stay the same during most of the day.

Even though the bright sun makes picture-taking easy, you may notice that your child is squinting or that shadows on his or her face are distracting. One way to eliminate these effects is to use fill-in flash. Place your subject with the sun at his or her back or side. Then use a flashbulb or an electronic flash unit on your camera. To preserve the natural sunlight effect, the light

H. Armstrong Roberts

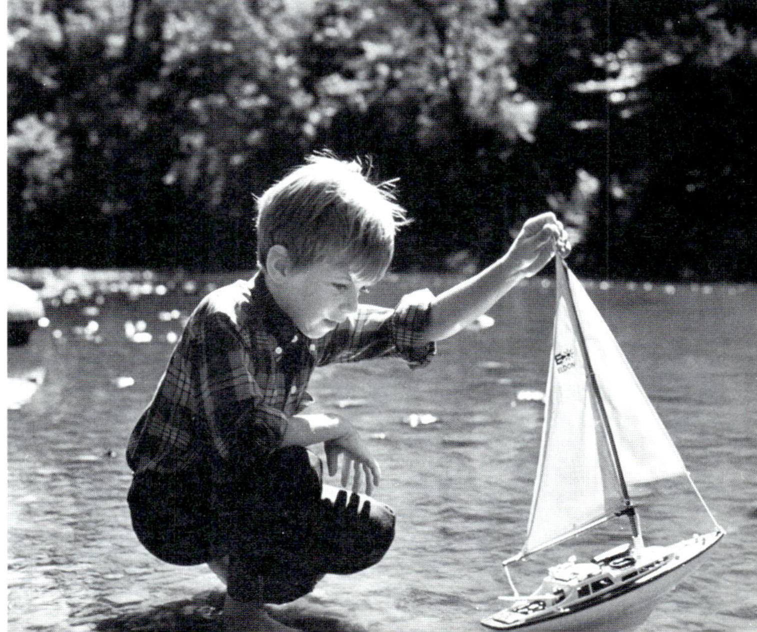

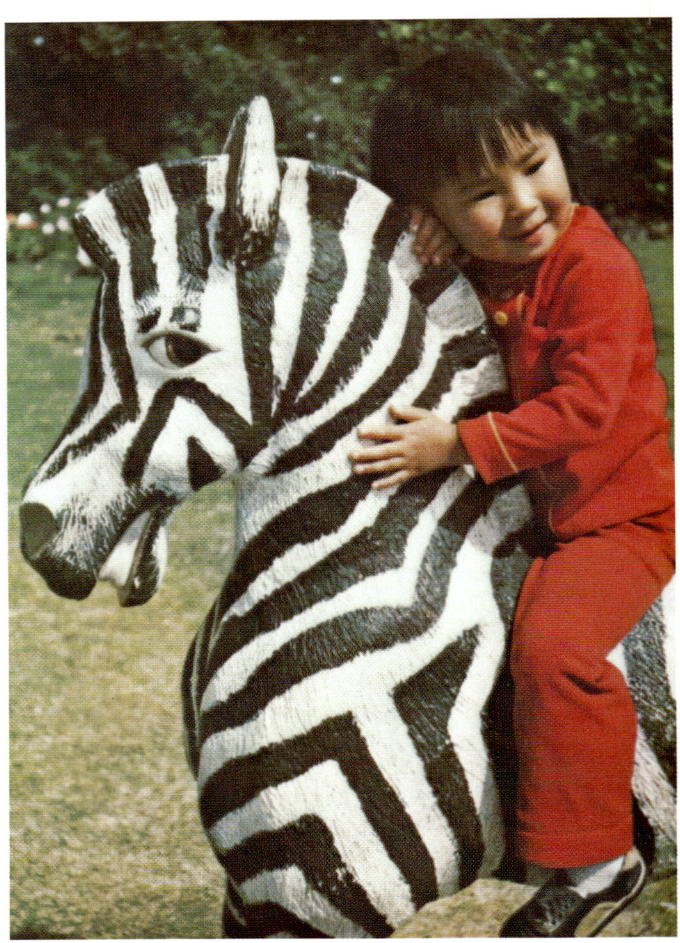

Peter Gales

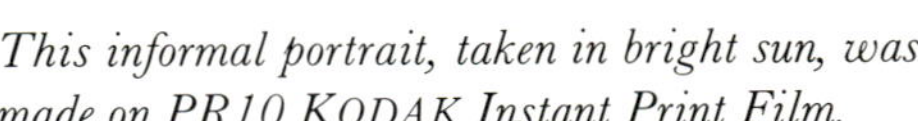

This informal portrait, taken in bright sun, was made on PR10 KODAK Instant Print Film.

Here the youngster was asked to direct his attention toward the toy truck, away from the sun. The result is a more natural pose—one that's free from a squinting expression. In each example, a 16 x 20-inch piece of white cardboard reflected light into the shadows to soften them.

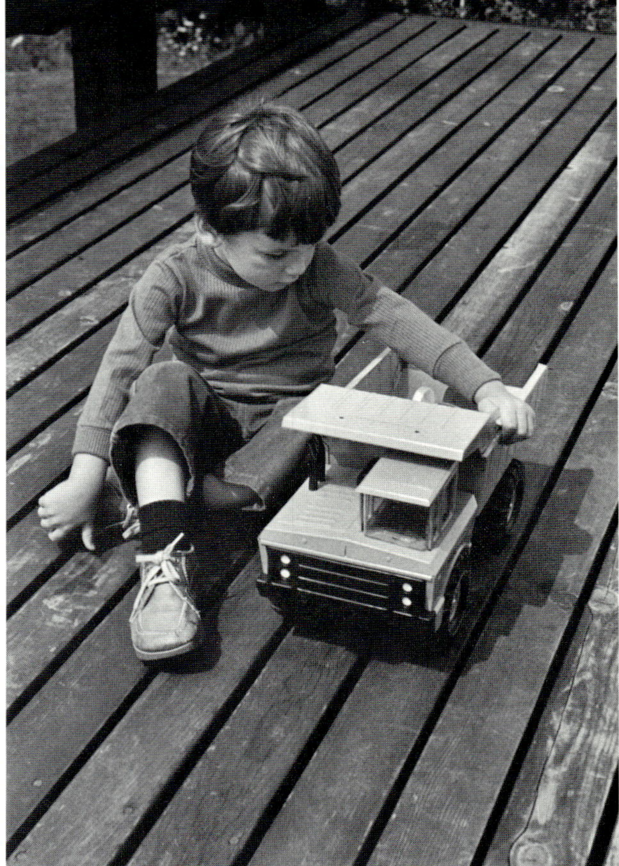

Keith Boas

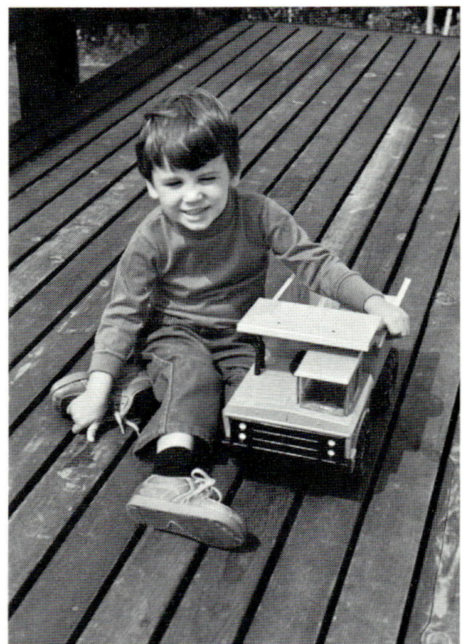

When your subject looks toward bright sunlight, you can usually expect some squinting.

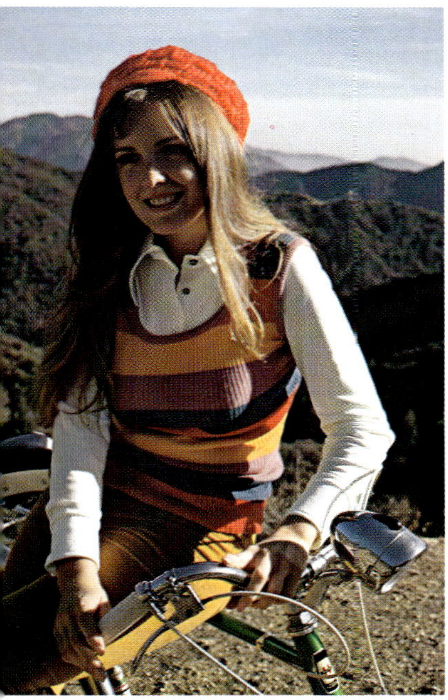

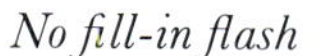

No fill-in flash

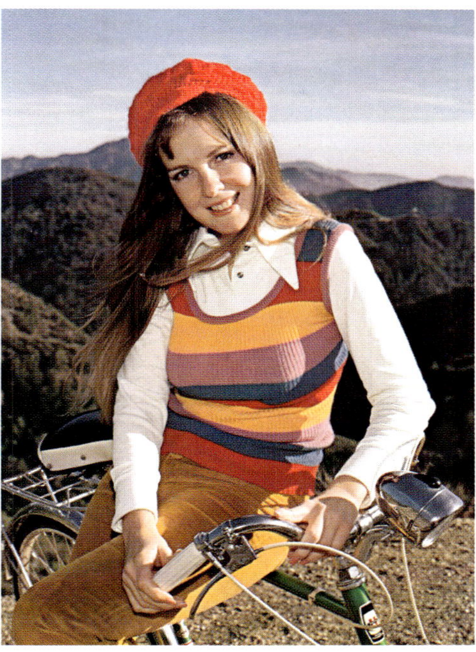

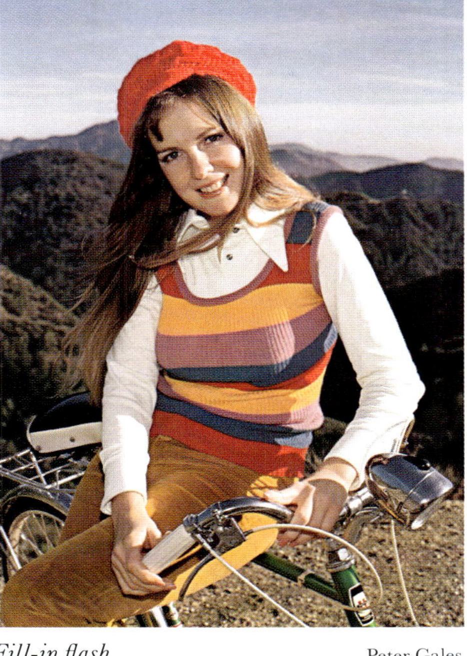

Fill-in flash

Peter Gales

Pete Culross

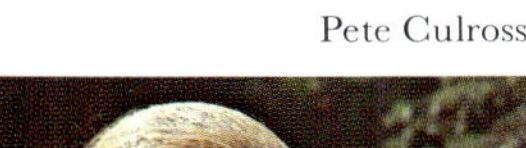

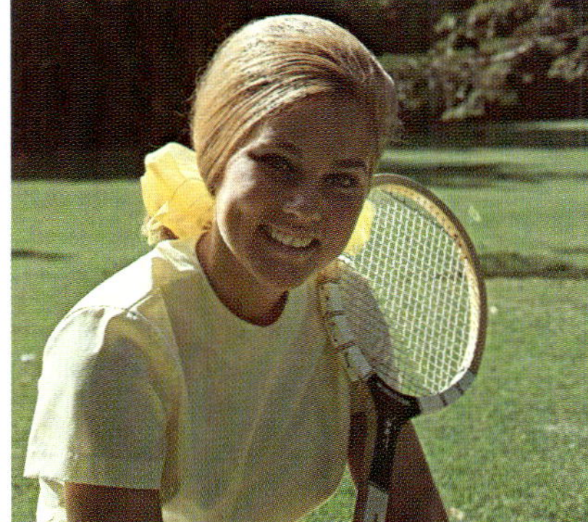

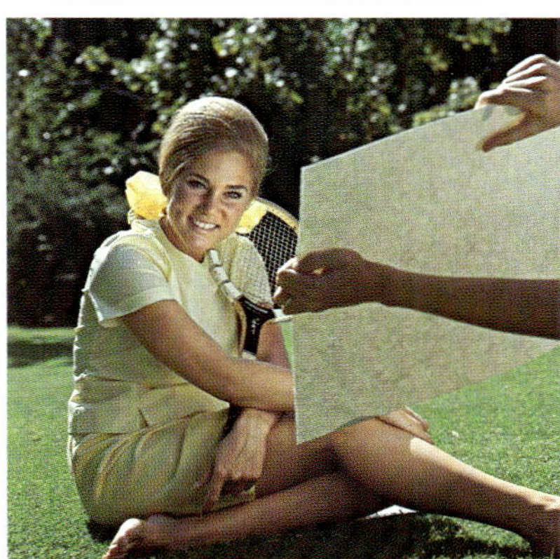

Notice how the shadows in the picture on the top have been filled in by the light reflected from a large white cardboard.

from the flash should lighten the shadows but not completely eliminate them. Check with your camera instruction manual for specific ways to set your particular equipment for fill-in flash.

You can also reduce shadows on the faces of your subjects on sunny days by using a reflector. As in the case of pictures made with fill-in flash, position the child so that the face is in shadow and the sun is at his or her back or side. The reflector can be almost anything that will reflect light. A sheet of white cardboard, approximately 16 x 20 inches (40 x 50 centimeters), makes an effective reflector. It also helps to have an assistant handy to hold the reflector while you are directing and taking the pictures. If you do not have a helper available, you can tape the reflector to an object such as a camera tripod leg.

When using the reflector, it sometimes is possible to bounce too much light into the child's face, creating unnatural lighting. Rotate the reflector back and forth slightly while watching the amount of light being bounced onto the child's face. If too much light reaches the face from the reflector, causing unnatural brightness and squinting, simply turn the reflector a bit away from the face to reduce some—but not all—of the bounce light.

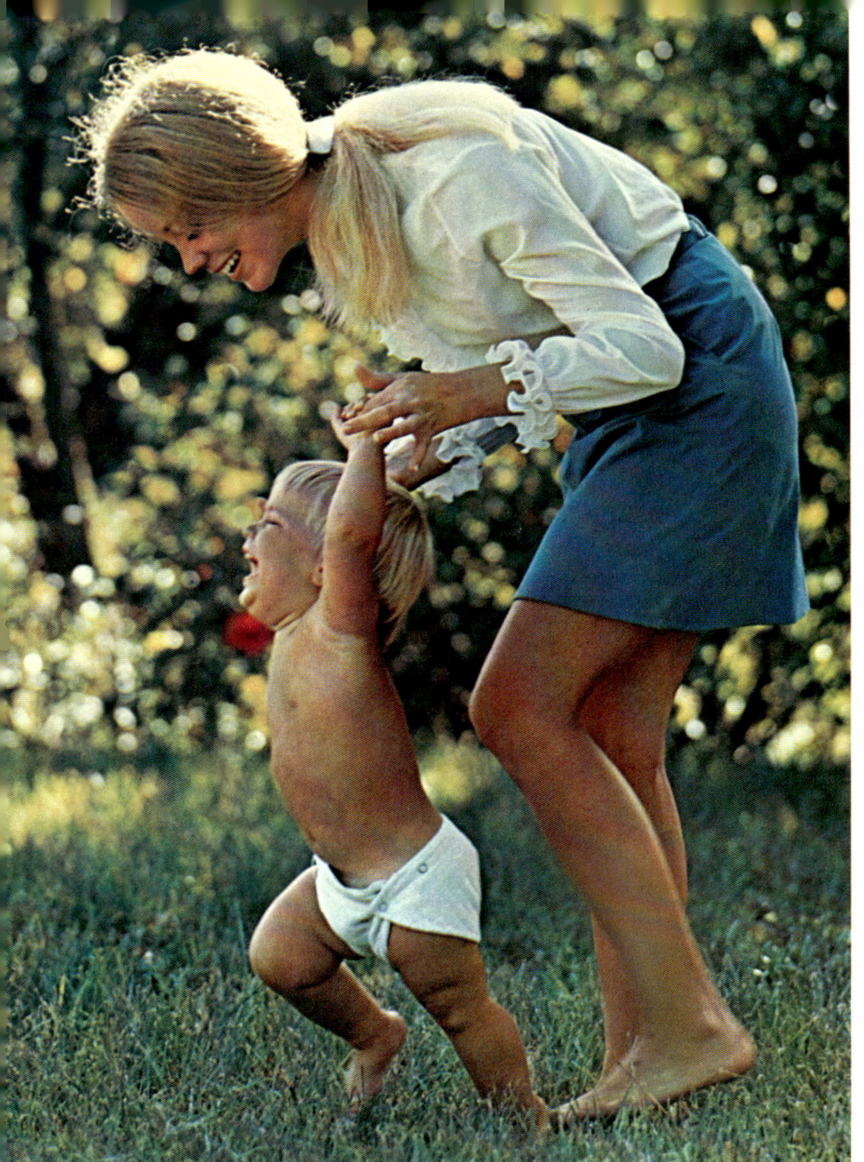

Dennis Hallinan

These pictures were taken in open shade, a lighting condition in which your subject is shaded from the sun by large nearby objects that are not overhanging the subject. Illumination comes from a large area of open sky overhead, in front of the subject. Open shade usually requires an exposure increase of 3 stops over that for bright sunlight conditions. If you don't have an adjustable camera, use a high-speed film such as KODACOLOR 400 Film to get good exposure.

Open Shade

Another way you can reduce lighting contrast is to have the child step out of direct sunlight and into the soft lighting of open shade. Open shade is the shade cast by large nearby objects; you should be able to see a large area of blue sky overhead. When you take pictures of children (or other subjects) in the shade, be sure that they are entirely in the shade, not partly in sunlight. A subject partly in shade and partly in sunlight has very contrasty lighting (often called "hatchet" lighting) which is usually undesirable for picture-taking.

Frank Cowan

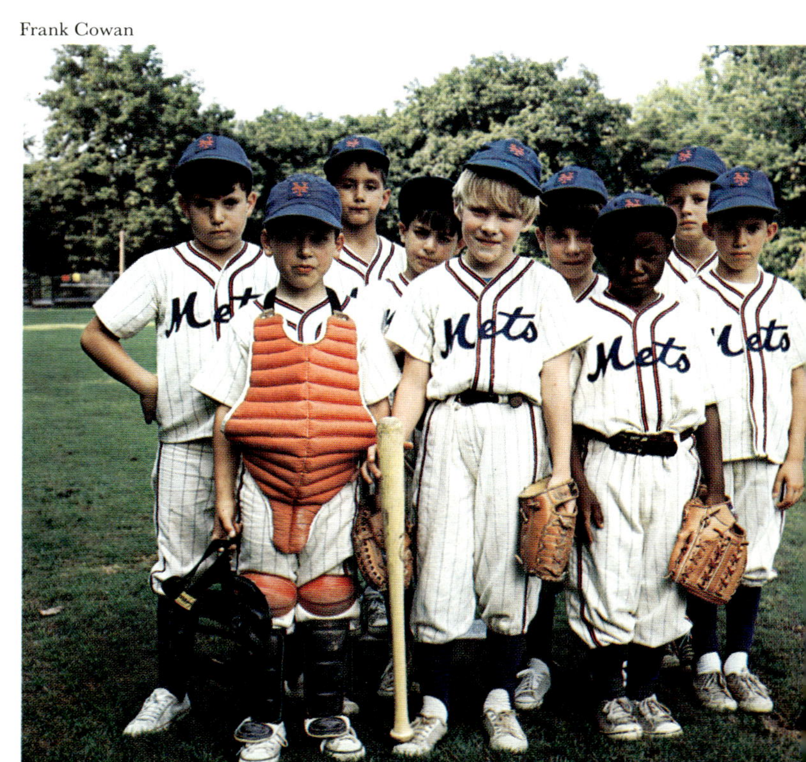

When the sun is obscured by light clouds so that it doesn't cast shadows, you'll usually get a good picture with an exposure of 2 stops more than the basic sunlight condition. With a nonadjustable camera, just use a high-speed material such as KODACOLOR 400 Film, which is available in 110 size (for pocket cameras) as well as in 135 size.

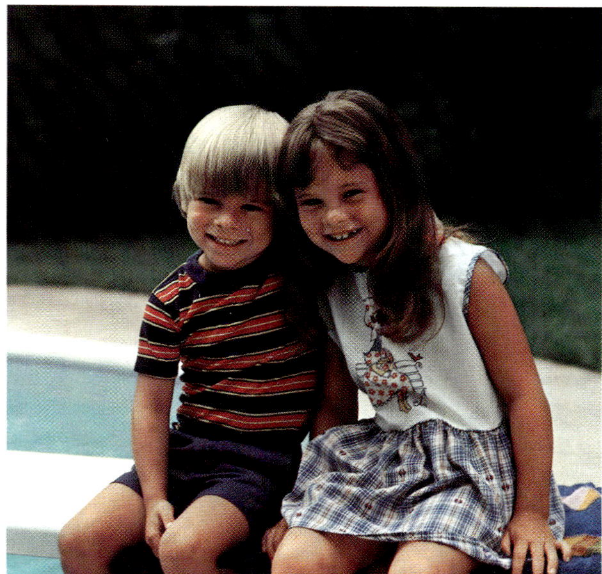

Don Maggio

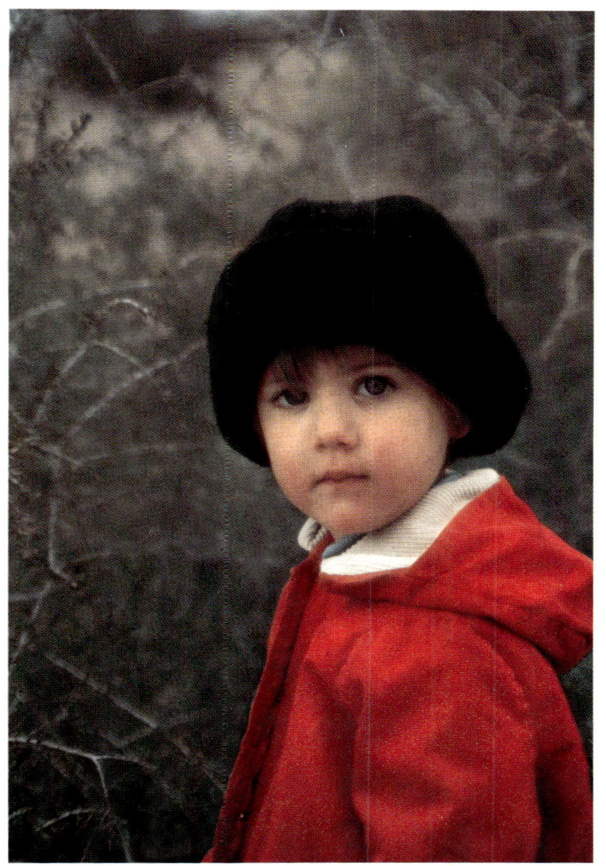

Thomas Ballard

Gary Boyd

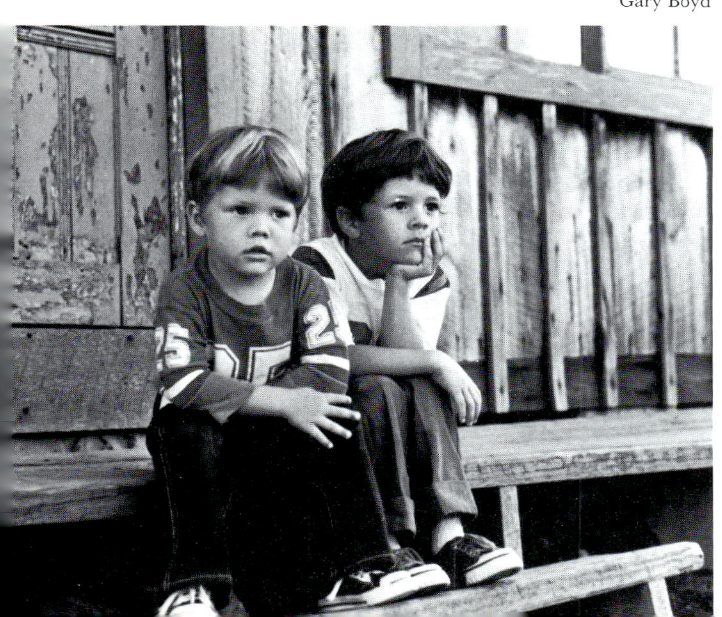

Overcast Days

An overcast or hazy day, from a photographic standpoint, can be one of your best friends. The light falling on your subject is diffused and even. Since there are no harsh shadows, you do not have to be concerned about using fill-in flash or a reflector. You'll find that colors are not as brilliant as they are in bright sunlight, but they tend to record on film as very flattering pastels.

If the lighting is only moderately hazy, your camera exposure would be the same as for bright sunlight. On overcast days when the sky appears white (a condition commonly referred to as "cloudy bright"), some extra exposure will be needed. The increase in exposure will probably be about 2 *f*-numbers. While adjustable cameras (including those with automatic exposure control) can easily handle this exposure increase, less expensive, nonadjustable cameras need a little help. If your camera falls into this latter category, use flash and restrict your picture-taking distance to the recommended flash-subject range for your equipment (usually between 4 feet/1.2 meters and 10 feet/3 meters).

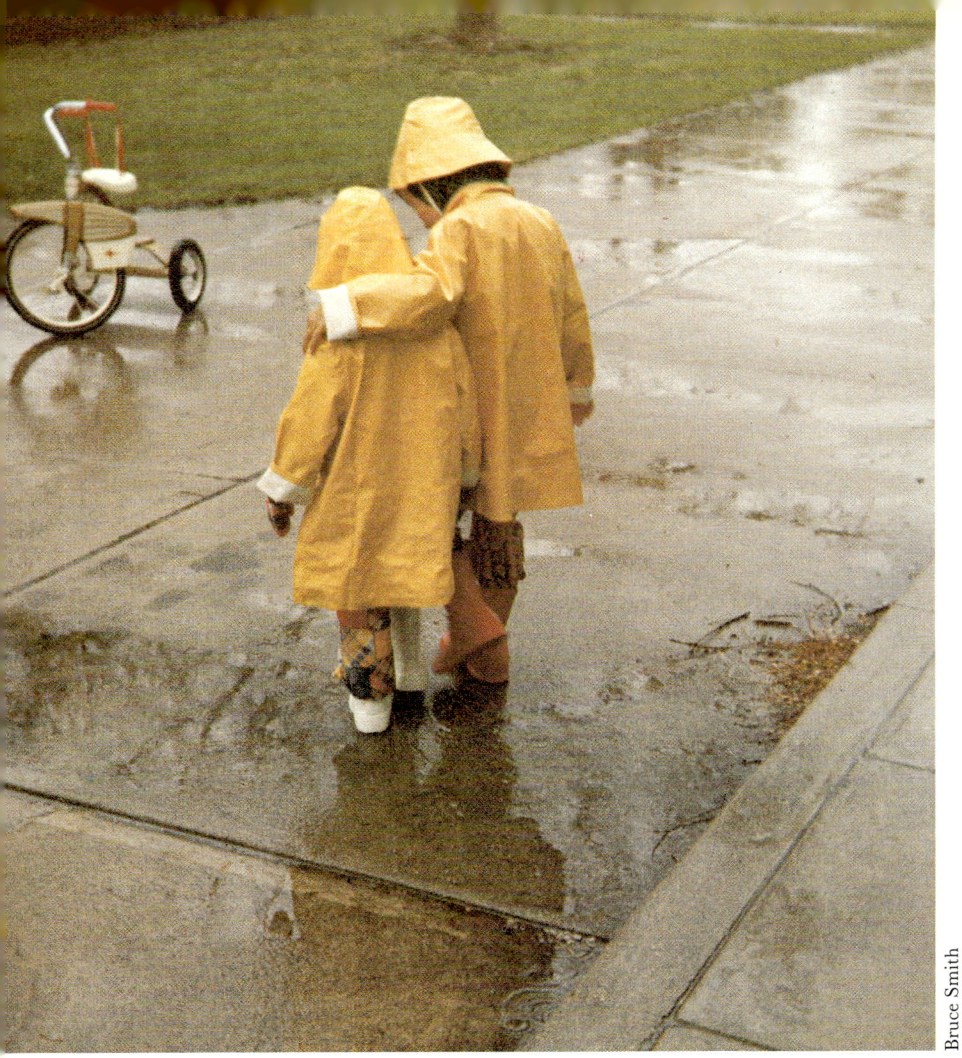

Bruce Smith

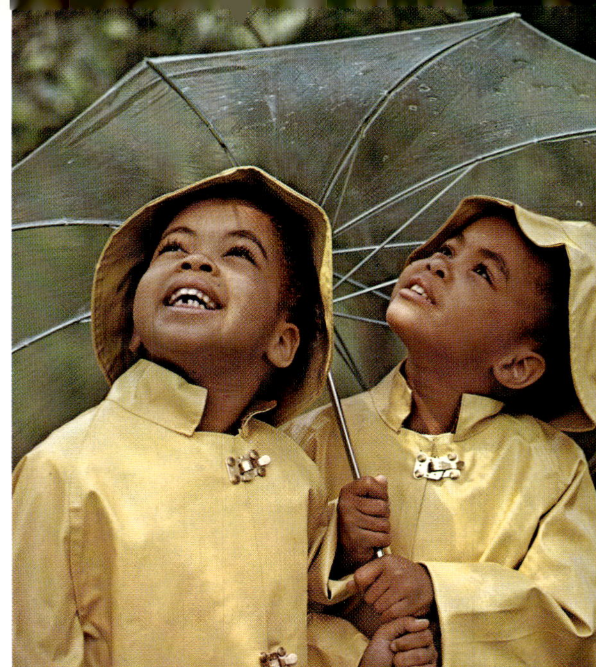

Joseph Schneider

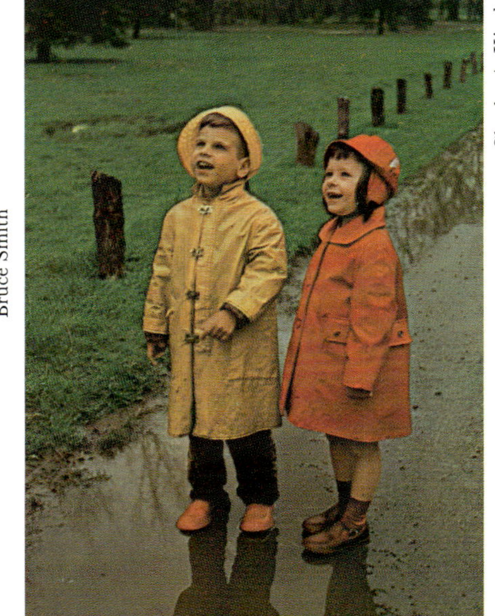

Charles A. Kinsley

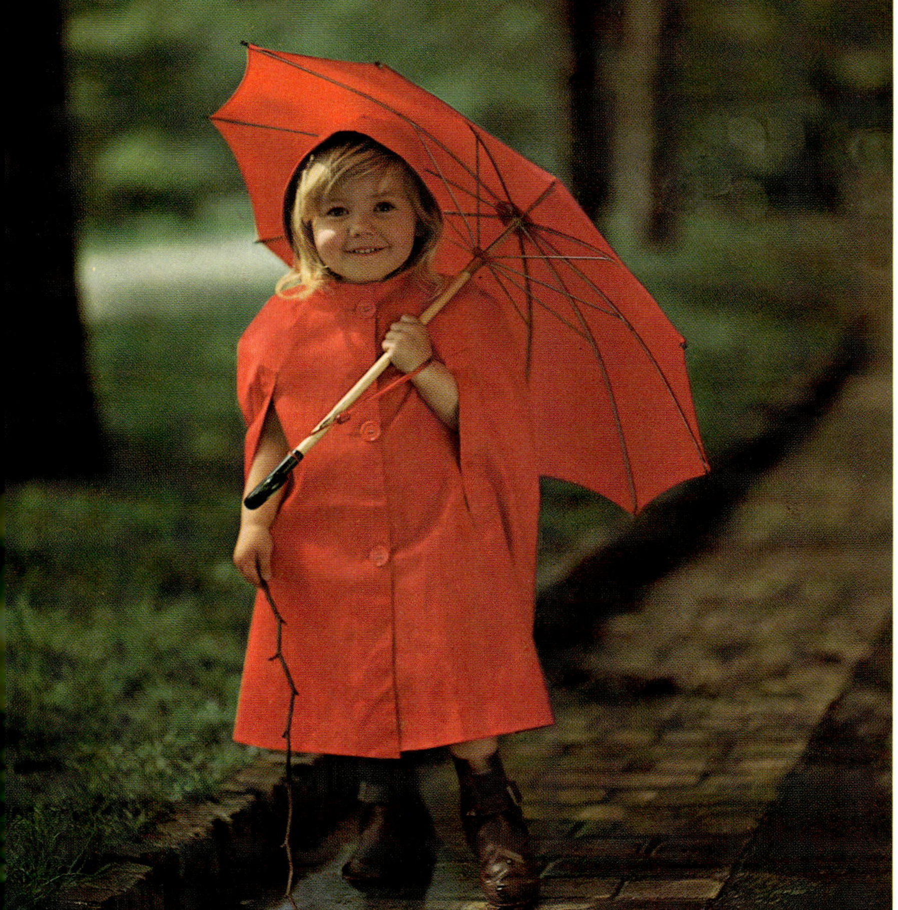

Tana Hoban

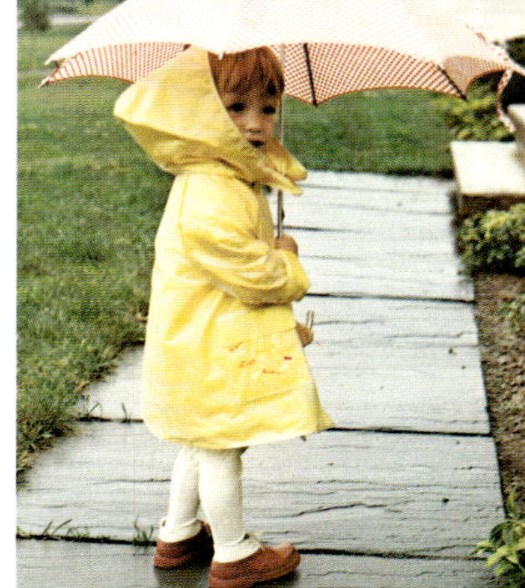

John Stampfli

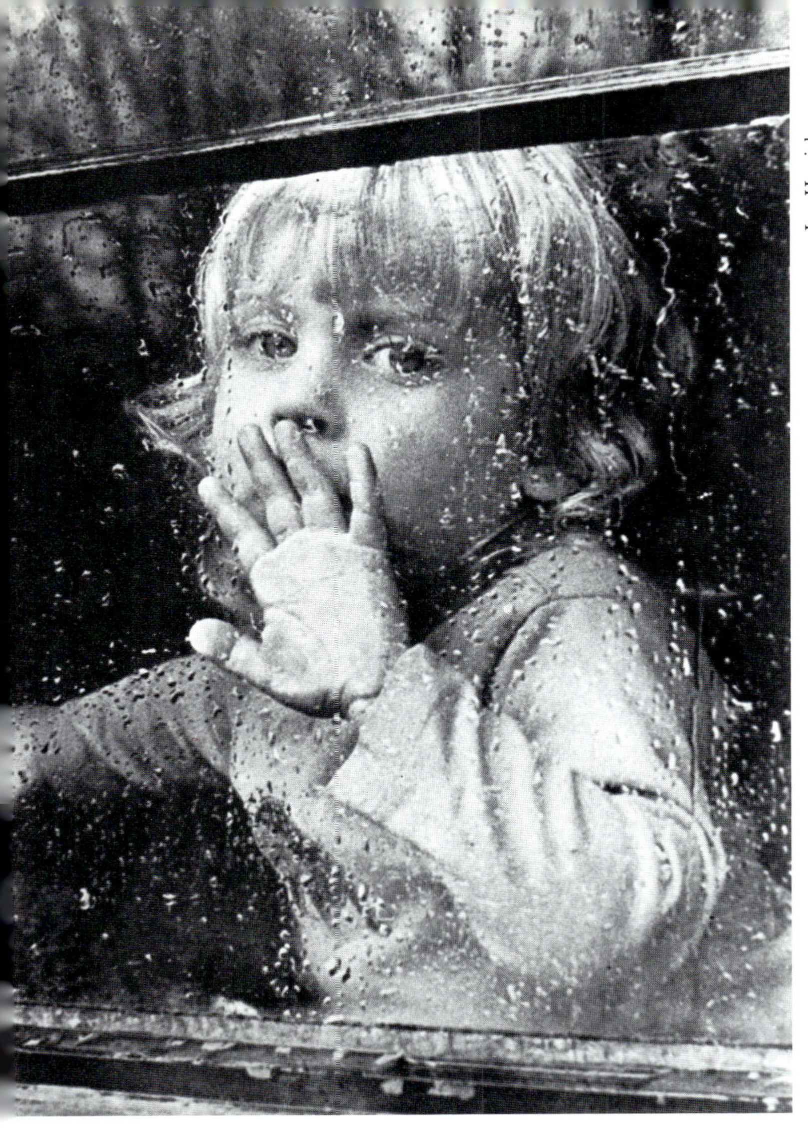

Lee Howick

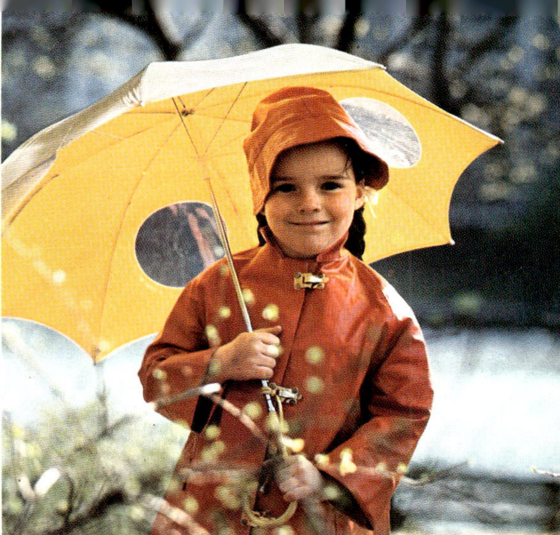

Dick Swift

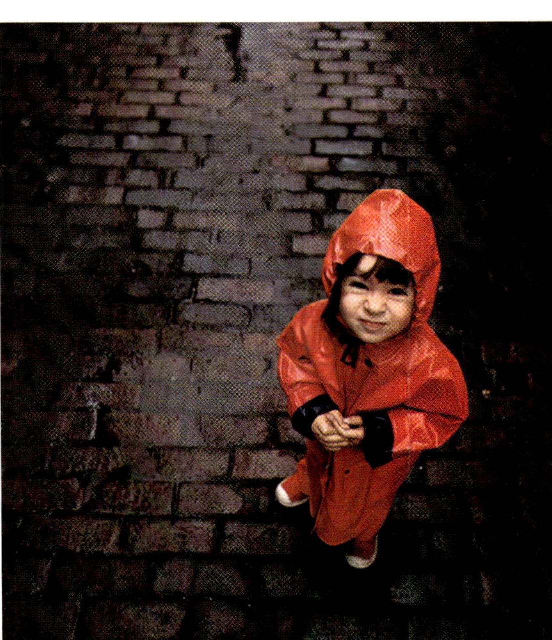

Peter Oliver

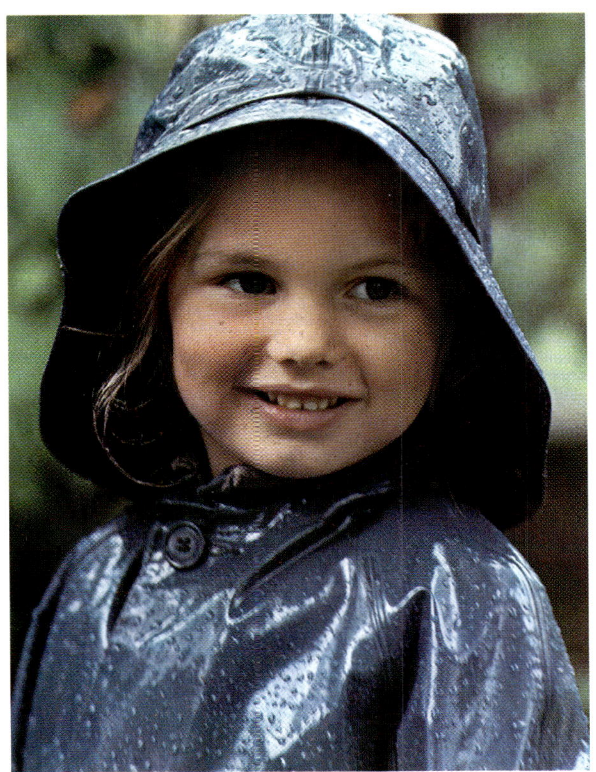

Rainy Days

Overcast days and rainy weather need not spoil your picture-taking fun. In fact, bad weather for some activities can actually be *good* weather for making pictures of children. Since the lighting is quite dim during or immediately after a rainstorm, either use flash or switch to a high-speed color film.

The next day the sun doesn't shine, take some close-up pictures of children outside. Chances are that the results will be among the very best pictures in your photo collection.

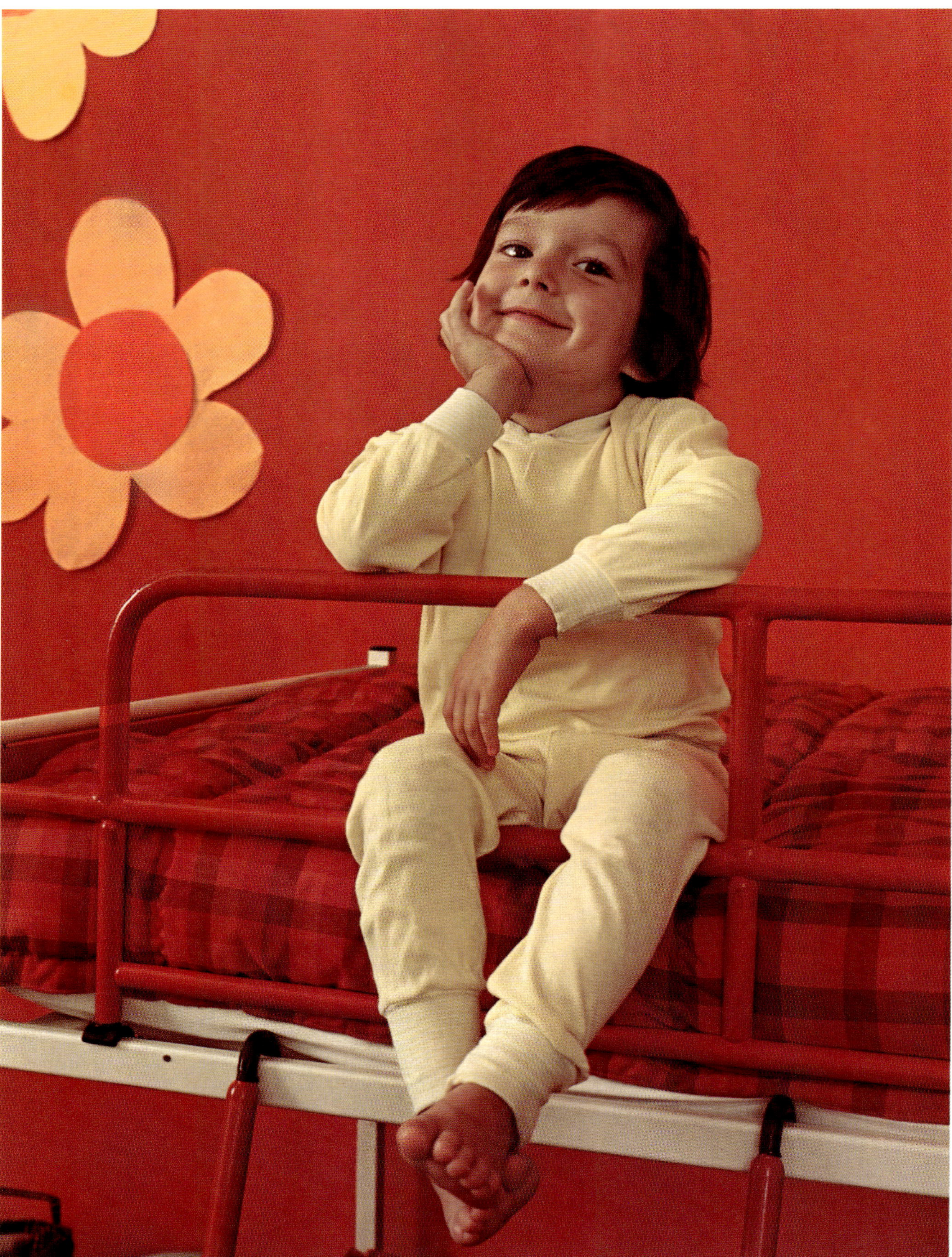

Norm Kerr

Lighting: Indoors

Assuming that the sun has set or that you have no way to let in the light from outdoors, you have three means of illumination—flash, photolamps, and the artificial light already existing in the scene. Let's take a look at each of these light sources as they relate to photographing children naturally—their ease of use, technical considerations, and quality of photographs possible.

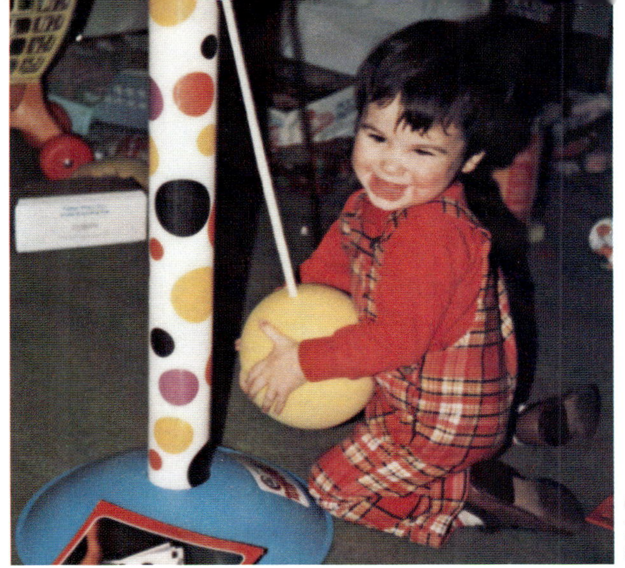

Keith Boas

Picture made with a KODAK Instant Camera, KODAK Instant Print Film PR10, and flipflash. The camera-to-subject distance was 5 feet (1.5 meters).

Direct Flash

Flash is by far the most popular method of making color pictures of babies and children indoors. Most people take flash pictures with the flash right on the camera. Flash on the camera produces even frontlighting on the child. It's especially useful when you might have to aim and snap quickly to capture just the actions and expressions you want.

You can take flash pictures with almost any still camera. The most important factor to keep in mind when taking flash pictures is the distance from the flash to the subject. A child close to the flash receives much more light than one who is at some distance from the flash. For the best possible pictures, you'll want to stand within the *proper distance range* from the child. This distance depends on the camera, film, and flash you are using.

If you have a simple nonadjustable camera, taking flash pictures with it is very easy. As a general rule, stand between 4 and 10 feet (1.2 and 3 meters) from your subject if you're using a magicube, flashcube, or flipflash. If you're using a HI-POWER FlashCube, stand between 5 and 12 feet (1.5 and 3.6 meters) from your subject. The appropriate camera-to-subject distance for the equipment you are using is explained in your camera manual. You should also read instructions supplied with flash equipment.

Automatic cameras have exposure control systems that automatically give you the proper

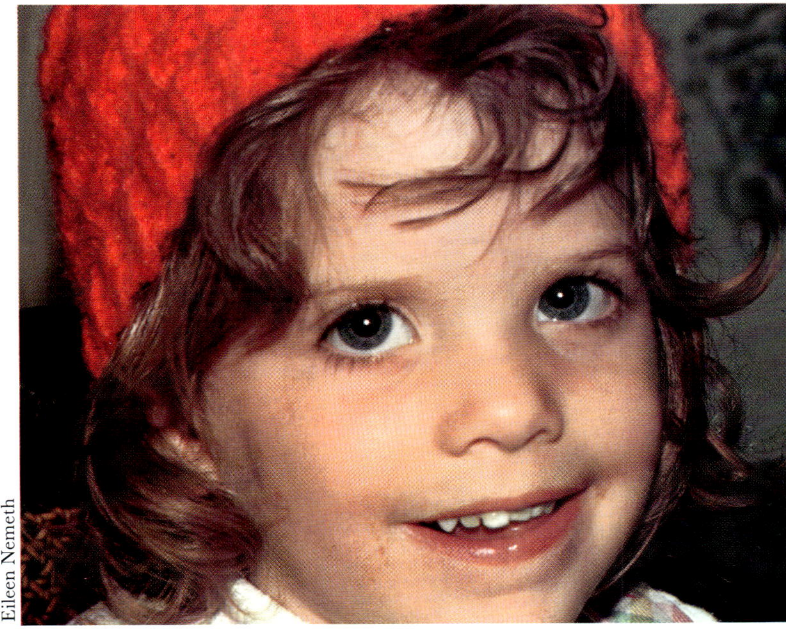

Eileen Nemeth

This close-up flash picture was taken with an adjustable camera. Check your camera manual for information on proper exposure with flash at close distances.

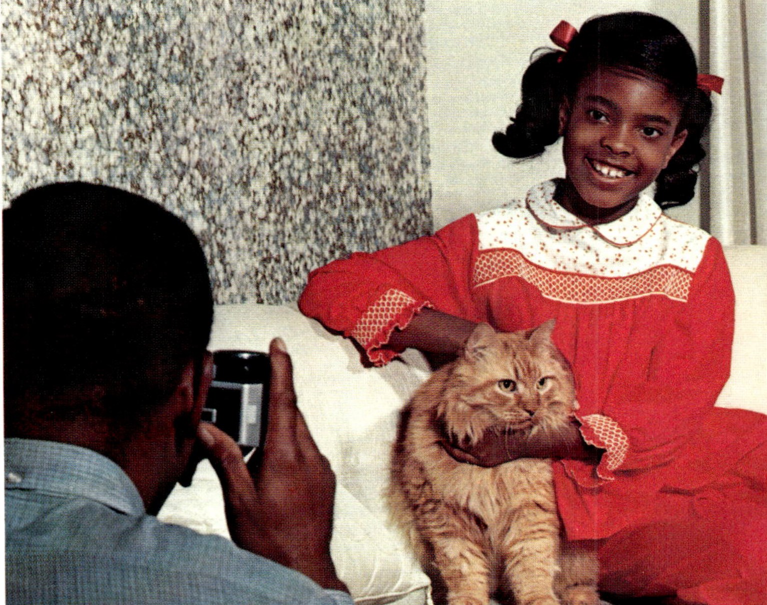

When taking flash pictures, be sure to stay within the recommended distance range from the flash to the subject (usually 4 to 10 feet/1.2 to 3 meters).

exposure for indoor flash pictures within certain distances. Because different automatic cameras allow you to stand at different distances from your subject, be sure to read your camera manual for specific instructions.

There are several settings to make if you're taking flash pictures with an adjustable camera. The settings for the shutter speed, lens opening, and flash synchronization will depend on your combination of film, flash, and reflector. Again, carefully read your camera manual, film instruction sheet, and instructions supplied with your flash equipment.

A startling effect occasionally appears in color flash pictures, in which the pupils of a person's eyes look red or amber. This phenomenon is caused by light from the flash being reflected from the retina of the subject's eyes. It's more prevalent in pictures of children than of adults. Such reflections can appear when the flash is close to the camera lens.

You can minimize this effect by moving the flash farther away from the camera lens axis so that the camera doesn't "see" the reflections in the subject's eyes. To increase the separation between the flash and the camera lens, you can use a Kodak Magicube or Flashcube Extender with a Kodak Instamatic® Camera, depending on the cube your camera takes, or with other cameras from which you can detach the flash.

If your camera takes the 8-bulb flipflash, you usually won't need an extender because one is built into the flipflash. Since the top 4 bulbs in the flash position are separated from the camera lens by the construction of the flipflash, this arrangement acts as an extender. However, if your subject's eyes are especially reflective, you can reduce the possibility of eye reflections even more by using a Kodak Flipflash Extender.

Red reflections in eyes are caused by the reflection of the flash in the subject's eyes.

Flipflash minimizes red reflections in eyes by extending the distance from flash to camera lens.

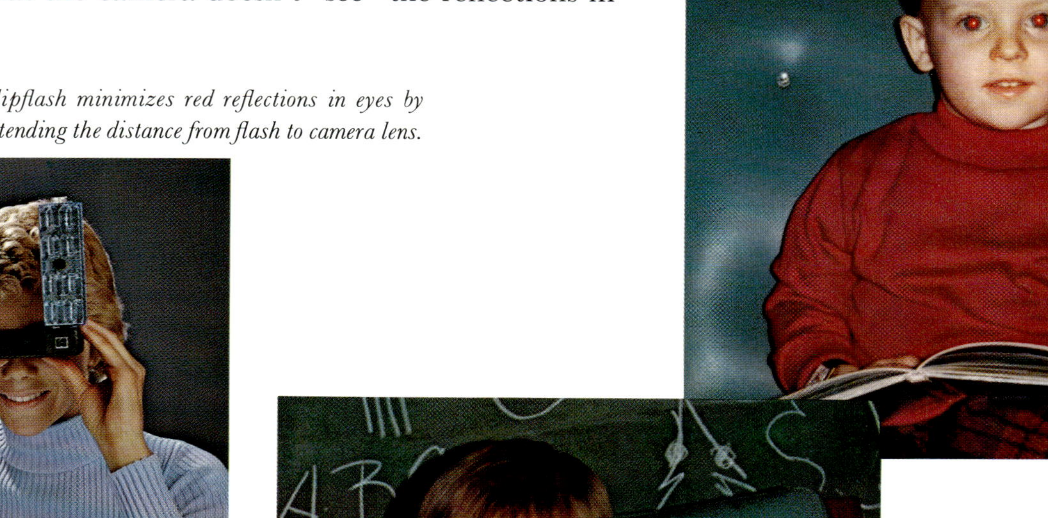

To minimize red reflections, use flipflash or a flash extender (available from your photo dealer's for cameras accepting flashcubes or magicubes).

Bounce Flash

In some cases when you use flash on the camera, portions of the background will appear in dark shadow and detract from your center of interest. You can improve the results by using a technique called bounce flash. You'll need a flash unit that can be detached from your camera so you can aim the flash at the ceiling of the room instead of directly at the child. The light bounces back from a high angle and reduces the background shadow. In bounce-light pictures, exposure depends on the power of the flash unit, the size of the room, the height of the ceiling, and the color of the ceiling and walls. For starters, use 2 *f*-numbers more exposure than you would use for direct flash pictures of the same subject. This type of lighting is similar to the soft, hazy sunlight that makes possible such pleasant pictures of children outdoors on overcast days. Bounce flash is especially appropriate for close-up pictures of most people.

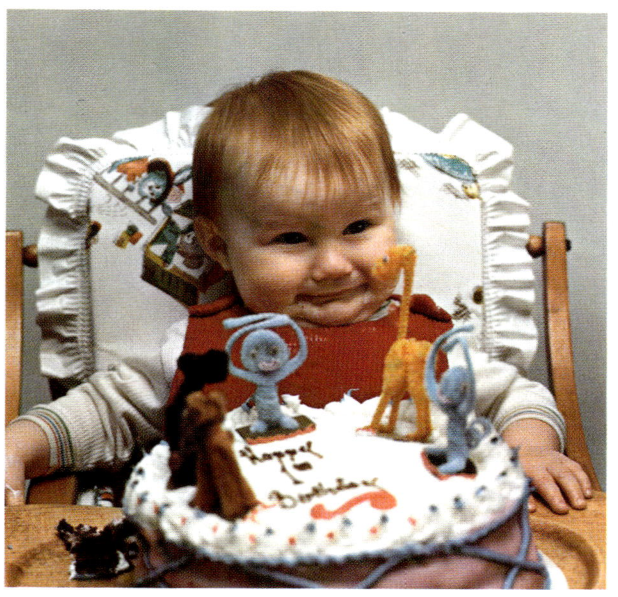

Emiel Blaakman

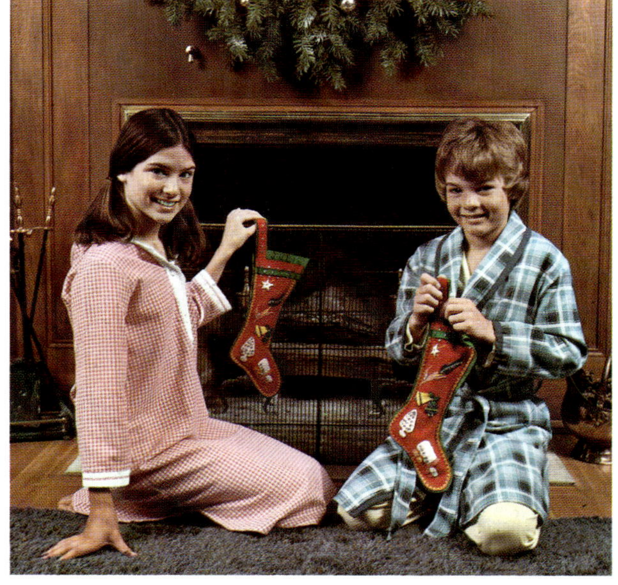

Don Maggio

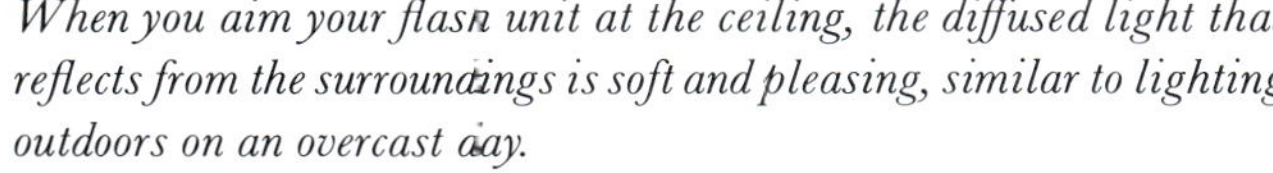

When you aim your flash unit at the ceiling, the diffused light that reflects from the surroundings is soft and pleasing, similar to lighting outdoors on an overcast day.

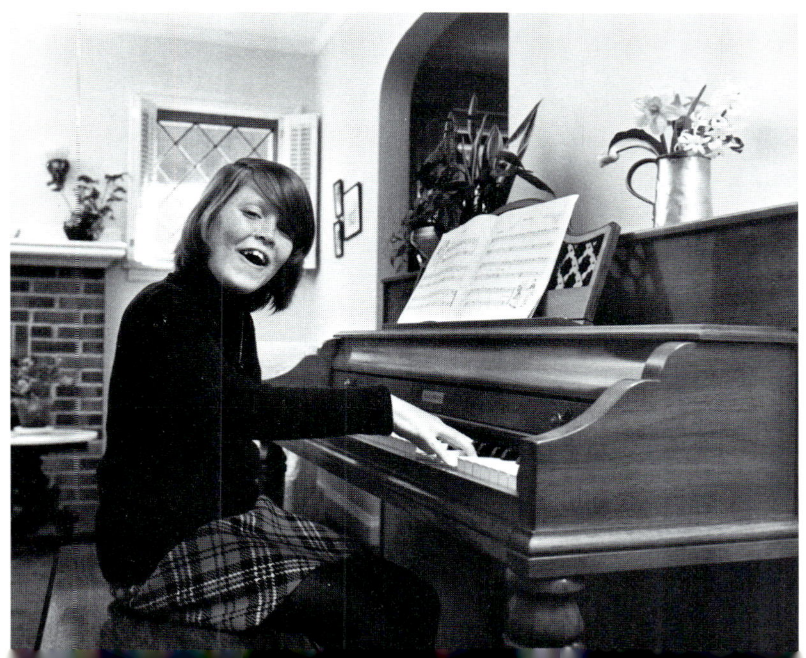

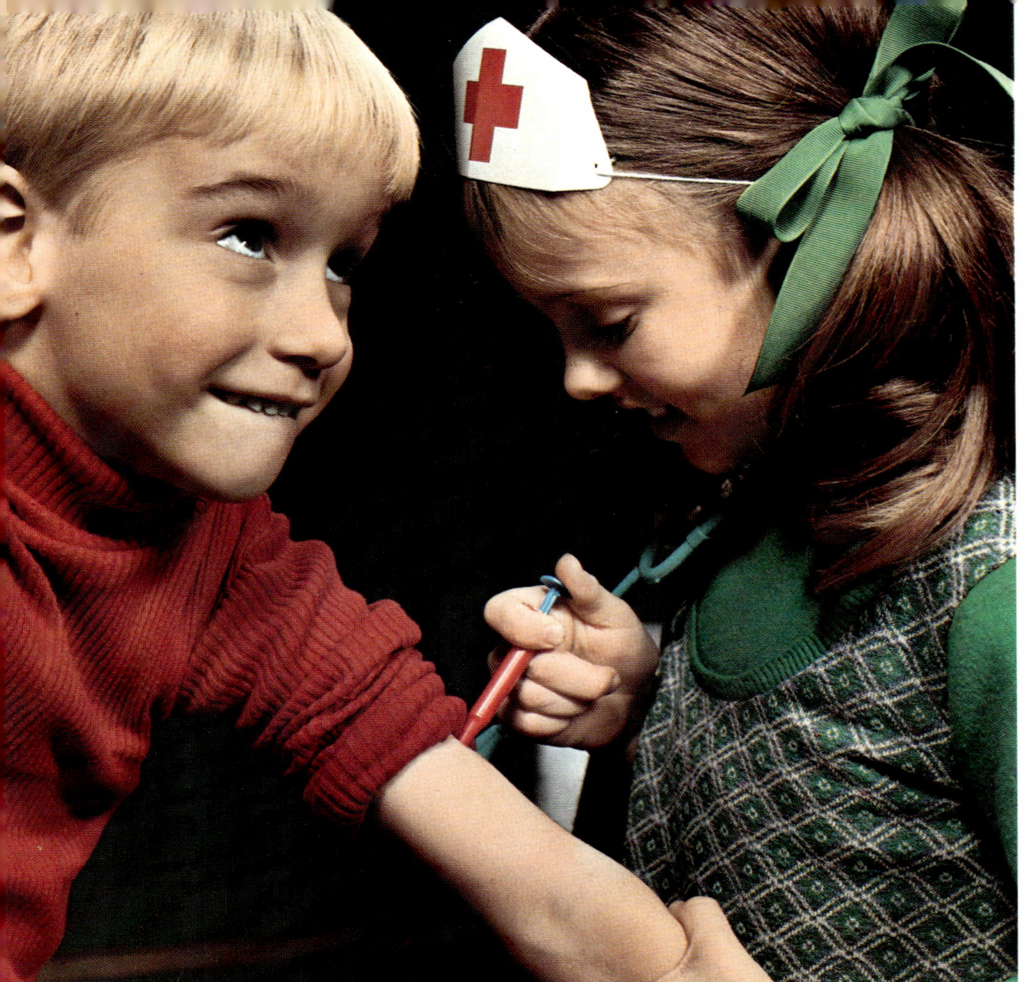

Emiel Blaakman

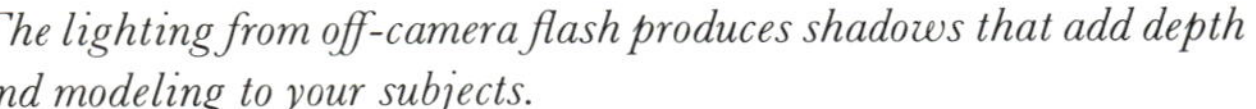

The lighting from off-camera flash produces shadows that add depth and modeling to your subjects.

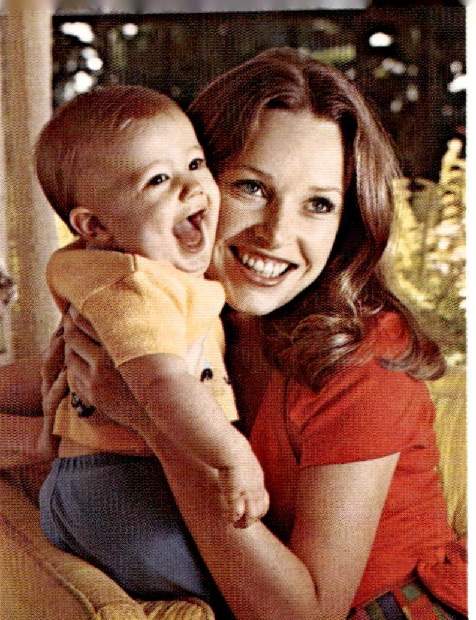

Neil Montanus

A KODAK Flipflash Extender being used for an off-camera lighting effect.

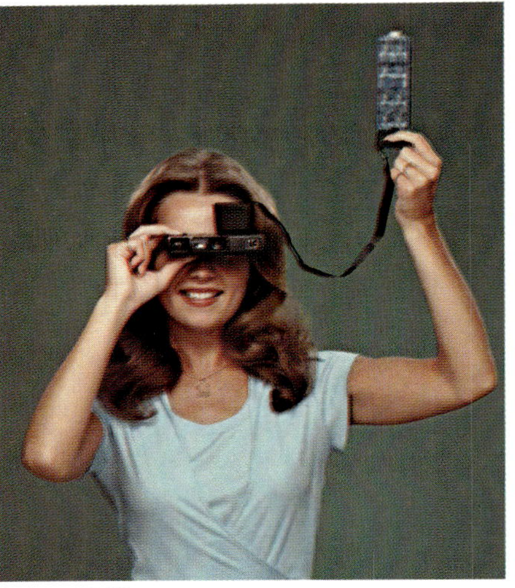

Robert Phillips

Off-Camera Flash

For quick and easy flash pictures, leave the flash unit attached to your camera. But for more dramatic lighting, you might like to try off-camera flash. If your camera has plug-in flash terminals, you can use an extension cord to place the flash as far away as several feet from the camera. This gives you the flexibility to place the flash in a location to simulate light coming through a window, for example. Or you can hide the flash in a fireplace to make realistic-looking "firelight" pictures with the young ones gathered around the hearth.

For pleasing lighting, point the flash at your subject, holding the unit at arm's length above and to one side of the camera. The resulting lighting is often more interesting than flash on camera because it brings out the form of faces. It also changes the position of the shadow of the flash on the background, hiding it behind your subject.

Umbrella Flash

While we have the flash unit off the camera, let's talk about umbrella flash for a moment. Here's a device that you can use to help improve your indoor flash pictures. You can buy a white or silver nylon fabric umbrella and use it as is for bouncing the flash onto your subject. Or you can coat the inside of an umbrella with aluminum spray paint. Photo dealers sell umbrellas especially designed for umbrella flash. Light bouncing from an umbrella produces soft, diffuse lighting similar to bounce flash. You can use it when it's not practical to work with bounce flash, such as when the ceiling is very high or when you don't want the picture to have the color tone of the ceiling. Umbrella flash also gives you more control over the direction of light than bounce flash does.

Use a clamping device to attach the umbrella to a small light stand or other steady object. Aim the shaft of the umbrella directly at your subject. Then use a second clamp to attach the flash unit to the umbrella shaft. The flash should be aimed at the center of the umbrella.

Exposure will depend on the power of the flash unit, size and shape of the umbrella, reflecting quality of the umbrella surface, and the umbrella-to-subject distance. Because there are so many variables to consider, make a few test exposures to determine the capabilities of your flash-umbrella combination. Start by allowing 1 more *f*-number exposure than you would use for direct flash.

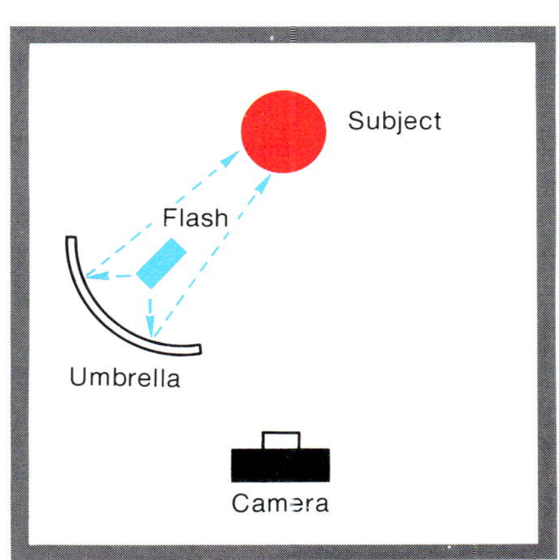

Notice the soft quality of this picture made using the umbrella-light setup shown in the diagram.

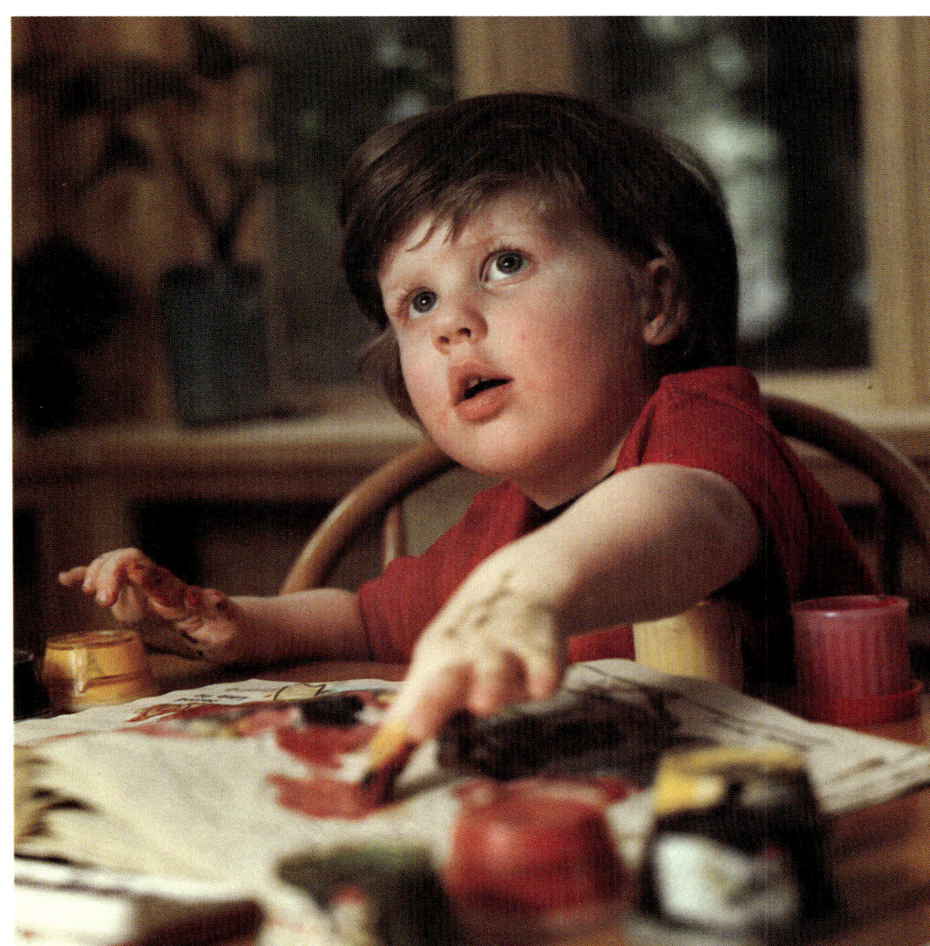

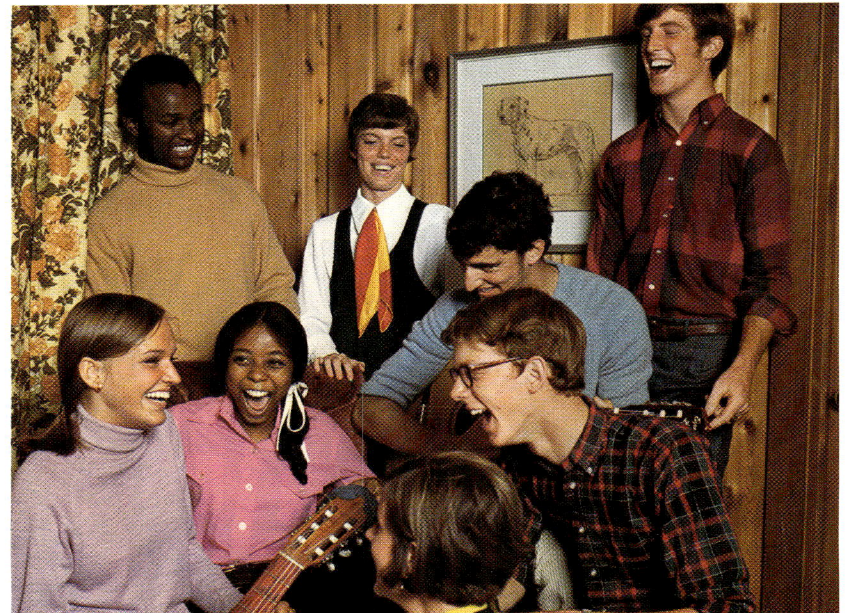

Frank Cowan

You can use a photolamp to raise the brightness level of artificial illumination in a room by bouncing its light off the ceiling. For a sparkling studio-portrait effect, use 2 or 3 photolamps pointed directly at your subject—highlighting hair and facial features.

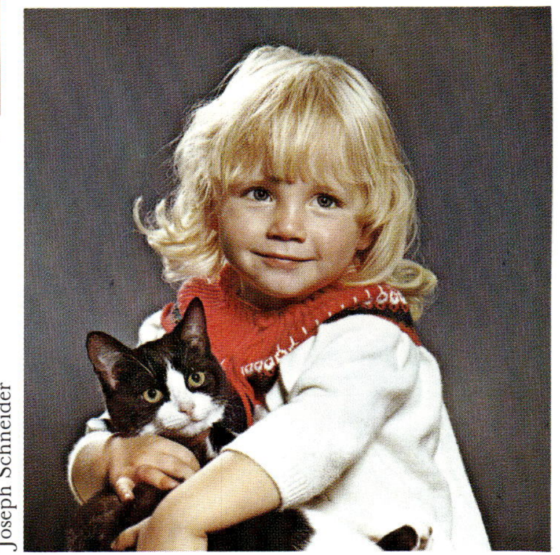

Joseph Schneider

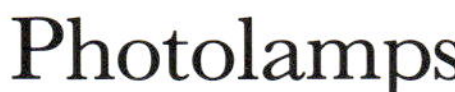

Photolamps

Traditionally, photolamps have carried a reputation of being those hot, bright lights that a person has to face if one wants to have a portrait taken or appear in a home movie. With recent improvements in film sensitivity and camera designs, it's no longer necessary to have your photographic models "cook" in front of hot lights. But photolamps continue to be popular for many picture-taking applications in and around the home. You can use all of the artificial lighting techniques we've previously mentioned with photolamps. The same basic lighting principles apply.

One popular use of photolamps these days is to bounce the light off a white ceiling as you would with bounce flash. This technique is particularly helpful for making movies indoors where there is not quite enough existing light for proper exposure. A single photolamp aimed at the ceiling will generally raise the ambient light in an average-size room high enough for acceptable exposures, providing you're using a movie camera with a wide lens aperture and high-speed film. The light falling on your subjects will be even and natural, generally appearing as though only normal room light is being used.

Keep in mind that photolamps produce a light far warmer in color (toward the red end of the spectrum) than does daylight. Whenever photolamps are used as the main light source for your pictures, be sure to select a film that is balanced for this artificial illumination or place the appropriate filter over the camera lens. To obtain a more natural color rendition when using 3400 K photolamps and a film balanced for daylight, for example, use a No. 80B filter and increase your exposure by 1⅔ *f*-numbers to compensate for the absorption of light by the filter.

Existing Light

Some of the best pictures of children taken indoors may be those you make without any flash or photolamps at all. The picture-taking possibilities that existing-light photography makes available to you open whole new horizons. Using a high-speed film and a camera with a large lens opening, you can make good pictures under almost any lighting condition—without the need for supplementary light. Besides enjoying the convenience of picture-taking by existing light, you'll find that your photographs look more natural because they include only the lighting that already exists on your young subject.

What is existing light? Well, it's the light that happens to be on the scene, such as the light from table and floor lamps, ceiling fixtures, fluorescent lamps, spotlights, windows, skylights, candles, fireplaces, and any other light source that provides the lighting. Existing light is the type of light found in hospital nurseries, homes, schools, meeting rooms, auditoriums—anywhere you find children involved in a potentially photographic situation. Existing light is characterized by lower light levels than you would encounter in daylight outdoors. For this reason, not all cameras will yield proper exposure under existing-light conditions.

If your camera does have low-light-level capability, give existing-light photography a try. Without accessory lighting equipment to think about, you can concentrate on getting the best pictures of children, and you have greater freedom of movement. Youngsters will really appreciate your existing-light approach to picture-taking because they won't be disturbed by the bright light from flash or photofloods. Chances are that they might not even notice you snapping pictures, which will give you an added bonus in relaxed, candid expressions.

With a high-speed color film and an adjustable camera you can make excellent candid pictures of children by existing light. Your subjects will also appreciate the absence of bright flash or photolamps.

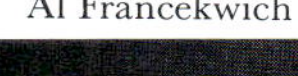

Al Francekwich

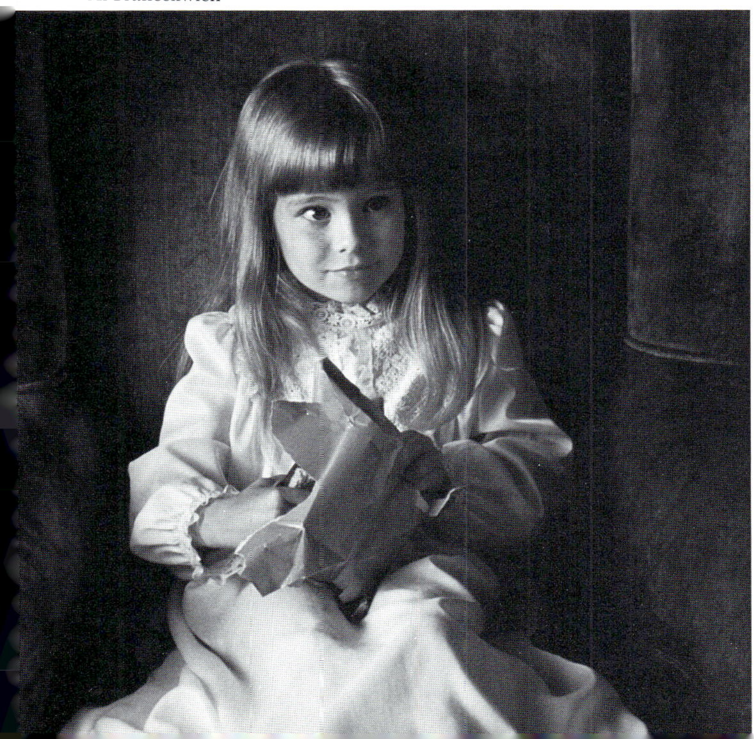

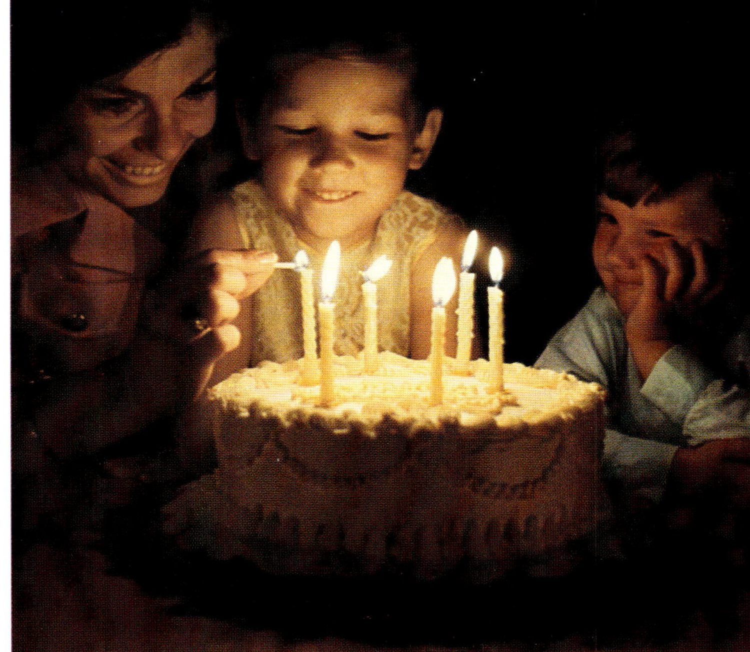

Lee Howick

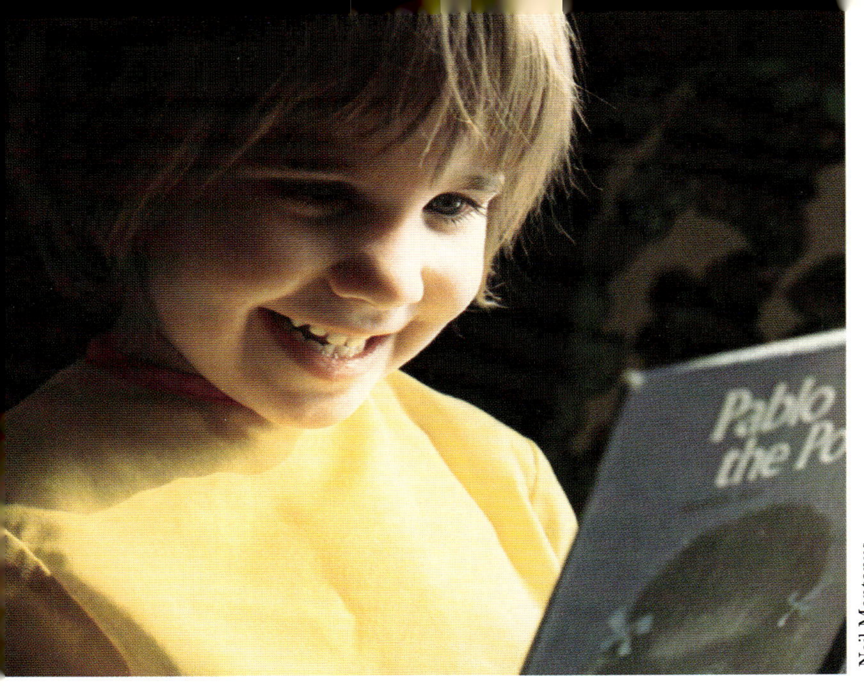

Neil Montanus

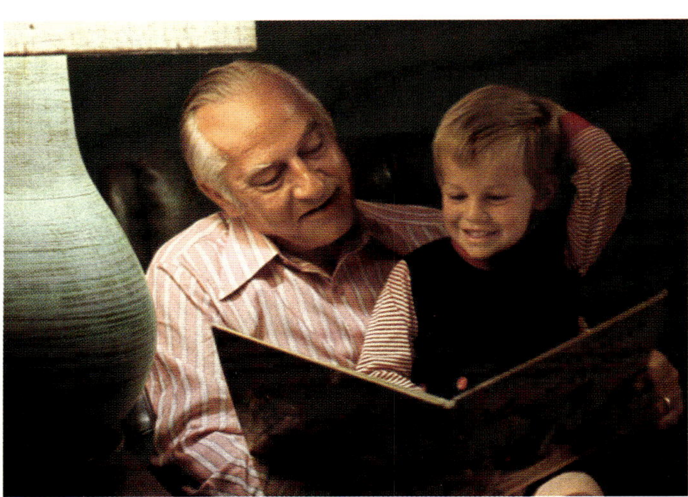

David Lichtenstein, Jr.

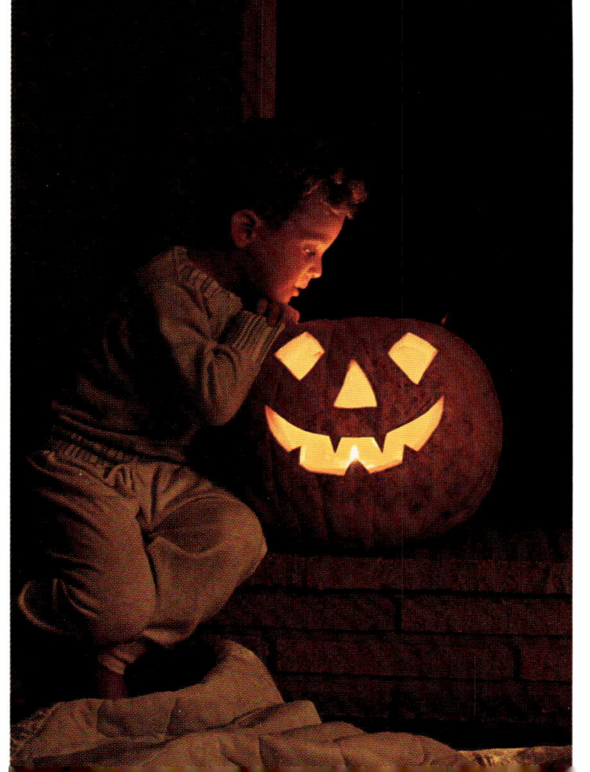

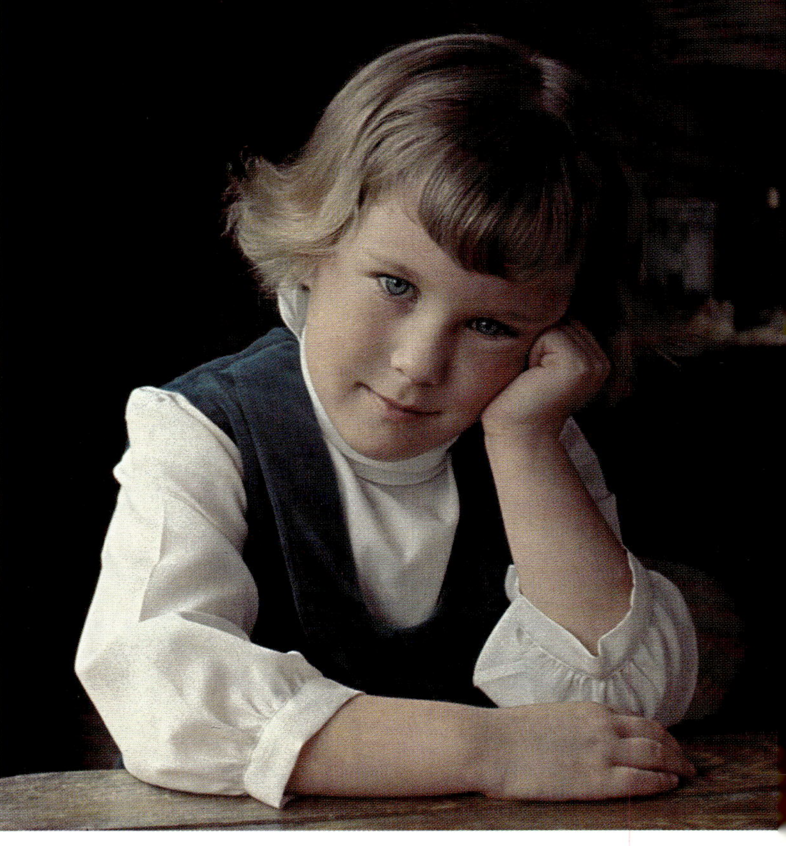

Because existing light is often quite dim, use an adjustable camera with an f/2.8 or faster lens and a high-speed film. Use a film balanced for daylight for scenes lighted primarily by daylight (window light). For subjects illuminated primarily by tungsten light (for example, pictures made in your home at night), use a film balanced for artificial light or use a high-speed color-negative material such as KODACOLOR 400 Film.

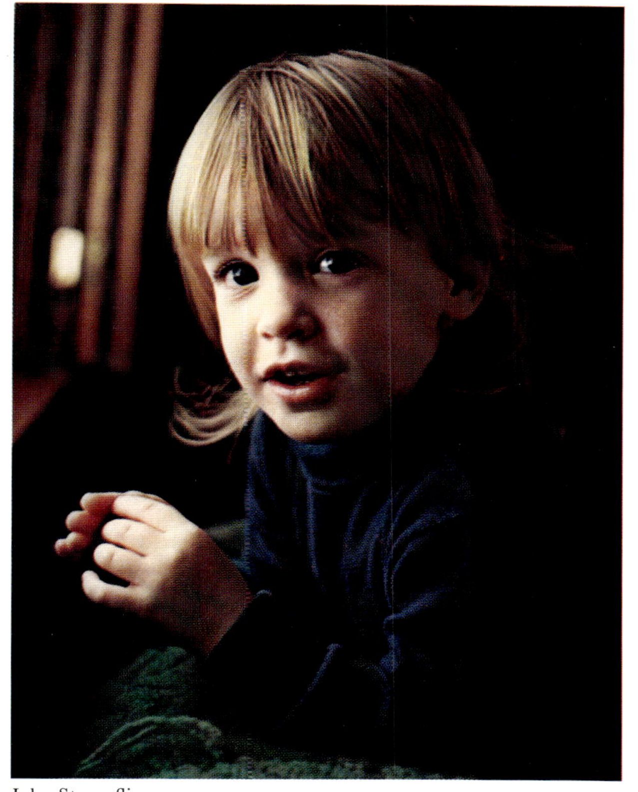

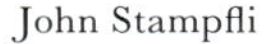
John Stampfli

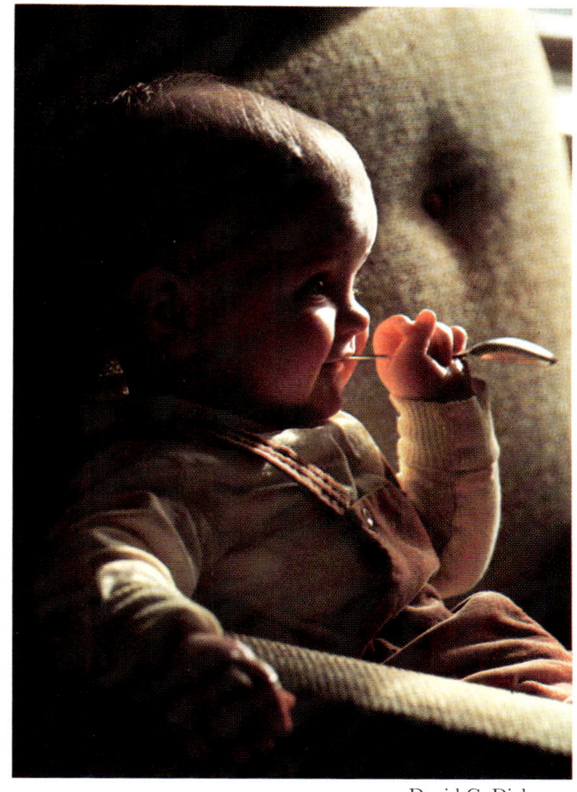
David G. Dickason

Window Light

With many cameras it's possible to take very pleasing pictures with daylight coming through the windows of your home and not to concern yourself with the weather. The lighting on overcast days is excellent for informal portraits indoors. It has a soft, diffuse quality which is flattering for pictures of children. It's even better when there is snow on the ground since this acts as a reflector.

Daylight coming through the windows is usually brighter than the artificial light in the home. Take advantage of the light from all the windows in the room by opening the drapes or curtains. This increases the light level in the room, making it easier to get enough exposure. It also makes the lighting more even.

If it is a sunny day outdoors, areas in the room that are not in direct sunlight usually are best for picture-taking. Lighting is less contrasty and is similar to the soft lighting found on overcast days. But you can also get good pictures when your subject is in direct sunlight near a window. Have the child turn his or her face toward the window. The bright sunlight lets you use faster shutter speeds and smaller *f*-numbers than you would use for most other existing-light pictures. You will benefit in having a better chance of getting a crystal-sharp picture.

Earlier, we talked about using a reflector outdoors to fill in the shadows. You can also use a reflector indoors to bounce the light coming through a window or glass door back into the shadow side of your subject. Reducing the shadows will usually produce a more pleasing picture.

When you are using an automatic camera, your subject may reproduce too dark in the final picture if a large window or glass door is directly behind the child (during the day). Change your camera angle or move the child so that the light from the window illuminates the front or side of the face, not the back of the head.

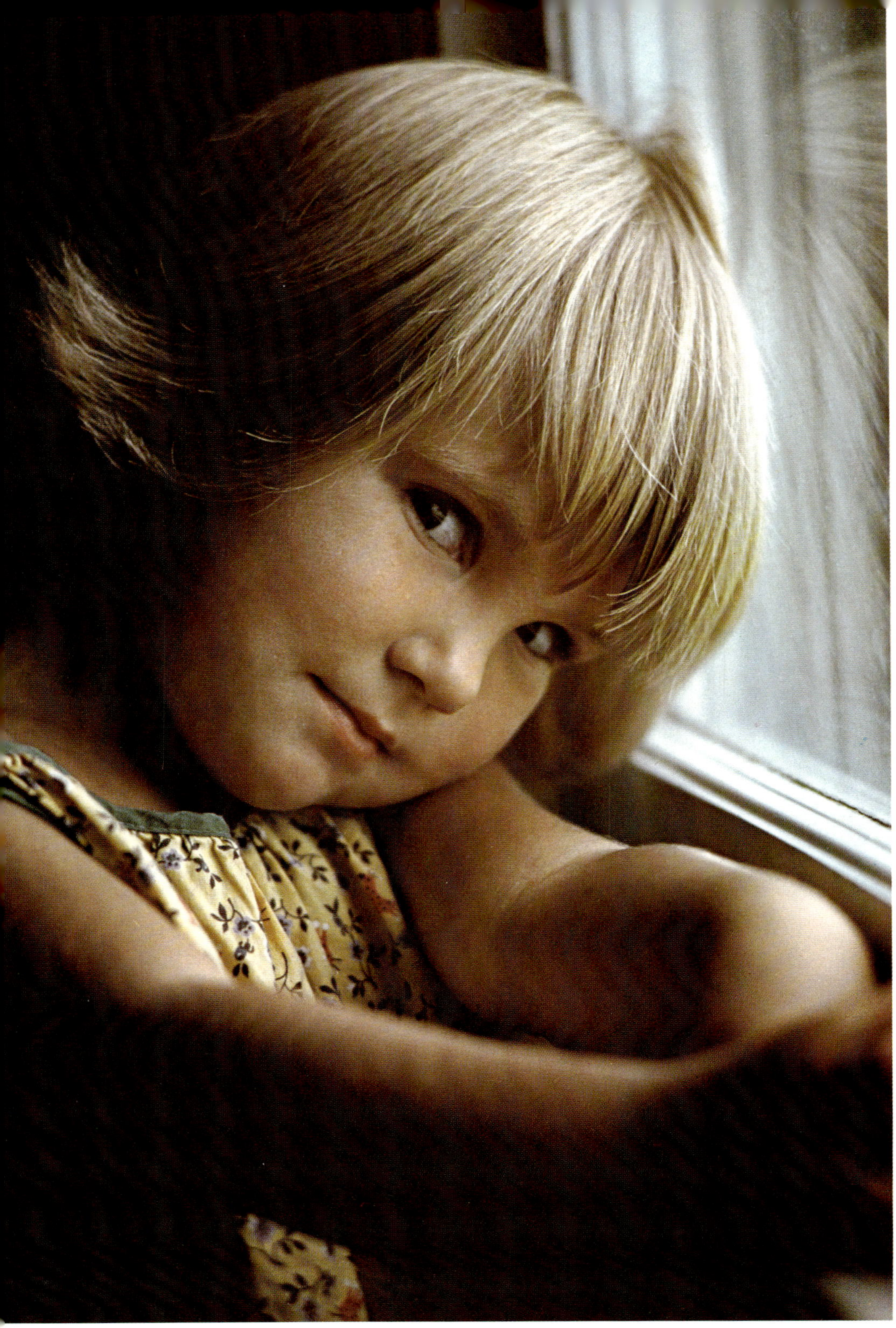

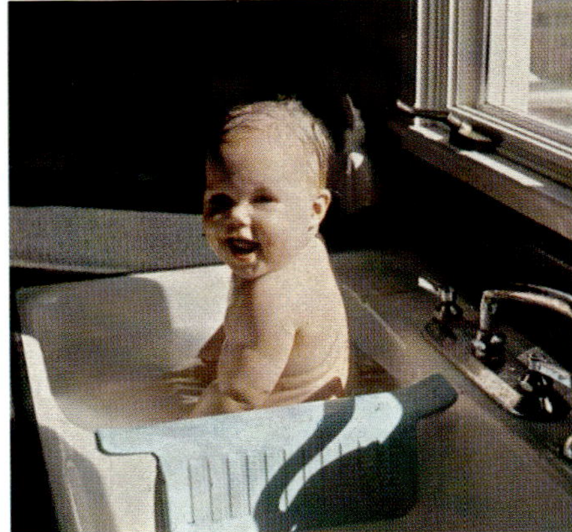

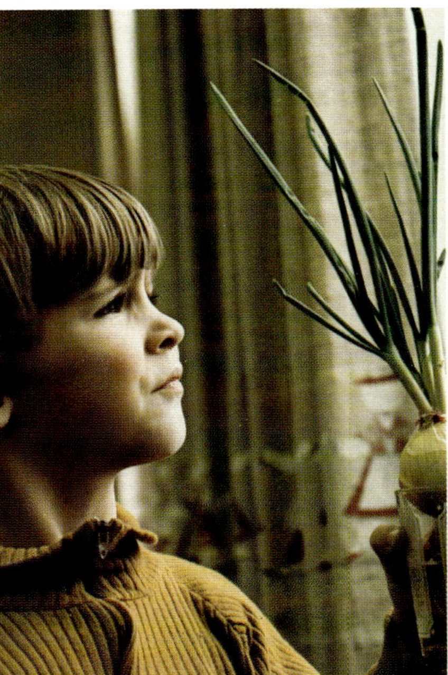

Philip James

Neil Montanus

Some important points to remember:

- *Take pictures of children by existing light for natural expressions and realism.*
- *Use a camera with a fast lens,* f/*2.8 or faster, and a high-speed film.*
- *For color slides, use daylight film for daylight or fluorescent illumination; use tungsten film for tungsten illumination.*
- *To make color snapshots, you can use* KODACOLOR *II and* KODACOLOR *400 Films for daylight or tungsten light or a combination of both kinds of light.*

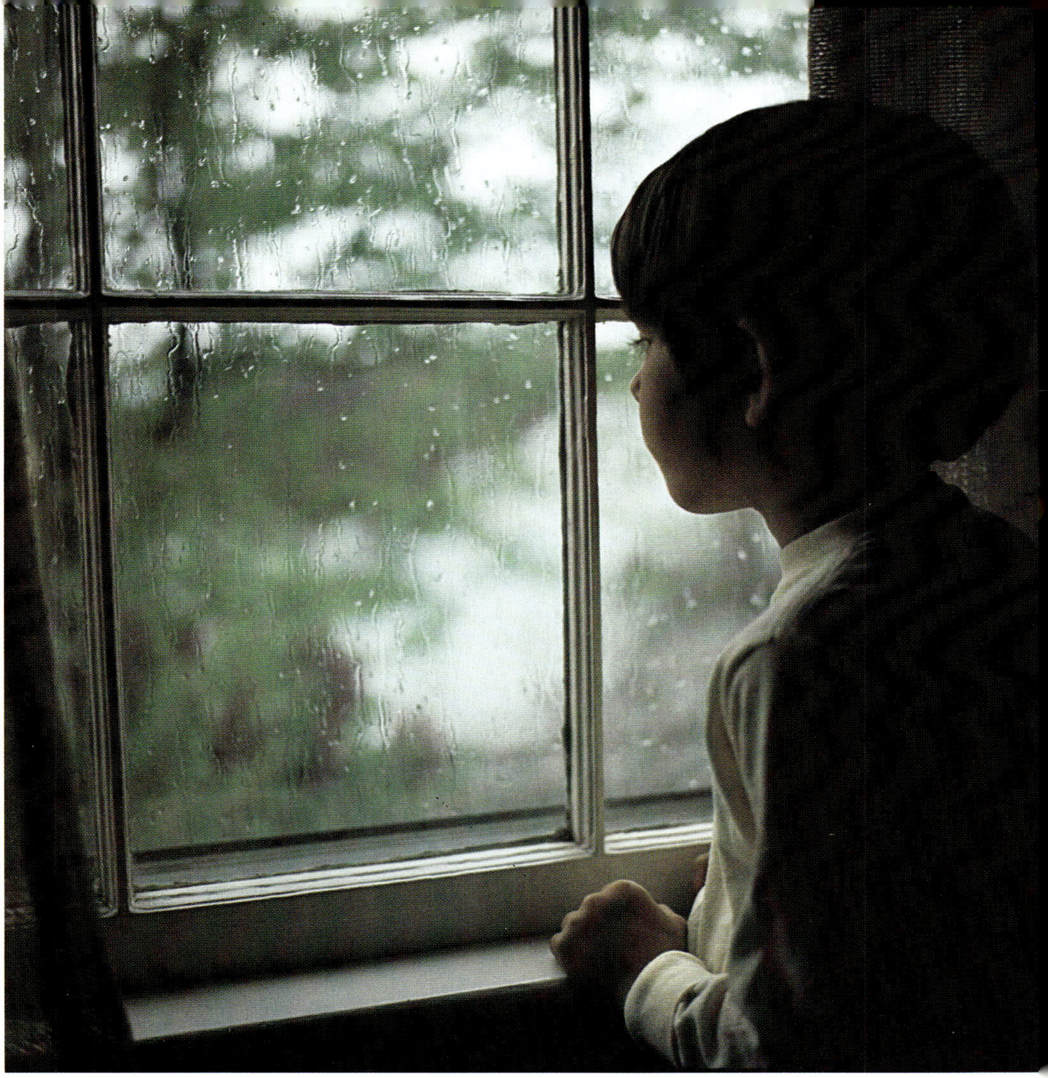

Jerry Johnson

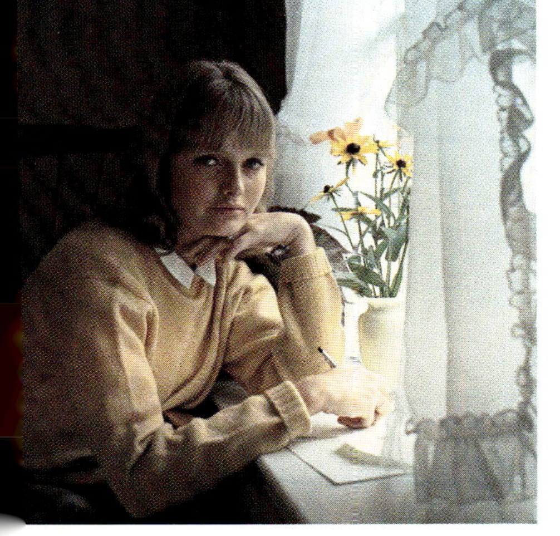

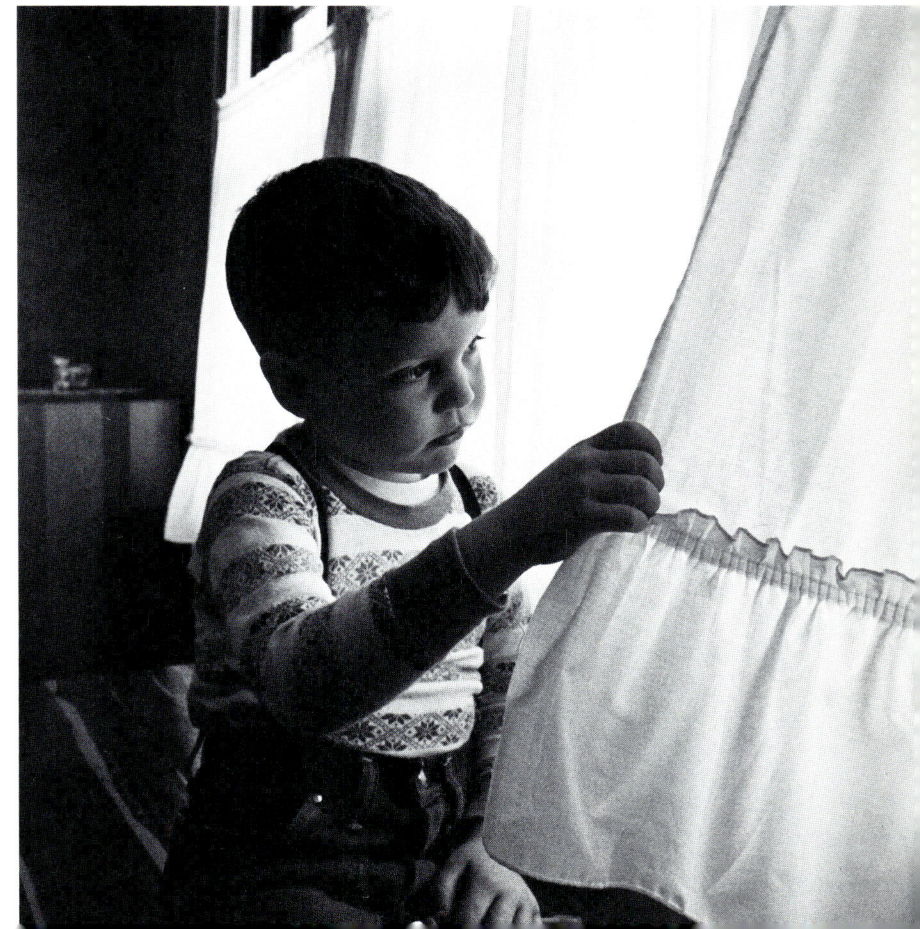

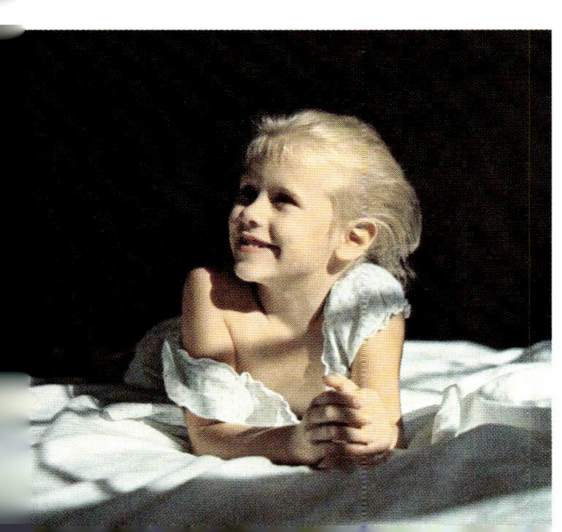

An uncluttered background will help keep the viewer's attention centered on the child. You can achieve soft, out-of-focus backgrounds by using a normal or telephoto lens and setting it at a low f-*number to produce a shallow depth of field.*

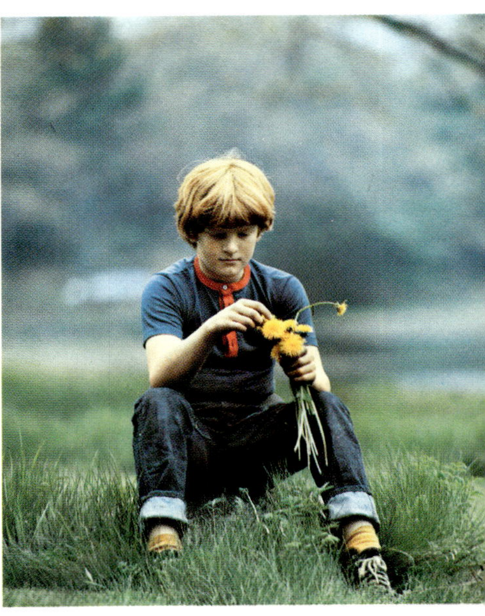

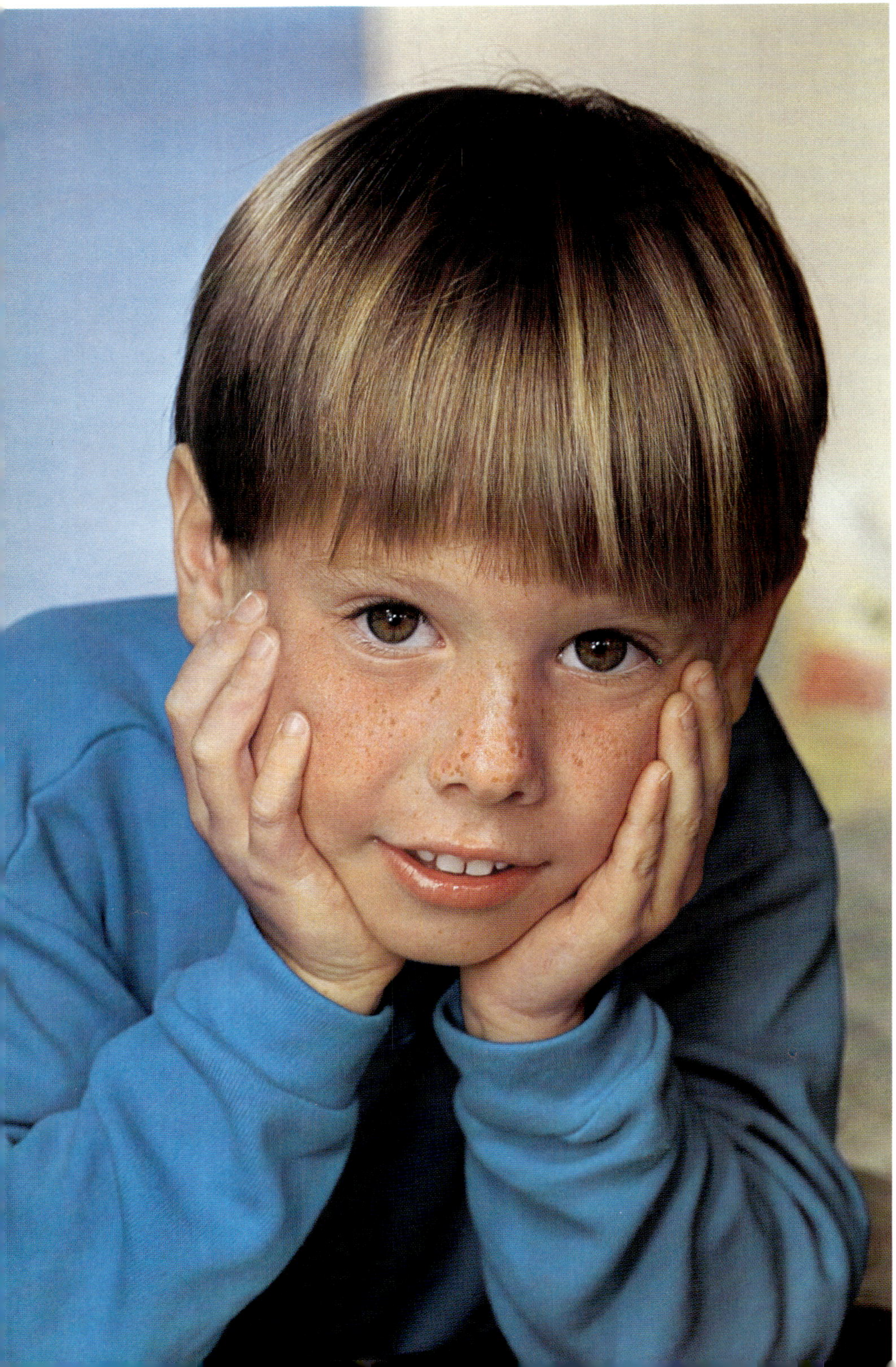

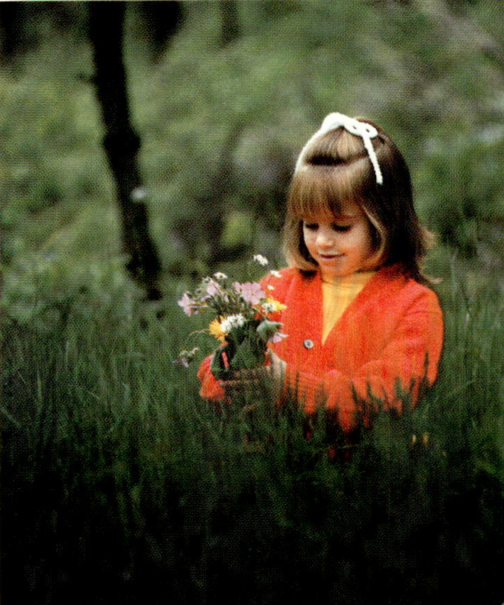

Choose Your Background

SIMPLE BACKGROUNDS

Wherever you happen to be photographing children—or for that matter any close-up subject—take your time and study the background before snapping the picture. A simple background can keep your viewer's attention centered on the subject, while a cluttered background can easily call attention away from the center of interest. Your eye tends to center on what you are most interested in, but the camera "sees"—and photographs—everything that the lens takes in. If you're not entirely pleased with how your center of interest relates compositionally with the background, walk around the child and choose a better point of view. Often when taking pictures outdoors, it's effective to use an extremely low camera angle to take advantage of the sky as a background.

Another good way to control the background in your close-ups of children involves the use of selective focus, which is a technique achieved by changing the camera lens depth of field. Depth of field is the distance range within which objects in a picture look sharp. For this technique you'll need an adjustable camera with a normal or telephoto lens. Since wide-angle lenses offer increased depth of field (as well as the exaggerated perspective we mentioned earlier), they are generally considered undesirable for making personalized, informal, close-up portraits of people.

With fixed-focus cameras everything in the scene from usually about 4 feet (1.2 meters) to infinity reproduces on the film acceptably sharp. With an adjustable camera, on the other hand,

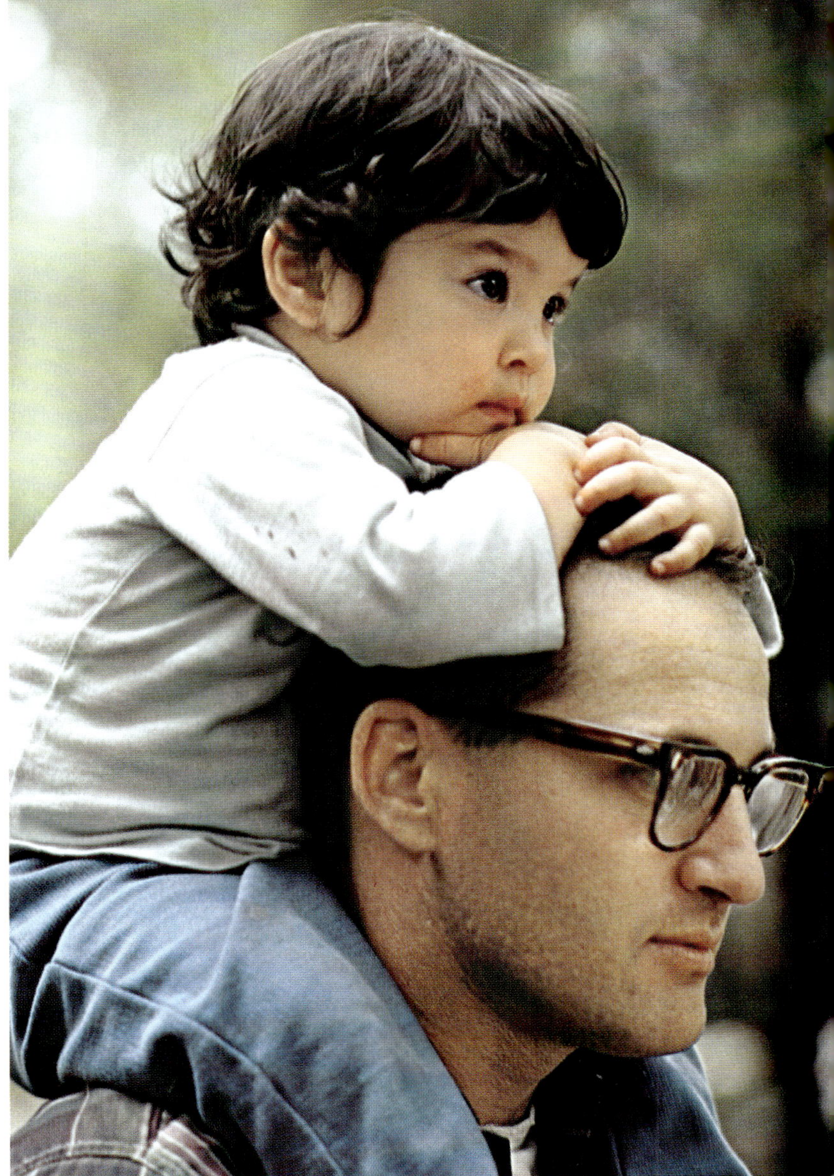

Suzanne Szasz

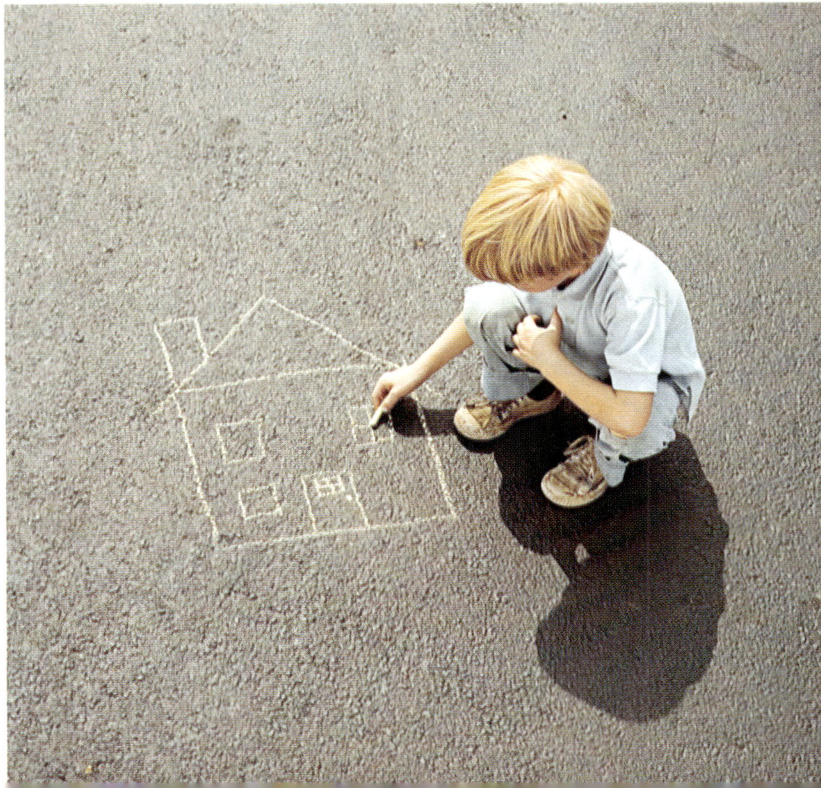

Here a high camera angle simplified the background, directing attention to the area within the photo.

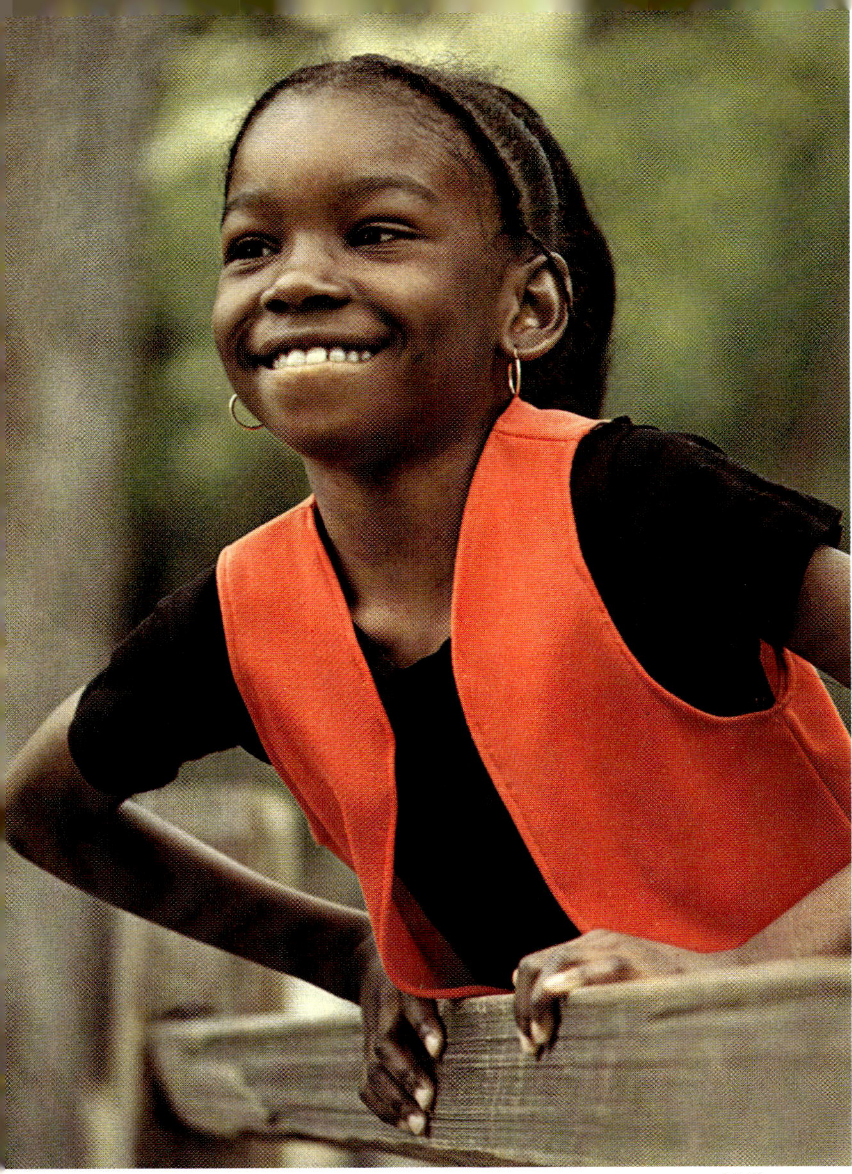

M. Peterson

In this example, the camera lens was set at its lowest f-*number for an extremely shallow depth of field. A low angle of view picked up a complementary background of blurred forest greenery.*

you can be selective in your depth of field. Depth of field decreases as the lens aperture gets larger. It's therefore possible with a large aperture to throw the background into an undistracting blur when you focus on your close-up subject. By your setting the lens aperture at a low *f*-number, such as *f*/2.8, the depth of field becomes very shallow. To compensate for this wide aperture, you'll have to choose a much faster-than-normal shutter speed; this shutter setting will depend on the brightness of light in the scene. In an outdoor situation on a cloudy bright (no shadows) day,

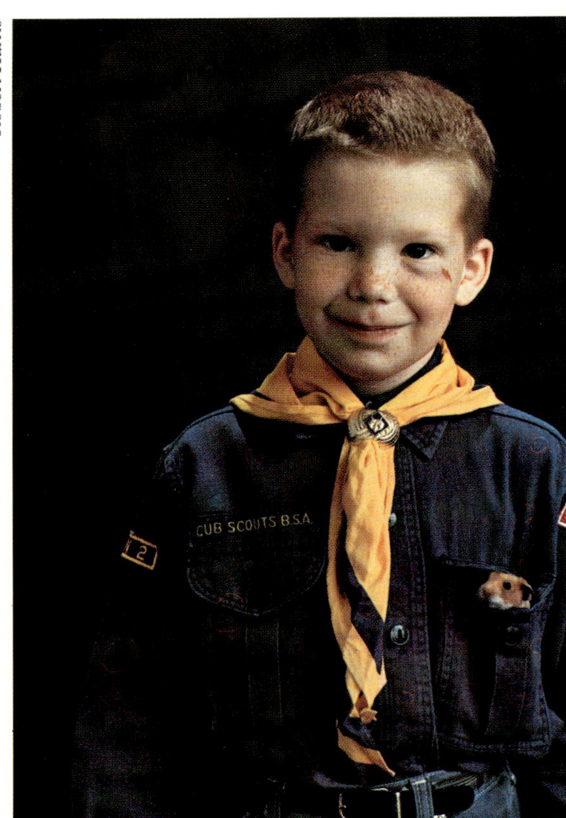

Robert Harris

Choose backgrounds indoors that are free from distracting glare and reflections. A matte-surfaced, fairly dark wall is an excellent choice for background simplicity.

for example, your normal settings for a medium-speed film, such as KODACHROME 64 Film (Daylight), would be *f*/5.6 at 1/125 second. Opening the lens aperture to *f*/2.8 for a shallow depth of field would require a corresponding increase in the shutter speed to 1/500 second.

When taking pictures indoors, a matte-finish background is an excellent choice for child portraits. It helps prevent glare and reflections from your lighting. A flat-painted wall also makes a fine background. Keep the child far enough away from the background so that no shadows fall on it. When taking color pictures, the child shouldn't be too close to the side wall either, unless the wall is white, because it could reflect some of its own color into important shadow areas. A background of a fairly dark color is usually a good choice, although you can make it appear lighter or darker by varying the amount of light you shine on it.

STORYTELLING BACKGROUNDS

Although we've been telling you to avoid cluttered backgrounds in your pictures, this doesn't mean that you must always select a plain background such as a blue sky, out-of-focus blur, or blank wall. You can, with careful attention to composition, choose an appropriate background that will help tell a story in a single picture. A child, for example, positioned against a storytelling background can make a very effective photograph, suggesting the activity he or she was involved in at the time the picture was taken. Pick an angle which shows the important features of the background to best advantage. Effective storytelling backgrounds for children might include a jungle gym, split-rail fence, pumpkin patch, bright red barn, beach or pool location, field of flowers—anything appropriate to the moment.

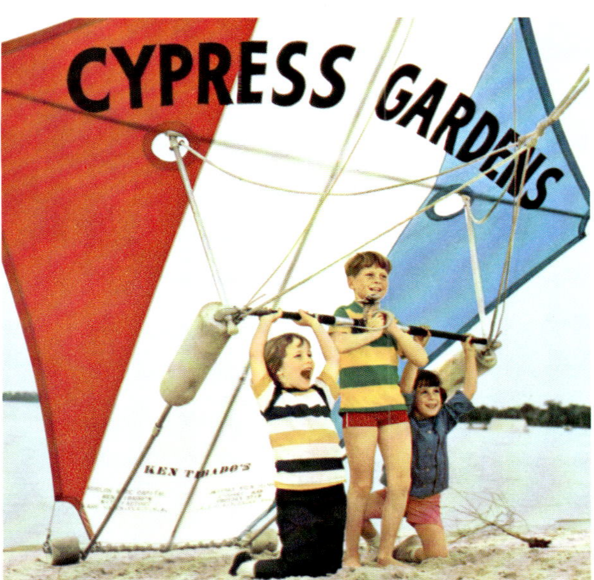

O. J. Roth

Don Maggio

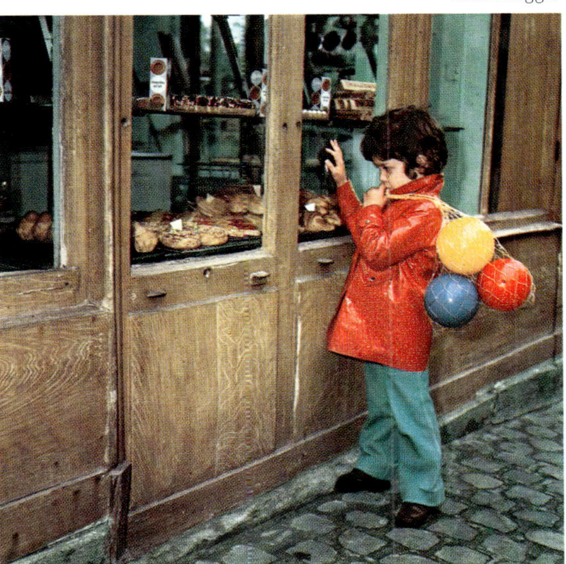

Grant Haist

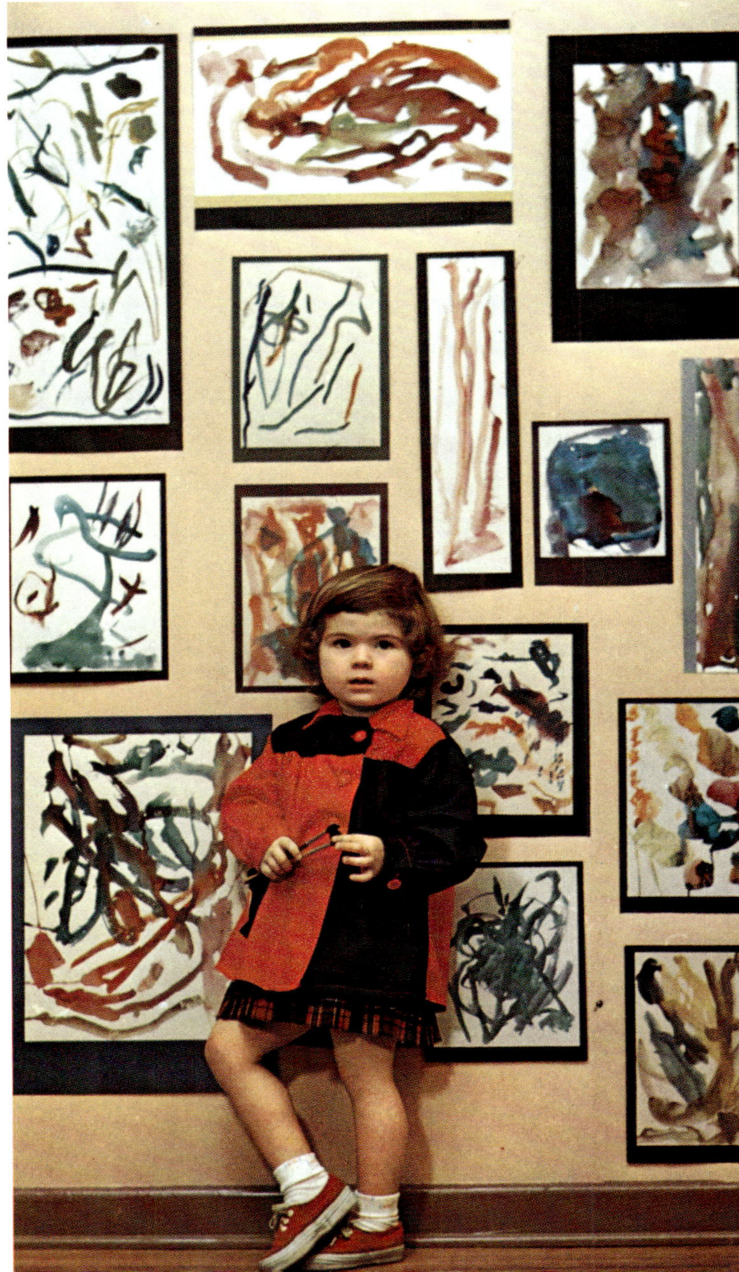

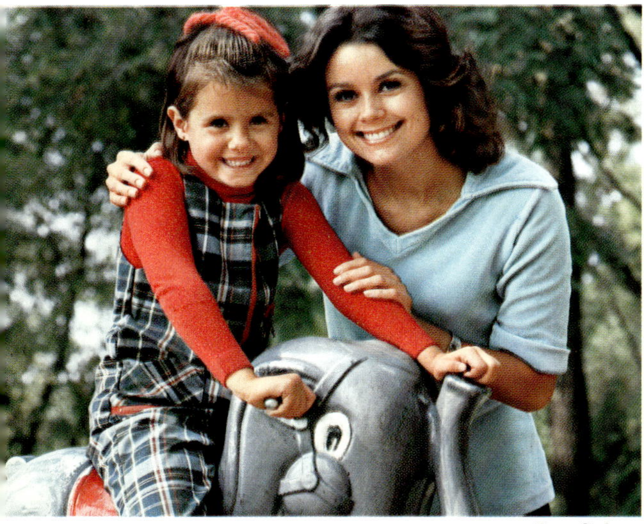

Pete Culross

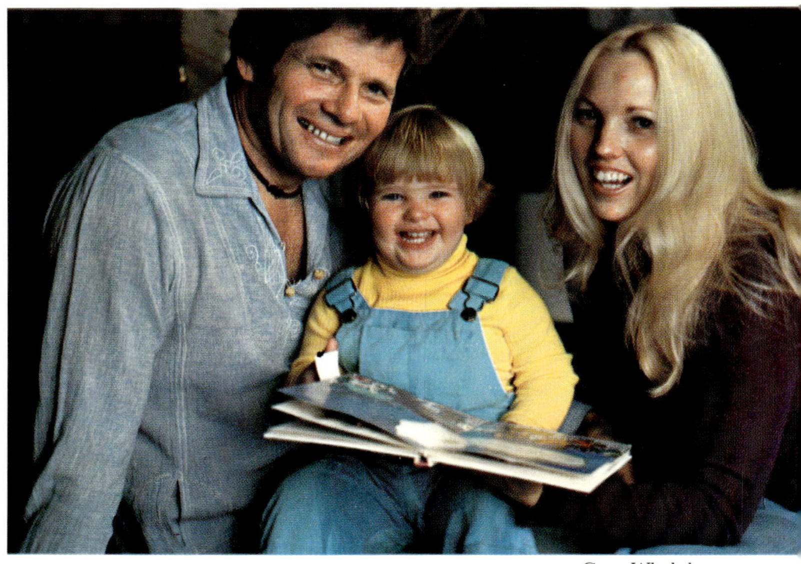

Gary Whelpley

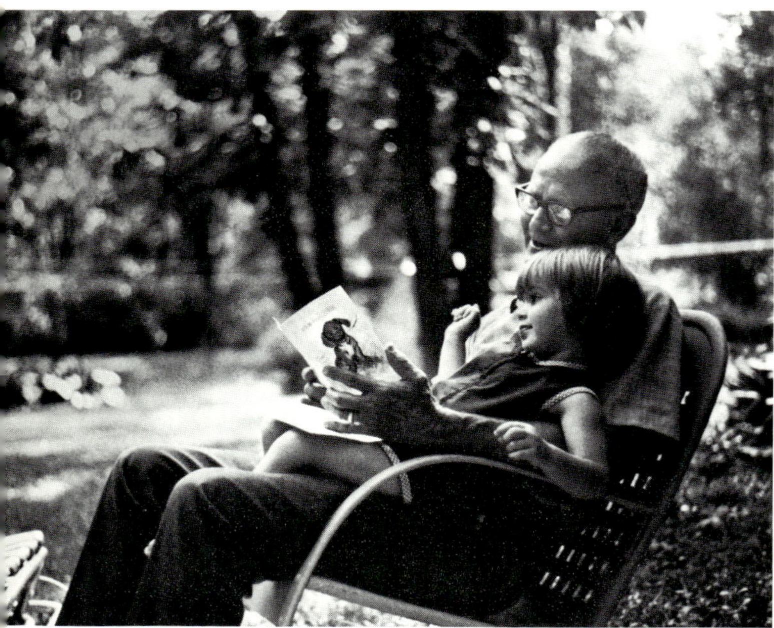

Mrs. David Davidson

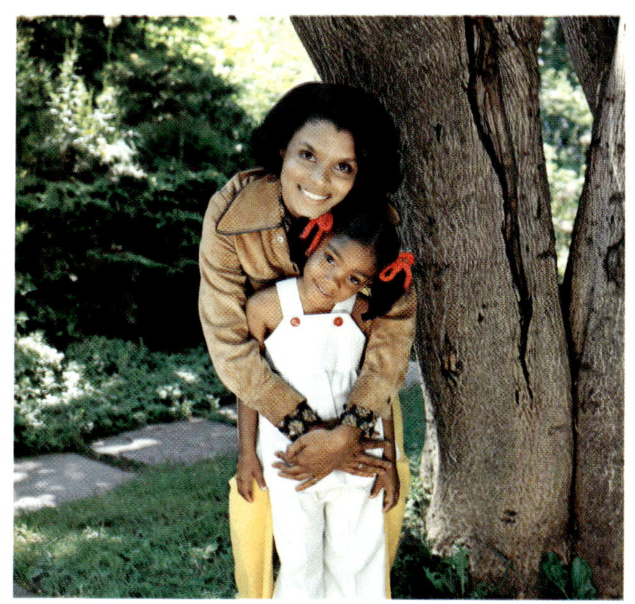

Jim Dennis

Don Maggio

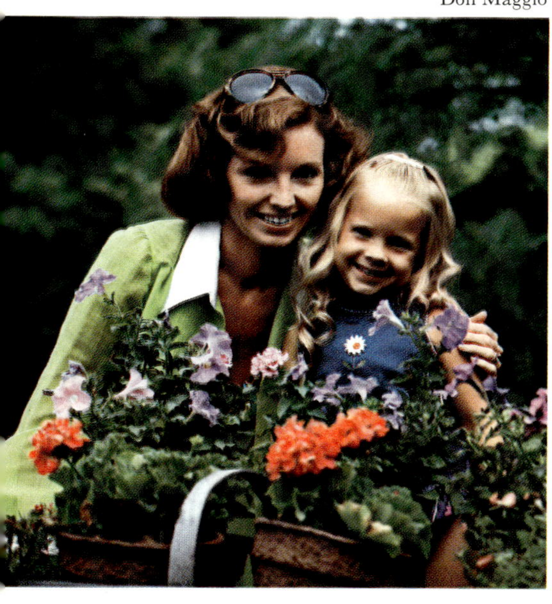

Emiel Blaakman

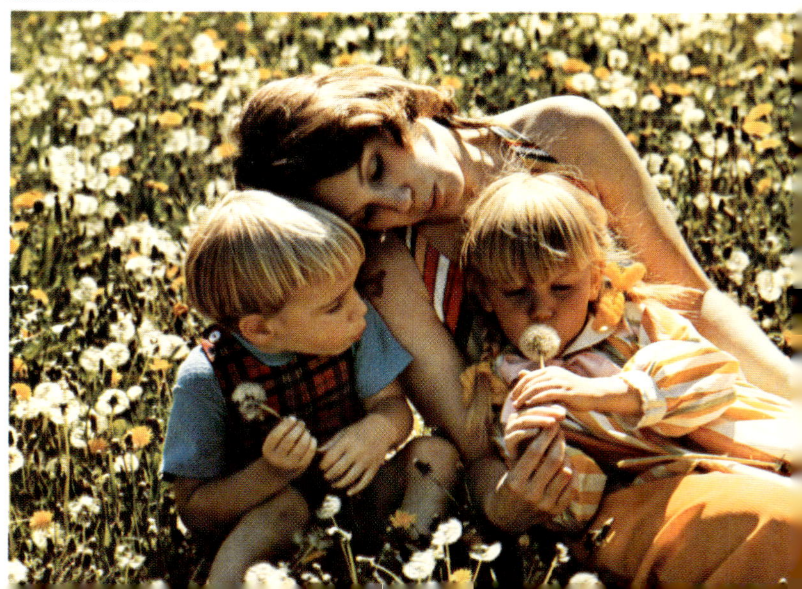

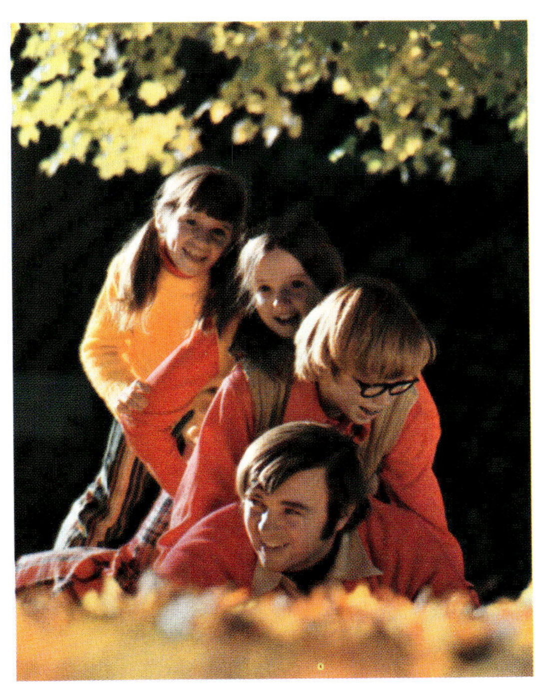

Part Three: Child and Family

Some of your most treasured pictures of children show them involved in activities with other family members. The kids helping Dad wash the car, the family dog taking your 5-year-old for a walk, Mom giving the baby a bath, the whole family building a snowman—all these things make good photographic subjects. Let's explore a few ways in which you can make your own child and family pictures more interesting and effective.

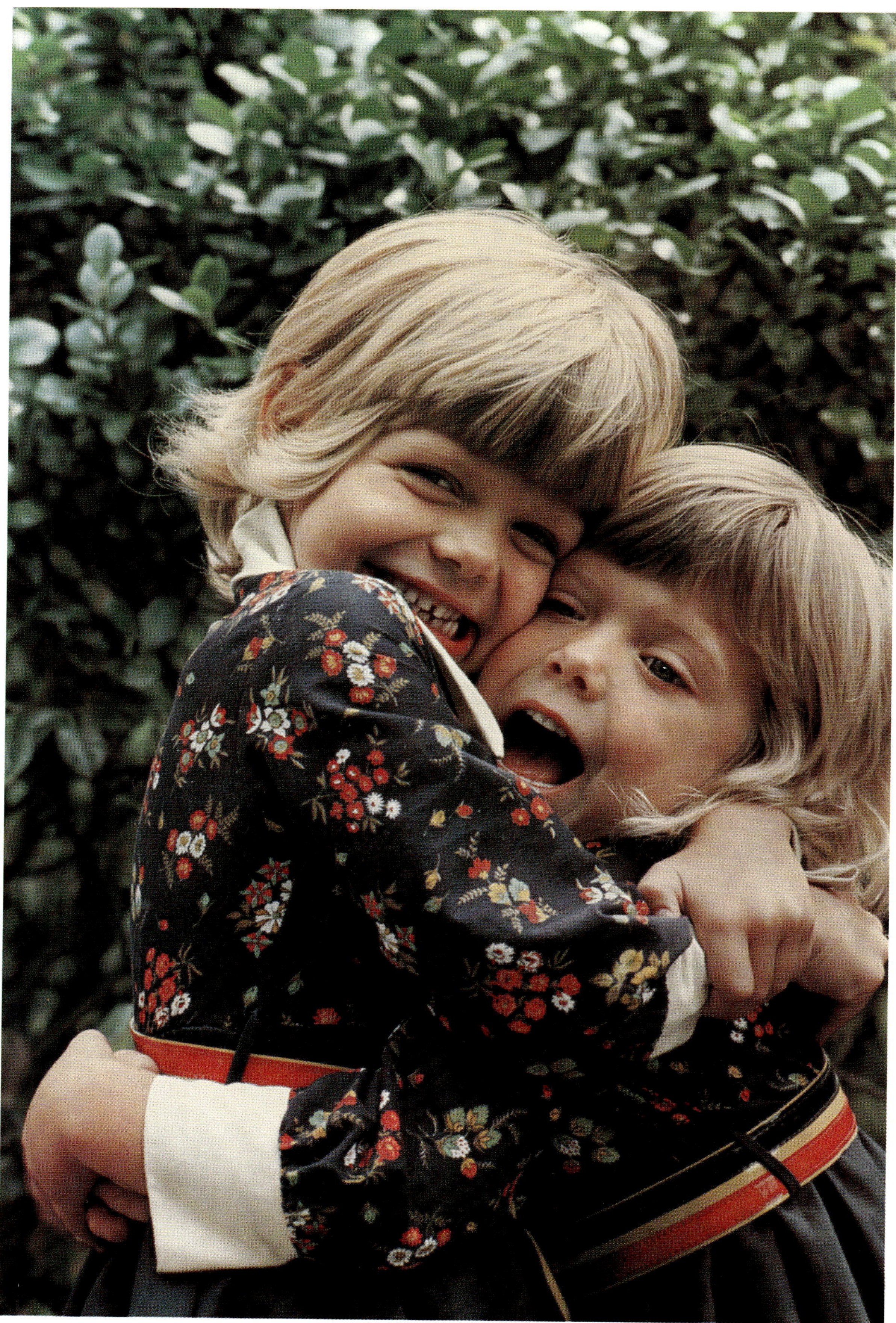

Anthony Mauer

The pictures on these two pages all have a couple of important compositional benefits in common:

- *In each picture, the subjects have been placed close together for a unified center of interest.*
- *Strong, often undesirable, horizontal lines have been avoided by arranging each subject's head at a different level in the scene.*

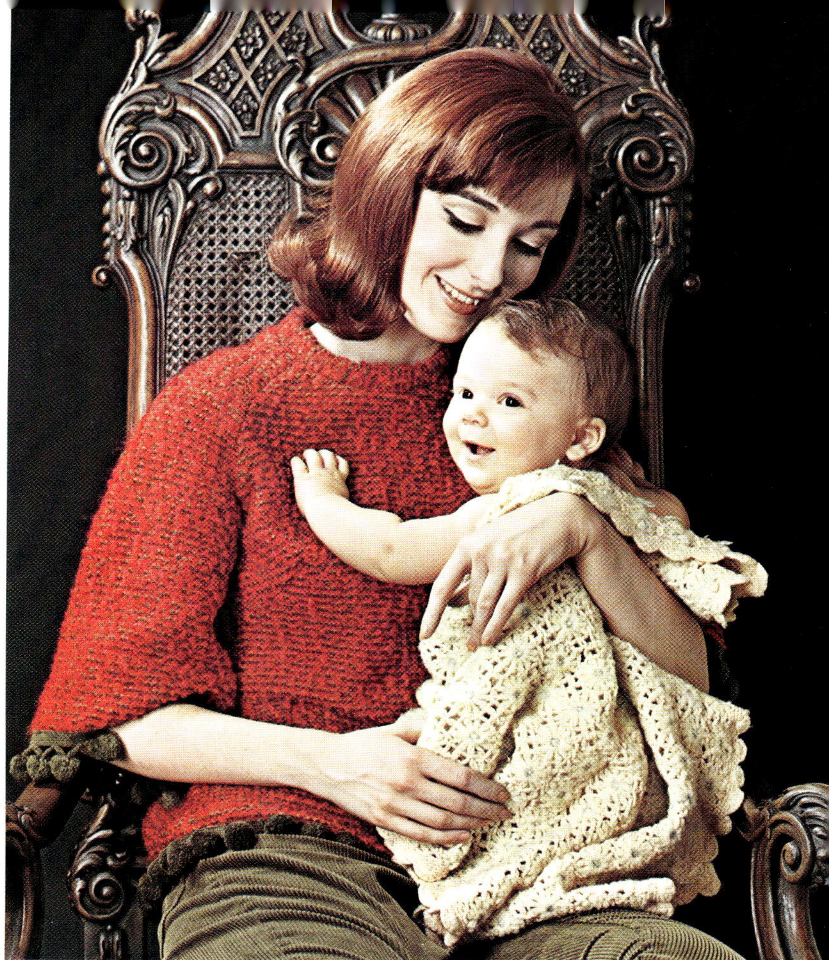

Composition

Good composition, simply stated, is *the pleasing selection and arrangement of subjects within the picture area.* Photographs with good composition are usually more enjoyable and they leave you with a comfortable feeling. While you probably already have a fairly good idea of what makes some pictures better than others, here are a few simple guidelines to refresh your knowledge and help you improve the composition in your pictures.

Center of Interest

Compose your images in the camera viewfinder to give importance to the center(s) of interest, so that your reason for taking the picture is clearly seen. Then before snapping the picture, arrange the other parts of the picture area to complement what you choose to be the center of interest.

While this premise for understanding good picture design applies to all pictures of children, it is particularly important when photographing multiple subjects. When your viewfinder image includes two or more people, for example, it's quite easy to arrive at a photograph having more than one center of interest. A picture with two or more centers of interest can be distracting because the viewer's eyes are forced to move back and forth. You can improve the composition by moving either the subjects, the camera position, or both, to bring the centers of interest closer together for a more pleasing picture.

This same eye-direction technique can work well for you when you set out to photograph your youngster who is happily playing with half the

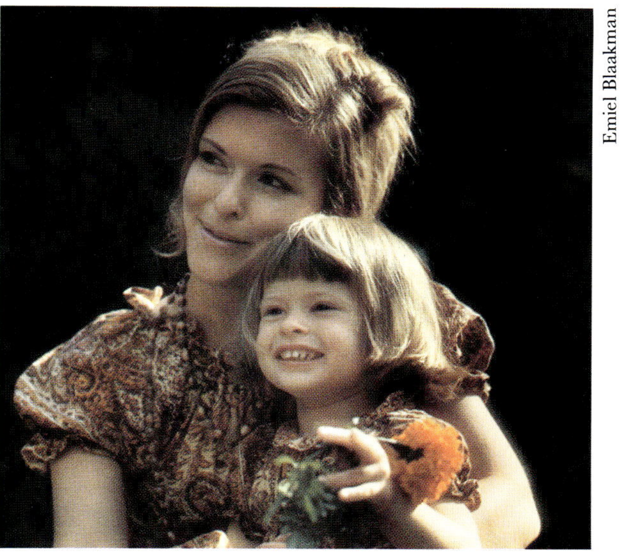

Emiel Blaakman

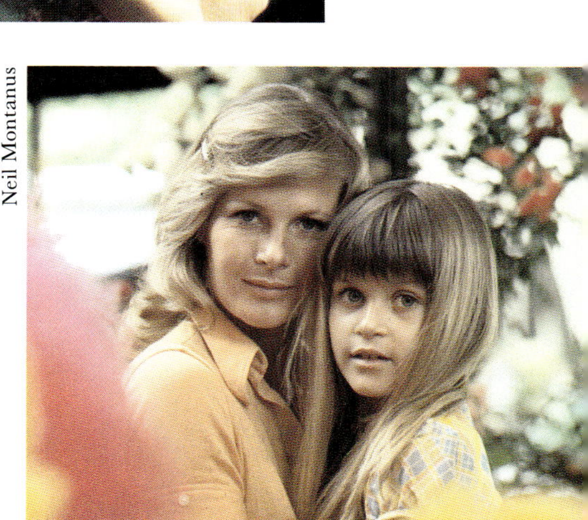

Neil Montanus

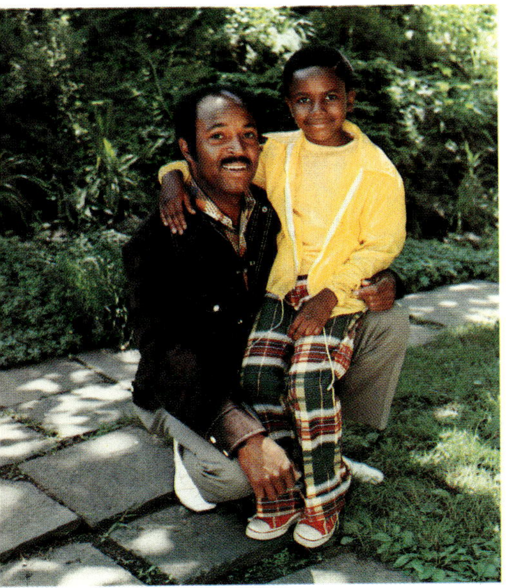

Jim Dennis

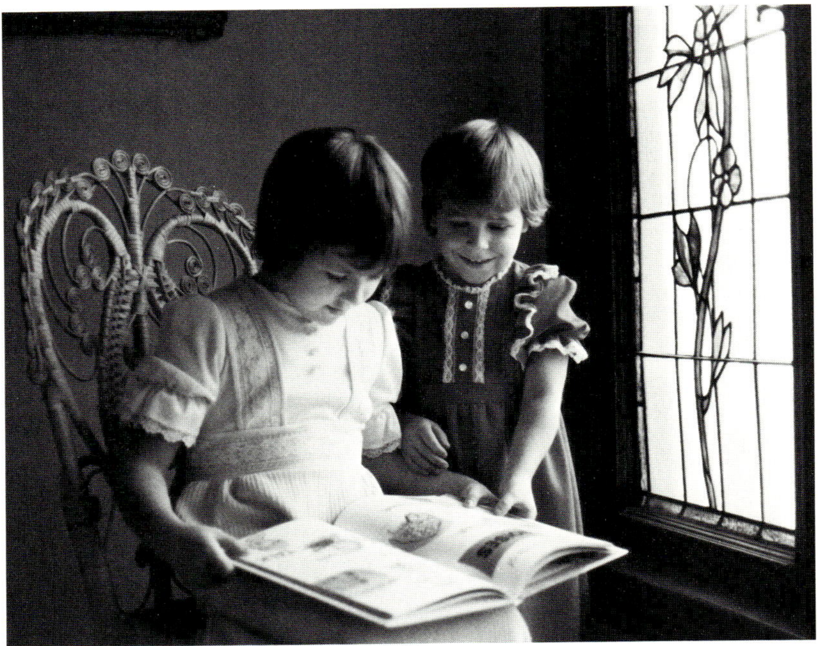

Robert Johnston

children in the neighborhood. Everyone will want to be in the picture (which is fine), but the unending display of laughter and enthusiasm could somewhat overpower the presence of your child who, after all, is your reason for taking the picture. Simply ask your child to continue an activity (building a birdhouse, making mud pies, blowing up balloons, painting a "Picasso"—anything appropriate to the moment), and then direct everyone else in the scene to watch that activity. All eyes will be on your child, the center of interest.

Before taking your next multiple-subject picture, quickly review these simple points, and make the required adjustments in composition before exposing the film:

- Arrange the subjects close together or wait until their activities bring them together.
- If possible, vary the head heights a little to add compositional interest.
- With larger groups, isolate your prime center of interest by having others look in that direction.

Let's take, as an example, a couple of perennially popular photographic subjects—a parent and a child. Try to avoid taking this twosome in a static, stiff-looking pose—such as standing at attention, side by side, staring straight at the camera lens. A better composition, one that would bring the two subjects together for a single center of interest, would be to have them get closer to each other. If both of their heads appear to be at the exact same height as you view them, you might ask one of your subjects to change positions by standing, kneeling, sitting, or whatever, to break up the strong horizontal line for a more interesting composition.

In many family group pictures, the youngest addition is often the most important element, simply because he or she usually receives most of the attention anyway. You can capitalize on this knowledge and, at the same time, make a better picture by directing the other subjects to center their attention on the little one. The result will be an effective picture of several individuals with the child as the center of interest.

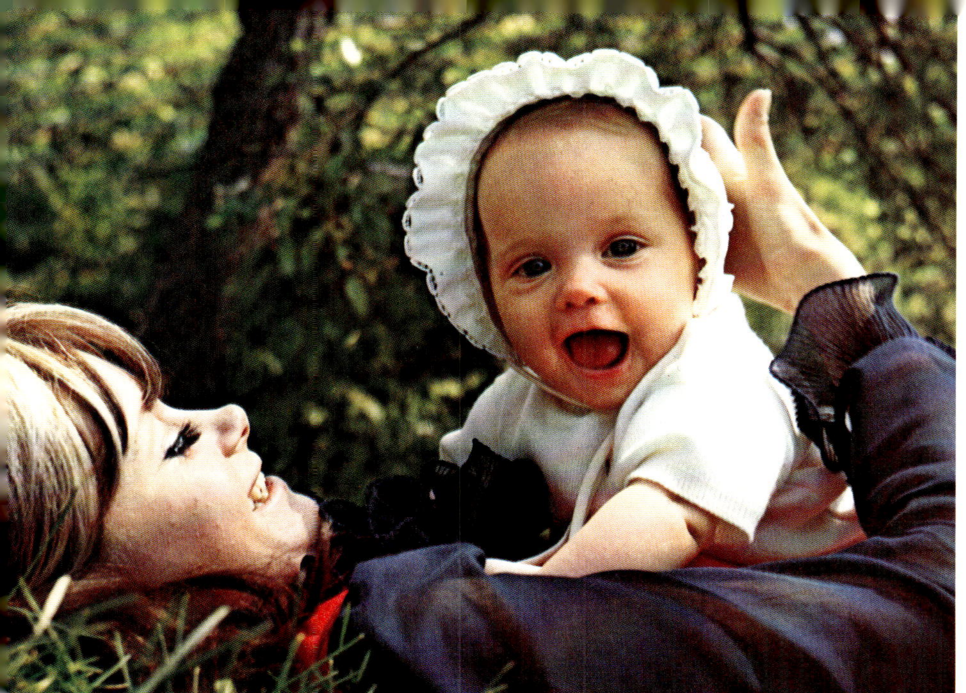

Dave Barone

Bob Clemens

When your viewfinder image contains two or more people, bring each element together for a stronger center of interest by moving either the subjects, the camera position, or both.

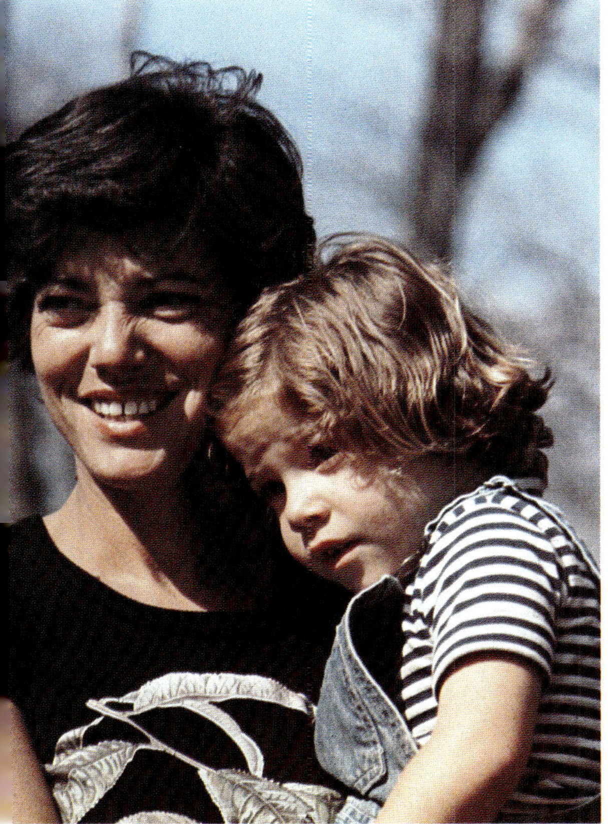

John Herman

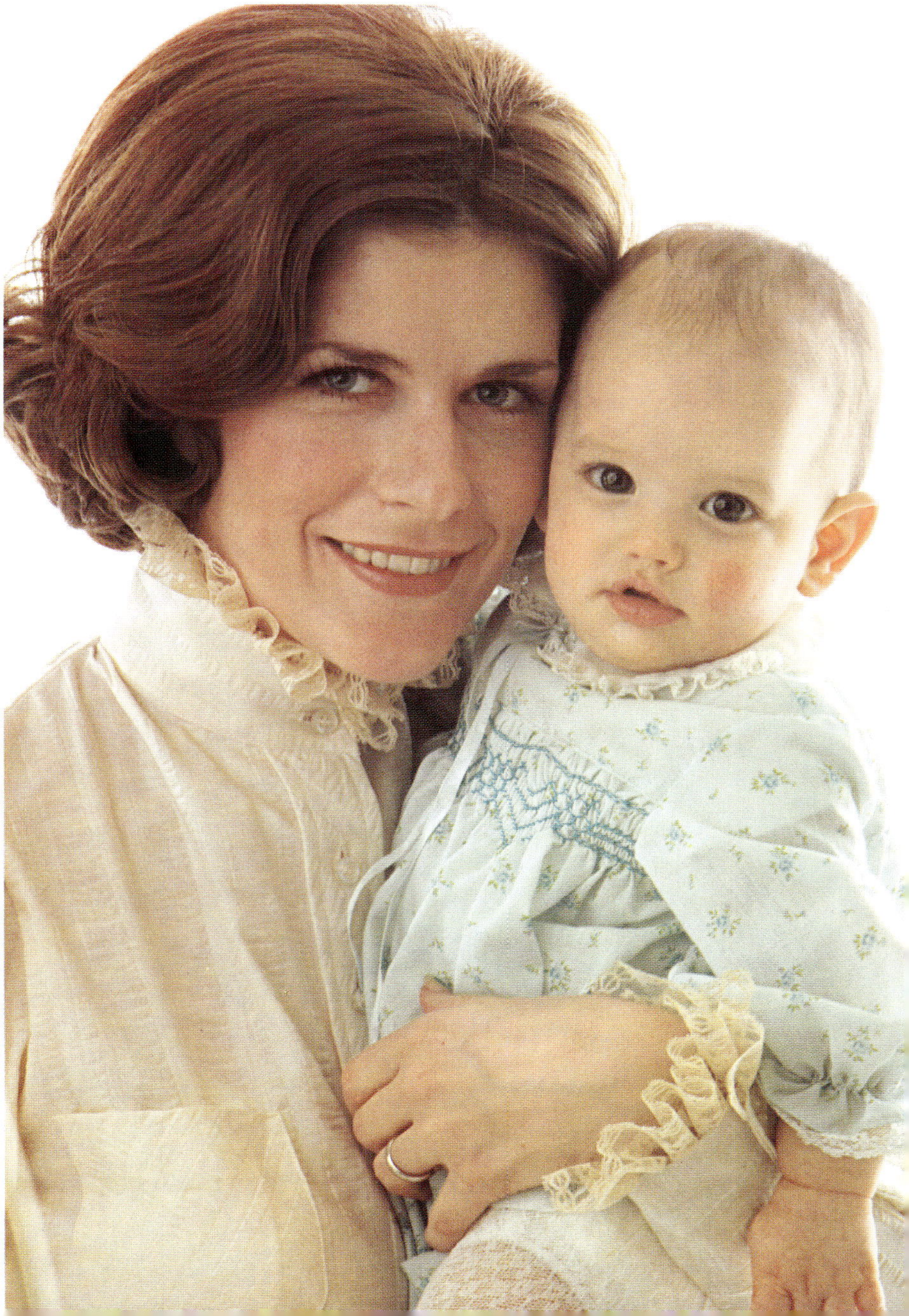

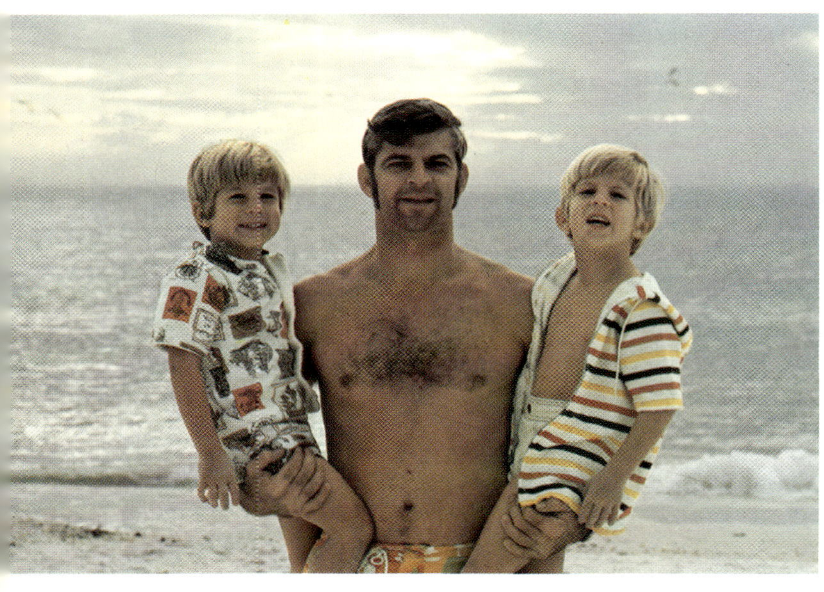

A horizon merger, in most cases, is very easy to correct by a simple shift in camera position.

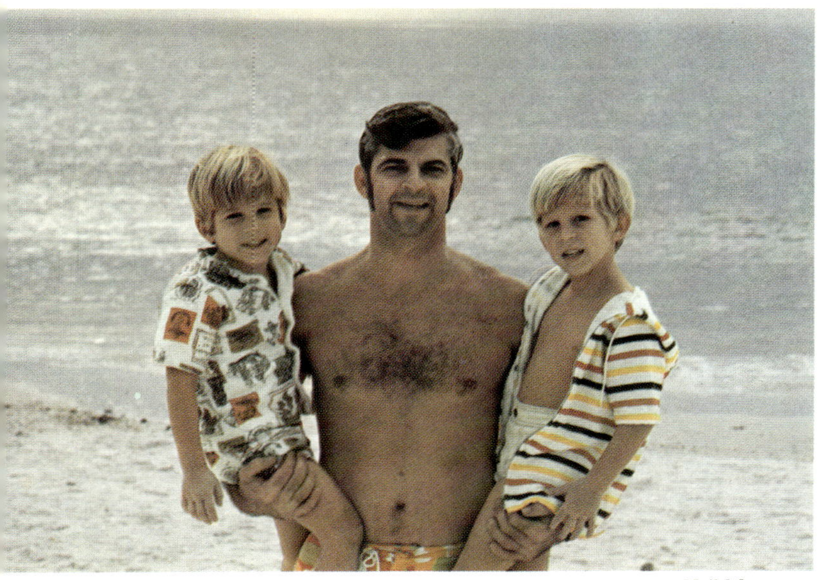

Neil Montanus

When you raise the camera position and aim slightly down, this horizon line is no longer a problem.

Here's an example of a border merger. The little girl's arm disappears into the left border of the picture, making an awkward composition. Watch for situations like this in your own photography. If you see an undesirable border merger in your camera viewfinder, change your angle to improve the composition.

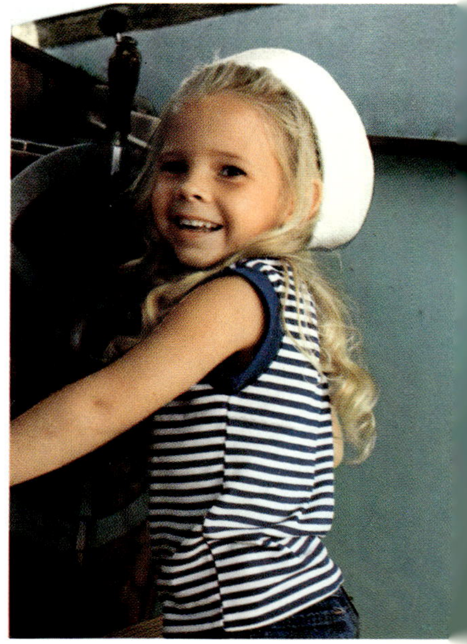

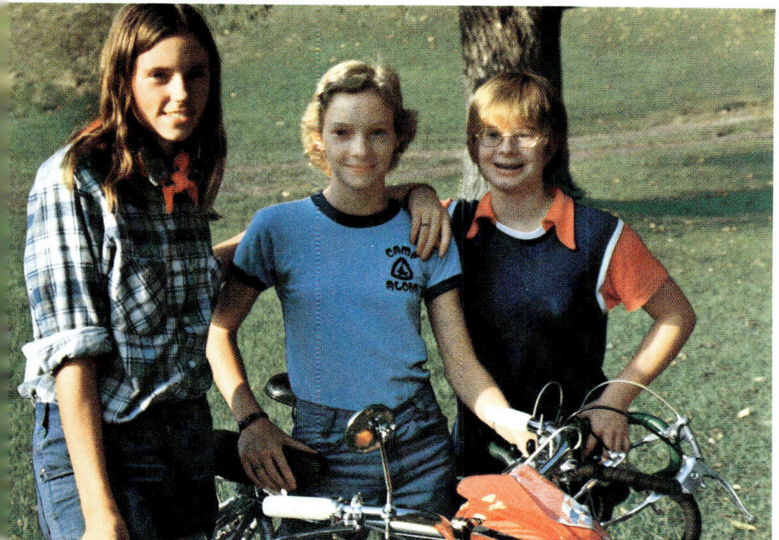

When the foreground (child on right) and background (tree) merge, the background can suddenly become an unwanted part of the foreground.

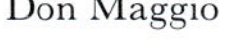

Don Maggio

The photographer corrected the situation and made a pleasing picture by simply taking a step to the right.

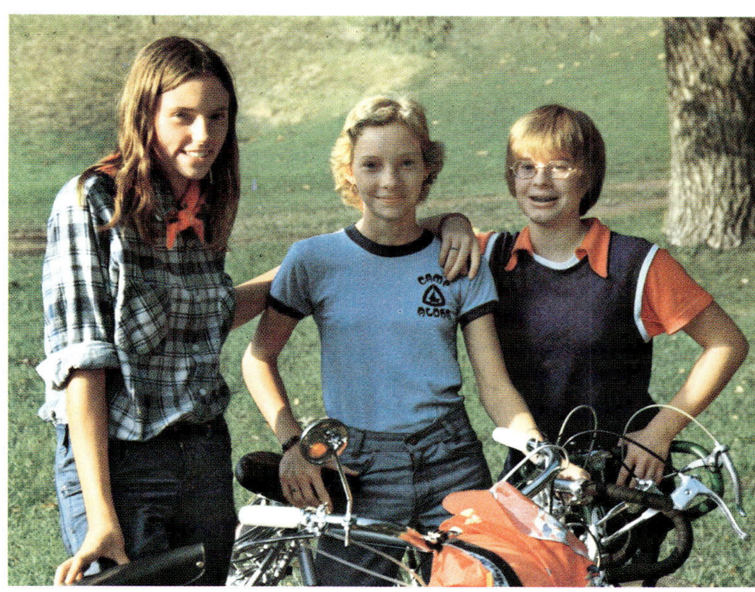

Avoiding Mergers

Earlier, we talked about how a plain, uncomplicated background can keep your viewer's attention centered on a subject while a cluttered background might easily detract from the center of interest. Mergers occur when unnecessary elements in a picture (usually in the background) interfere with the main subject. When the foreground and background merge, an object in the background can suddenly become an unwanted part of the foreground. You've probably seen at least one snapshot in the past where it appears as though a tree or post is growing out of a person's head. You can easily avoid mergers of this type and achieve a more pleasing photograph by simply changing the camera position slightly to the right or left. Check the scene carefully in the viewfinder. If you see a distracting object near any of your subjects, correct for it by adjusting your viewpoint before taking the picture.

Another type of merger occurs when one or more of the subjects in your picture are partially cut off by the picture borders. For example, the hand of a child, who is pointing with an outstretched arm, disappears into the picture border. And then there's the situation in which you are trying to get a close-up of a small child and a tall adult without arranging them very close together. This could easily result in a photo containing the child but perhaps only half of the adult's head (or the other way around). To avoid unwanted border mergers, you must—in addition to practicing good subject control—carefully frame the scene in the viewfinder before snapping the picture. Make sure, before depressing the shutter release, that your eye is properly centered in the viewfinder window so that, at a glance, you can see all four edges of the picture area. When these borders are visible to you, it's a very good bet that you will record on film the image you are seeing with no surprises later when you first view the resulting picture.

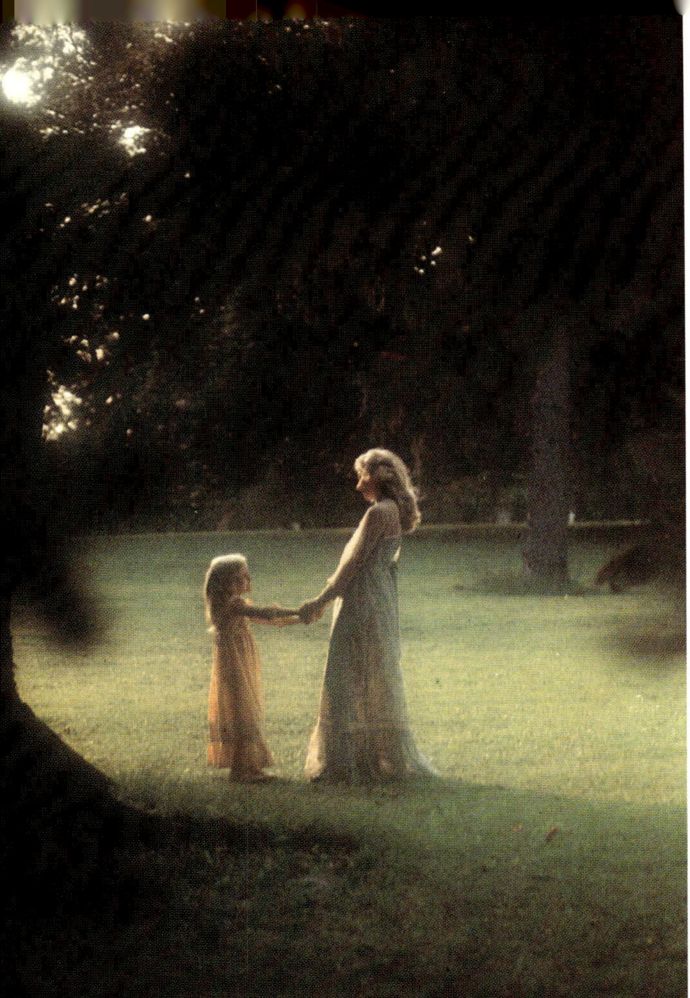

Robert Johnston

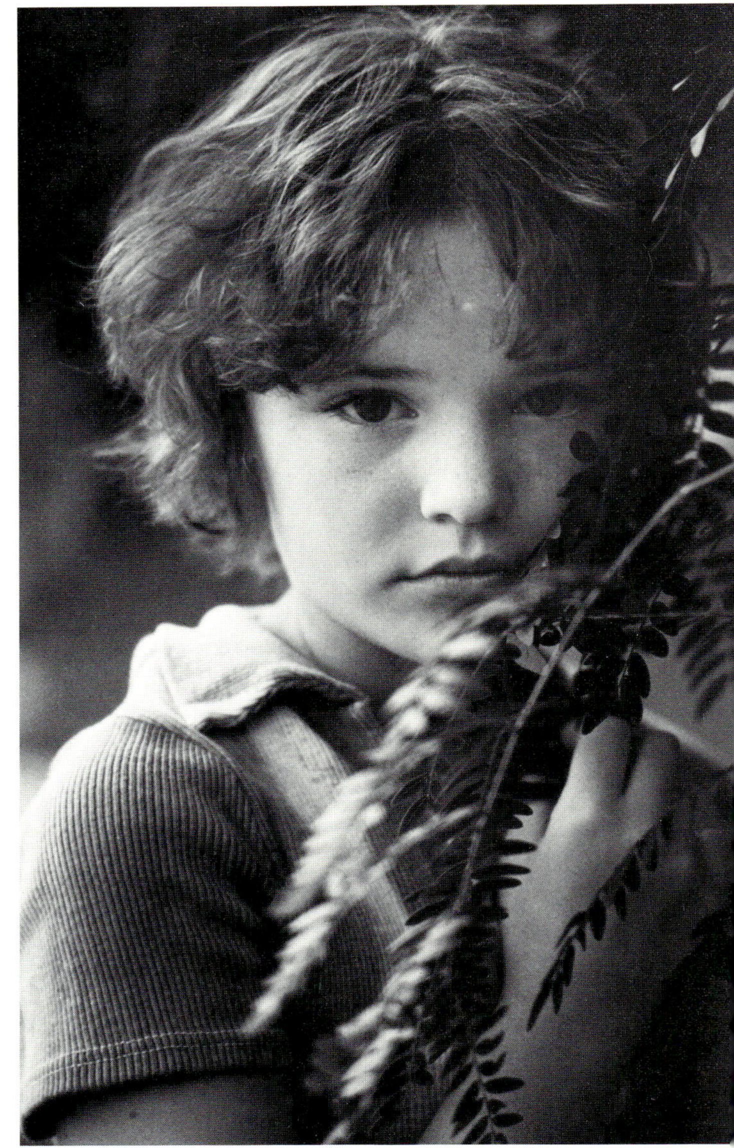

Don Maggio

Framing

To give your outdoor family portraits some feeling of depth and make them more than just snapshots, you can frame the setting with an interesting foreground. Good foreground elements include overhanging tree branches, tall grass, flowers, doorways, and even some fences. A foreground frame can often provide the picture with a new dimension, making your photo worth more than a second glance. If you use a frame in the foreground, be sure to choose one that would be appropriate for the subject and the situation.

Another tip: Foreground framing elements near the lens should be either extremely out of focus or very sharp. Anything in between usually looks like a mistake and makes the frame distracting rather than helpful.

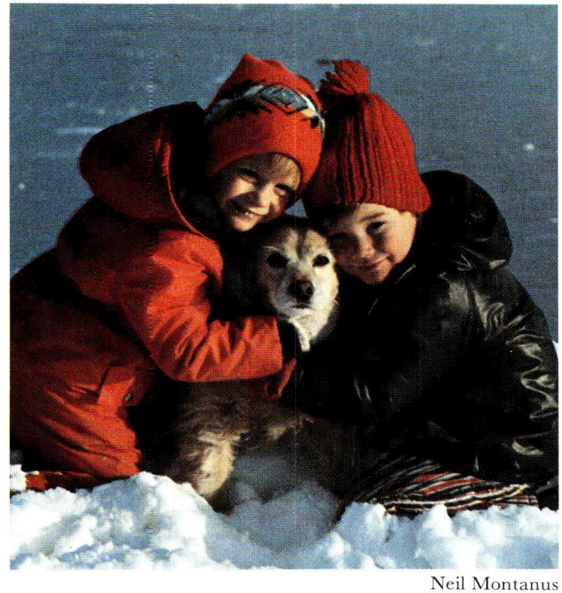

Neil Montanus

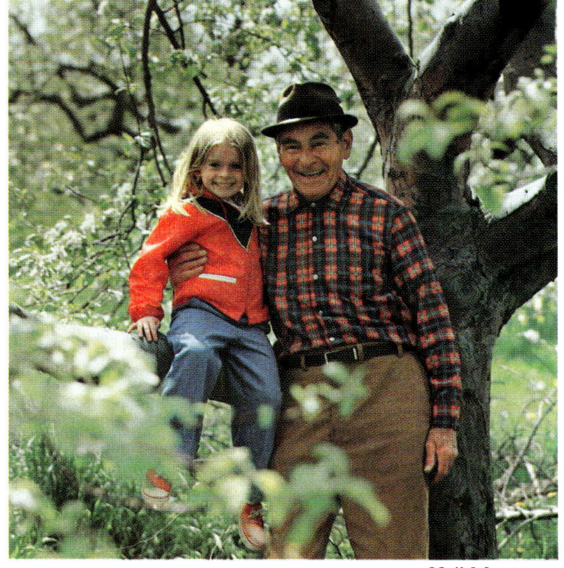

Neil Montanus

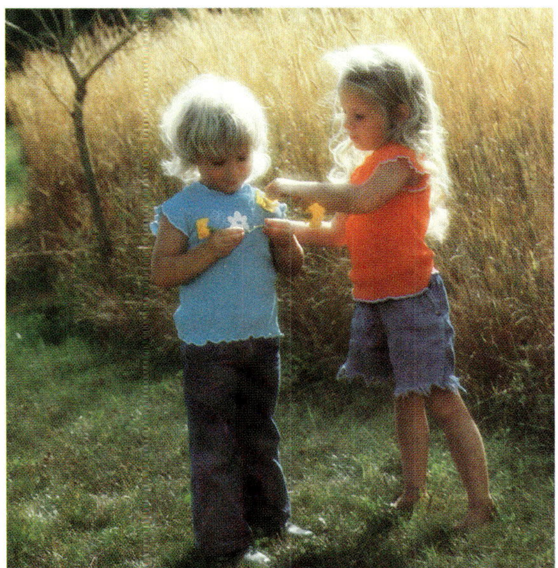

Jim Dennis

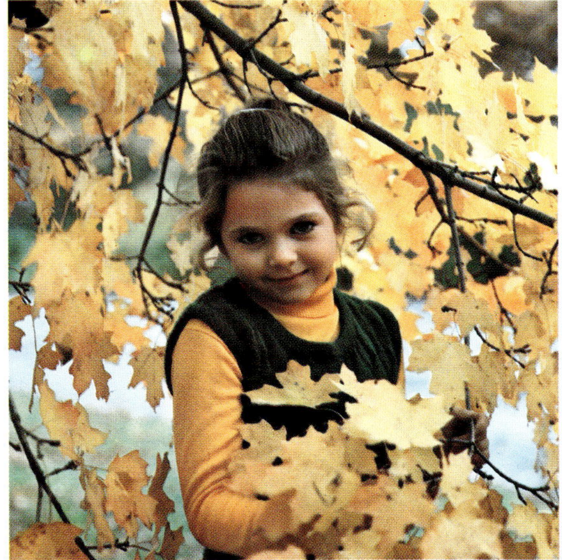

Pete Culross

Take Advantage of the Season

Each season of the year brings a new parade of family recreational activities, many of which offer natural picture-taking opportunities. Spice up your photo album with images of everyone enjoying the snow, the sunshine, the spring and autumn color—whatever it is about the day that sends children and parents alike bursting into the great out-of-doors. You don't have to live in a National Park or on a tropical island to take great environmental family portraits. Just maintain a positive attitude, show a touch of imagination, and take advantage of the multitude of natural props available to you at the moment. With proper camera handling and a little general enthusiasm, you can turn an ordinary family outing into a handsome photograph, ideal for a holiday greeting card (more on this later) or an album, wall, or desk-top display.

Pete Culross

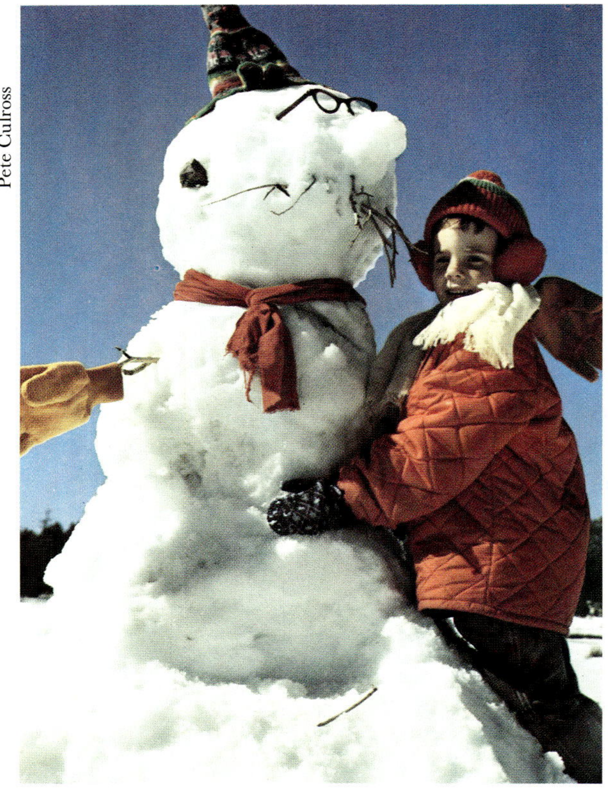

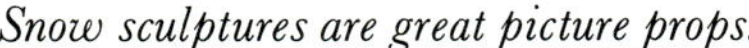

Snow sculptures are great picture props.

Neil Montanus

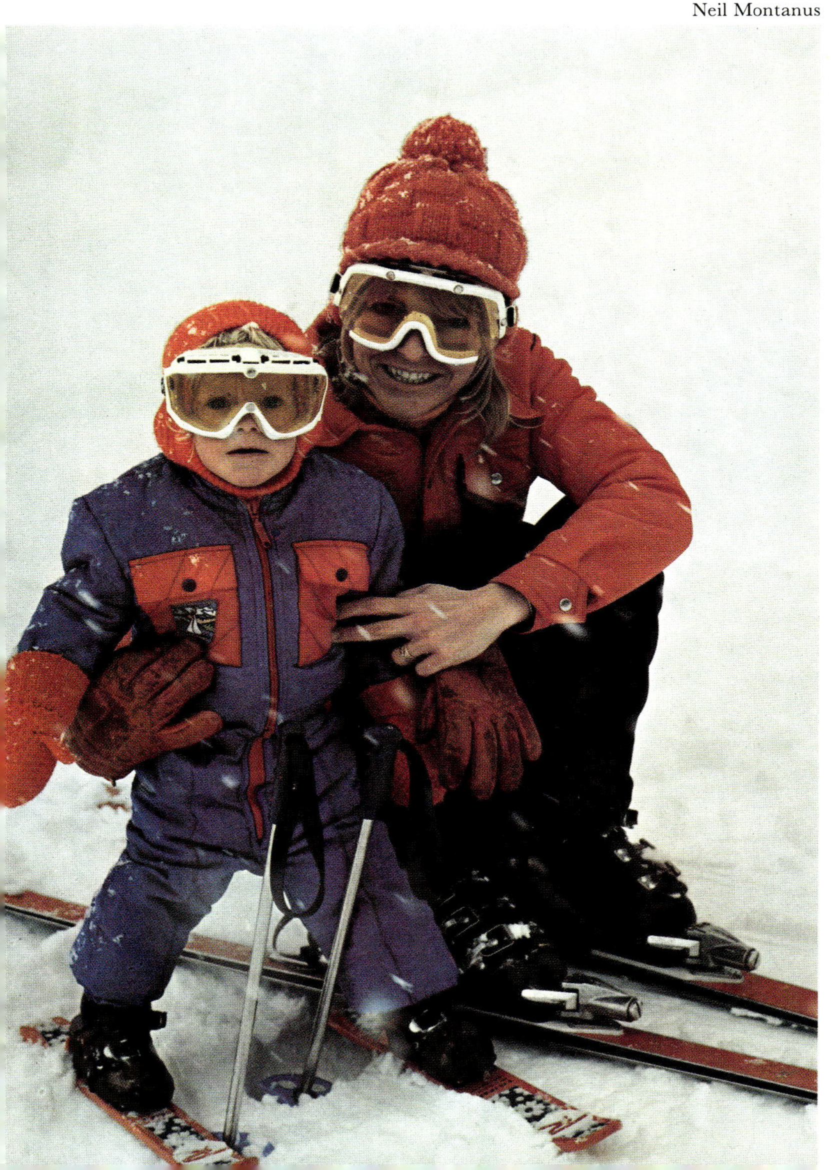

Bright clothing makes pictures colorful.

Winter White

Suppose the temperature hasn't been above freezing in 3 weeks, the snow is knee-deep, and you haven't photographed your children in so long they no longer resemble their dog-eared images you carry next to your credit cards. "I'll take a new picture of the kids in the living room," you say. Not a chance! You can take indoor pictures any time of year. Now is the time to meet the winter blahs head-on by dressing everyone in warm clothing and sending them out the door. You, of course, will go right along with them, *camera in hand.*

As your family pursues their chosen form of winter fun, watch for those moments when the action will be at its best, their expressions the happiest, and the background scenery both simple and storytelling.

Although picture-taking on a chilly February day is technically no different from recording a picnic in August, there are some camera-handling techniques and aesthetic considerations that can help you improve your winter family pictures. The following tips are applicable to most picture-taking situations and types of photo equipment:

- If there's a snowfall under way and you're plagued by a snow-covered camera, put your camera into a plastic bag, leaving the lens and viewfinder exposed. If you carry your camera under your coat, you may not need the case, which can be in the way when you're trying to take a candid picture.

- A cold temperature can have an effect on the quality of instant pictures. If you are using products such as a KODAK Instant Camera and KODAK Instant Print Film PR10 on a cold day, place the prints inside your coat pocket or a similar warm place *as soon as* they are ejected from the camera. Leave them there during development (about 8 minutes). Otherwise, the prints will appear too light.

- The smaller your camera is, the easier it is to hide from the elements. KODAK TRIMLITE INSTAMATIC and KODAK TELE-INSTAMATIC® Cameras are ideally suited to outdoor picture-taking in the cold. You can easily keep one warm and still accessible. The controls on the more advanced models are simple to locate and manipulate with gloves. You can carry a day's supply of film and flipflash in one inside pocket. Drop-in cartridge loading makes a film change short and simple.

- Personalize your scenic pictures with your family members. Ask them to pose in the foreground (15 to 20 feet/4.5 to 6 meters away) and look into the scene. Have them wear their brightest clothing to add a dash of color to your pictures.

- If you have an adjustable camera, your film instruction sheet or film carton will indicate approximate exposures. If you're posing your subjects against the bright snow, your exposure will record detail on faces *or* in the snow, not in both. To achieve accurate exposure for your subjects, move in close to their faces to make your meter reading.

- Take plenty of pictures. It's the best way to remember all the fun and to share it with others.

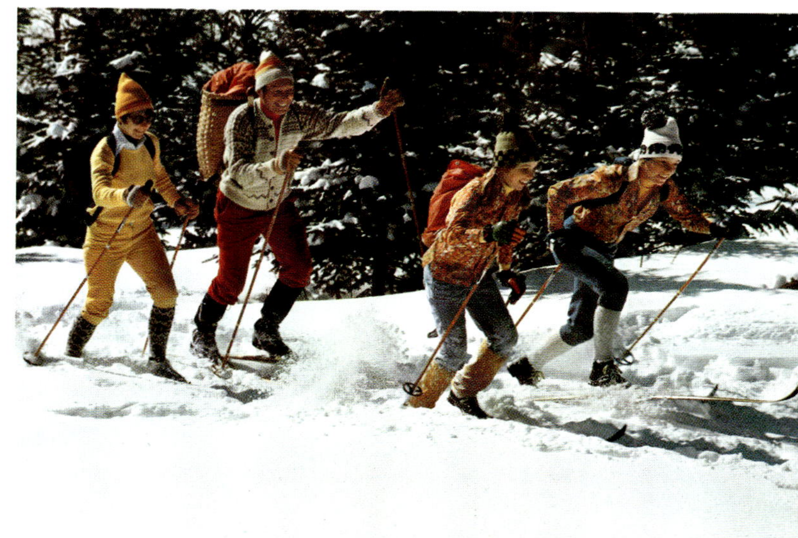

Take pictures of people doing things. Norm Kerr

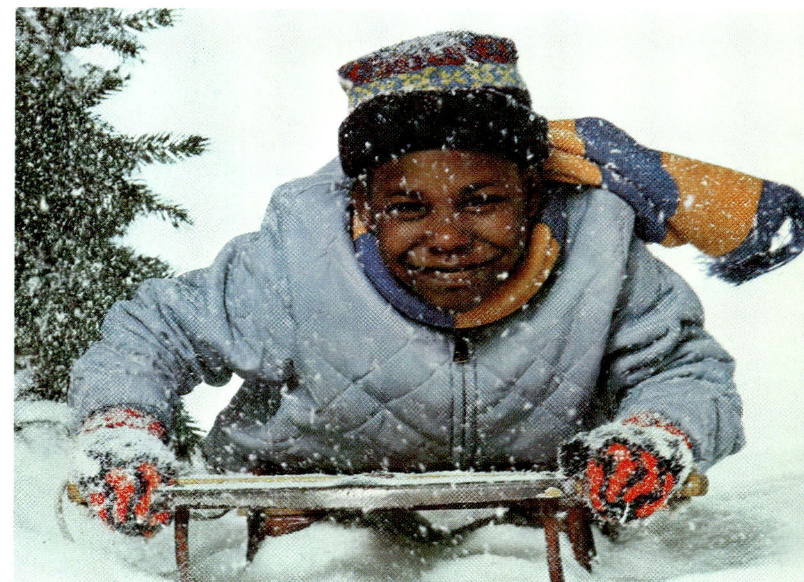

You can take good wintertime pictures even during a snowfall. Menkin Seltzer

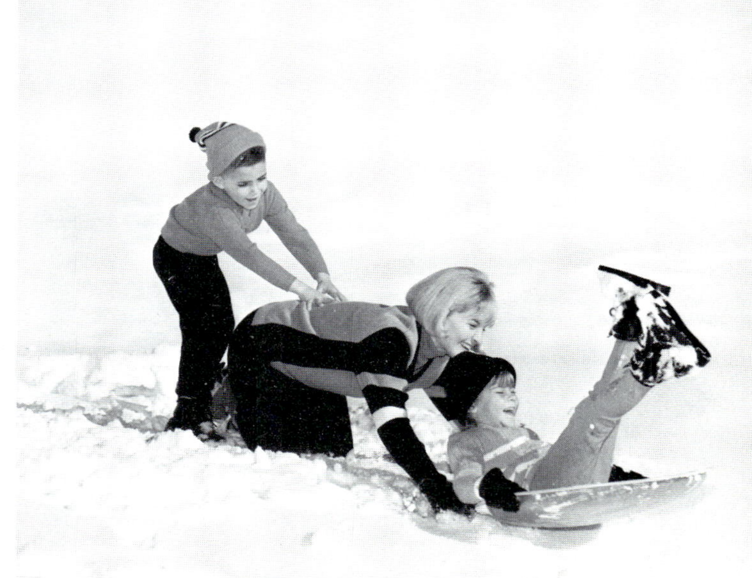

Choose the best viewpoint to get a simple, uncluttered background.

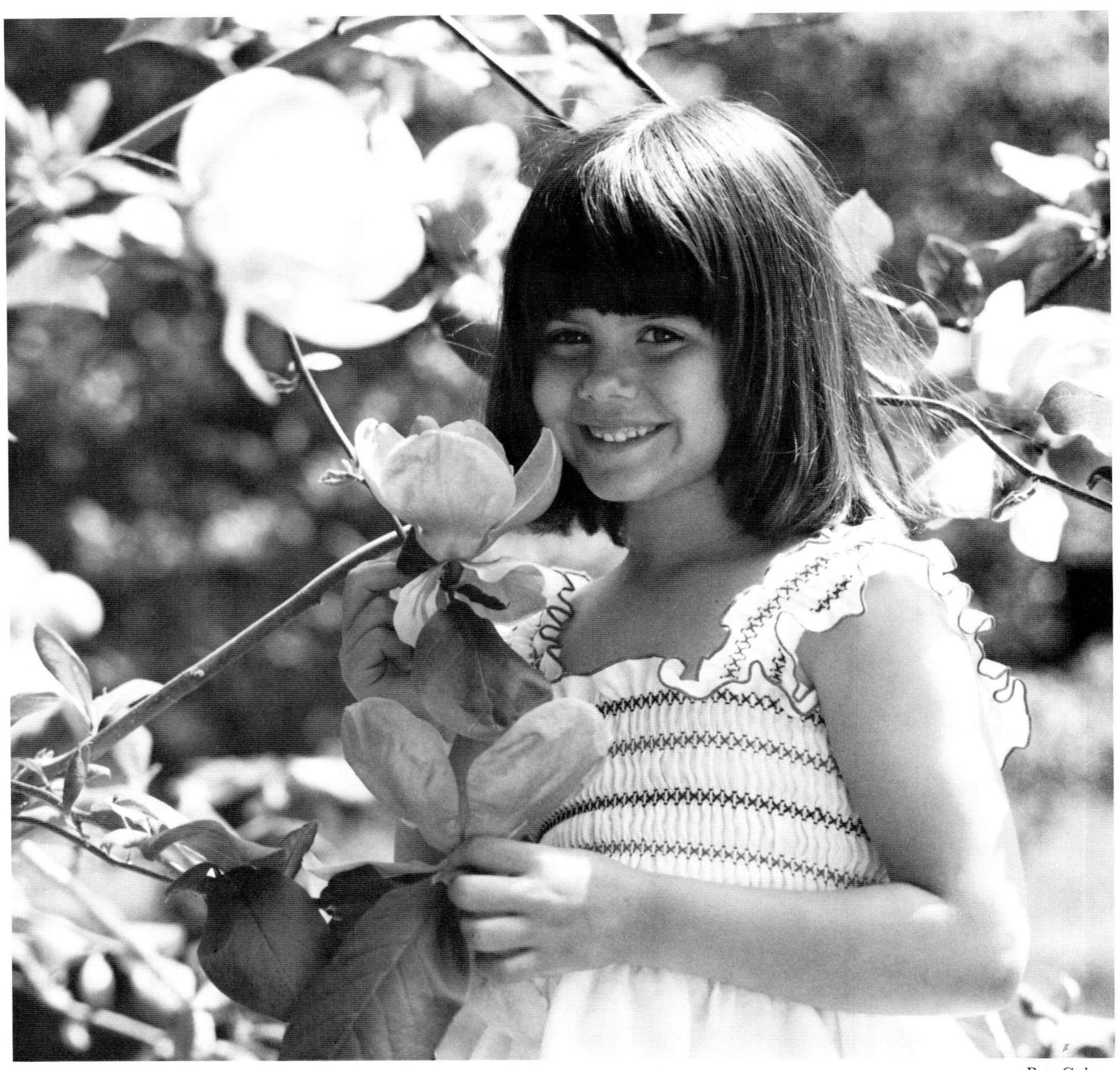

Pete Culross

To concentrate on your subject, move in close.

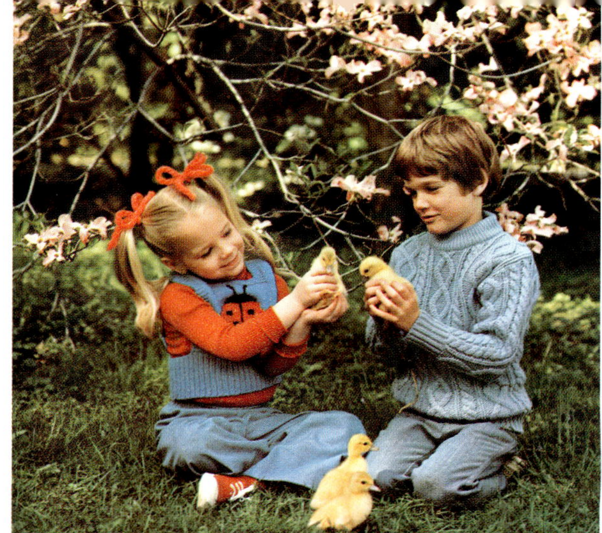

The soft light of open shade is great for taking pictures of children.

Spring Color

Springtime is one of the most exciting times of year for every family member. With the arrival of warmer weather, colorful flowers pop from the ground, children run in the fresh air, and nearly everyone becomes involved in some form of cleanup operation or the start of a new project.

Yes, springtime is *the* time to be out of doors. It's also a good time to capture on film the fun of family activities as they blend with the bright and cheerful colors of the season. Around home, there are plenty of good opportunities for child-and-family pictures. Have your camera ready to record images of Mom helping a youngster learning to ride a new bicycle, close-ups of Dad and the kids getting the garden ready for planting, and perhaps a handsome portrait of the entire family wearing their new spring clothes, about to leave for church. (Ask a neighbor to take your family group picture so you can be in the photo, too.)

Interesting springtime activities to photograph away from home might include a family excursion to the local zoo, a group walk around the pond in a nearby park, or maybe a bike ride to no place in particular. Perhaps you might have a youngster or two involved in organized sports, such as Little League baseball. Take the camera along to a practice session or game and make an official team picture.

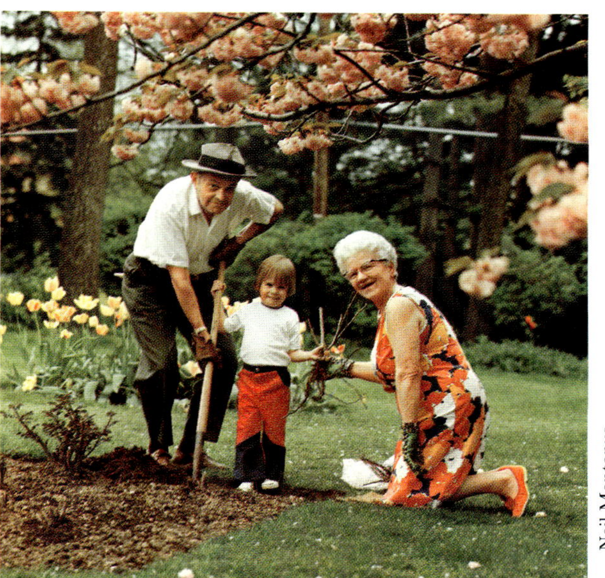

Neil Montanus

Springtime is a good time to capture family activities on film.

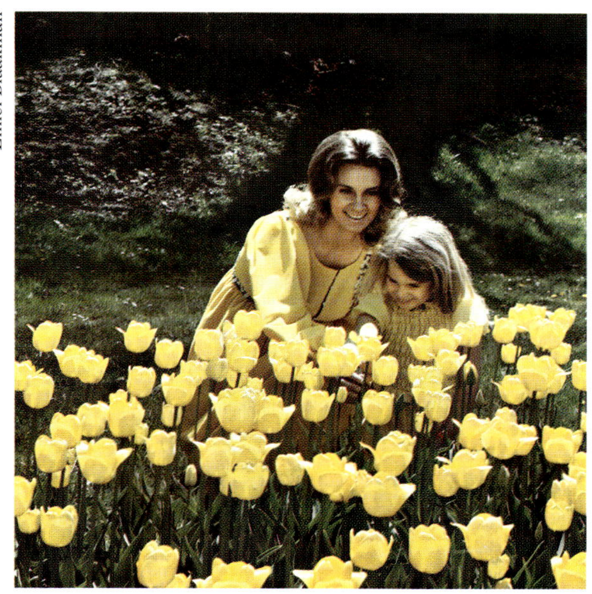

Emiel Blaakman

Use plenty of foreground color to add a sparkle of springtime to your photos.

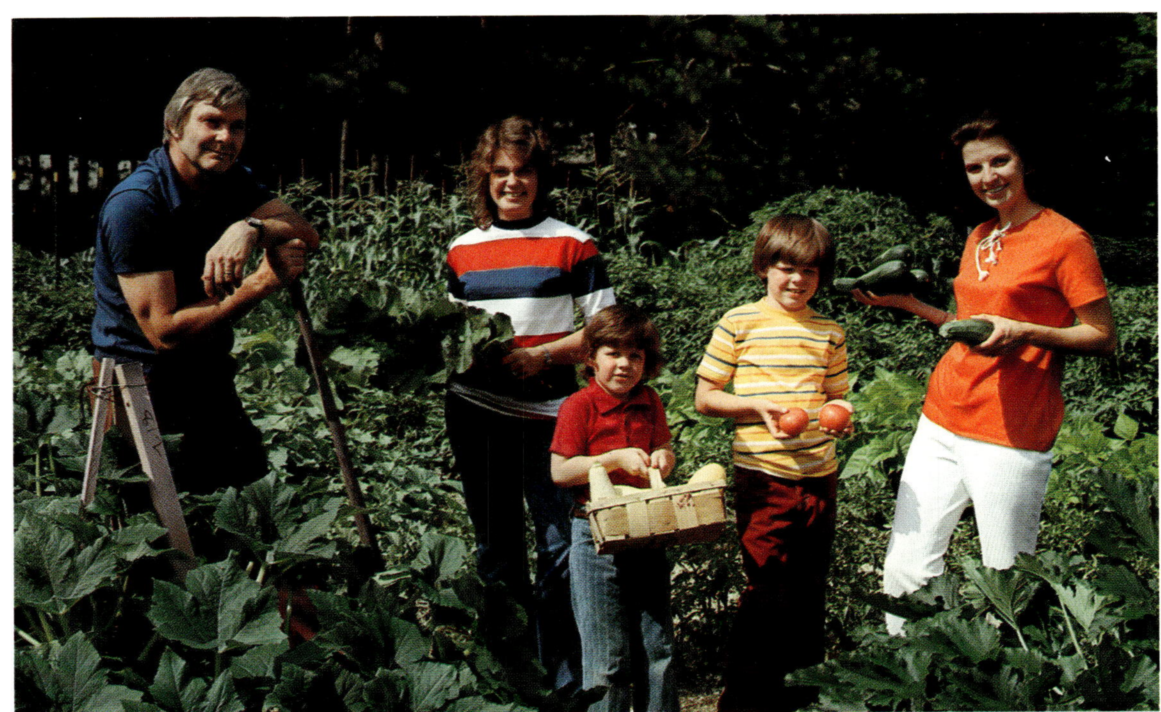

Neil Montanus

Sunny Summer

A glance into just about any family's photo album will show you that more pictures of children are probably taken during the summer months than at any other time of the year. And it's no wonder when you consider that the weather is generally warm and sunny, and there are long hours of daylight each day. Summer is the time of year when families are together more since children are not in school and parents are often on vacation. Whether your summer plans call for vacation travel and adventure or a quiet rest around home, you'll want to make the best picture records possible of family happenings—pictures that you'll be proud to share with faraway friends and relatives or keep in a special place along with other keepsakes that reflect the times of your lives.

To help you visually capture your family in summertime, keep in mind the photo tips we've already covered—particularly those involving outdoor lighting, background control, composition, and capturing natural expressions. Then add to these basic techniques a few of the following ideas to give some additional zip to your picture collection.

Foreground Color

Place your subjects behind a few pots of bright colored flowers. A patio or deck planter filled with red geraniums, for example, can add plenty of eye-catching color to the picture and help frame your center of interest. Depending on the activity, other effective foreground props might be a striped beach blanket, checkered picnic tablecloth, and possibly even a balloon or two.

Silhouettes in the Sunset

Summertime may find you and your family enjoying a sunset at the shore, on a mountaintop, or perhaps right in your own backyard. Family members appearing in the foreground of a dramatic sunset picture will be silhouetted against the sky. Have your subjects turn so their profiles will be recognizable. The resulting photograph will be both pictorial and personal.

These kinds of pictures are easy to take because exposure is not very critical. Overexposure makes the sunset appear lighter and earlier, while underexposure gives deeper, richer colors, making the sunset look more advanced. In either situation, your foreground subject should stay fairly well silhouetted. A typical exposure for a setting sun partially obscured by clouds would be 1/60 second at *f*/5.6 for KODACHROME 25 Film (Daylight) or 1/125 second at *f*/5.6 for KODACHROME 64 Film (Daylight).

When you use an exposure meter, the reading should be based on the brightness of the sky and clouds. This will render your foreground subject dark and the sun slightly overexposed, with rich colors in the clouds.

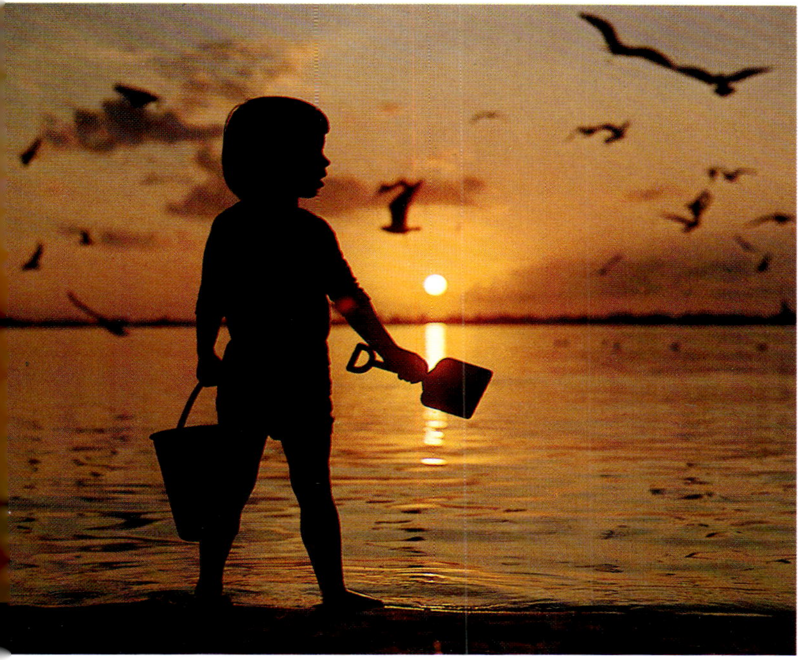

Dennis Hallinan

Photograph your child in silhouette at sunset for an appealing vacation photointerpretation.

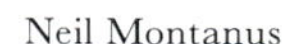

Neil Montanus

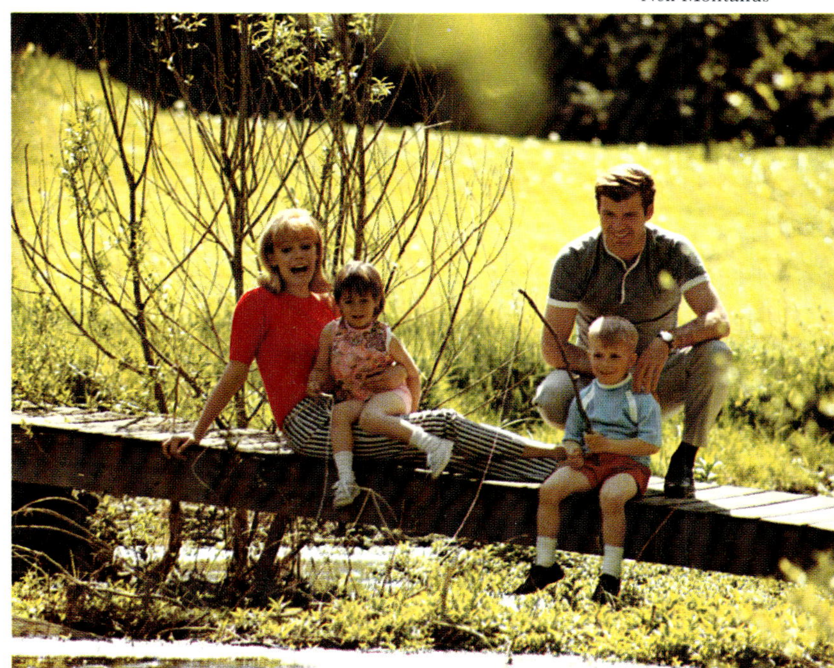

For natural-looking pictures, capture your family subjects while they're at work or play.

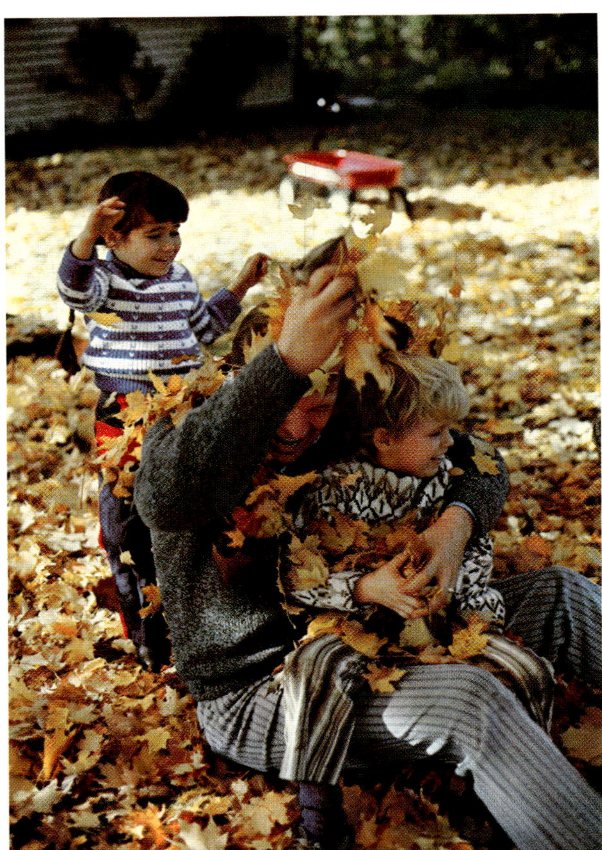

Neil Montanus

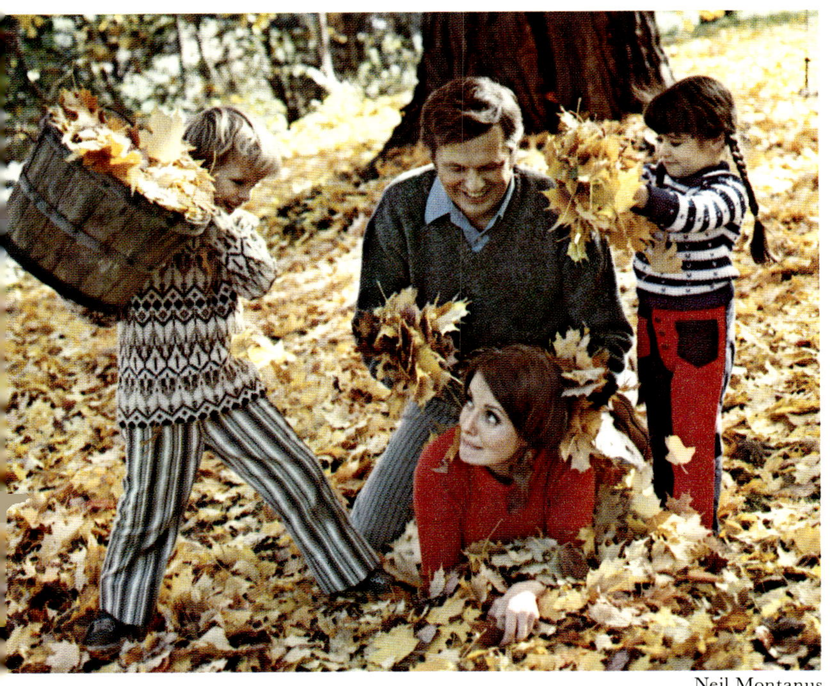

Neil Montanus

Arthur Whitty

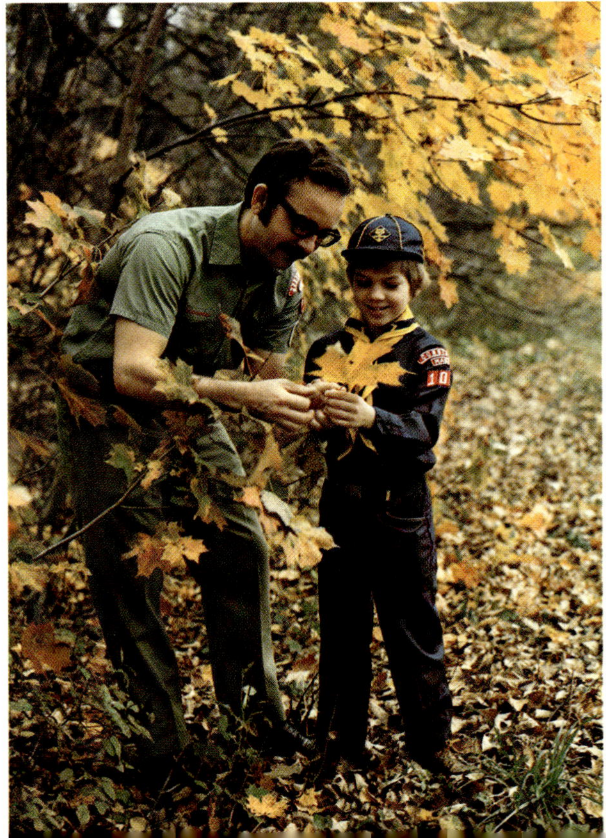

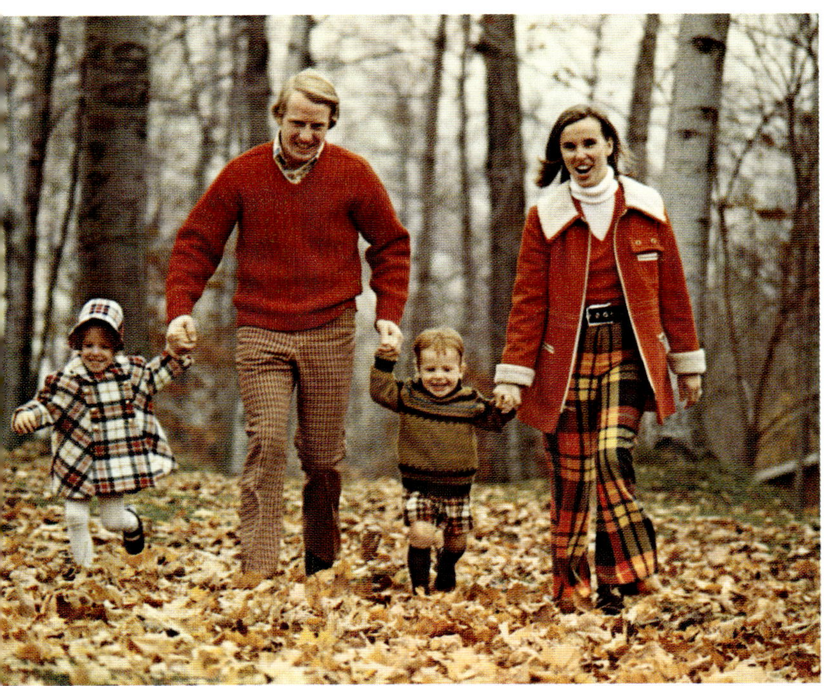

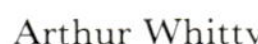

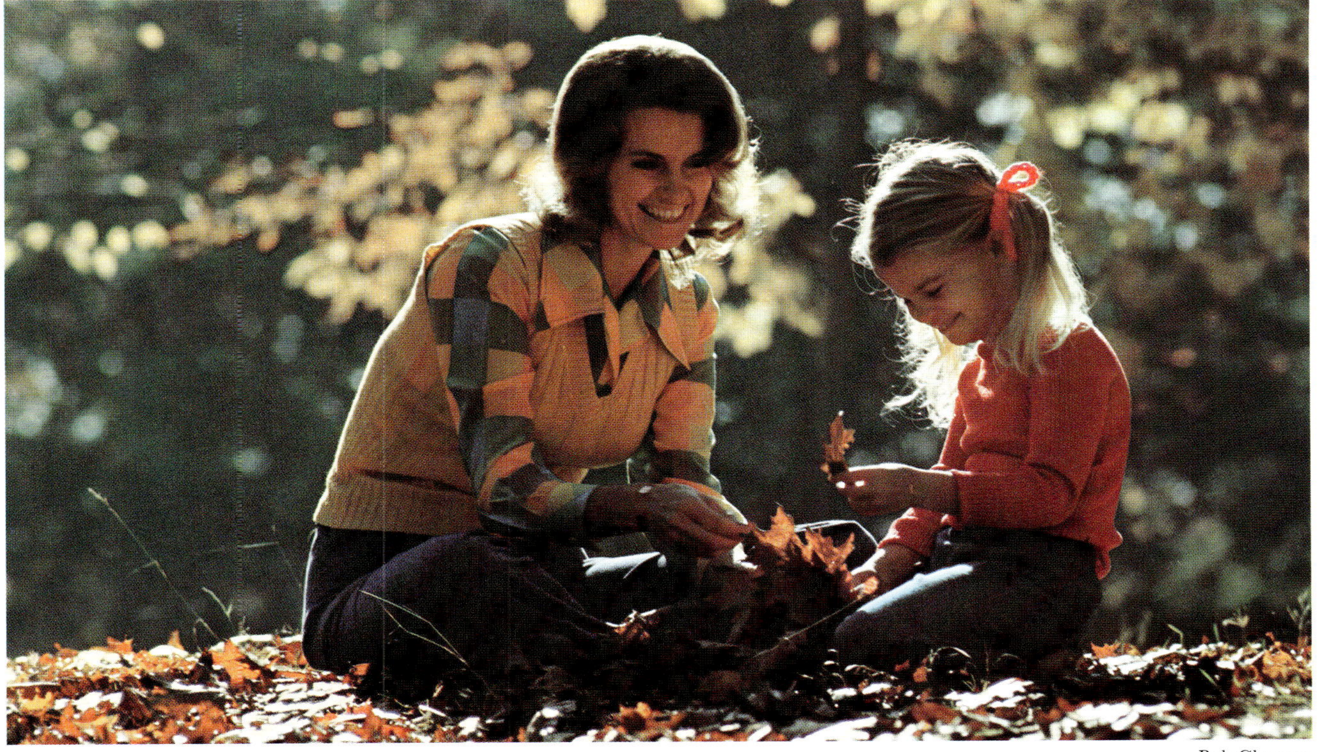

Bob Clemens

Autumn Leaves

A rustle of brilliant yellow foliage against a clean, blue sky, a field of fat pumpkins flanked by acres of dried corn stalks, a lawn blanketed with fallen leaves that you can kick your feet through—these are just some ingredients of autumn that offer ideal opportunities for family pictures. It's the time of year when your 5-year-old might be boarding the school bus for the very first time or when older children put on their uniforms to play football or march in the band. Stock up on color film and be ready to meet these photo opportunities.

To give your pictures color and interest, remember these important tips:

- Keep your subjects active for happy, natural-looking expressions.
- Encourage your subjects to wear bright-colored clothing to accent the scene, particularly on overcast days.
- Take plenty of close-ups for attention-getting results.
- For an uncluttered, rich-colored background, take pictures of your clan from a low angle to take advantage of the blue sky or a blaze of autumn foliage.
- Don't put off good opportunities for picture-taking. When outdoor color is at its peak and the youngsters are eager for that nature walk, act fast! A heavy rain is often common at this time of year and can quickly destroy the splendor of autumn foliage (and the lighthearted mood of your models).

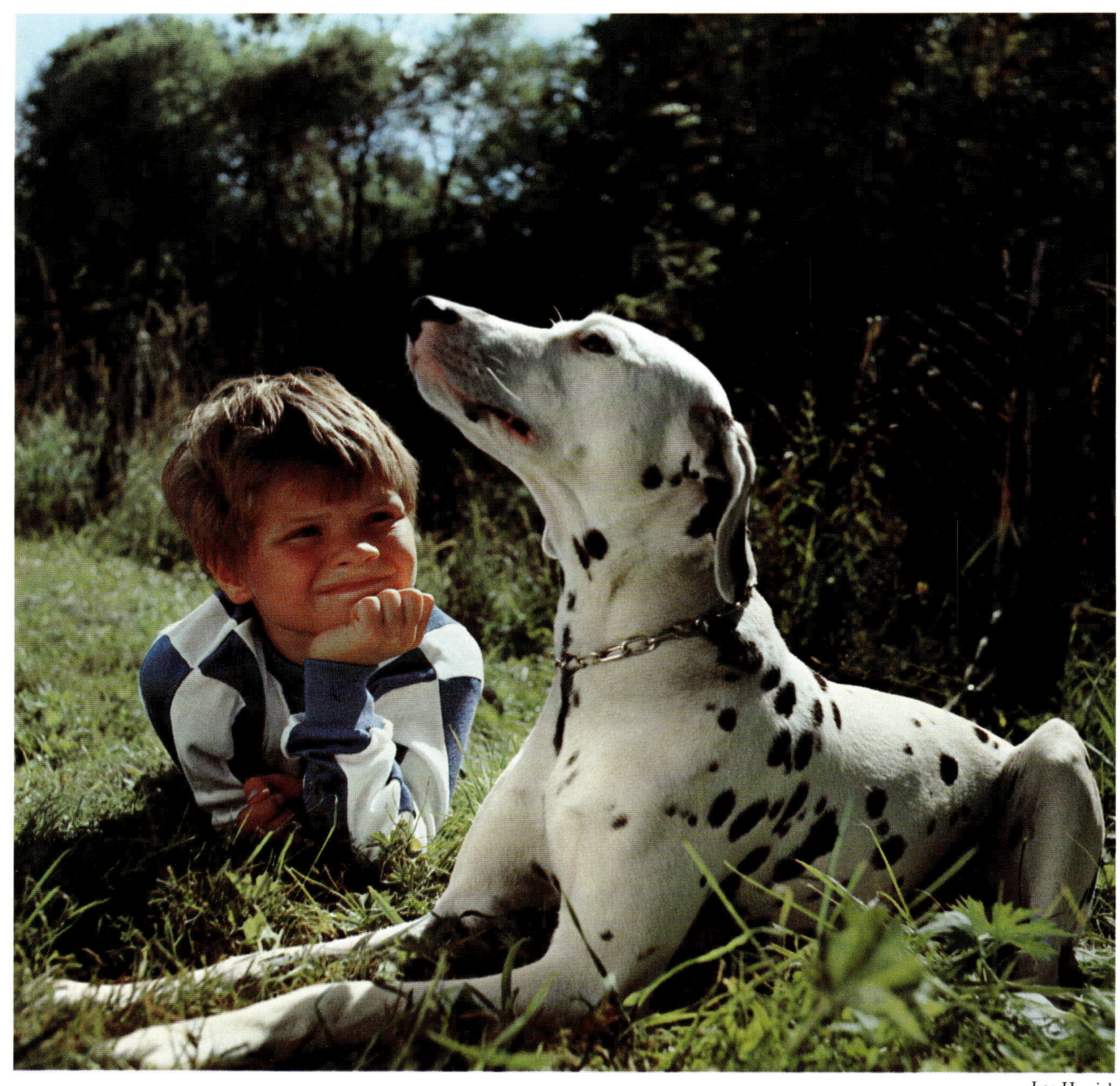

Lee Howick

Children with Pets

Pets aren't people, but they are important members of the family. The same tips that help you get good pictures of children alone can also be applied in capturing the antics of the animal that shares your home.

Right along with children, pets are among the most appealing subjects for pictures. You'll get your best pictures of pets and children together by getting down to their level. Remember that photos taken from the child's and animal's viewpoint will show their faces, which are much more interesting than the tops of their heads.

You'll need lots of patience to get good pictures of children and pets together because animals seldom stay in one place for very long. If the animal won't cooperate, have the child either sit with or hold it while you take a picture of both subjects. Move in close with your camera and fill the viewfinder with both pet and child. At a distance of about 4 or 5 feet you can get excellent close-ups of most small animals receiving attention from a child.

Outdoors, use a low camera angle for a blue-sky background. Or try a higher angle to use grass, foliage, sand, snow, or water as your background. Indoors, position your subjects in front of a plain wall. Always remember that the simpler the background, the easier it is to direct attention to your centers of interest.

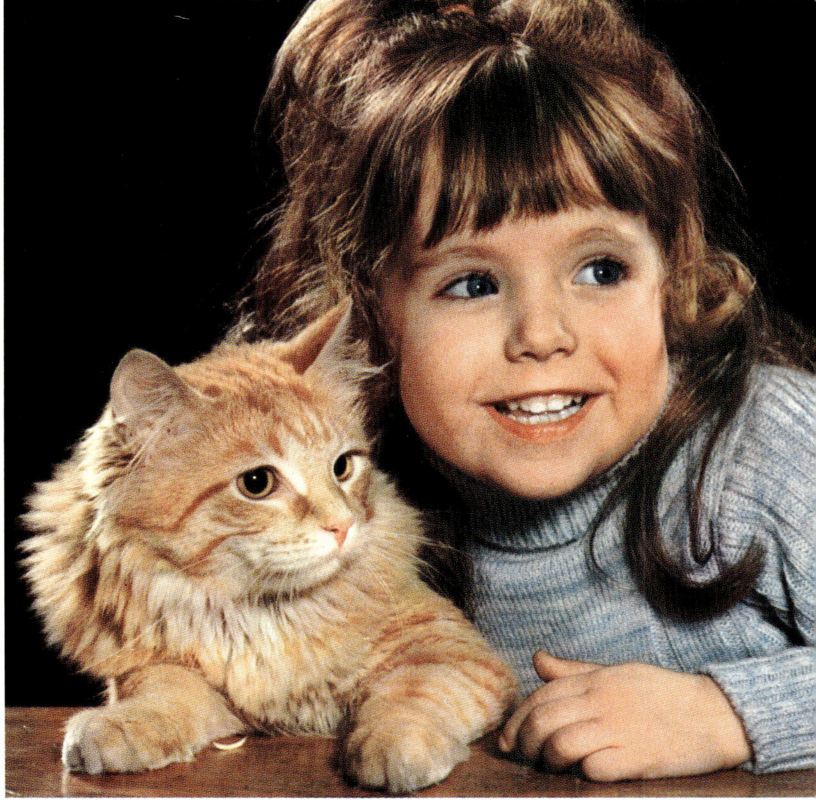

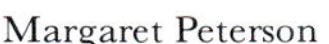

Margaret Peterson

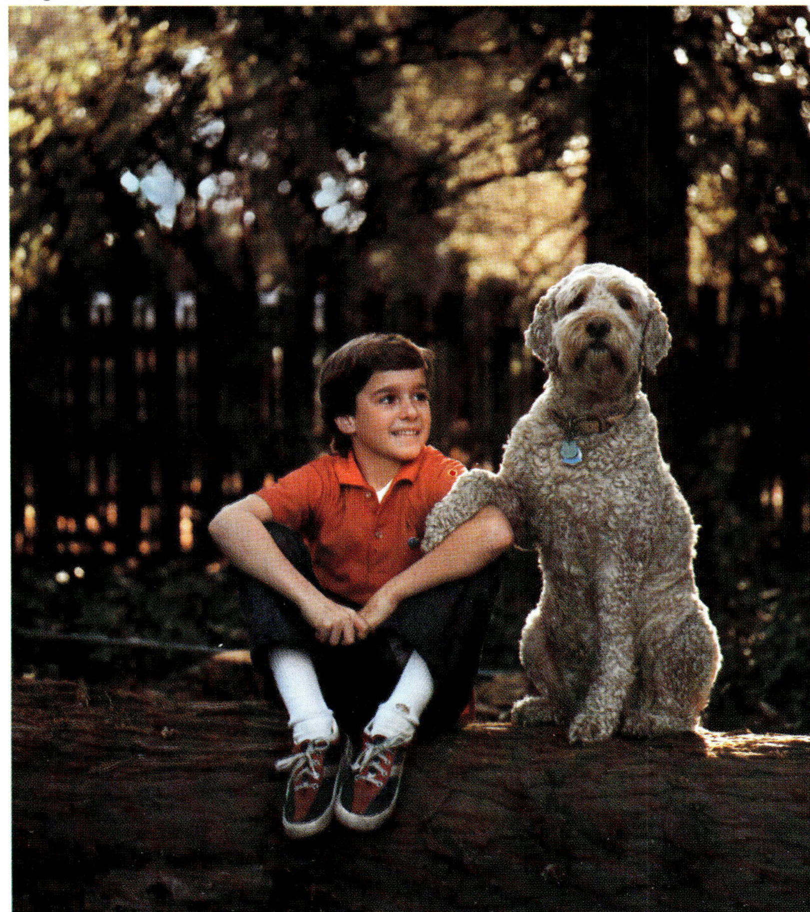

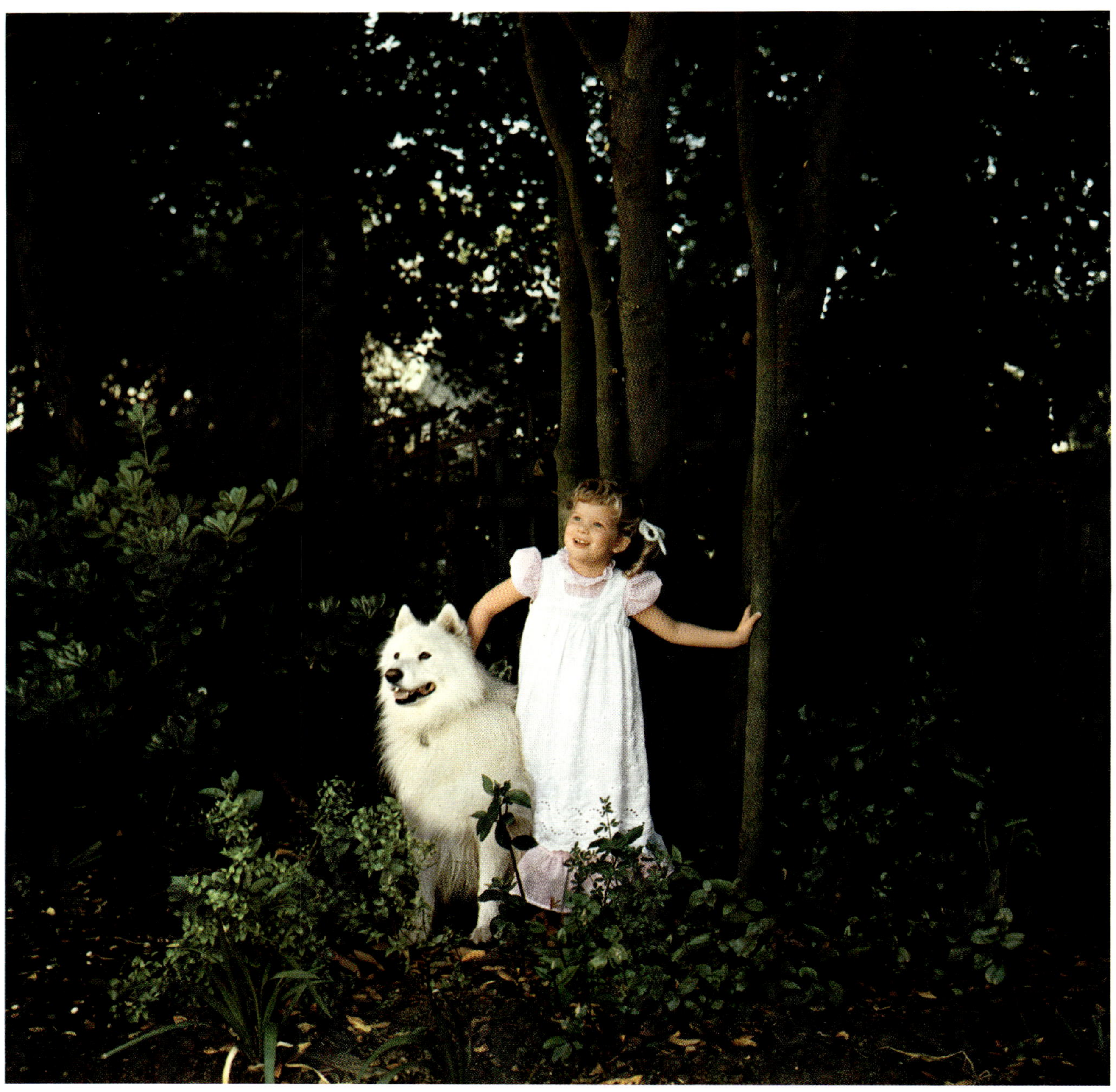

Margaret Peterson

Children and pets, in addition to making good companions, provide excellent subject ingredients for successful pictures.

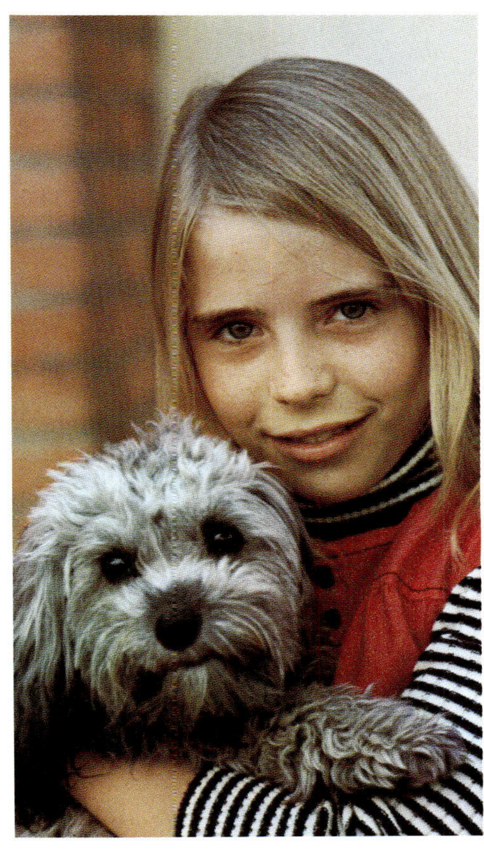

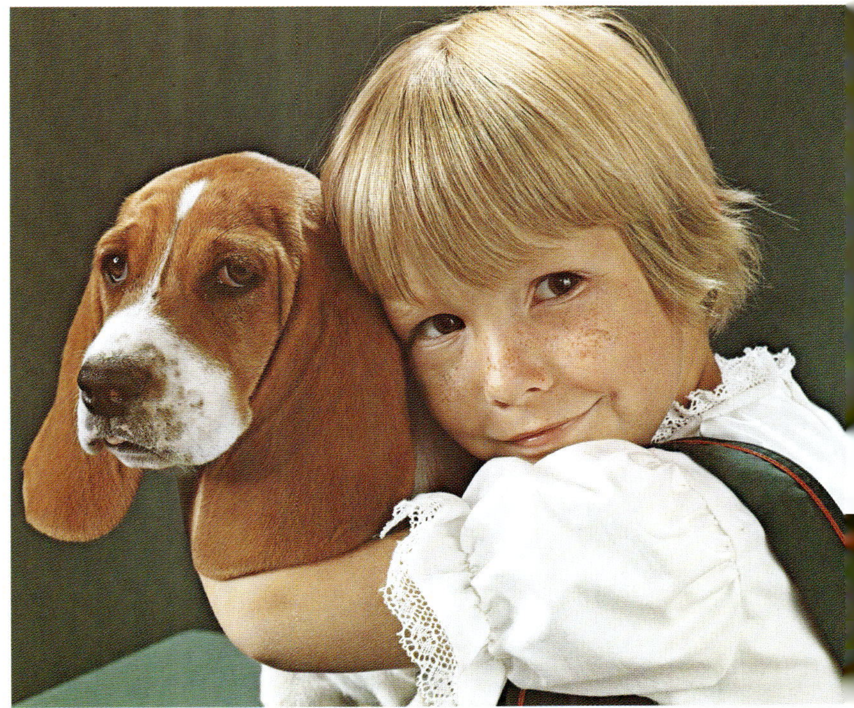

Neil Montanus

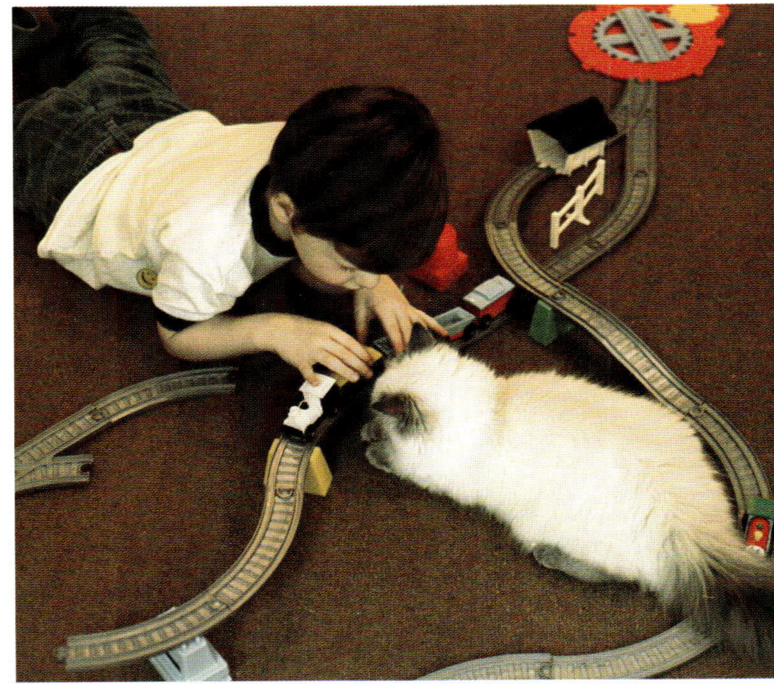

Neil Montanus

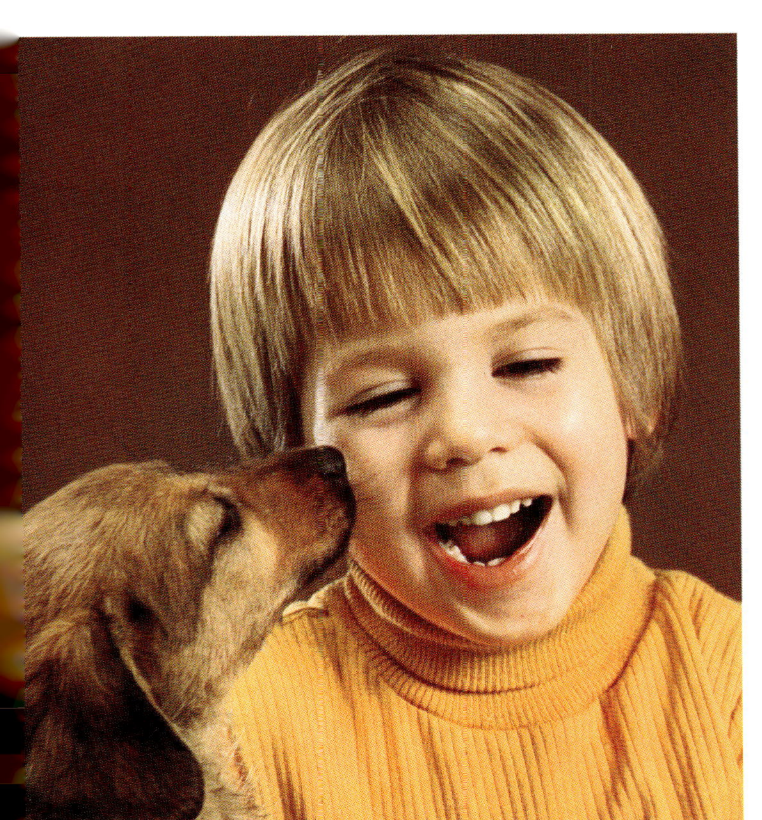

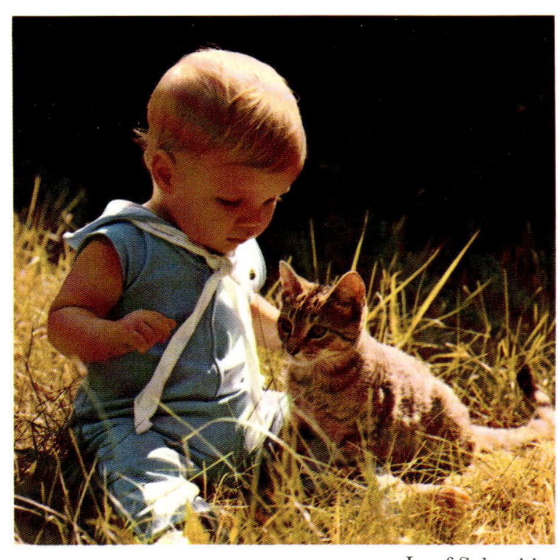
Josef Schneider

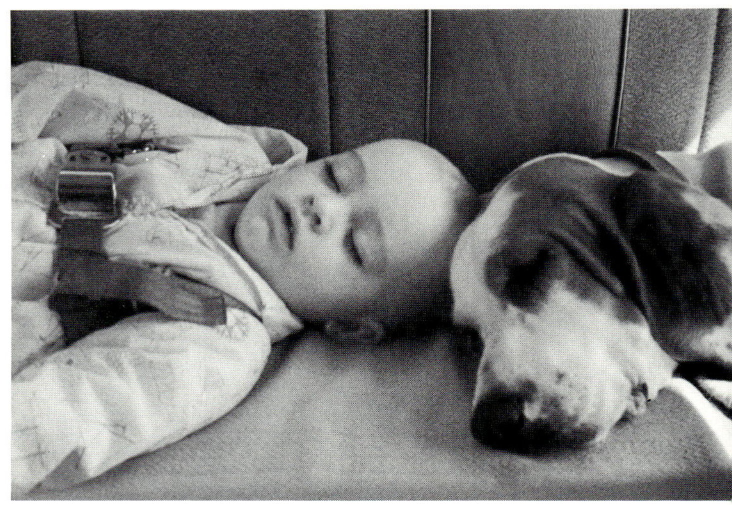

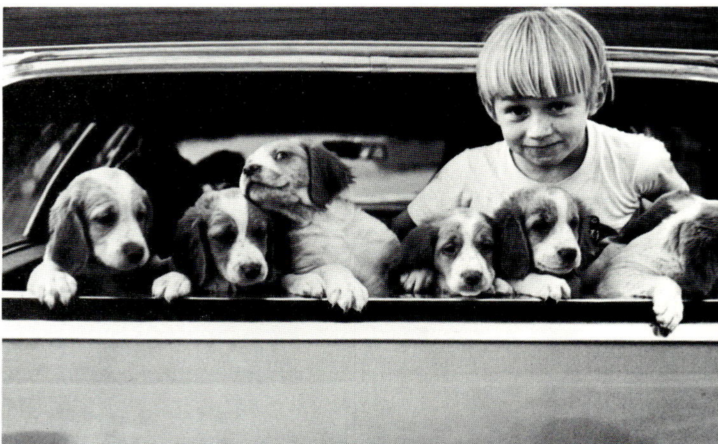
Patsy Brewer

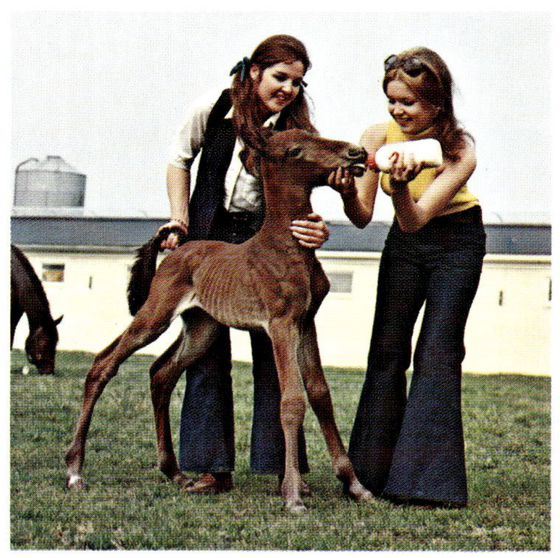
Neil Montanus

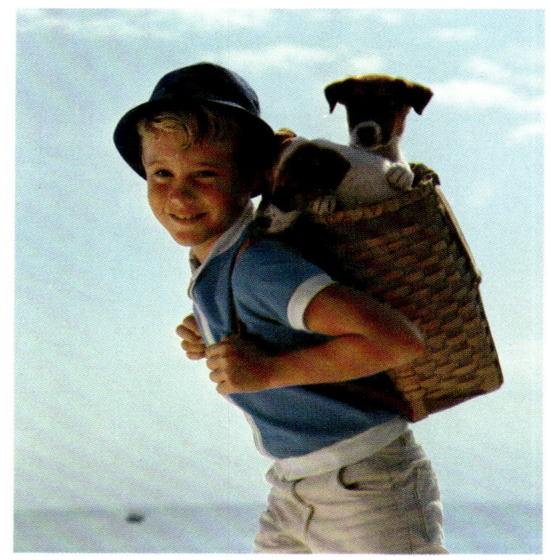
Ozzie Sweet

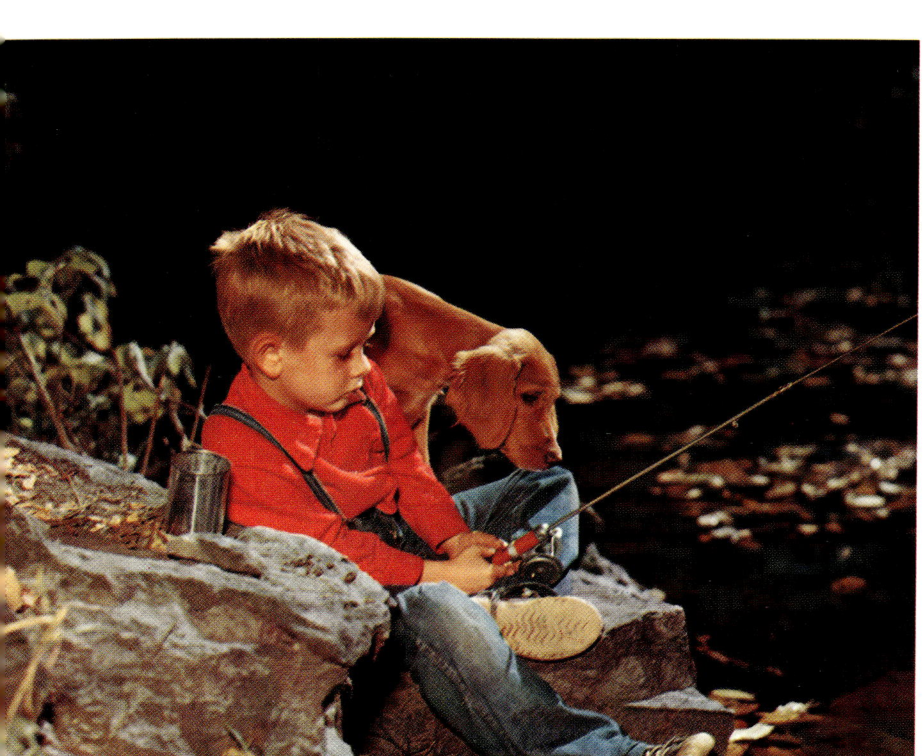

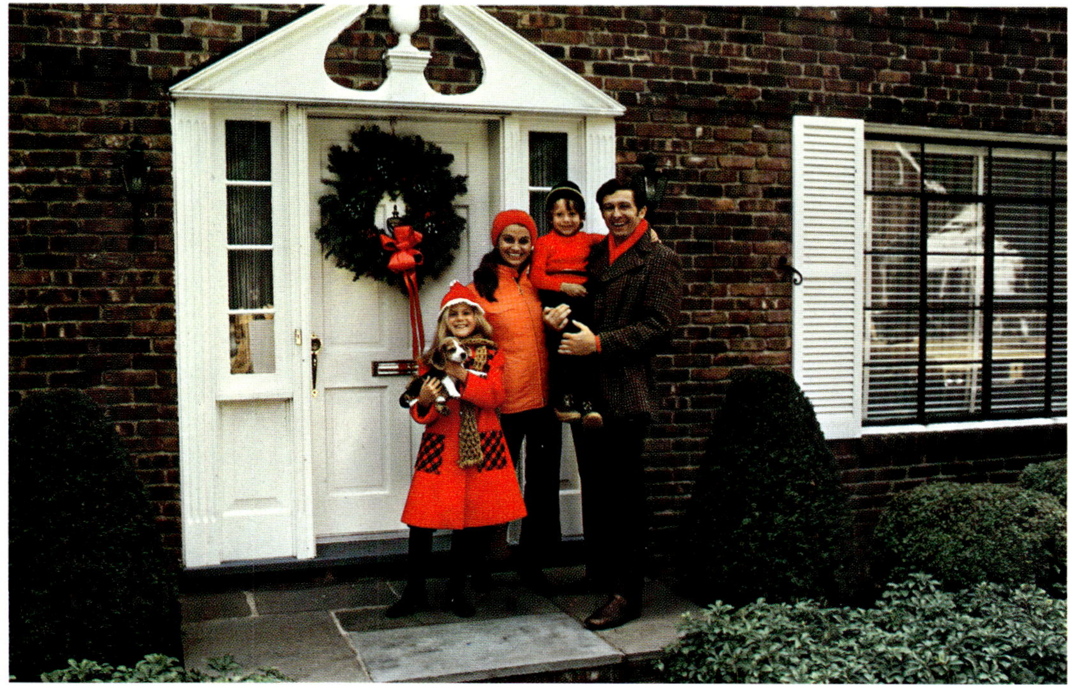

Tony Petrocelli

Props such as ribbons and pine boughs can suggest the spirit of Christmas indoors. Snow and colorful, warm clothes are naturals for dressing up a photo greeting made outside.

Photo-Greeting Cards

Whether you're welcoming a new baby or a new graduate, a photo-greeting card will get the picture to everyone. This kind of personal greeting will mean more and be remembered longer than the standard greeting card. Photo greetings can be as simple as a family snapshot enclosed with a card or as deluxe as a commercially processed holiday card. But no matter what the occasion or the technique, photo-greeting cards are both attractive and personal.

Maybe you already have a personalized picture that is just right for a photo-greeting card. But if you don't have one, now is the time to get out your camera. Well in advance of most occasions, there are many opportunities for snapping appropriate pictures for photo-greeting cards. When you're planning a Christmas photo-greeting card, for example, pictures showing the children dressed in winter clothing and enjoying winter activities can be just as seasonal with or without snow. Props such as a carefully placed bough of greens decorated with an ornament or two, some candles, a wreath, or a few pine cones will provide the needed seasonal touch. On the other hand, the pictures you use for Christmas photo-greeting cards don't really need a Christmas or winter theme. A picture showing the kids (go ahead and include Mom, Dad, and the dog if you like) enjoying summer vacation can be a welcome sight in the middle of winter. Or a picture of your family with a background of fall foliage can make a colorful card. Many people tuck away ideas and suitable snapshots all year long. Then when the occasion

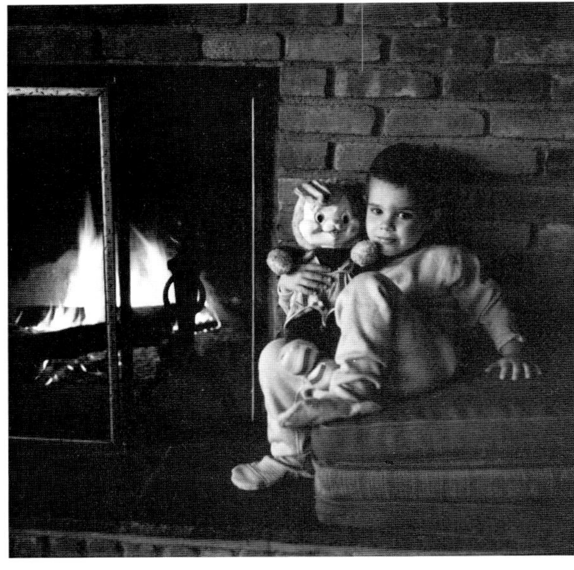

Daylight, entering from the left, produced this soft, flattering illumination. See Window Light, pages 63-65.

approaches, they have a plentiful stock of material with which to make a greeting card.

So remember—don't wait until the last minute to start your photo-greeting card. Take your picture early. The photograph is the heart of any photo greeting, so the better the picture, the better the greeting. The best pictures show your family doing something rather than just standing stiffly. When you get them all together, have them concentrate on each other or an activity—not on the camera.

SPECIAL IDEAS FOR PICTURES

Greeting Reflected in a Mirror

If you have a large mirror on your wall, you can use it to create an unusual greeting-card picture. Print or tape a greeting right onto the face of the mirror, and have a child or the whole family stand facing the greeting. Take a picture of the reflection of your subject in the mirror while standing at an angle to the mirror. Make sure you can't see the camera or flash unit in the mirror because anything you see in the mirror will appear in the finished picture. With nonadjustable cameras, make sure the combined distances from the subject to the mirror and from the mirror to the camera don't add up to more than your recommended flash distance. The recommended flash distance is usually from 4 to 9 feet (1.2 to 2.7 meters), so if your subject is 3 feet (.9 meter) away from the mirror and you are 4 feet (1.2 meters) from the mirror with the camera, you'll be within the range. With an adjustable camera, figure your exposure on the total distance from the subject to the mirror and back to the camera.

Fireside Pictures

An attractive fireside glow on your children's faces will portray the warmth of the holiday season—and you won't even need to light the fire. If you have a camera that can be used with an extension flash, put the flash unit into the fireplace and aim it at the subjects in front of the fireplace. Base your exposure on the distance from the flash to the subject. You can also use a photolamp in the fireplace. In this case, use an exposure meter to determine the exposure.

You may want to include a blazing fire to add color and interest to a fireside picture. (Of course, you'll have to build a fire for this picture, and you can't put any photo equipment in the fireplace!) You can illuminate the scene with flash or a photolamp located so that the light appears to come from the fire. If you can adjust the shutter speeds on your camera, use a slow shutter speed such as 1/30 second to allow the fire to record in the picture. Most nonadjustable cameras automatically use a slow shutter speed for flash.

For a very natural, warm-looking fireside picture, photograph the scene with existing light and color film. Turn on all the lights in the room and use an exposure meter to determine your exposure. Home lighting is dim compared to sunlight, so your exposure times may be long. For exposures longer than 1/30 second, put your camera onto a firm support, such as a tripod, and ask your subjects to remain as still as possible.

Pictures Through a Window

A picture taken through a window can convey a cozy feeling of family togetherness, and the edge of the window can make a natural frame for the subjects. Chances are that the first picture you'll take of a new baby will be through a window—the nursery window (see page 13). This type of picture is perfect for a birth-announcement card because it shows the new arrival in a storytelling surrounding.

When you want to take family Christmas-card pictures before the snow flies, you can make an indoor scene look wintry by shooting from outside a window that you have frosted with one of the many commercial preparations on the market. Or hang a wreath in the window and pose your family around it.

The best time to take frosty-window pictures is at twilight. You can turn on the lights in the house to illuminate the subjects inside, and the twilight outdoors will illuminate the frost on the windows.

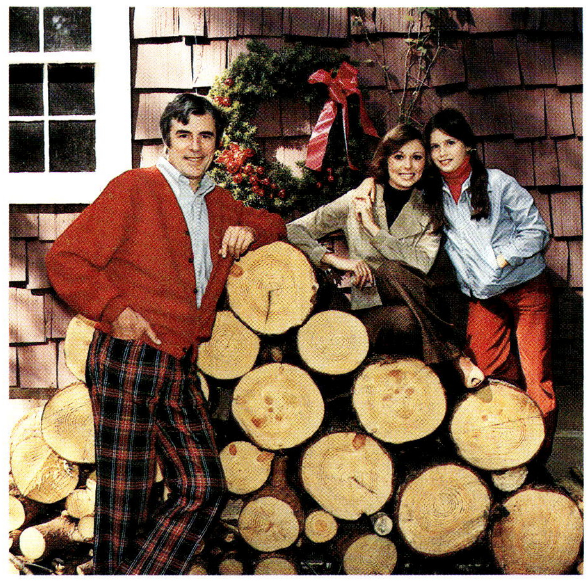

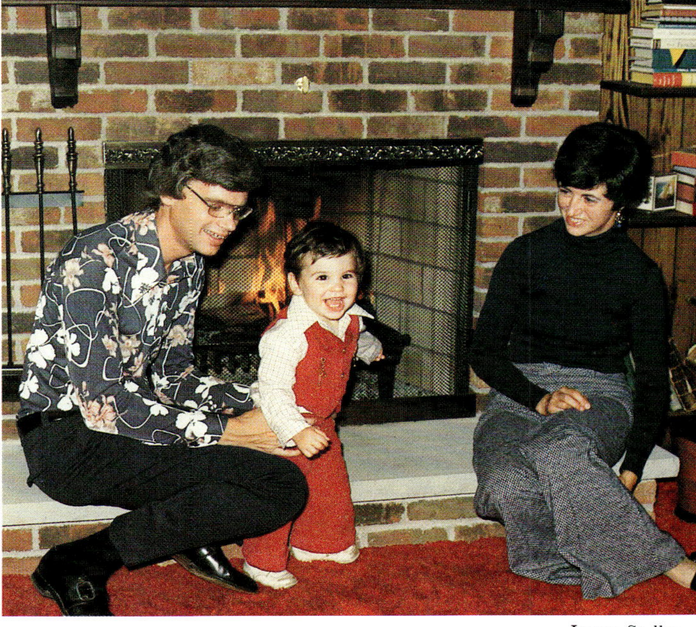

James Sadler

Make a habit of photographing the family each year for your greeting cards. Your recipients will enjoy this personal approach.

George Butt

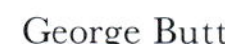

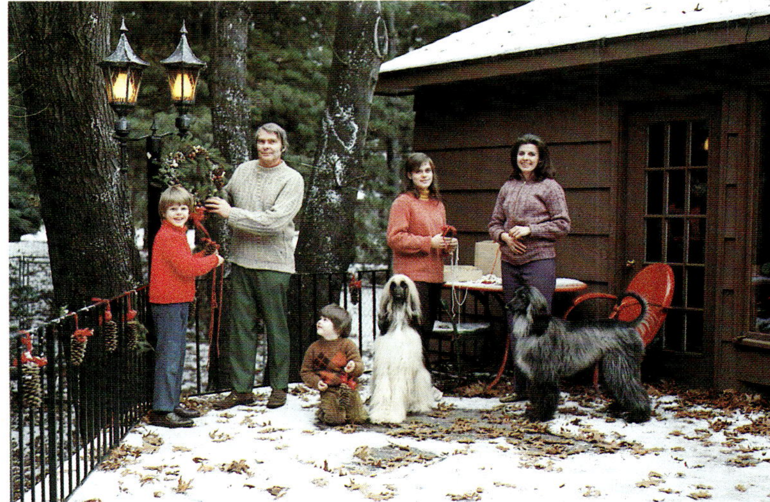

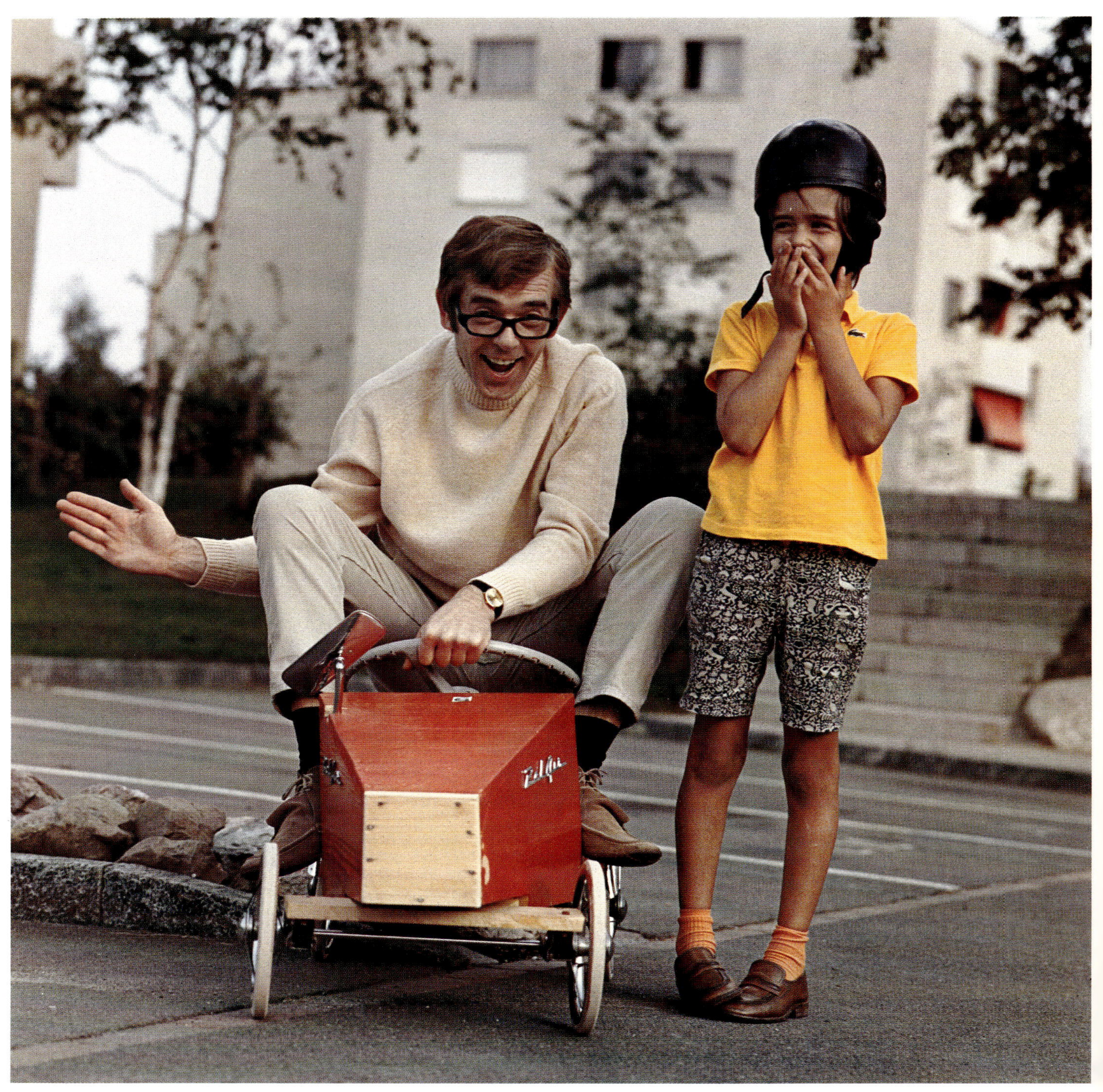

Capturing Natural Expressions—See pages 40-41.

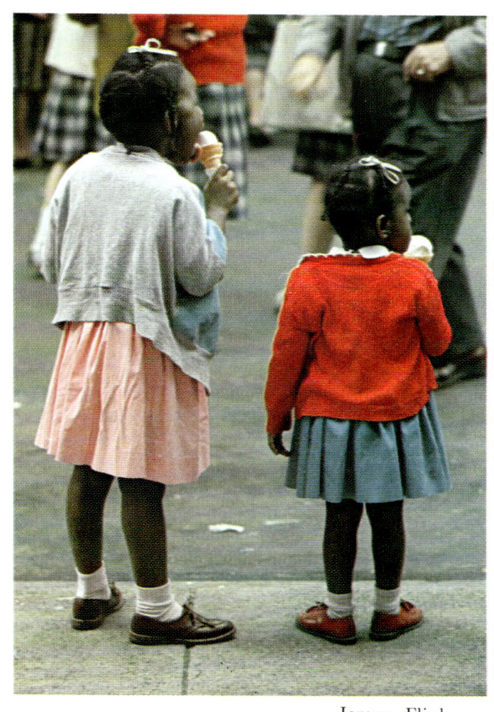

Jerome Flinkman

Part Four: Candid Opportunities

Here is one area where you, the parent photographer, have an edge over the professional. You are there. Indoors and out, there is hardly a day that passes when you won't see an opportunity to catch your child or family group in an unconsciously funny or heartwarming situation. Of course you can't capture all of them, but you can *take many fine, natural pictures for your album by making sure to keep your camera loaded and ready.*

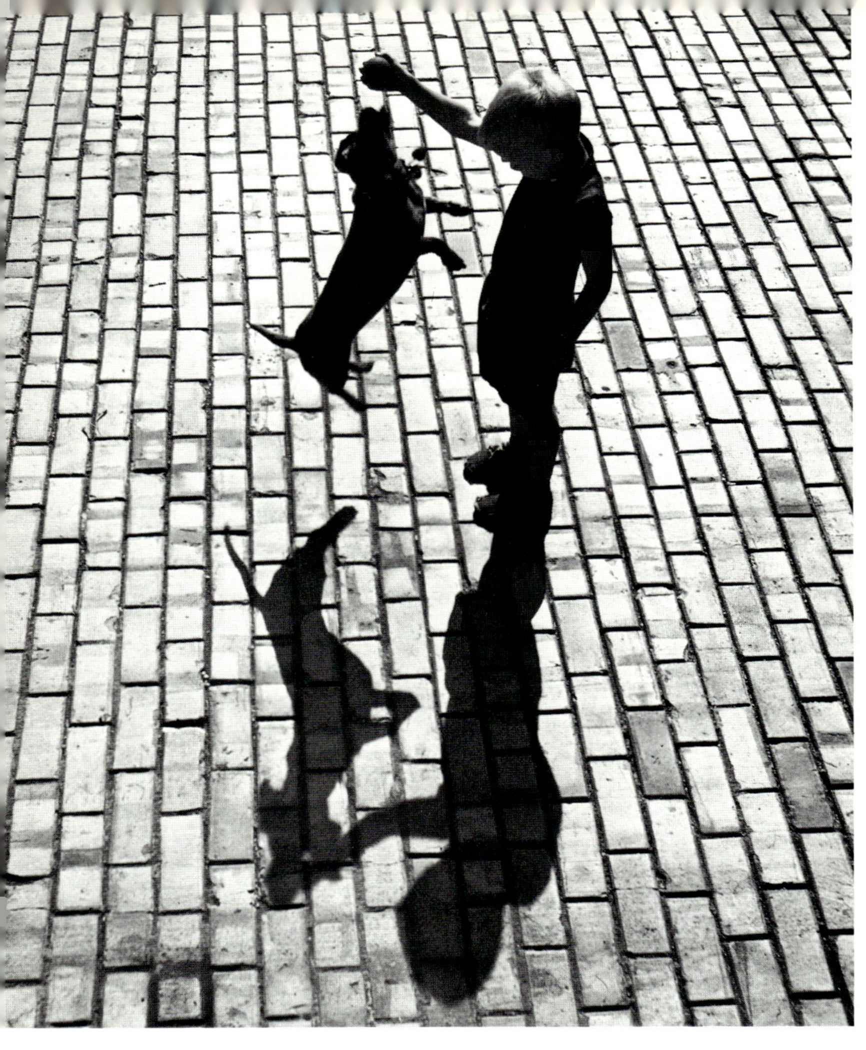

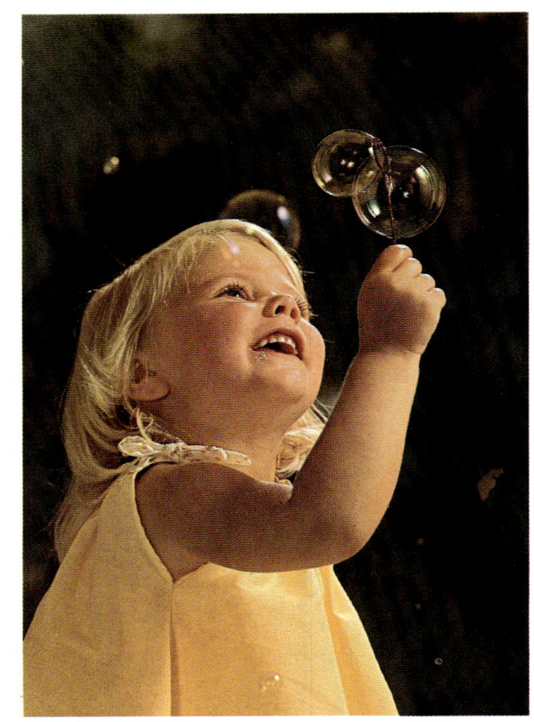

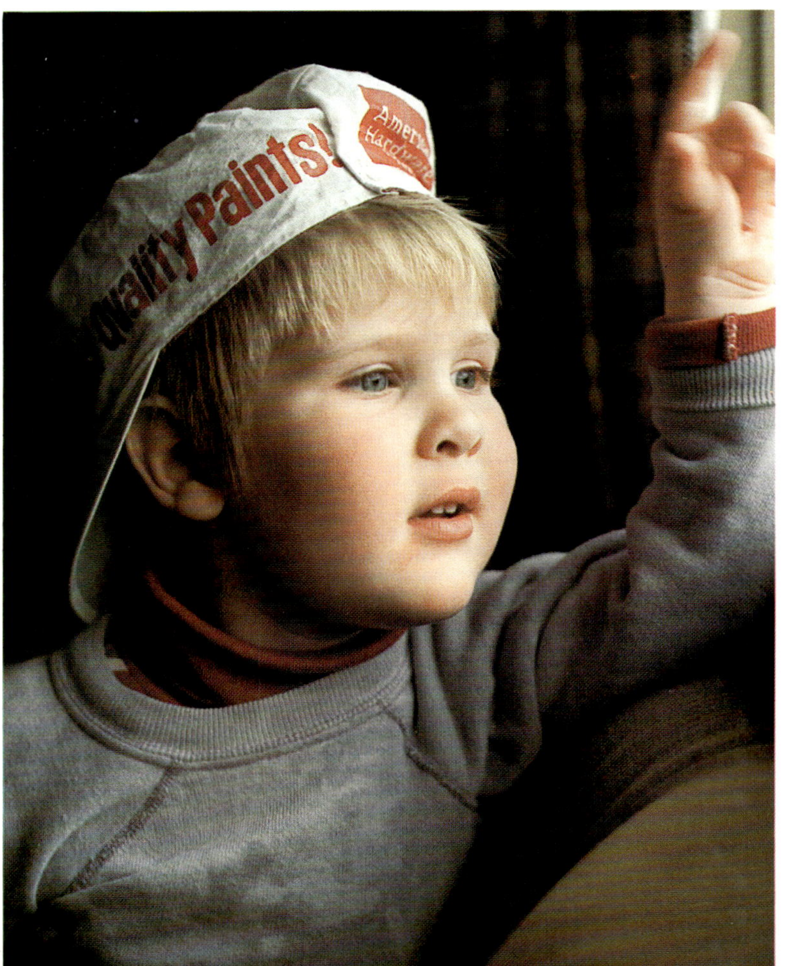

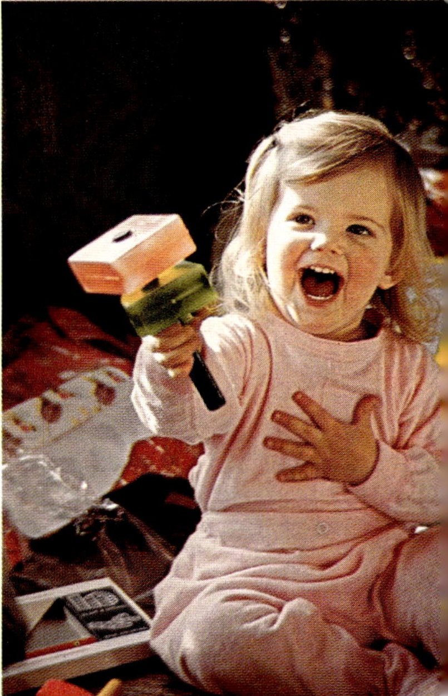

Be the family historian for your family and snap pictures of everyday events. If your initial reaction to an incident around the house is to reach for the camera, you'll probably get a good picture for the family album.

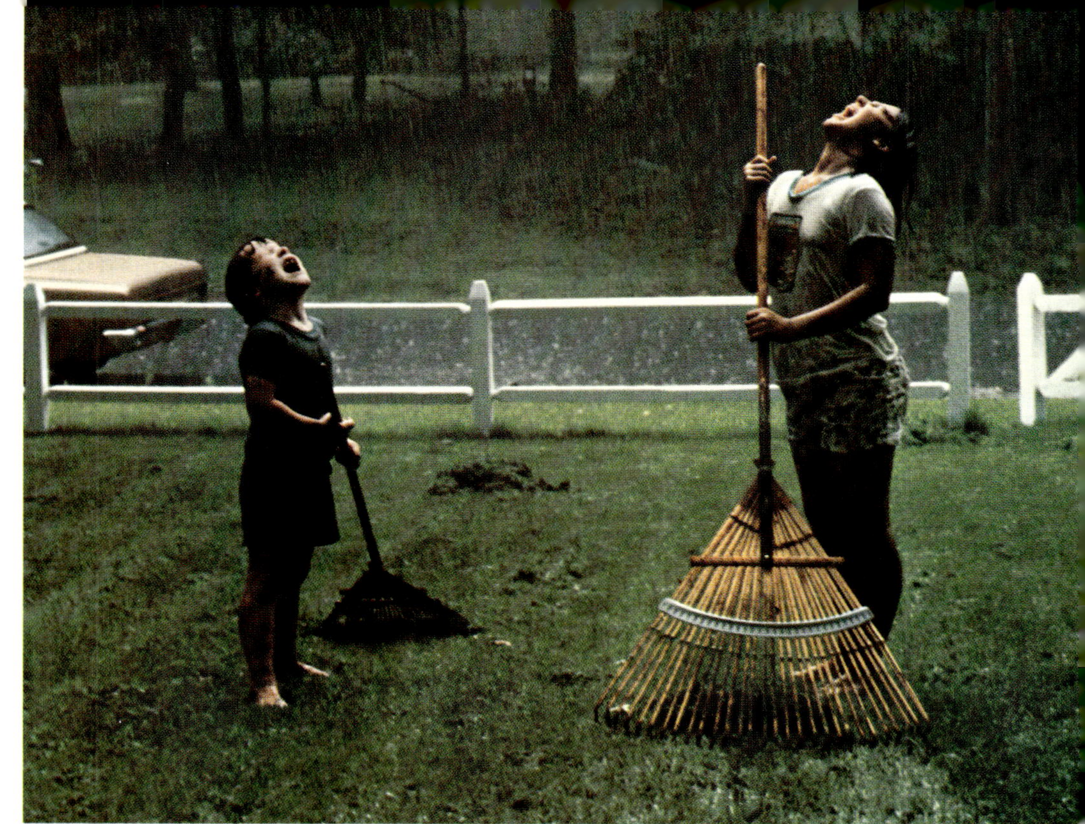

M. Richards

In and Around Home

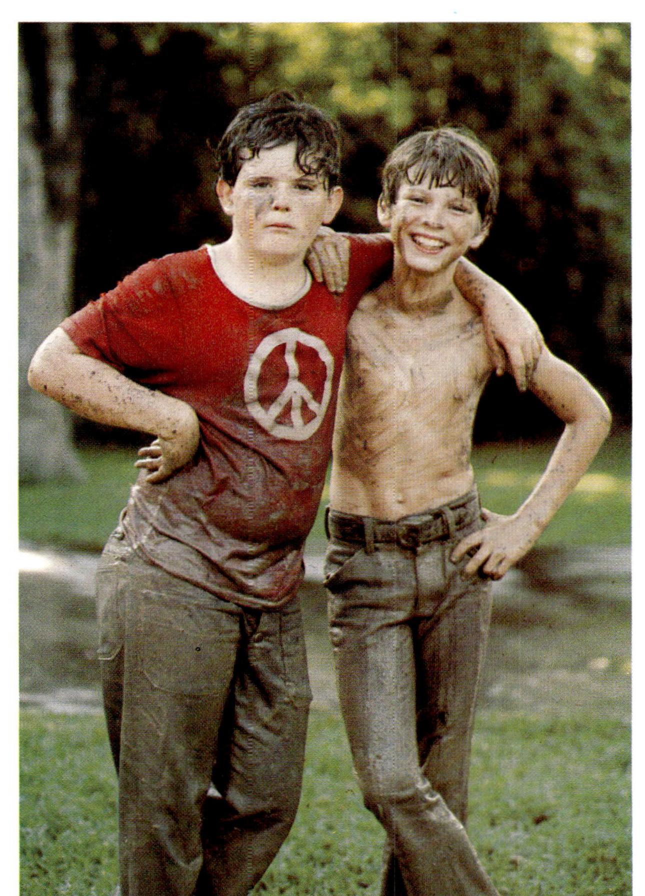

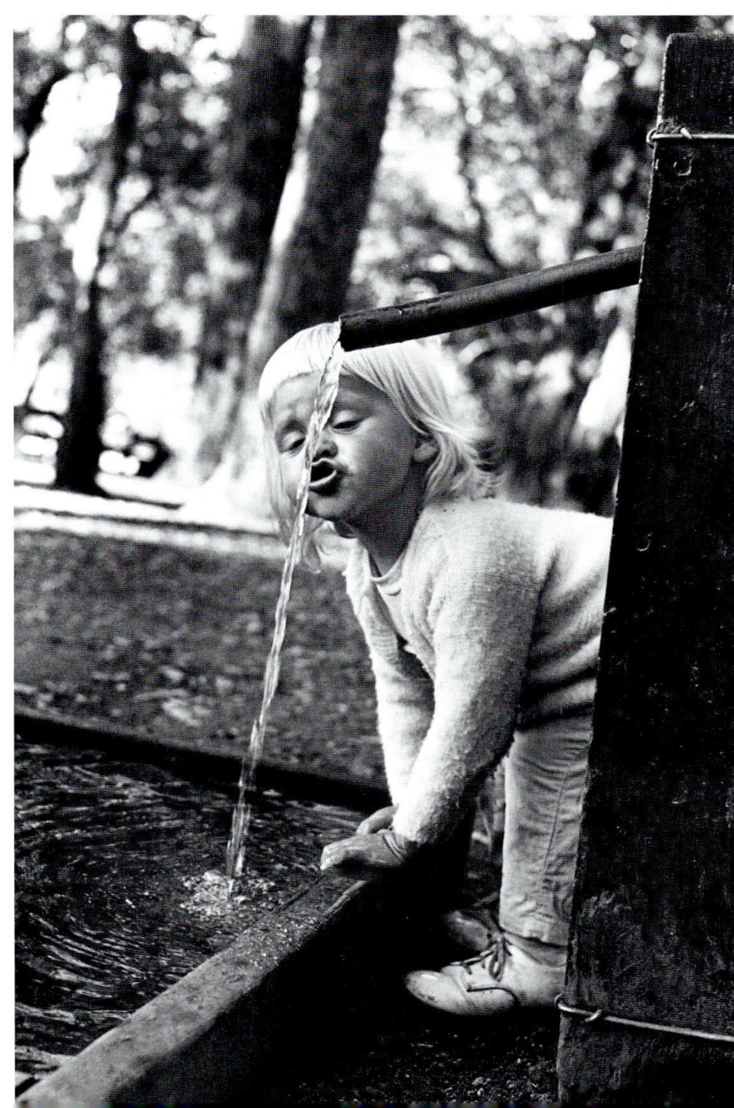

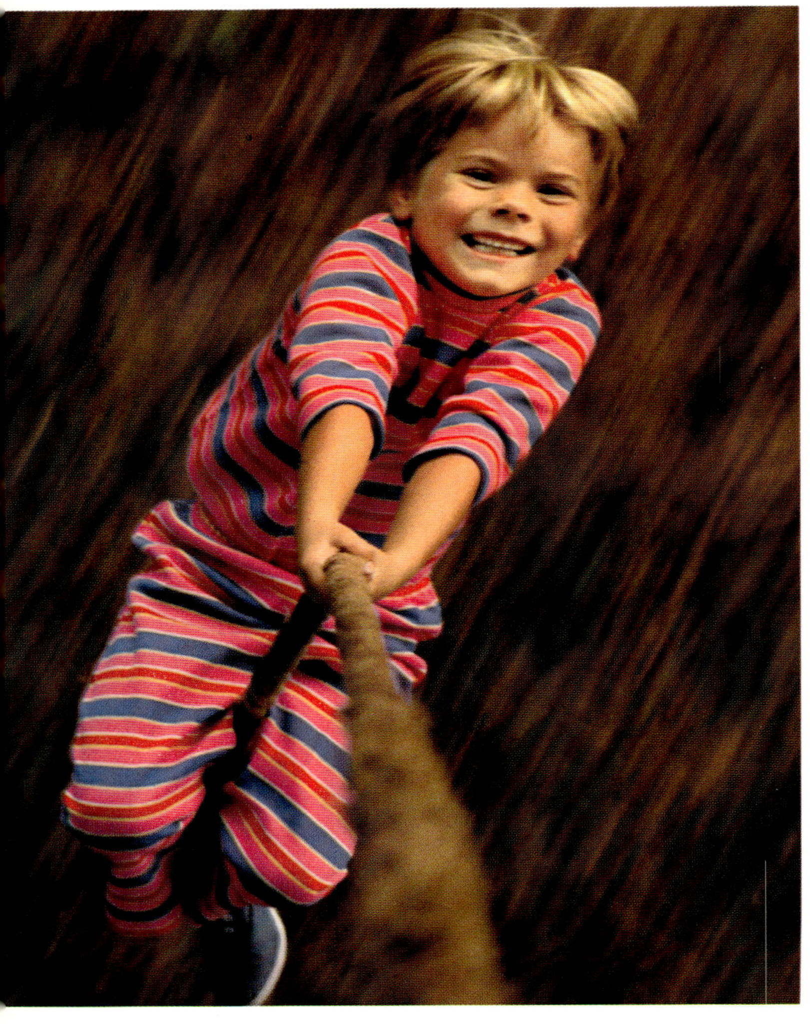

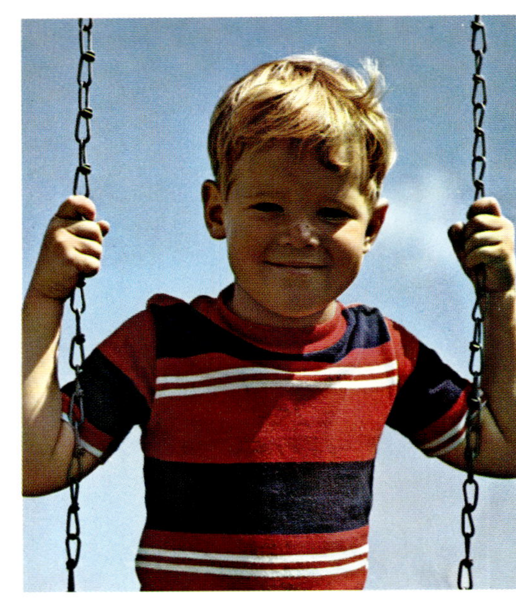

At the Playground

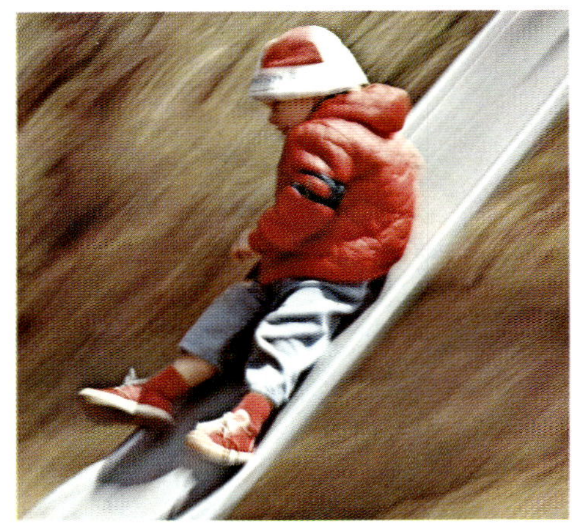

Emiel Blaakman

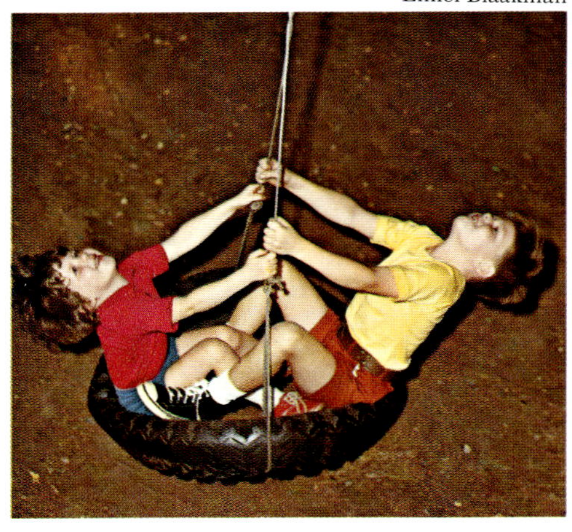

Portions of some of these pictures are intentionally blurred to create a particular impression. The technique involves using a slow shutter speed while panning the camera to follow the action.

Bob Clemens

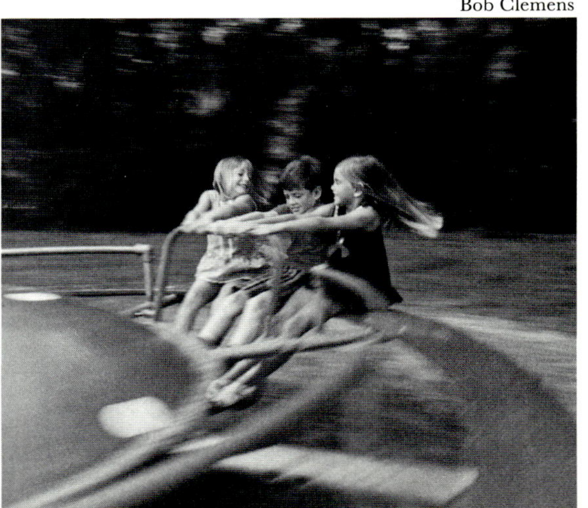

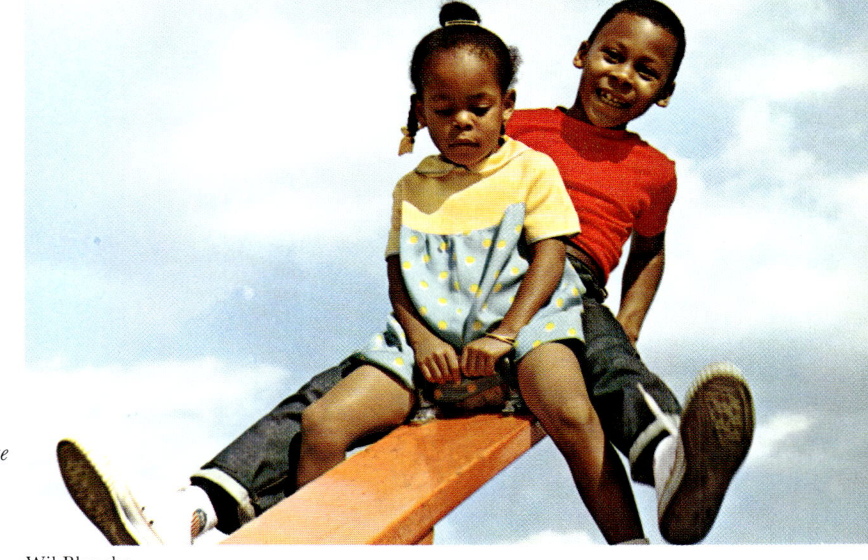

Wil Blanche

Look beyond your subject before you snap the picture. *For more information on effective uses of backgrounds, turn to pages 66-69.*

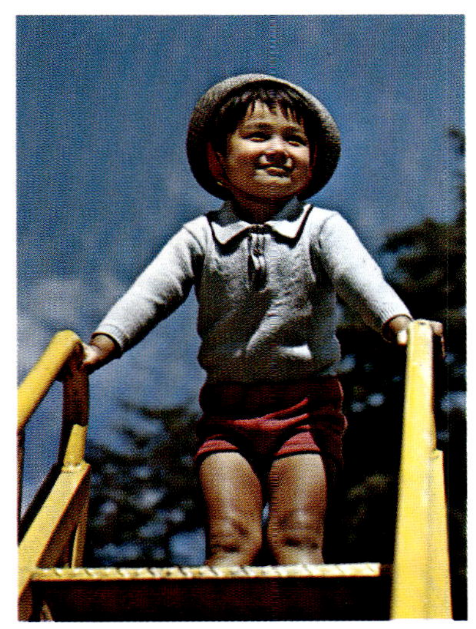

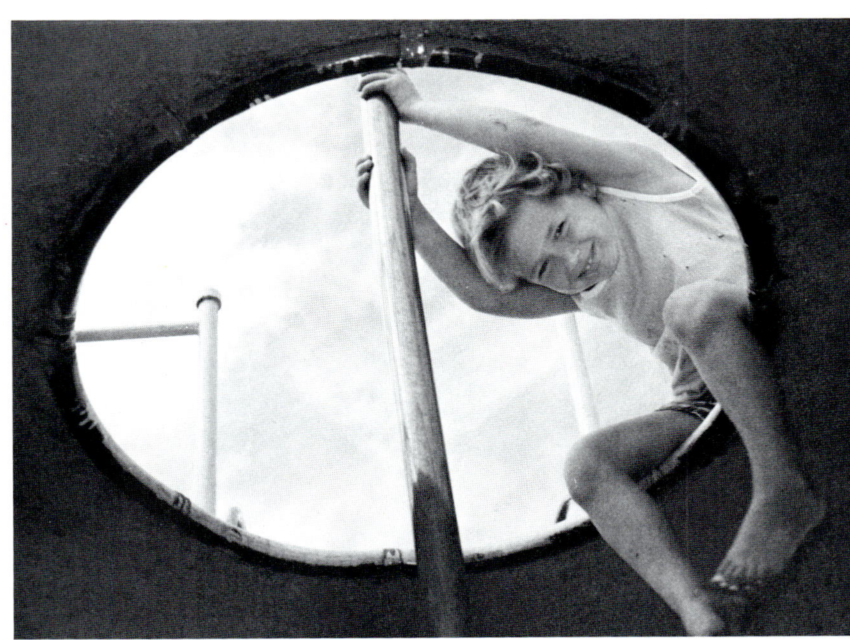

Emiel Blaakman

Thelma S. Myerson

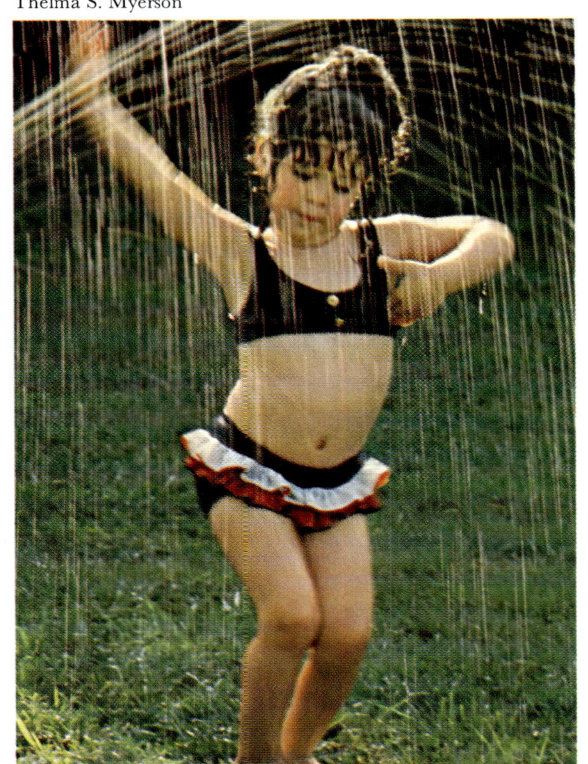

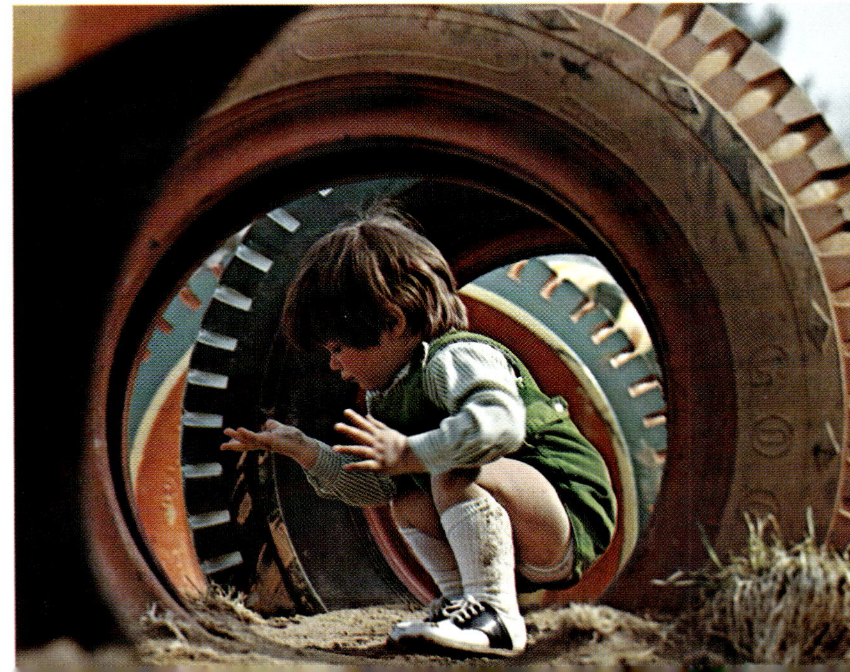

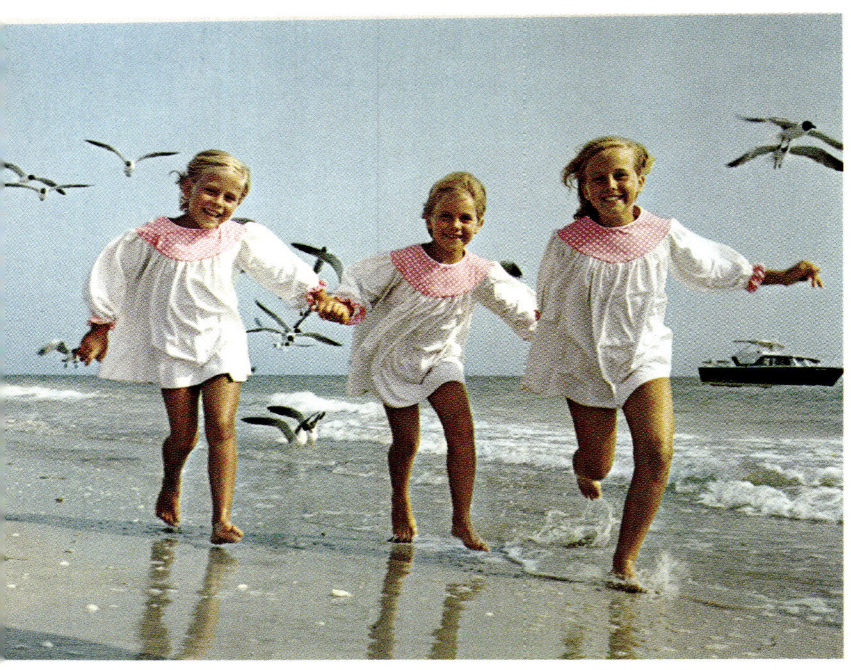

Ozzie Sweet

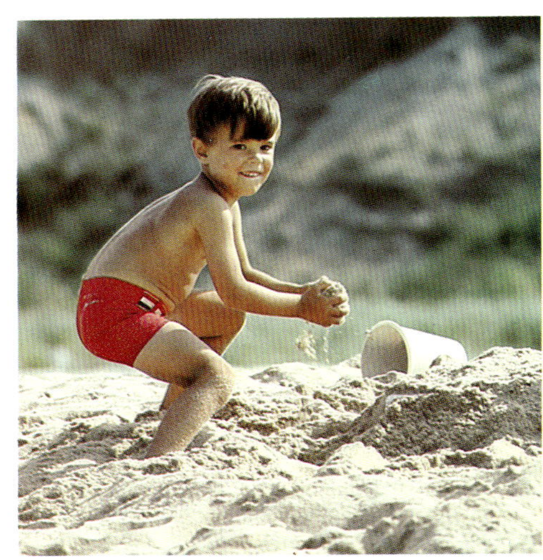

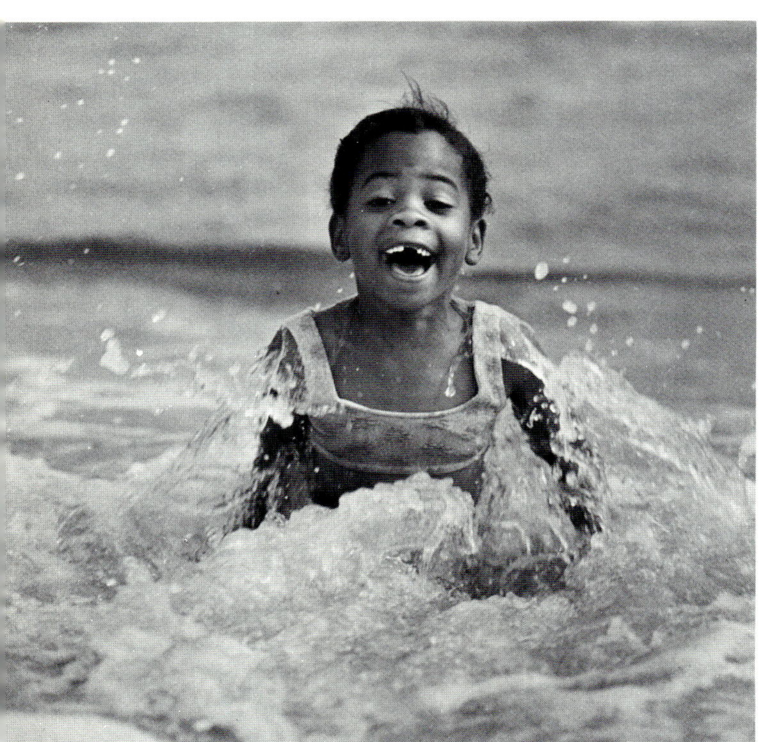

Phoebe Dunn

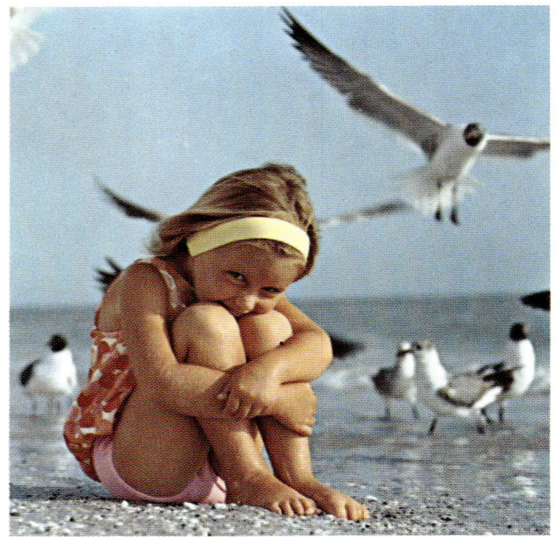

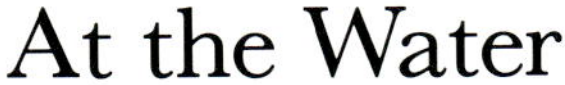

At the Water

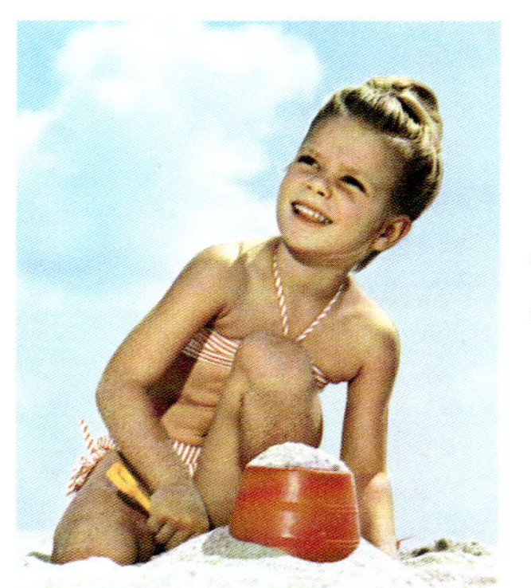

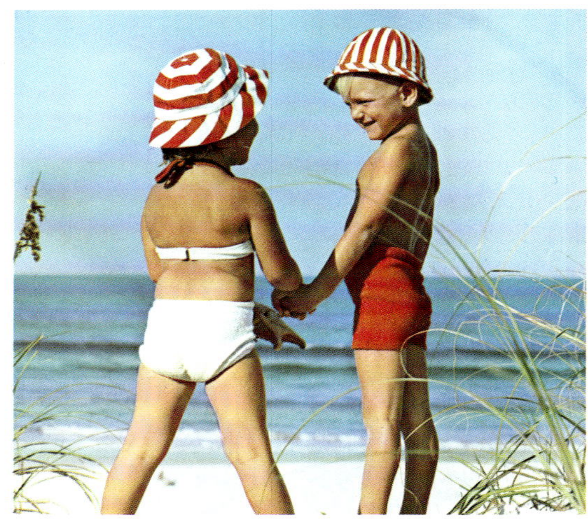

Since children are moving almost all the time, don't ask them to ac like statues—take pictures of them in their active, natural state.

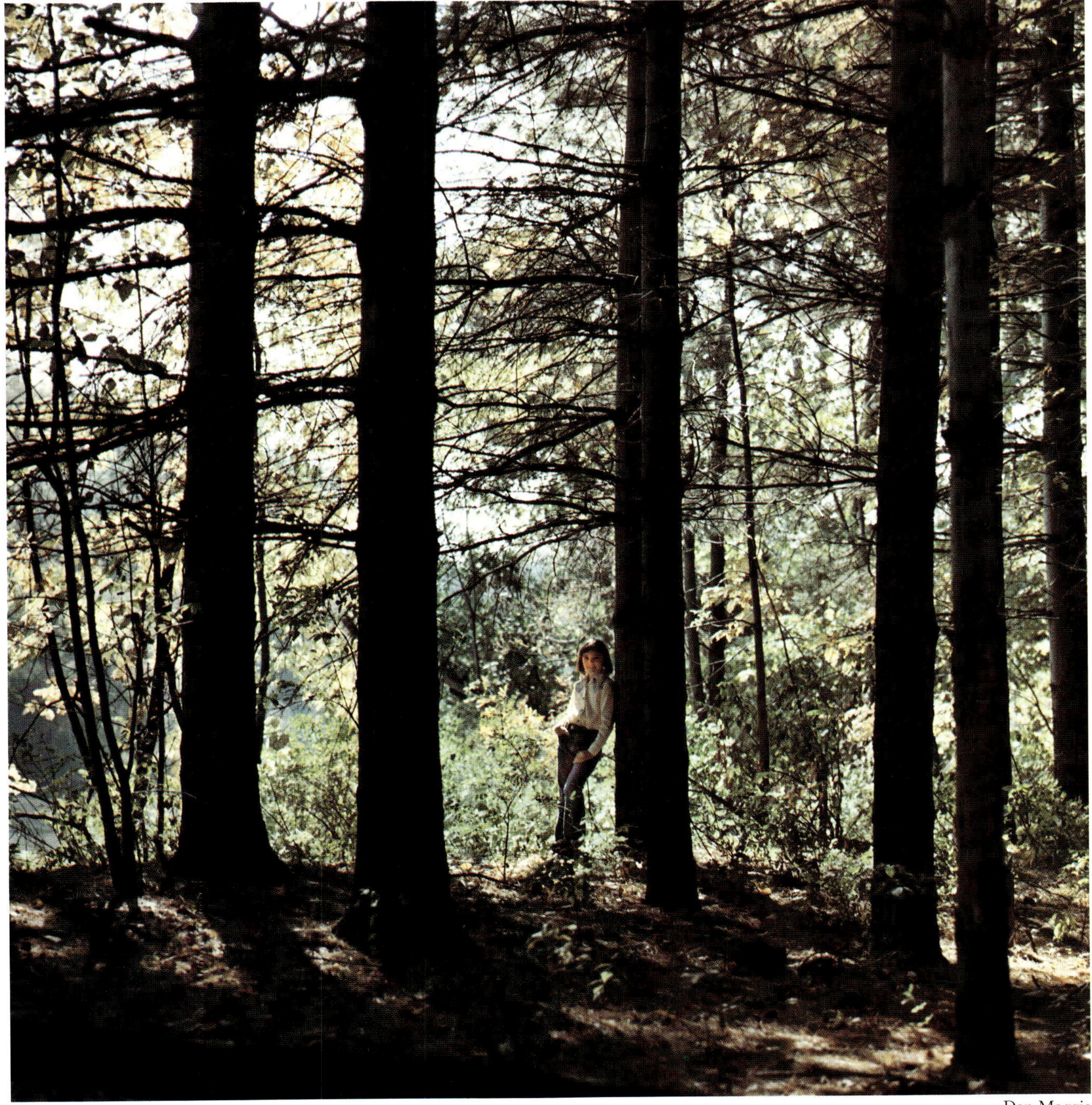

Don Maggio

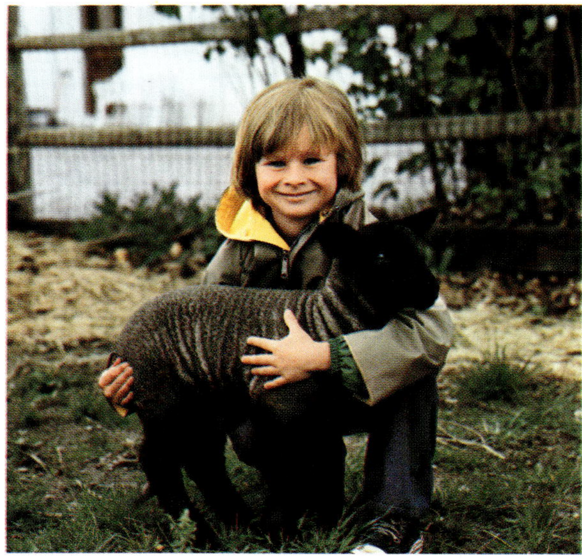
Don Maggio

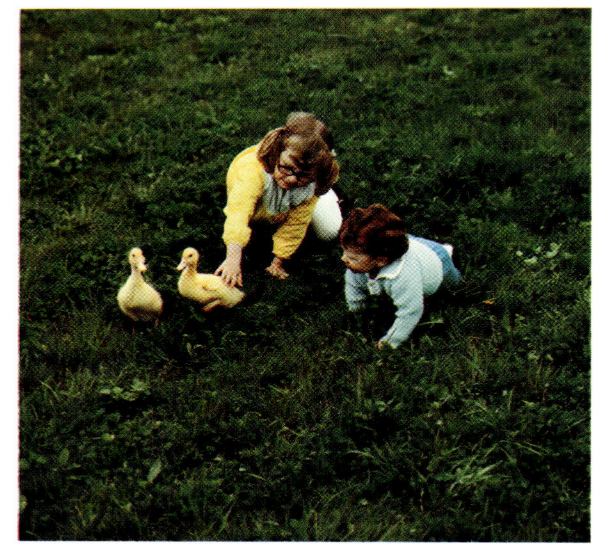
Neil Montanus

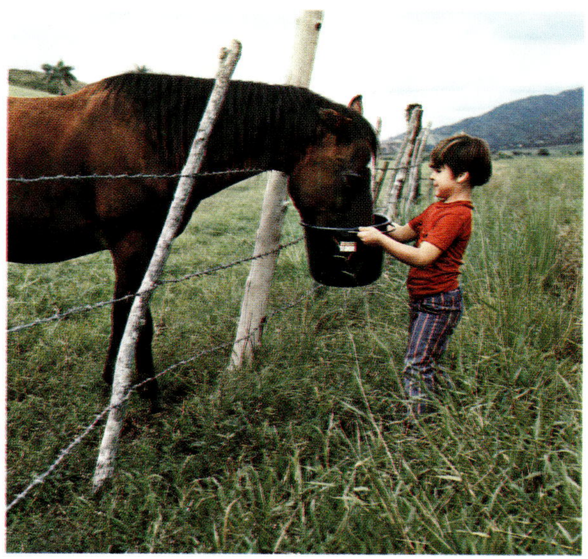
Don Nichols

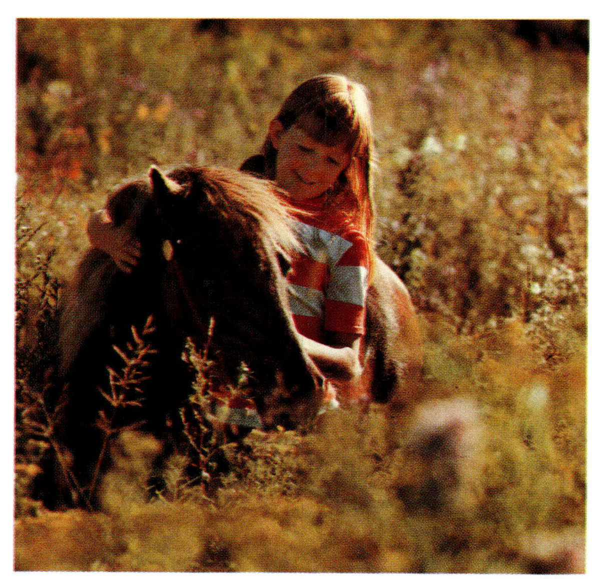
Bob Clemens

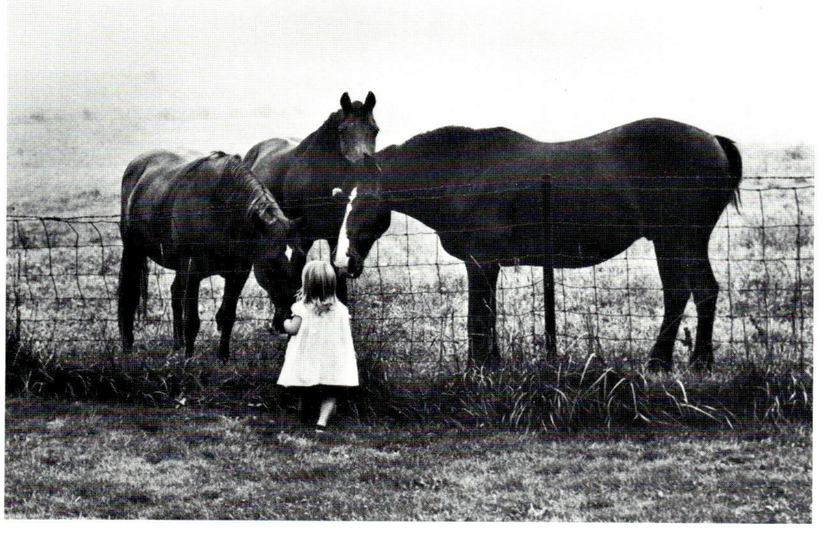
Margaret Sawyer Vick

Down on the Farm

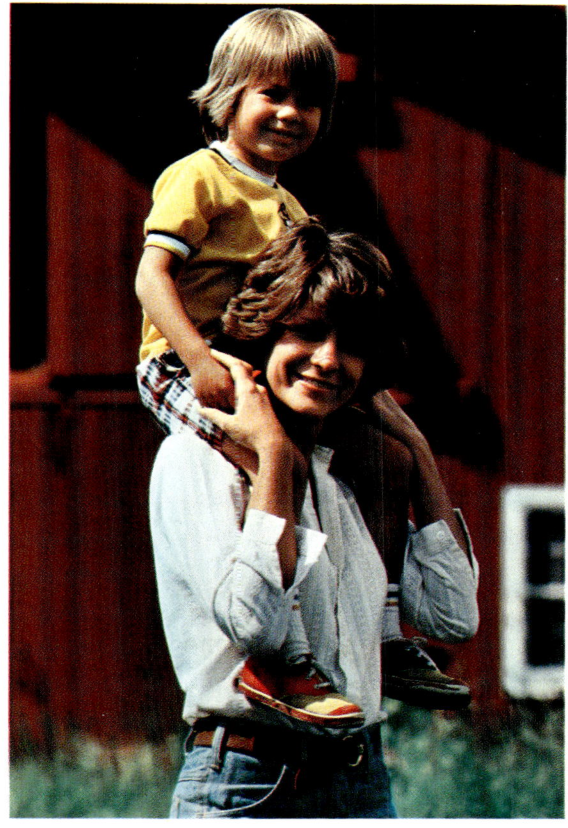

Bob Clemens

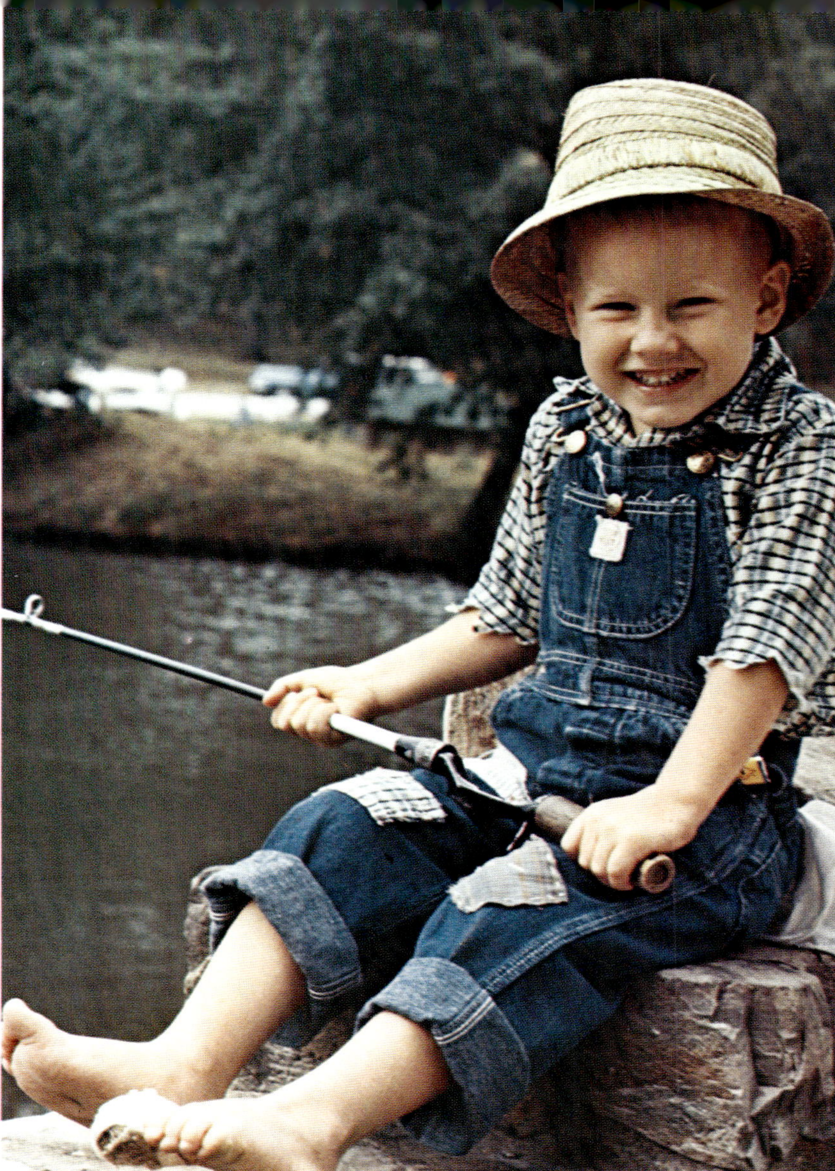

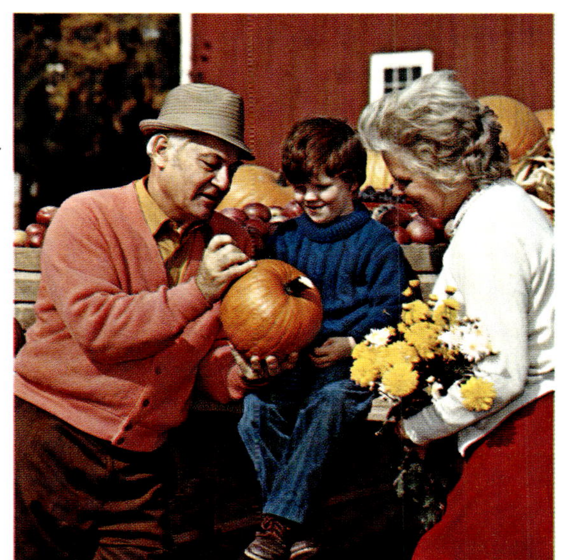

Neil Montanus

You can make memorable, informal portraits by combining children with animals. (See pages 88-92.) Remember, too, that simple props can help relax your subjects and tell a story.

Beverly Schultz

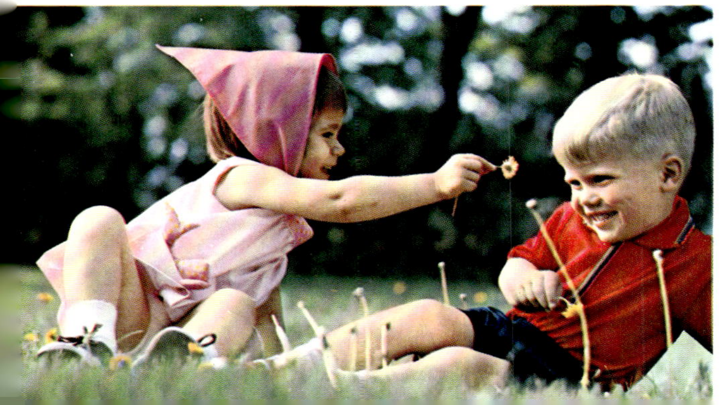

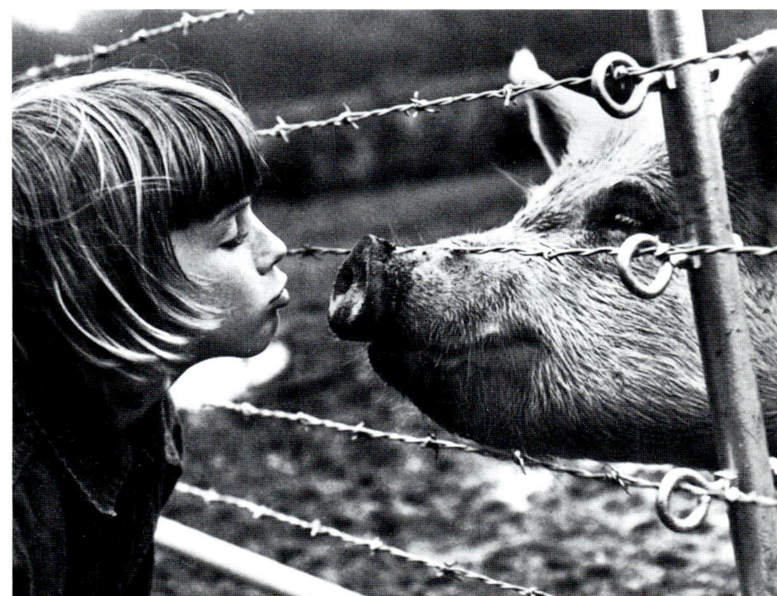

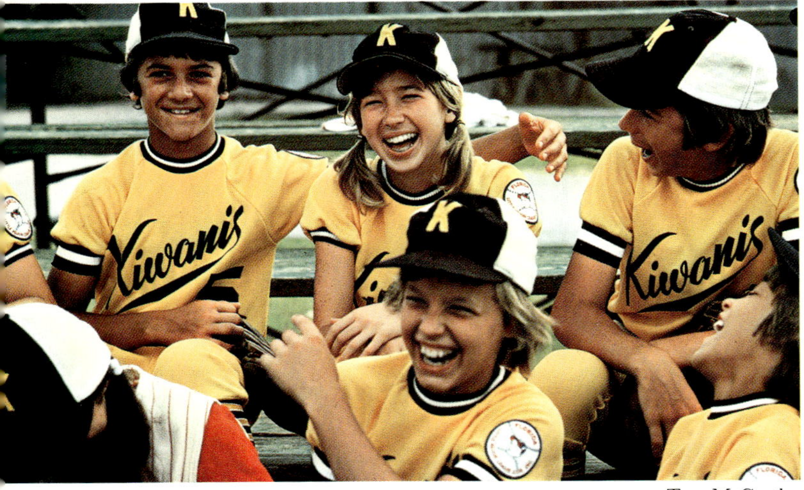

Tom McCarthy

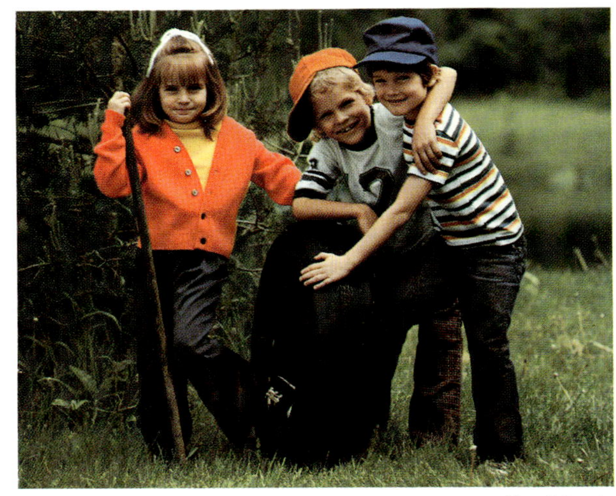

Don Maggio

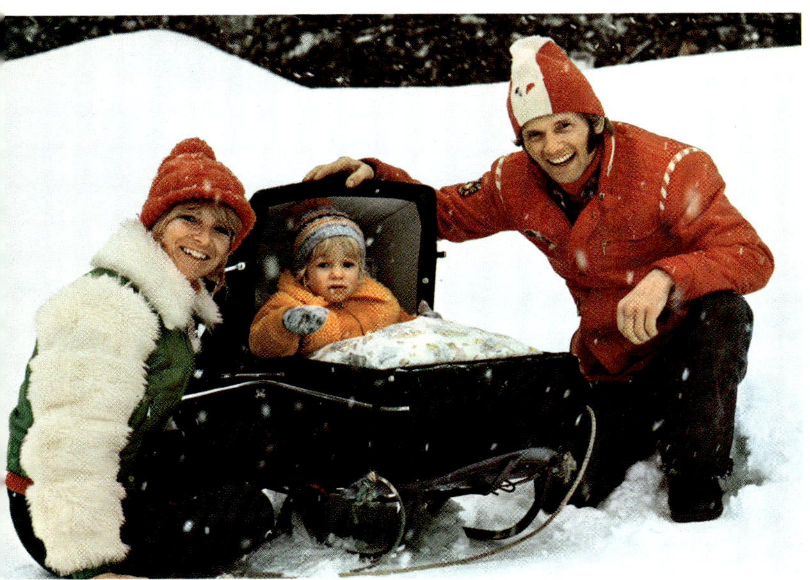

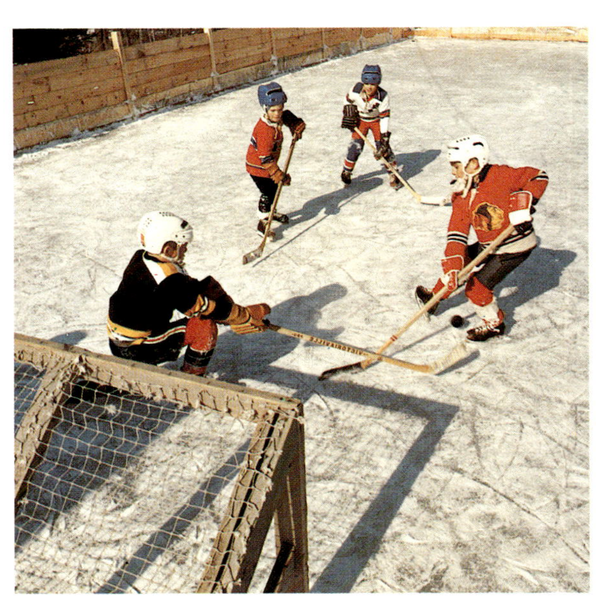

Neil Montanus

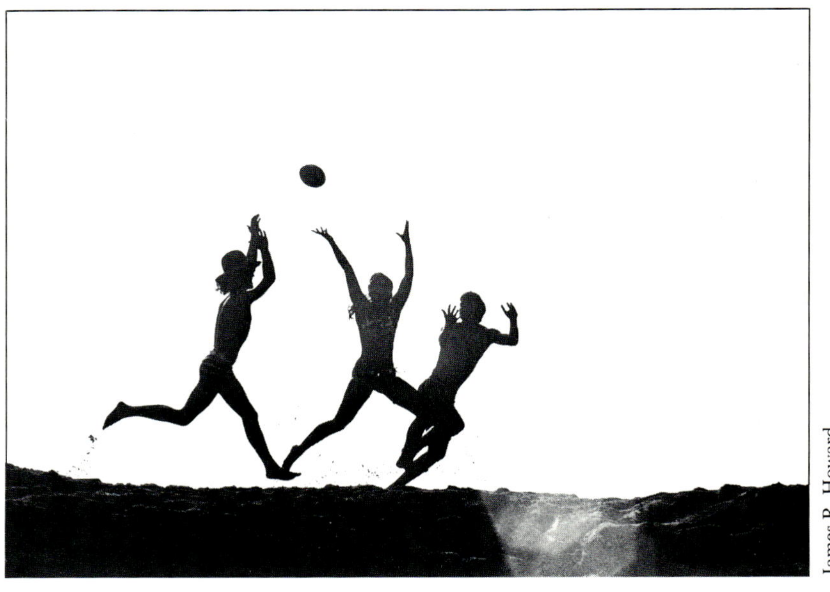

James R. Howard

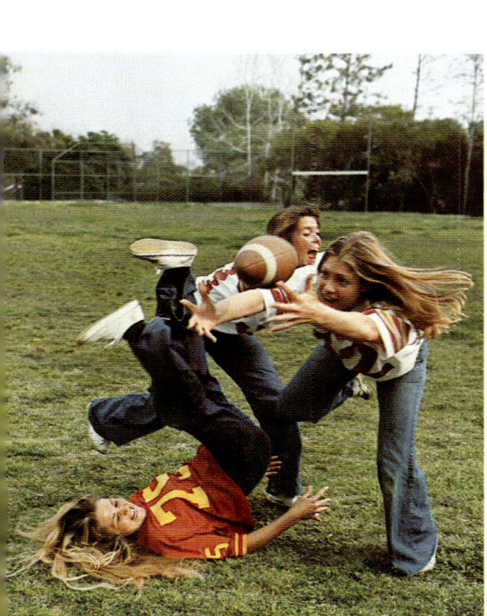

Peter Gales

Jon Abbot

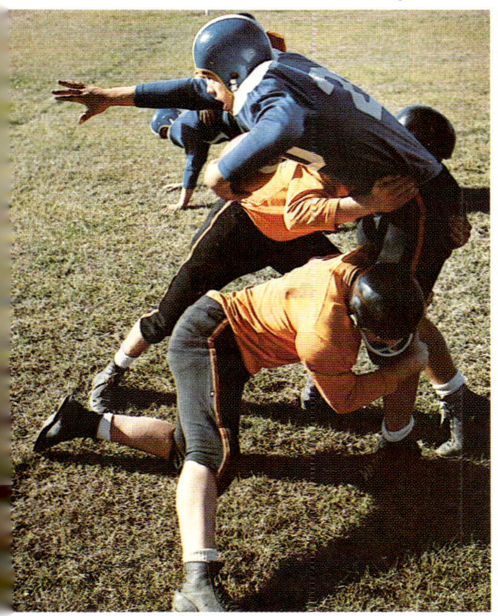

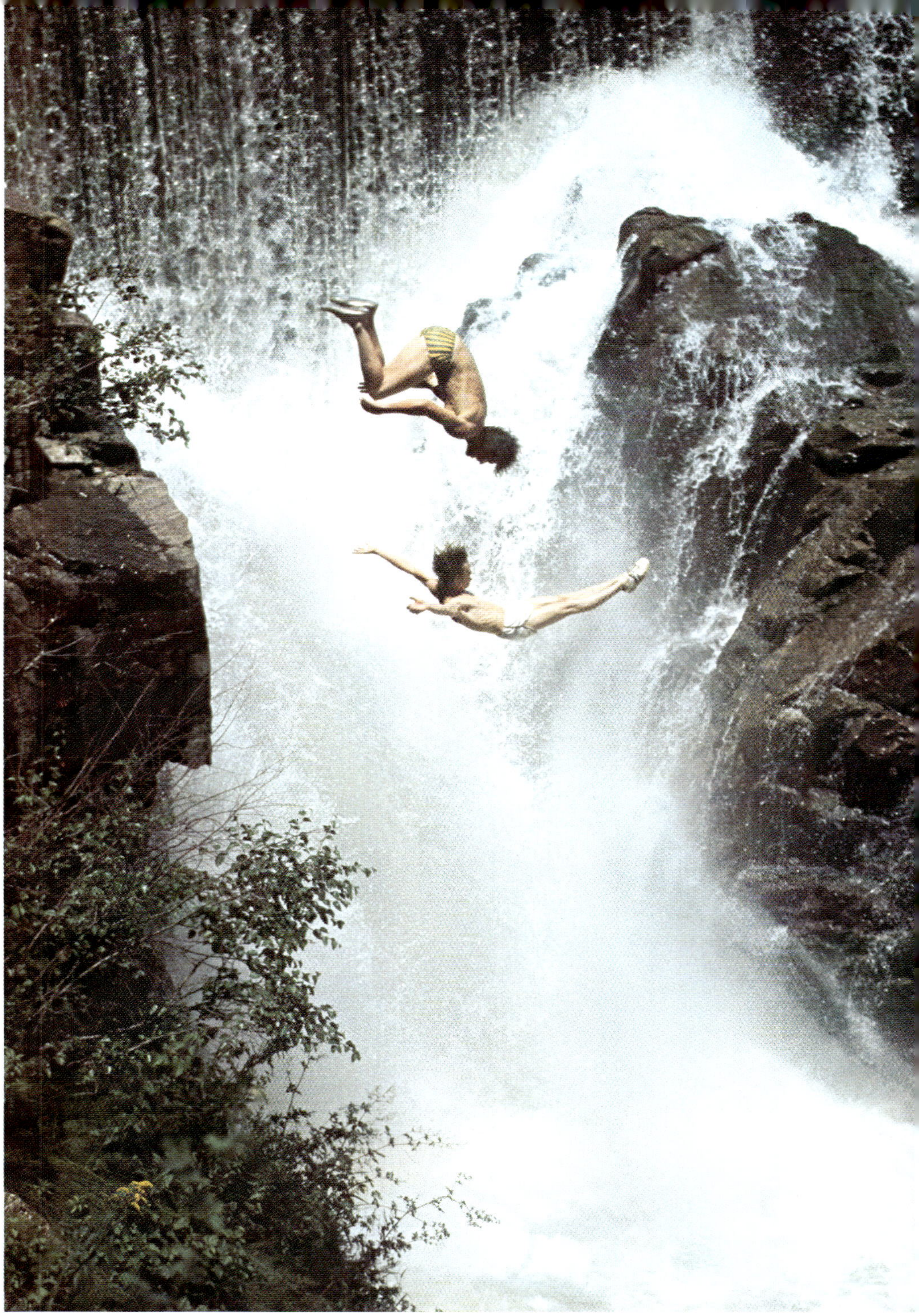

Bobby Adams

Sports and Games

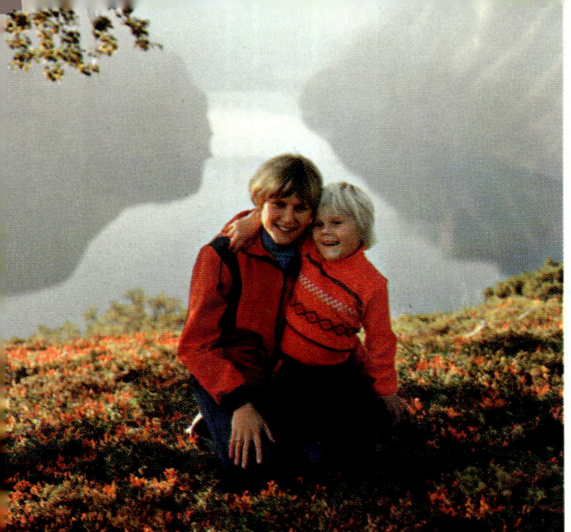
Norm Kerr

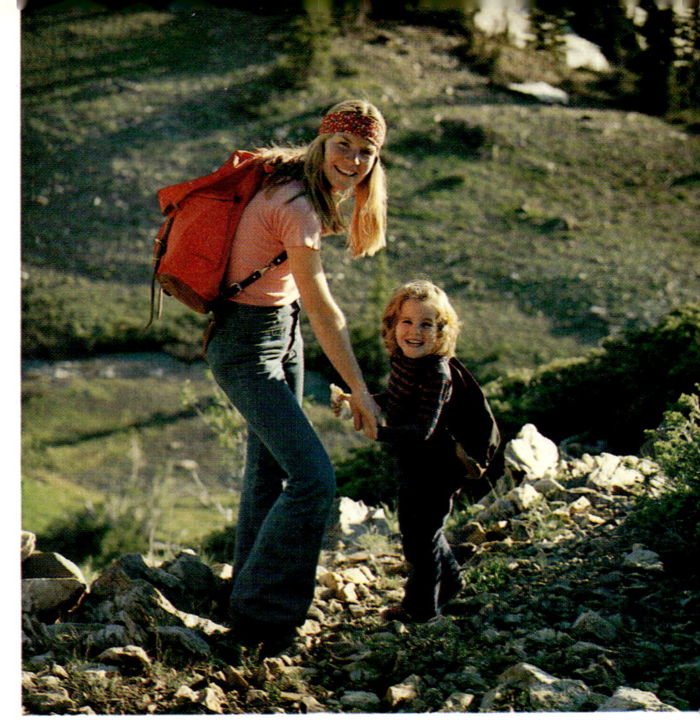
Norm Kerr

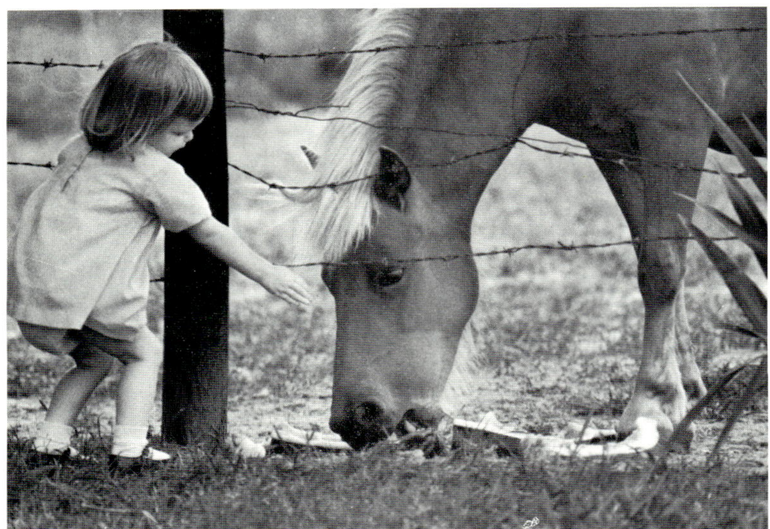
Marion L. Brown, Jr.

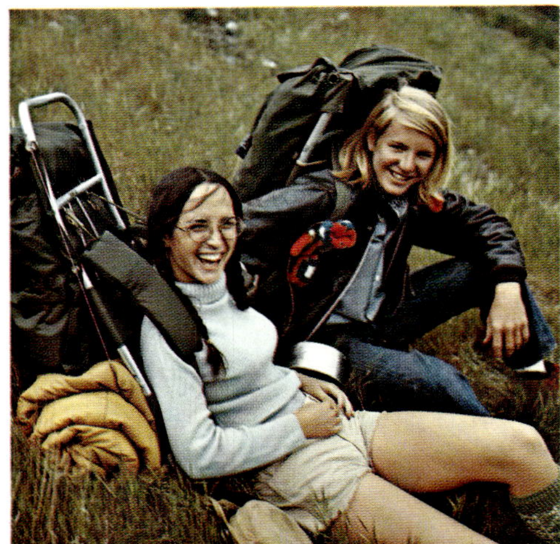
Peter Gales

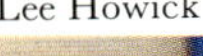
Lee Howick

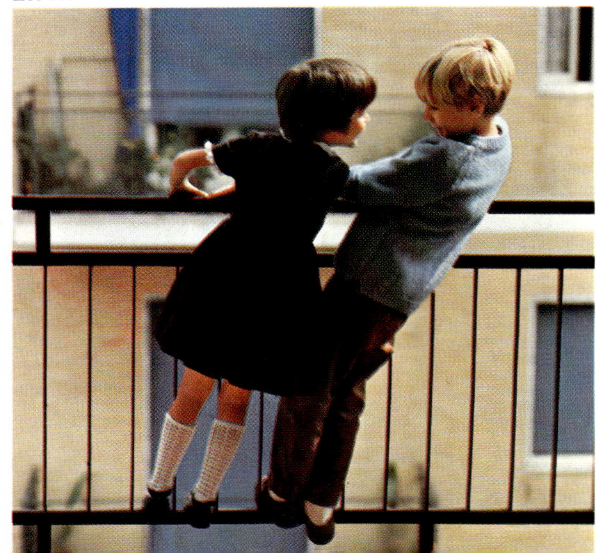

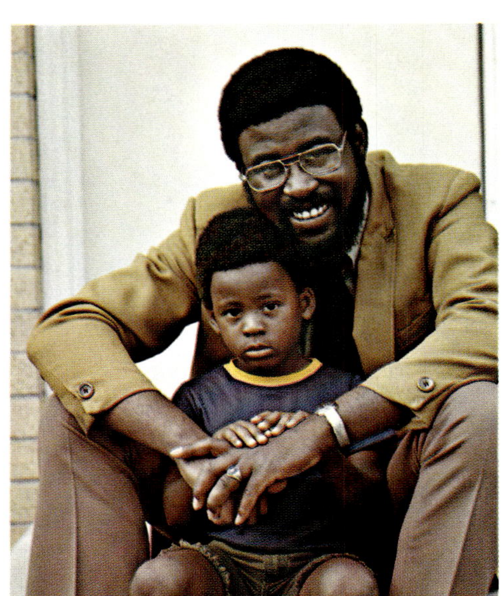
Norm Kerr

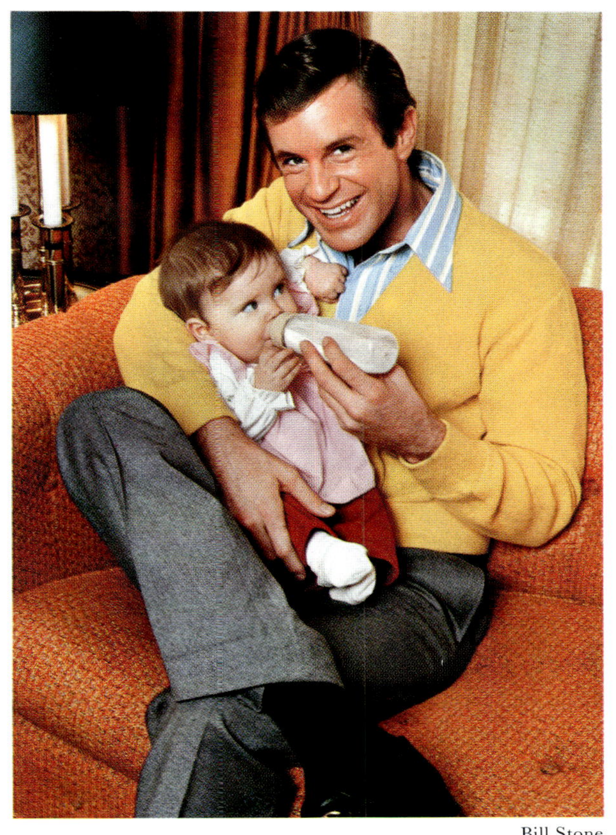
Bill Stone

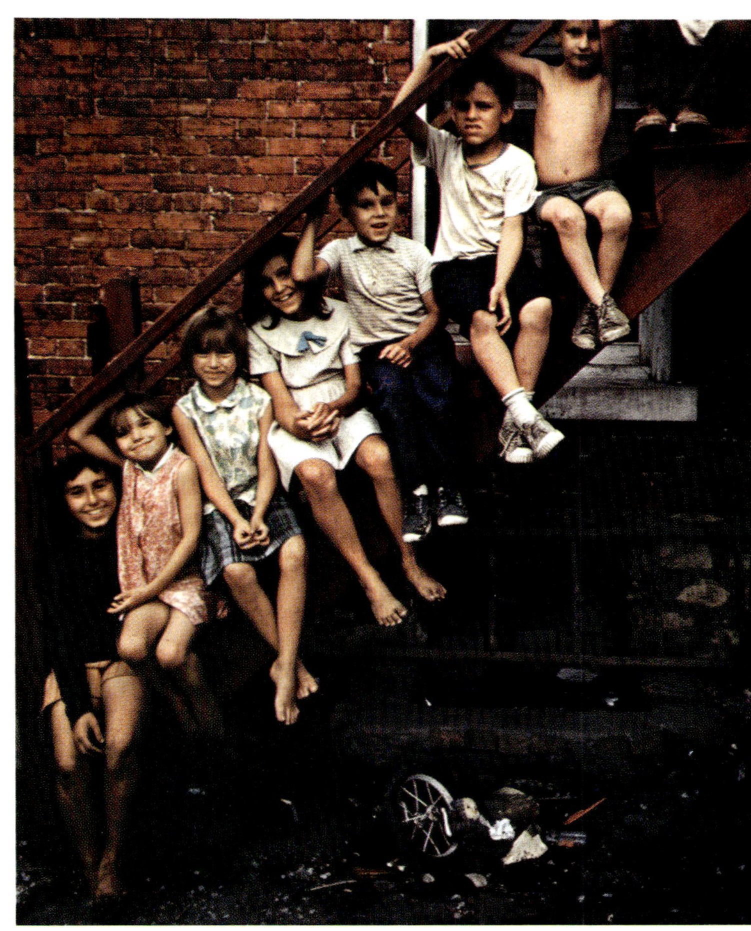
Louis S. Swenson

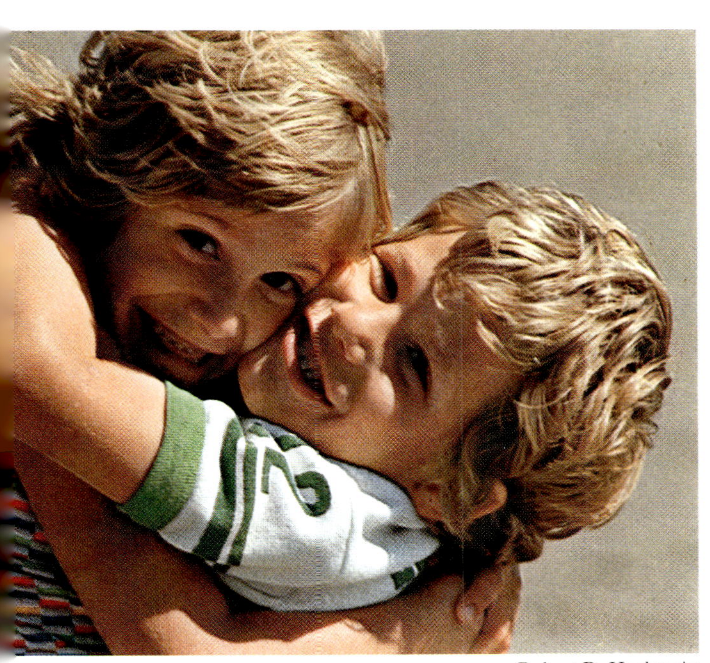
Robert R. Healequist

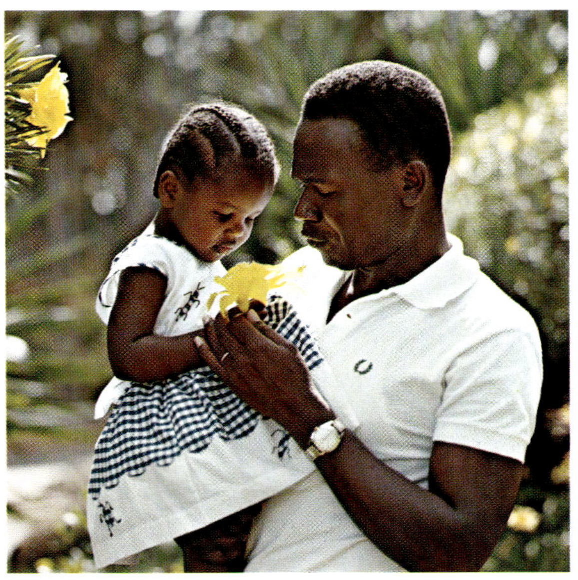

Togetherness

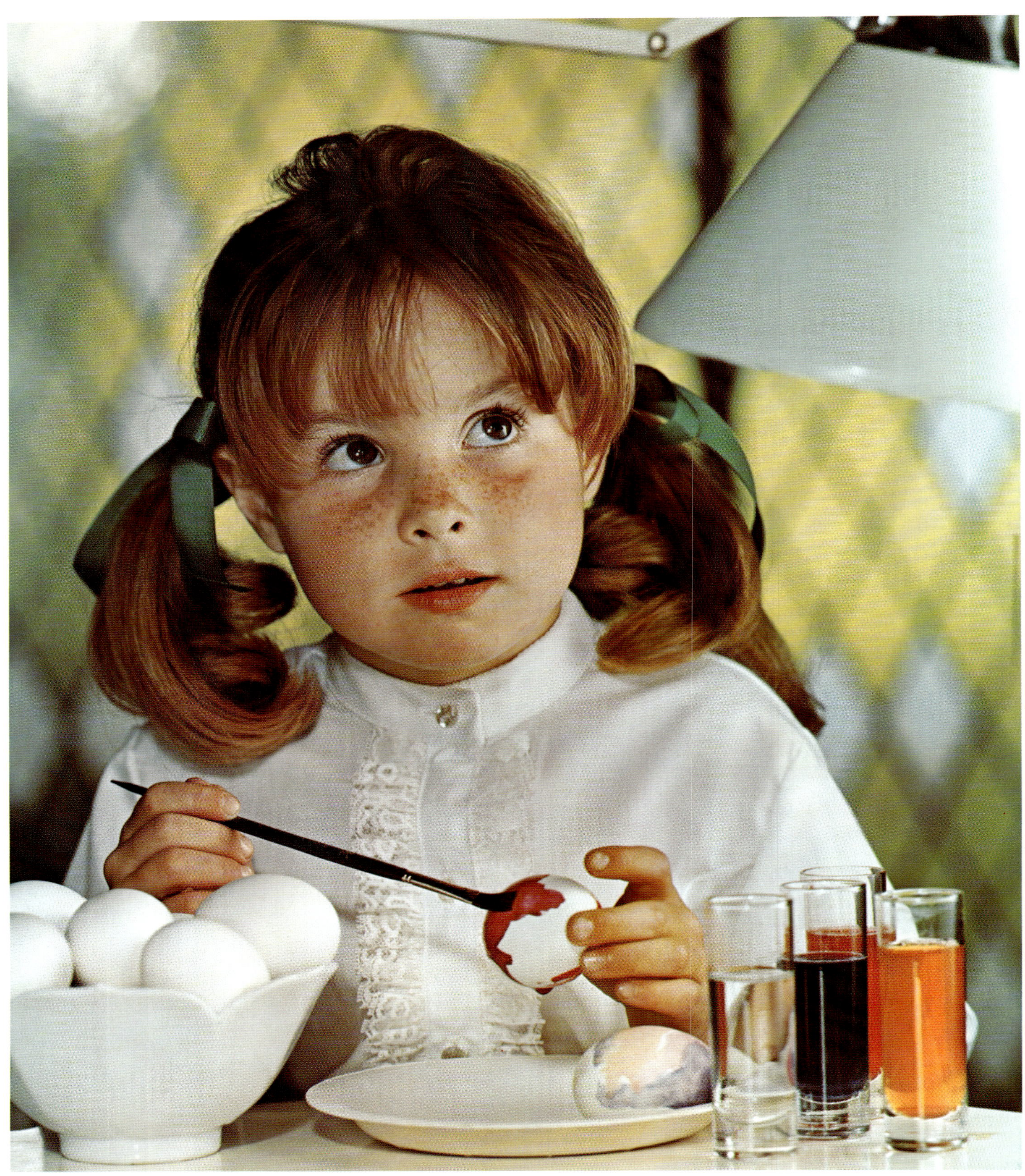

John Mechling

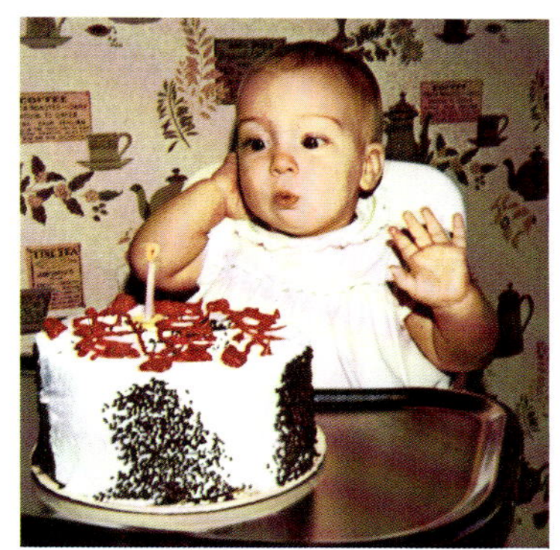

Part Five: Special Occasions

Birthdays, holiday festivities, sports events, parties, and many other special activities bring children together in situations you'll want to remember in pictures. A snapshot of your child, for example, hilariously costumed for Halloween, captures a milestone event and gives you a picture that you'll cherish for years. In fact, pictures taken wherever children gather for fun will be some of your most popular photos.

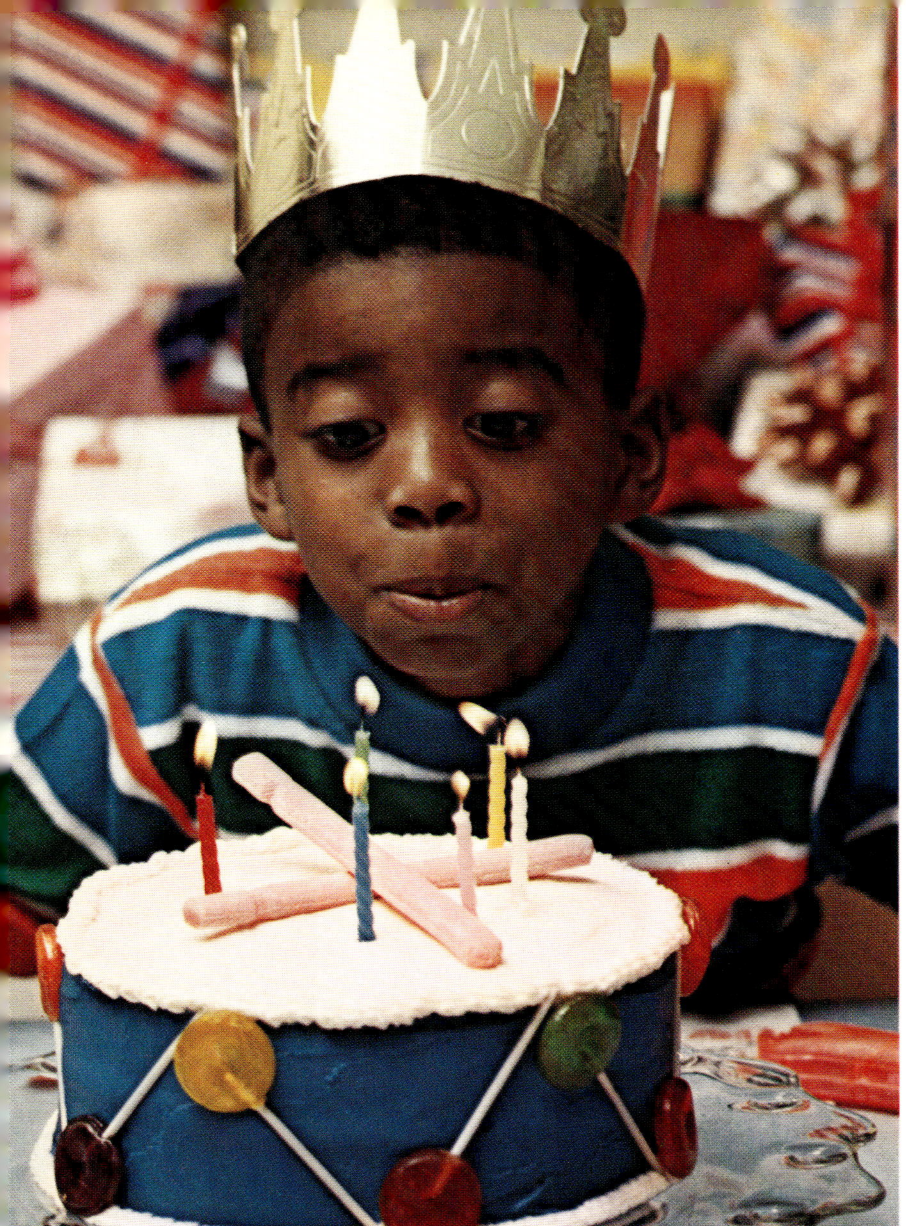

Birthday parties and Easter-egg preparations provide natural opportunities for good pictures. Take lots of snapshots—you'll enjoy them for years to come. (See pages 61-62 for tips on taking indoor pictures by existing light.)

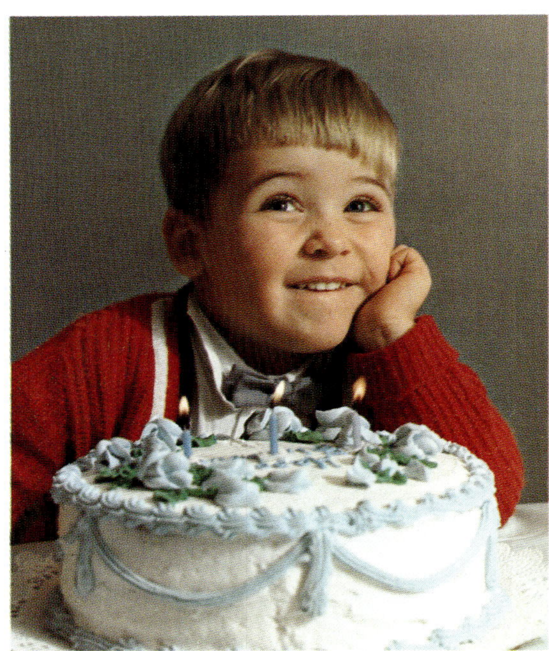

Neil Montanus

Party Time

Childrens' parties are always special occasions and deserve good photo coverage. Make your picture record more interesting by snapping several pictures throughout the event.

You'll want to feature that part of the event that has the greatest attraction—for example, the birthday-cake episode, opening presents, or playing a group game. Take a picture or two of the preparation. Then anticipate the action by having your camera in hand, and start capturing all the party fun as soon as it starts. Children often move quickly from one interest to another, so don't wait for that perfect picture opportunity to come along. You might photographically miss the entire event.

Children who are doing something will have relaxed, natural expressions. Parties usually provide those activities that let your subjects be natural. Take pictures of the youngsters while they're involved in conversation or a game rather than standing in stiff poses waiting for the flash to fire.

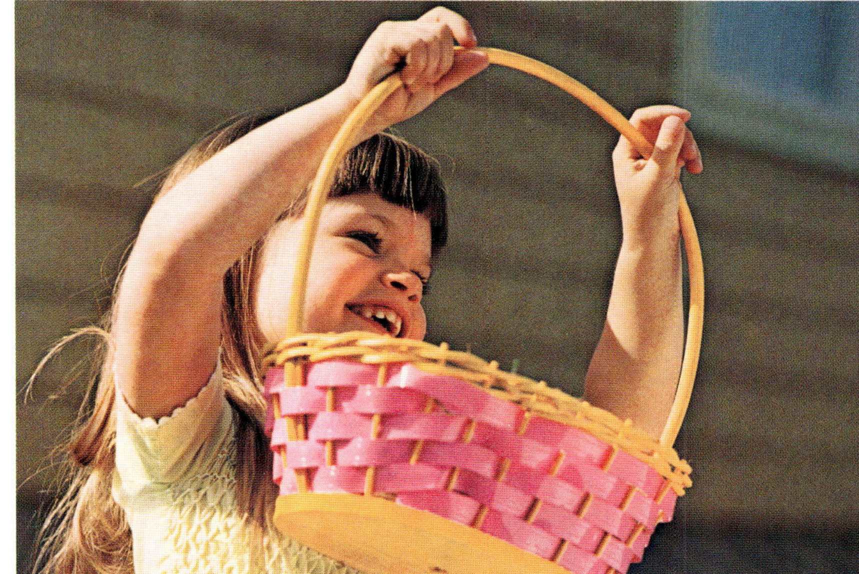

Emiel Blaakman

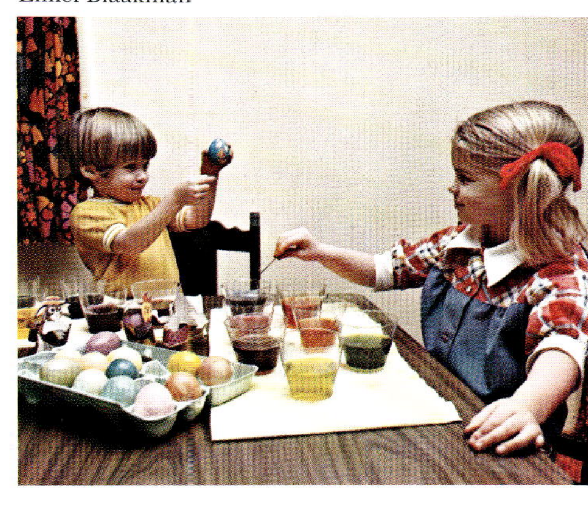

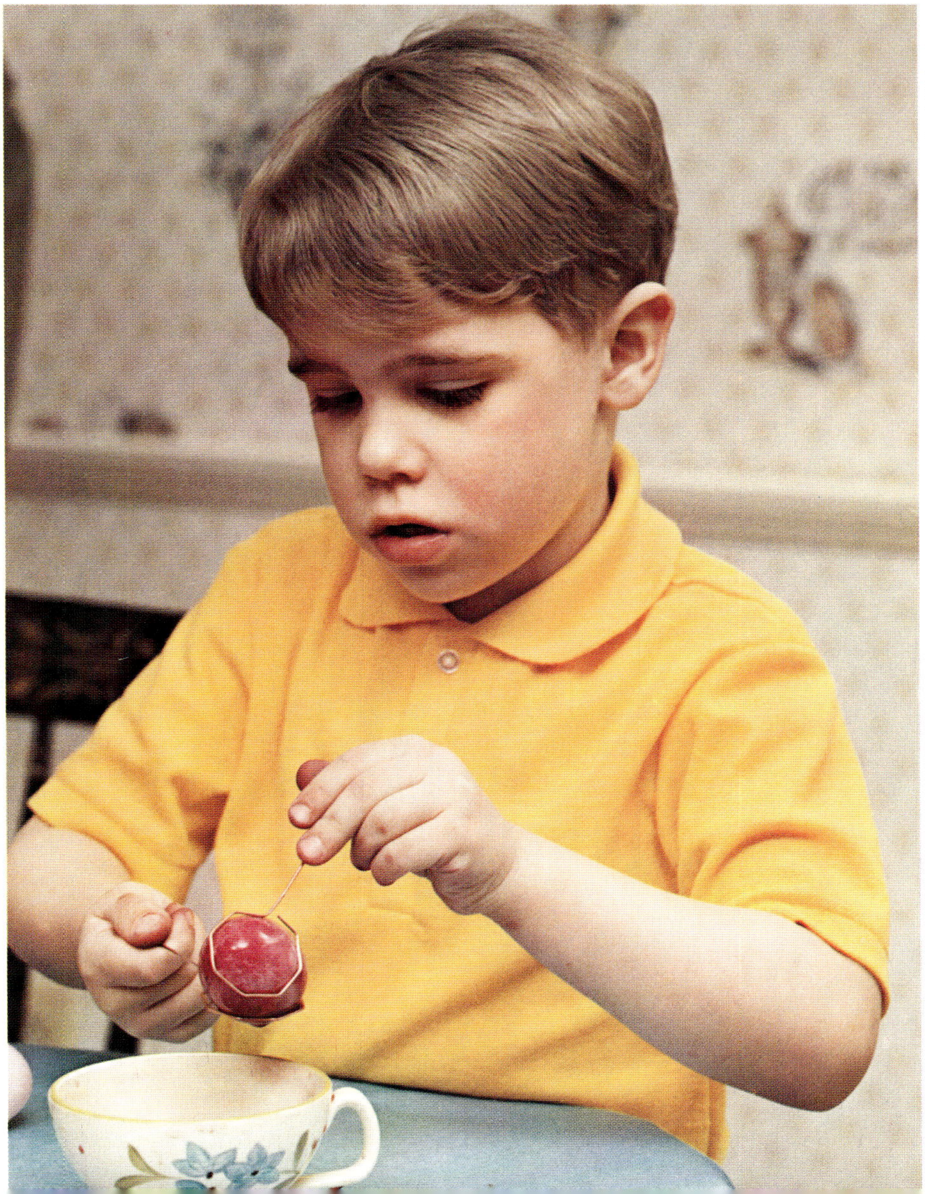

Emiel Blaakman

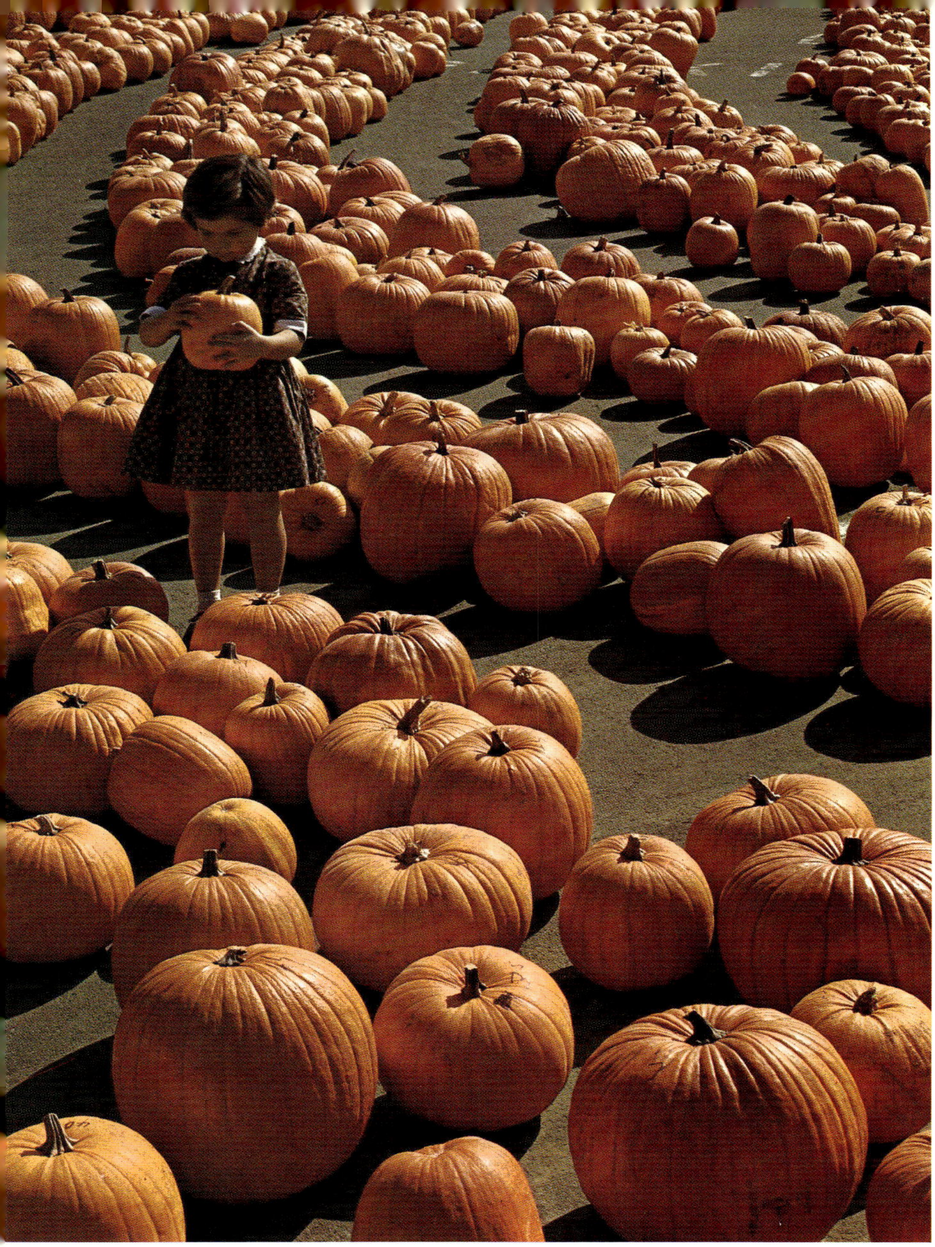

Grant Haist

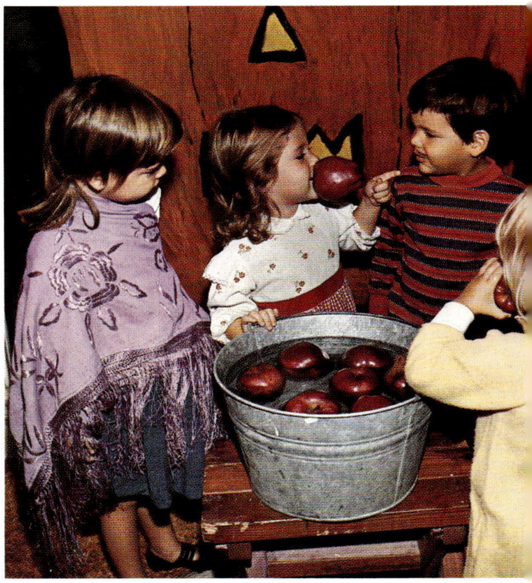

Peter Gales

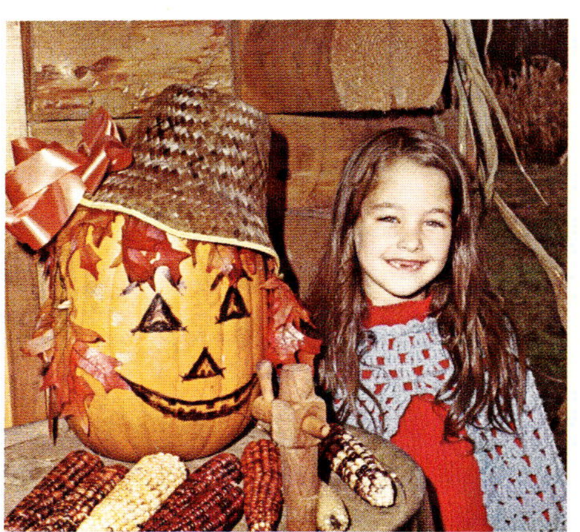

Robert Chaet

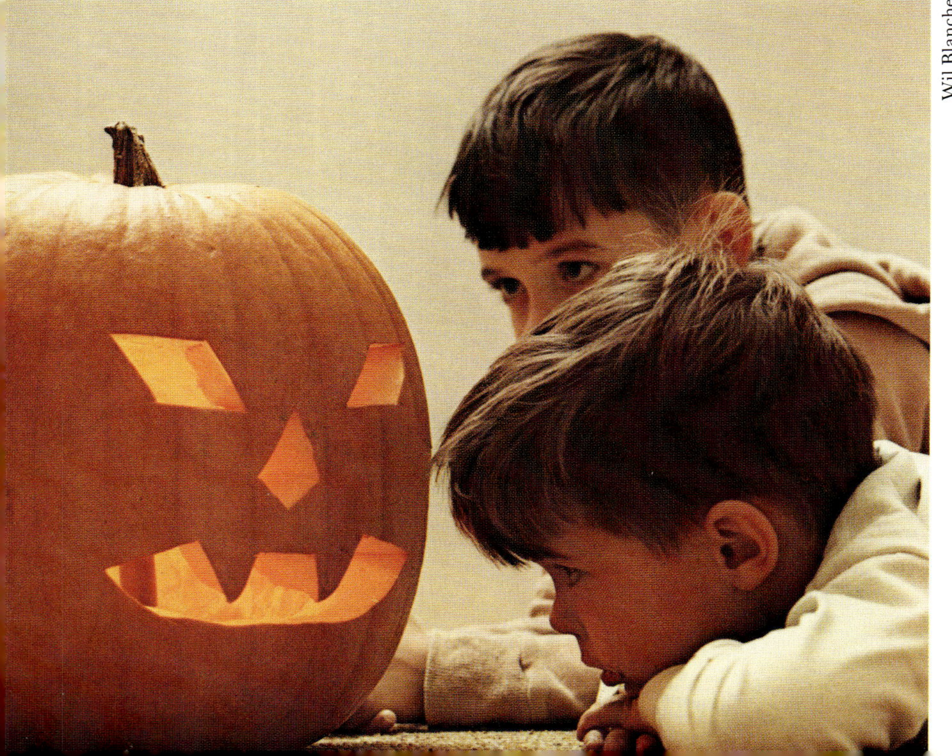

Wil Blanche

Special occasions place children in situations you'll want to remember in pictures. If you're taking pictures with flash, remember to stay within the flash range recommended in your camera manual. Using an adjustable camera and high-speed color film, you can often take natural-looking photos without the need for flash, like the picture on the left. (See pages 61-62 for details.)

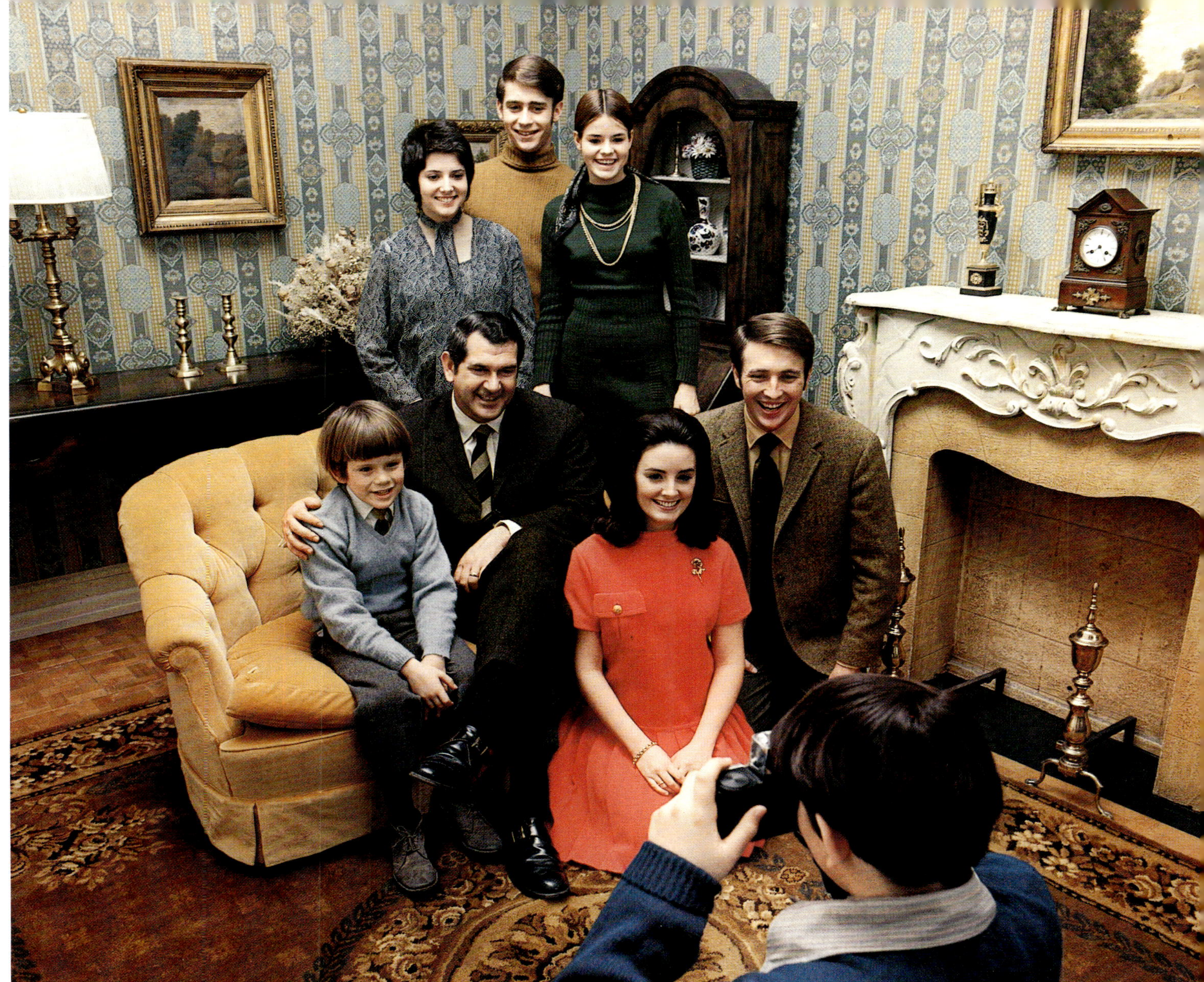

Tony Petrocelli

The Family Reunion

Family reunions, as do parties and holidays, bring children together. And if the occasion is a wedding reception, anniversary party, full-scale picnic, or other event where lots of relatives gather, you can generally be sure to find plenty of young ones around. The trick is to get good pictures of the children for the sake of memory without making a Hollywood epic.

Try to avoid squeezing the entire group into a single picture. With your camera ready to go, first take a good look around you to notice who is doing what and where. Chances are the multitude of youth present has broken up into distinct play groups (assuming that it's not mealtime). Several children might be engrossed in a game in one area while in another, three or four little cousins are busy playing in the sandbox or scribbling with crayons. A third group might be sitting quietly off to the side, contemplating the gathering over a soft drink. Focus on situations like these. They're the kind of natural activities you'll want to seek out with your camera to record those moments when children are relaxed and being themselves.

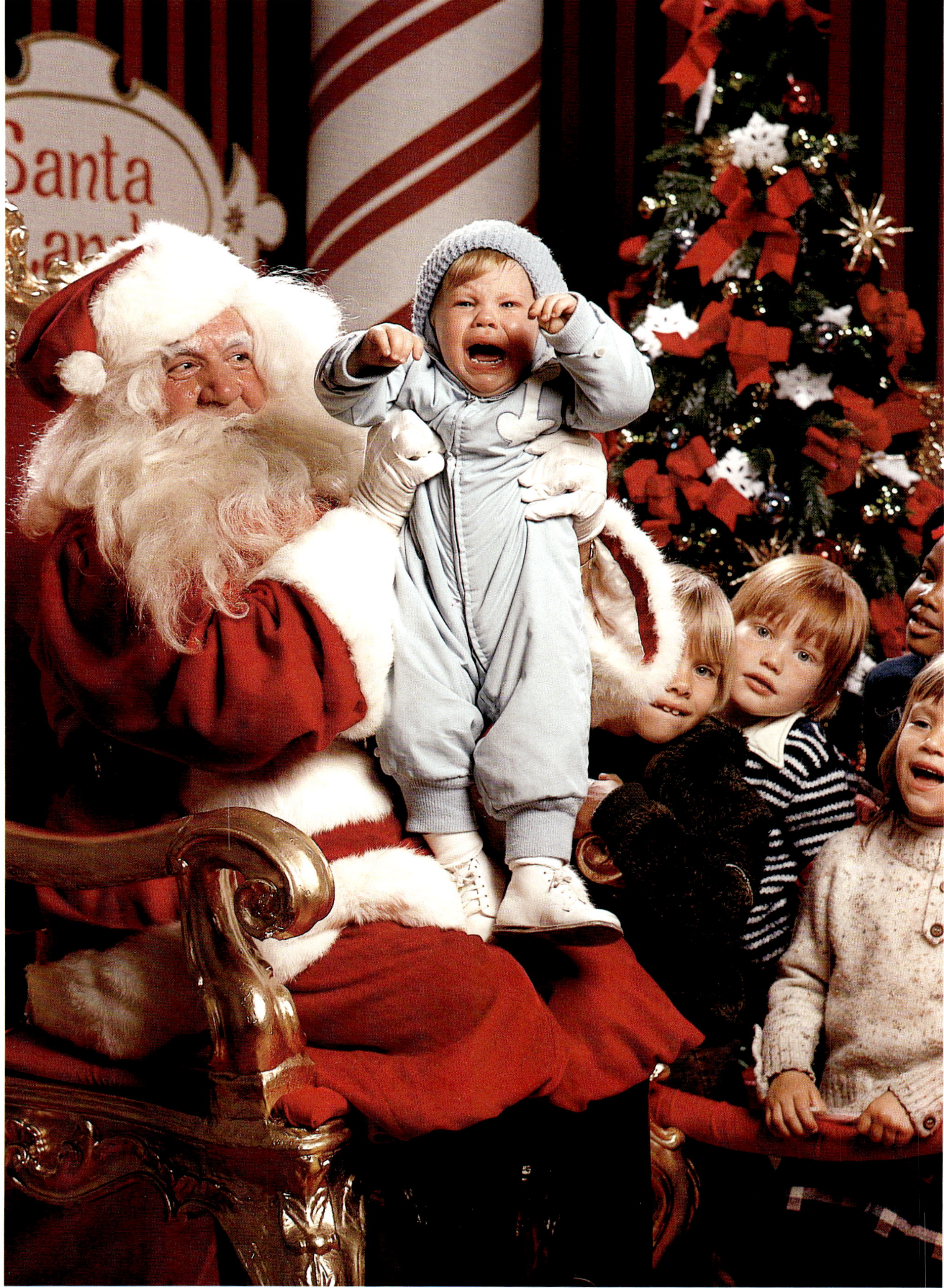

Bill King

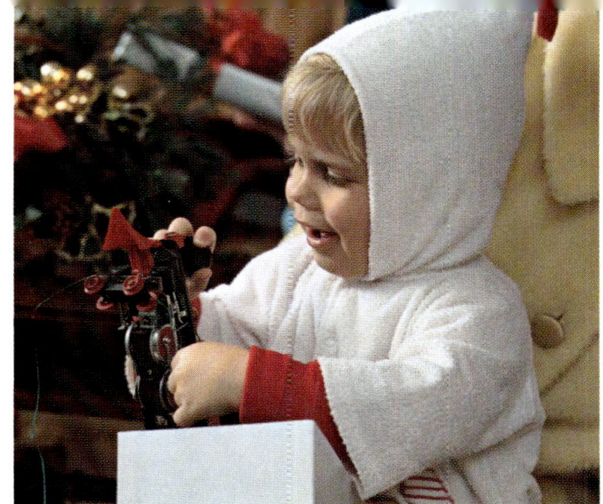

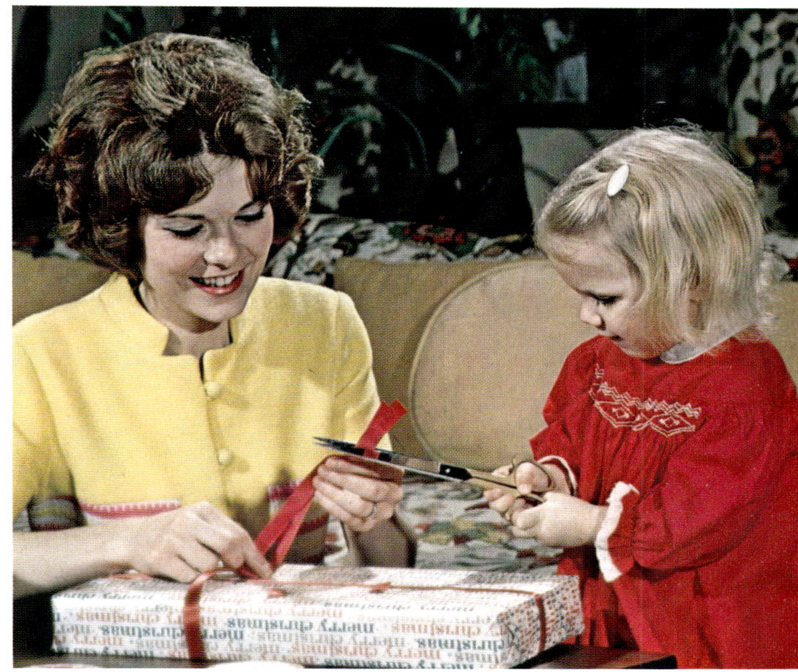

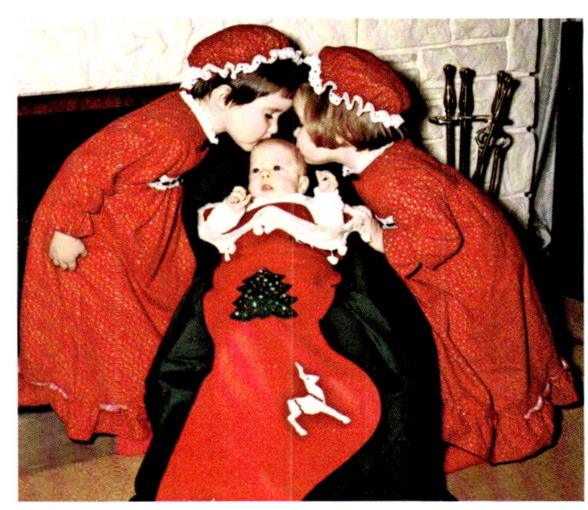

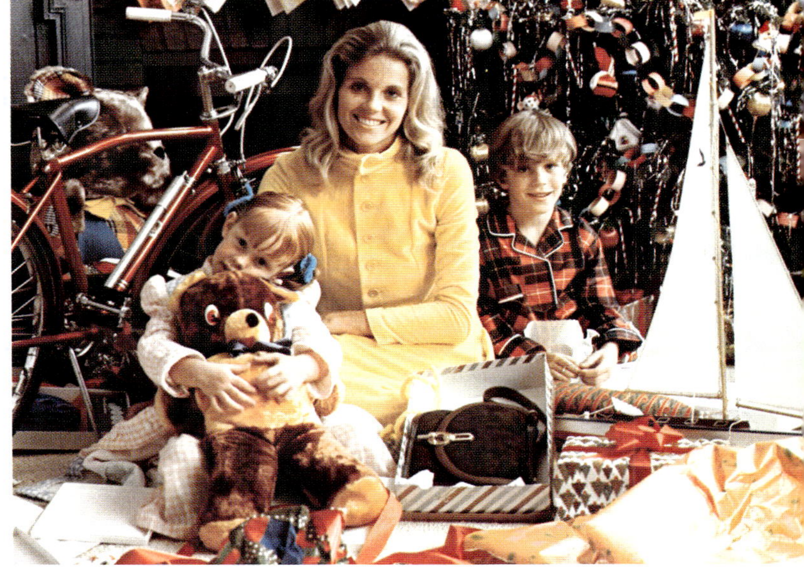

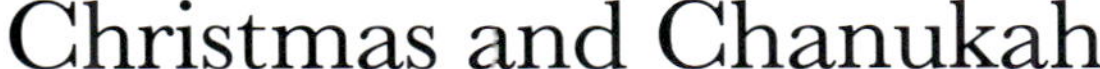

Christmas and Chanukah

Christmas and Chanukah are perhaps the best times of the year from a picture-taking standpoint. Presents, colorful decorations, the fancy dinner—all these and other happy festive themes make ideal props for holiday pictures of children. Keep your camera ready with plenty of extra film and flash supplies on hand to meet this multitude of picture possibilities.

Of all the events taking place during the holiday season, Christmas morning shines brightest in the eyes of many young ones. If you're using an adjustable camera, set the focus scale in advance to the distance you plan to be from your subjects. Then when children begin to open their gifts under the tree, you can record the look of anticipation on their faces and their happy smiles of delight. Remember to move in close and lower the camera to their eye level for a strong center of interest.

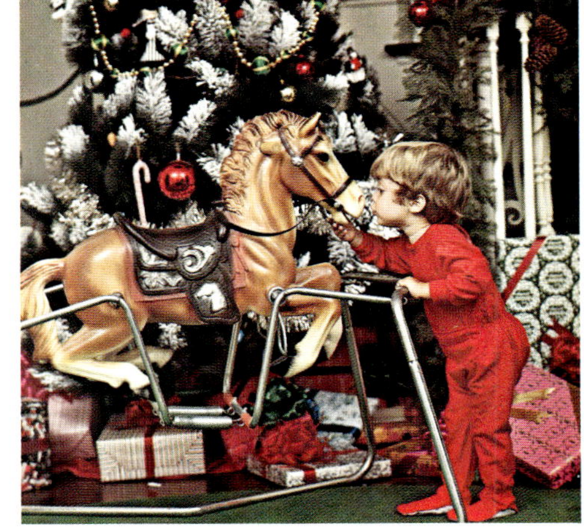

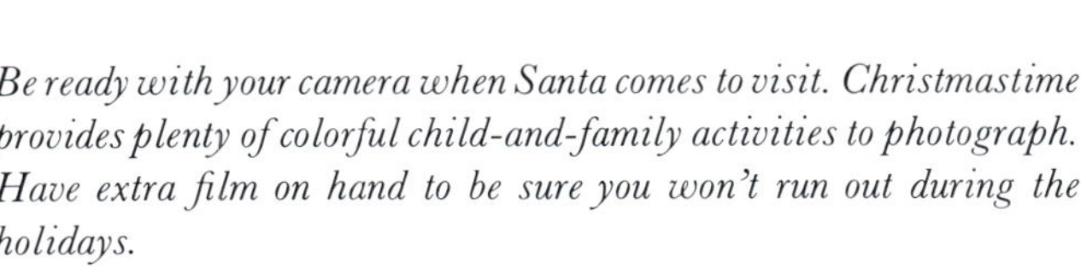

Be ready with your camera when Santa comes to visit. Christmastime provides plenty of colorful child-and-family activities to photograph. Have extra film on hand to be sure you won't run out during the holidays.

Make your picture record more interesting by snapping several pictures throughout the event.

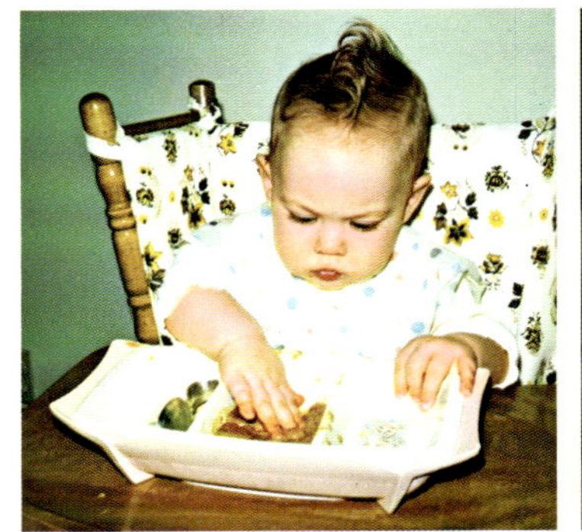

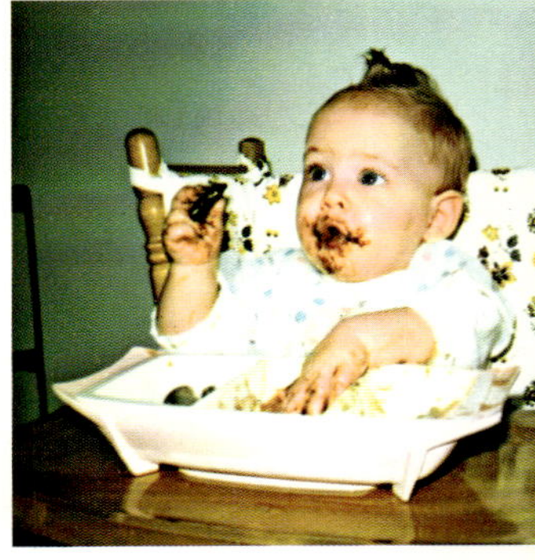

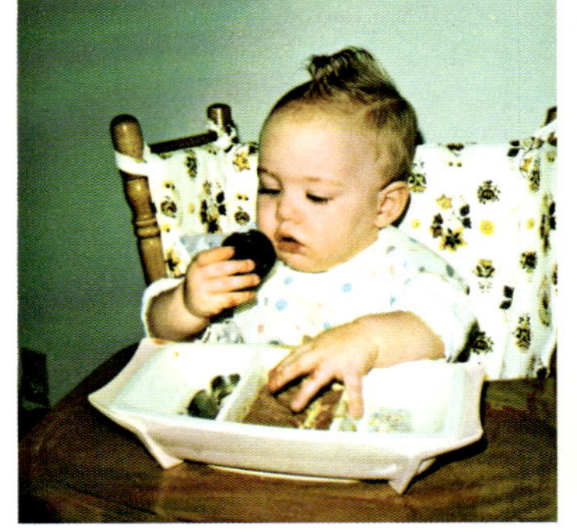

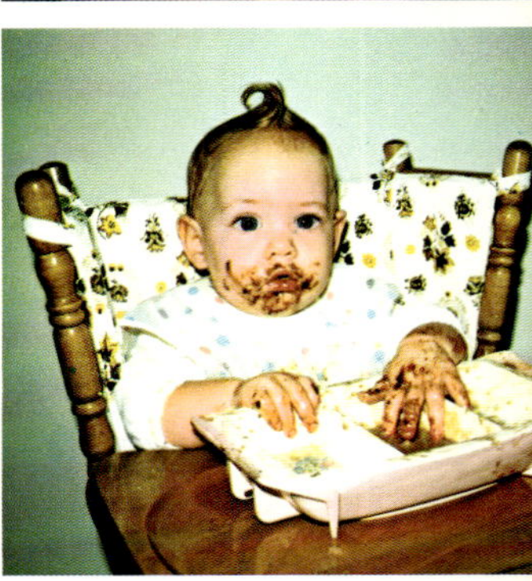

Part Six:

The Picture Series

Do you want to take some natural photos of a child who is at the camera-conscious age when the presence of a camera might produce a forced, unwanted response? To avoid unnatural poses, encourage the child to participate in a favorite activity, such as looking through a picture book, playing with blocks, or eating an ice-cream cone. Then capture the event from beginning to end on film, taking several pictures along the way to make a complete story. Let the child casually enjoy all the activity rather than be instructed to pose in a certain way. The child will soon become quite accustomed to the frequent click of the shutter, and you will have an interesting series, with at least one picture suitable to stand alone as a striking, informal portrait.

To show a complete story, make your first picture set the scene, and then follow it with a few more of the continuing action. Your final picture should conclude the activity. Begin by taking a picture showing the child or children with all the props about to be used to establish the location of the story. Then move in for some close-ups of the activity and some intent expressions. Your final picture should wrap up the story by showing the logical result of the previous activity. If the story suggests no logical completion, watch for an expression or action which might serve as a humorous climax to the sequence.

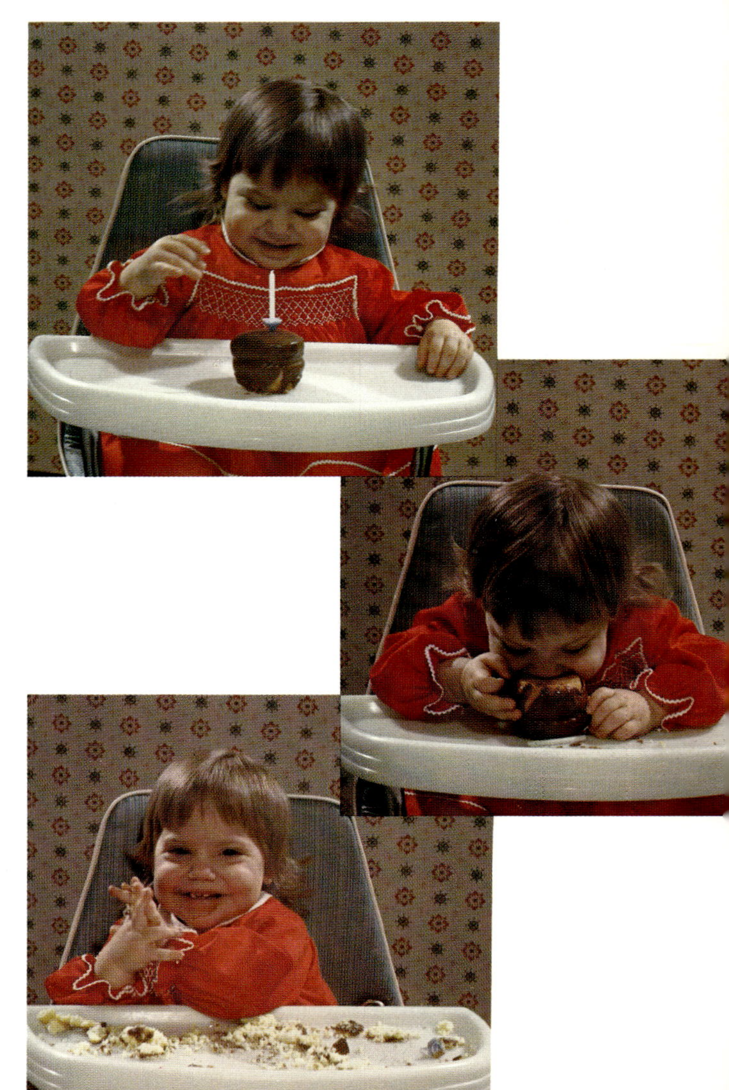

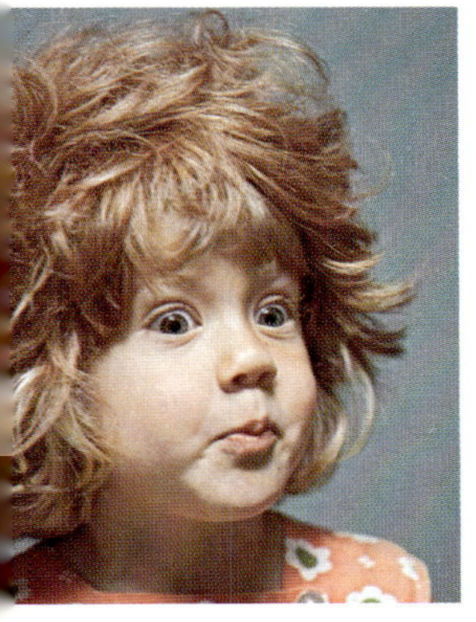
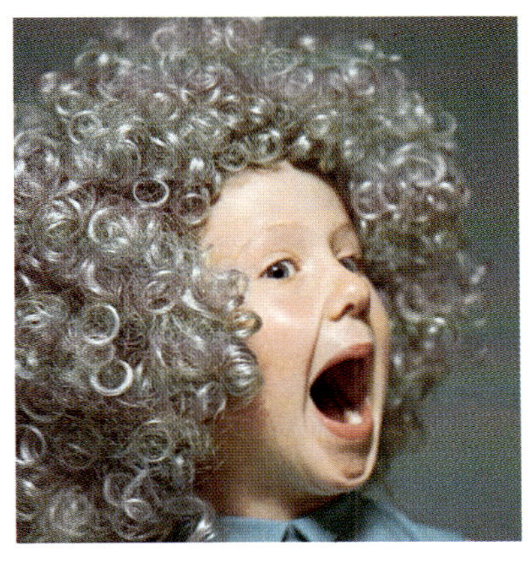
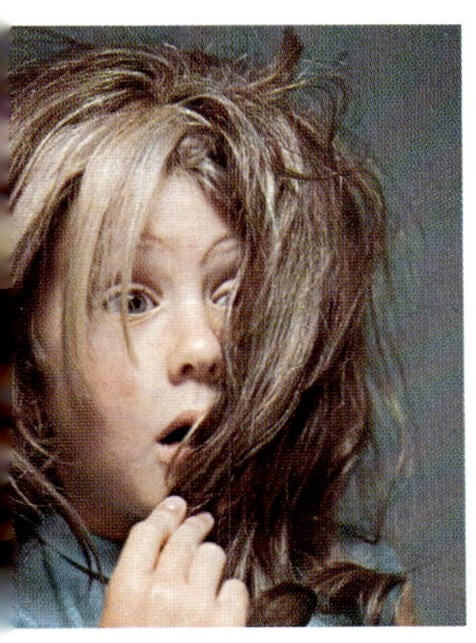
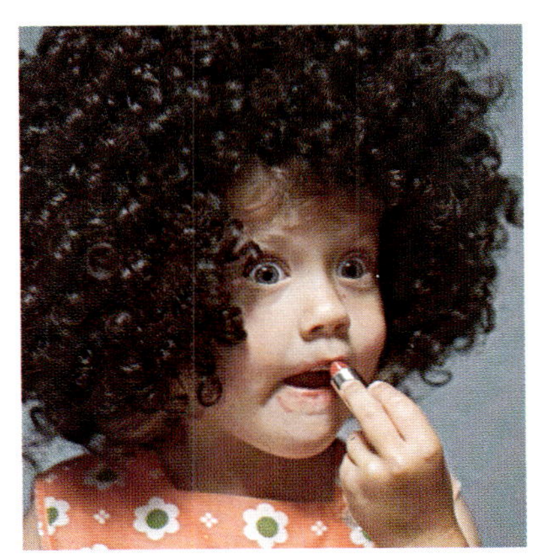
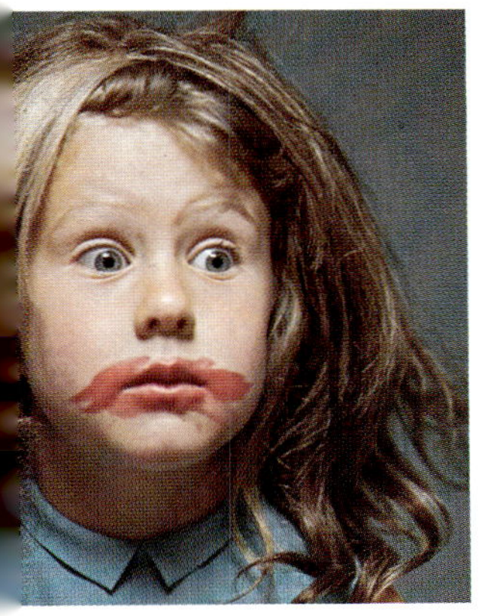
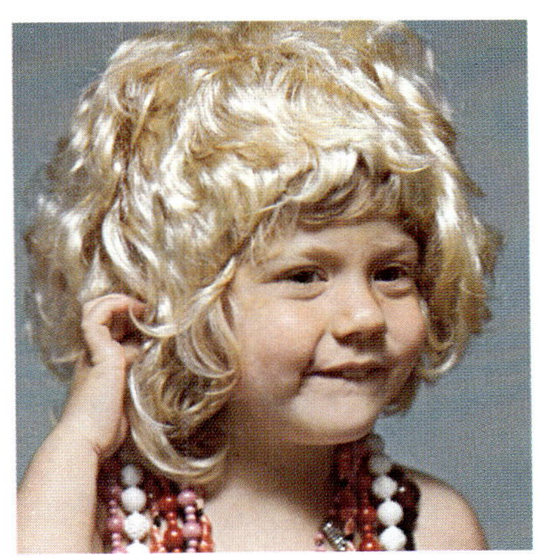

Emiel Blaakman

Finding Picture Opportunities

Events that have the makings for a good picture story are very plentiful. In fact, nearly everything that a child does in the course of a day has storytelling potential. Make an effort to watch a child's daily routine and take note of any good picture possibility.

While some enjoyable activities will be repeated many times by a child, don't limit your picture opportunities to these events. Learn to know what toys or projects bring out the most animation in a child. Then present the youngster with the appropriate gift. For example, a new toy sailboat in the hands of a future old salt, combined with a field trip to a nearby pond, will provide you with enough picture-series material to last half the afternoon.

Have your camera, extra film, and any other photographic equipment you wish to use ready ahead of time before you present your gift. When the child first receives this new diversion, enthusiasm will probably be at its peak. Start your picture-taking immediately to record all of the fun.

Working With a Helper

To capture those priceless images of youth on film, you must have a cooperative model—a child who is both happy and interested in working with you to meet a mutually pleasant goal. But still there are a multitude of important little things that can go wrong. You need a helper to assist in spotting unwanted elements and make instant corrections so that you can devote all of your attention to concentrating on good composition, lighting, exposure, and facial expressions. Your subject's mother or father can usually serve as your assistant, adjusting the child's clothing, redirecting a wild wisp of hair, smoothing a shirt wrinkle, or wiping a runny nose.

Your helper should be close at hand during those moments when you are actually taking pictures, too, possibly helping you to coax a tired or self-conscious little one into a smile. Even if your helper is not required to assist in directing the child, he or she should remain close by, preferably slightly behind you to avoid distracting the child.

Making a Slide Show

Organizing and presenting your slides of children effectively can go a long way toward making the show a success. Your young subjects may have all the makings for strong audience appeal, but chances are that the picture series of them will not be well received by your audience (usually family and friends) unless you present it well. The polish that results from good organization, pacing, and careful picture selection will be at least fifty percent responsible for the success of your slide presentation.

First, of course, take some pictures—plenty of pictures! Vary your subject distance and camera angle. This will give you a wide selection of slides to choose from when you edit your results. Interesting close-ups of children's faces can provide valuable material for a change of pace in your finished show.

Besides taking plenty of pictures to tell your story, strive for quality in every frame. A good slide show should be clever, entertaining, and storytelling—it should also represent your very best picture-taking efforts. There's little excuse for showing your audience a poorly exposed or composed, unsharp slide just because it happens to be a picture of one of your favorite people.

To add variety to the pace and give some polish to your slide show, add a few title slides. By viewing an entire slide sequence (or a group of sequences) at one time on an illuminator, you'll quickly see where titles are needed. (Small illuminators, which are easy to use and store, are available through most photo dealers.) Many titles are ready-made for your camera. Just take a picture of them. Include a child in your title pictures to add a dash of color and interest.

Here are a few ideas for making slide shows that feature babies. Below each subject, we've included a suggested shooting order of appropriate scenes for telling the story.

Even when one picture can tell a story, you can usually make a better story with several pictures. You can make a photo sequence of any children's activity—a birthday party, cookie-baking project—you name it.

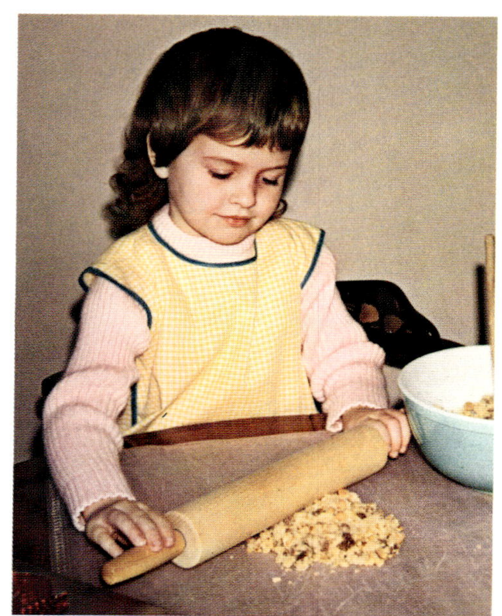

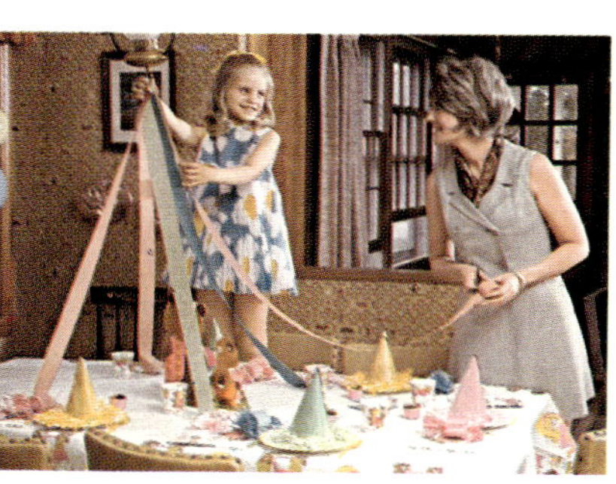

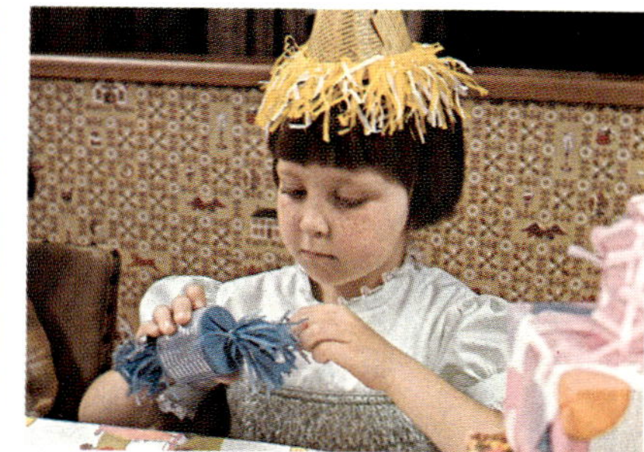

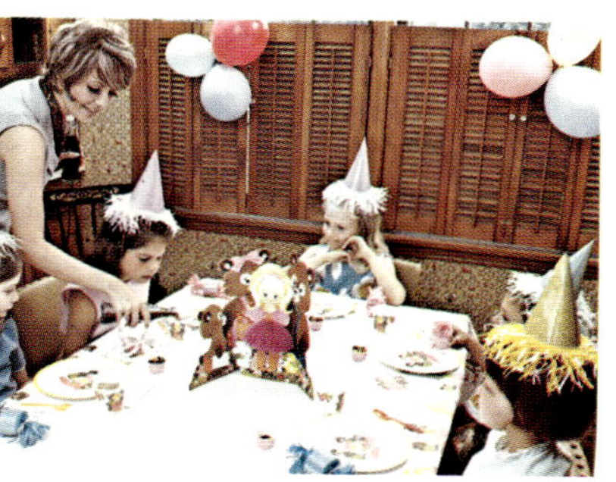

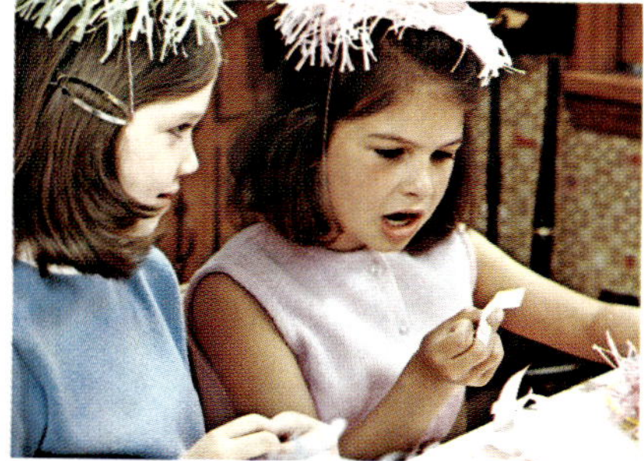

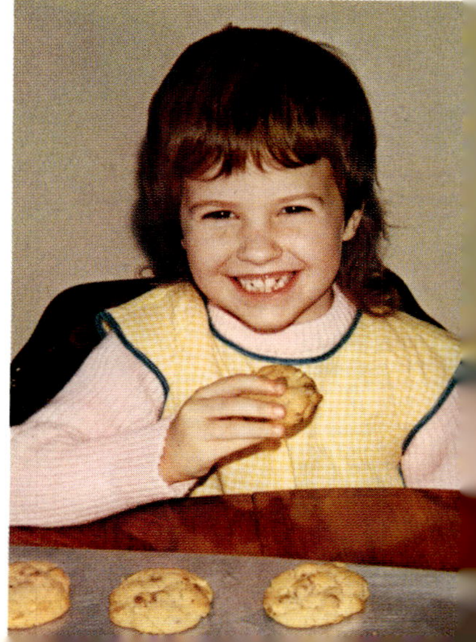

Our Newborn Comes Home

- Close-up of birth announcement
- Scenes of Baby's room with crib, dressing table, toys, and other paraphernalia
- Long shot of hospital entrance, preferably with hospital name included in scene
- Sequence of Mother and Baby leaving hospital and entering car
- Scene of Mother bringing Baby into house
- Mixture of medium shots and close-ups of Mother and Baby sitting on sofa
- Scenes of relatives and friends looking at Baby
- Sequence of Mother putting sleeper onto Baby

Baby Gourmet in High Chair

- Close-up of Mother preparing Baby's bottle
- Medium shot of Mother setting warming dish onto high chair
- Mother putting food into dish to warm
- Dad getting Baby from crib
- Dad placing Baby into high chair
- Close-up of Mother putting bib onto Baby
- Sequence of Mother feeding Baby
- Close-up of Baby's face covered with food
- Close-up of Mother wiping Baby's face
- Close-up of Mother's approving face
- Baby drinking from baby bottle

Baby's First Steps

- Baby standing in crib
- Dad picking up Baby and standing Baby on floor
- Sequence of Dad holding Baby while guiding Baby's first few steps
- Close-up of Dad's hands holding Baby's hand
- Medium shot of Dad releasing grip as Baby toddles onward
- Baby walking
- Sequence of Baby stumbling, getting up—with a little assist from Dad—and walking again

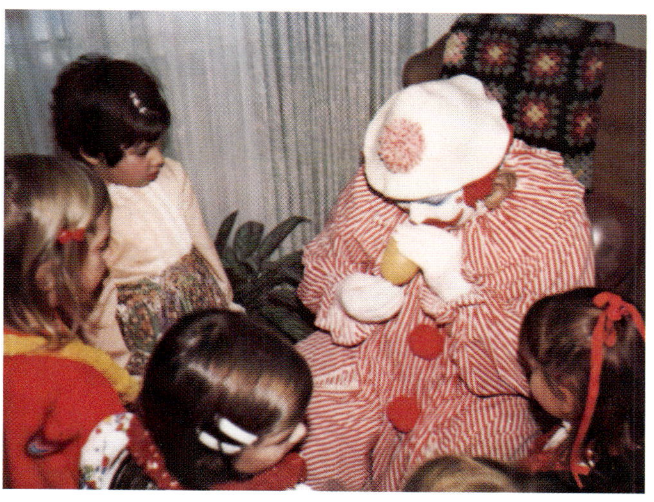

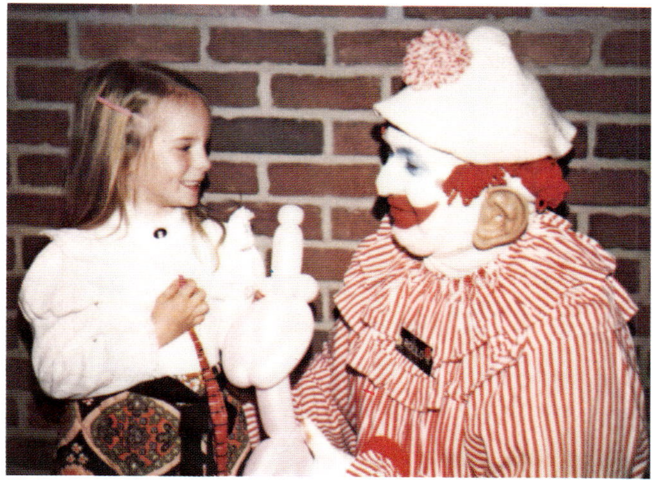

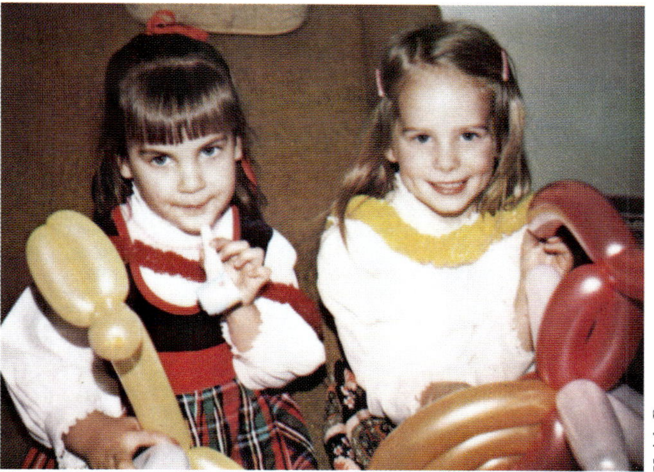

Keith Boas

When there's a houseful of youngsters gathered for a party and special entertainment planned, take several pictures of the event so you will have a complete photo record of the big day. (Series taken with a KODAK Instant Camera and KODAK Instant Print Film PR10.)

Part Seven: Pictures on Display

Stationery stores and photo shops offer a variety of photo albums to suit your needs.

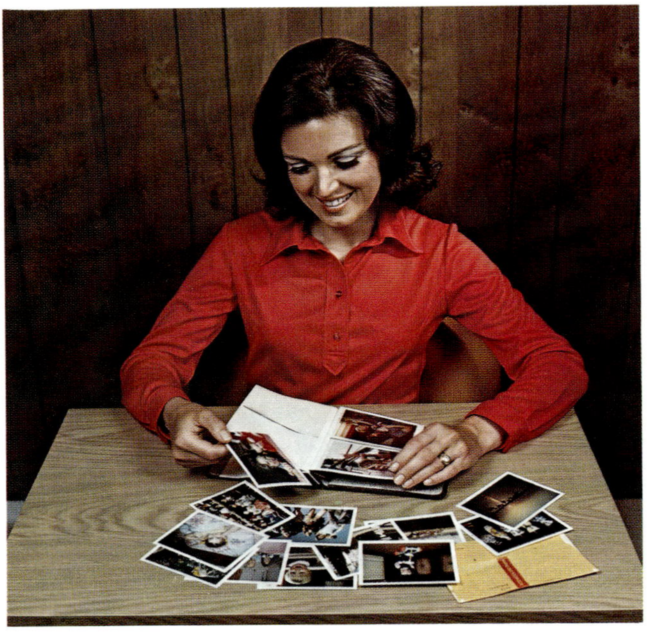

You might prefer to make your own album by using colorful construction paper and general-purpose white glue or double-sided tape (sticky on both sides). After gluing the prints in place, put the pages into a three-ring binder or folder.

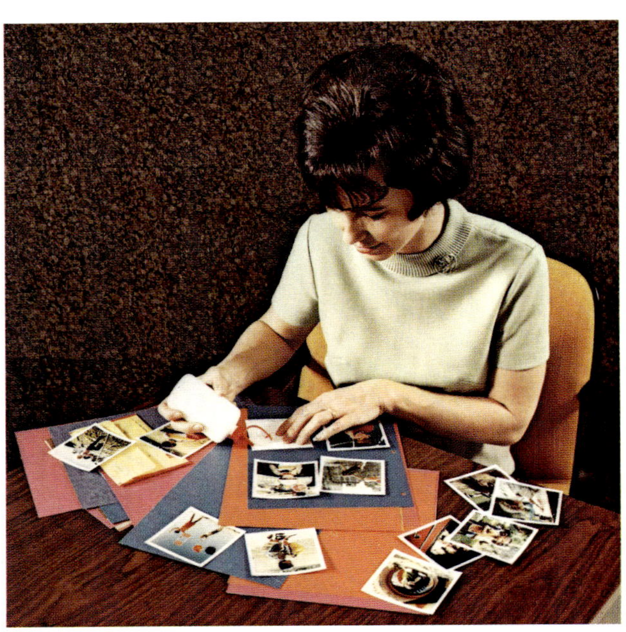

Albums Keep 'Em Together

When you take good snapshots of children, don't keep them hidden in a shoe box in the bottom desk drawer. Show them off! One good way is to keep them in photo albums. Then display your latest albums on an end table or coffee table where everyone can browse through them. Try it. You'll be surprised how many times you hear "What a good idea!" Chances are that your children will be much more cooperative during the next picture-taking occasion, too.

Your album will be most interesting if you organize your pictures in a logical sequence as we've suggested earlier in Part Six. You may even want to add captions to your pictures. To do this, you can buy adhesive-backed paper from stationery stores. After you write or type your captions on the paper, cut them apart, peel off the backing, and stick them into place.

If you don't have a photo album for the pictures of children that you've already taken, now is a good time to start one. To assist you, we've included a section of album pages for you to use in the back of the book. Gather all your loose pictures of the kids together and sort them. Group the best ones into sequences by date or subject and—keeping everything in order—stick them onto the pages.

For ease in mounting most pictures, use a tape, such as Scotch brand double-coated tape, that is sticky on both sides. Just apply a bit of the tape to the back of the print near the corners, turn the print over, and press it into place on the album page.

You can also mount your prints into the album using a cement specially for that purpose, such as Kodak Rapid Mounting Cement, sold by photo dealers. Don't use rubber cement or pastes that contain water or penetrating solvents.

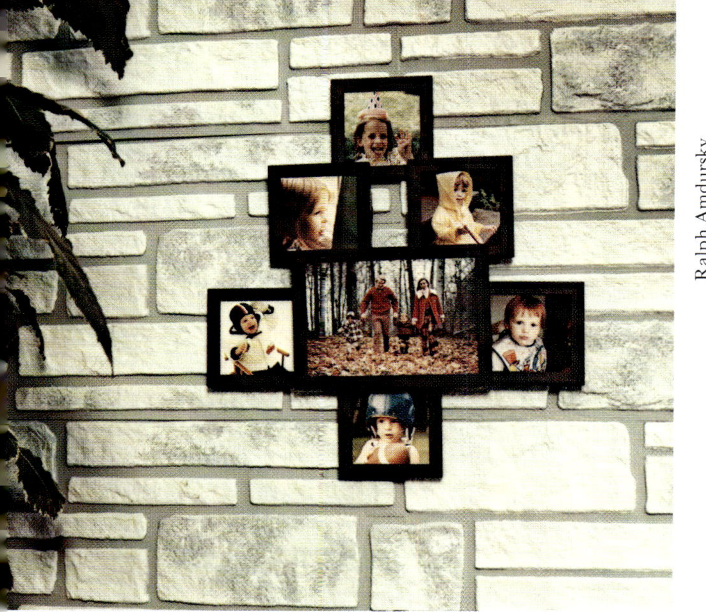

Ralph Amdursky

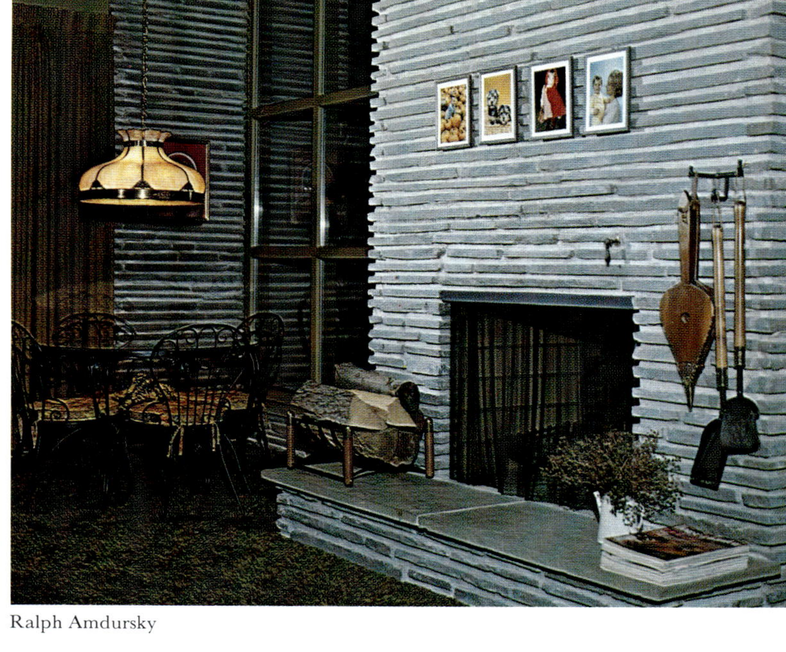

Ralph Amdursky

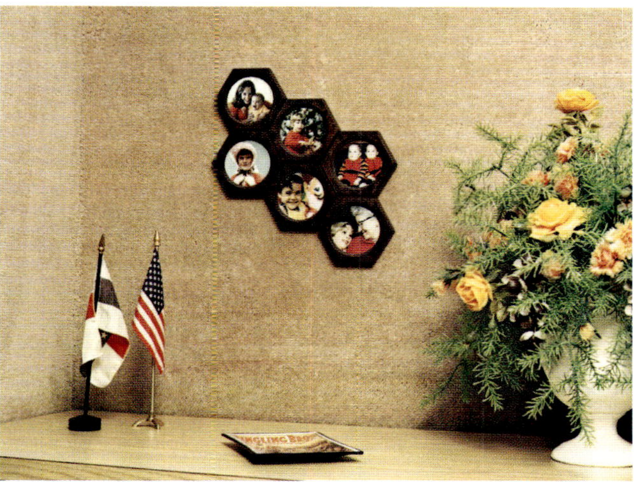

Pictures on the Wall

There are many different and interesting ways to display pictures of children on a wall. Display one large picture, or combine several pictures into an interesting grouping. You can get many ideas for grouping pictures from the photographs of home interiors that you see in magazines.

Pictures usually look most pleasing if they're centered when hung over a piece of furniture such as a sofa or a chair. With a long piece of furniture such as a buffet or stereo, you may want to hang the picture off-center and balance it with a planter or a flower arrangement placed on the other end of the furniture.

Most photographs look best when hung at eye level, although there are some special situations in which a print appears pleasing when hung slightly below eye level. Pictures hung above eye level give the impression that they're not part of the room.

Mounting Pictures

Mounting can enhance the visual effect of a picture. Some pictures look attractive when mounted onto a white mat and put into a frame; others look better if they're flush-mounted and displayed without a frame. Choose a mount that suits your personal taste and keeps the emphasis on the subject of the photo.

Mounting boards are available in a variety of colors at art-supply stores (avoid brightly colored mounts that might steal attention from the subject of your photograph). There are several materials that can be used for attaching prints to mounting boards, such as mounting tissue and various kinds of cement. The mounting material you use should be determined by the type of paper used to make the print. For the latest information on mounting materials and methods based on the paper used for *your* prints, consult your photo dealer.

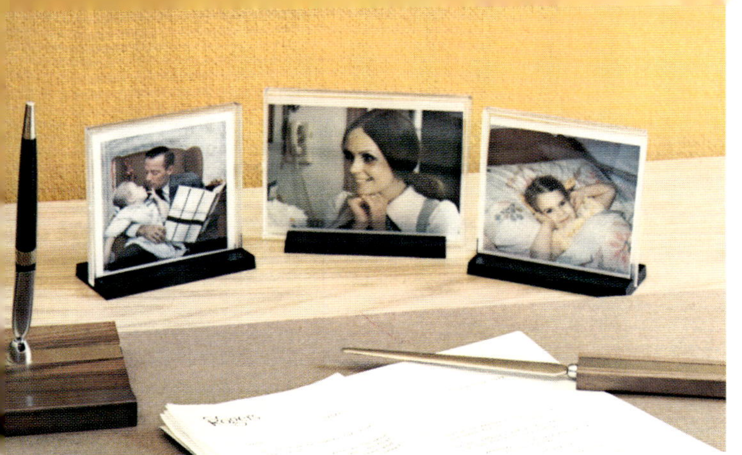

KODAK Print Frames are ideal for displaying snapshots on a desk. You can use photocubes to display your favorite pictures of the little ones on any shelf, tabletop, or counter surface in your home.

If you have your pictures framed, the mounting is usually included in the framing. Many ready-made frames come with mats, and you just slip the picture into place under the mat.

For a simple, modern look, flush-mount your print onto cardboard ⅛ or ¼ inch (1.5 or 3 mm) thick. Cut the print a little larger than the mount and then use a sharp knife, razor blade, or paper cutter to trim off the excess print after mounting. Finish the edges of the mount with a black felt-tipped marker.

Bulletin Boards

One of the easiest ways to display prints of the young ones is to tack them onto a large bulletin board. To keep the display current with fresh pictures of your fast-growing, constantly changing offspring, you simply remove the old snapshots and pin or thumbtack up the new ones. Bulletin boards come in many sizes and you can buy them already framed. If you prefer something more original, try covering a piece of wallboard with colorful burlap or yard goods which match the draperies of your room.

Cork

Insulating cork has become a popular decorating accessory, and it's often used in place of wood paneling. Install a cork wall in the kitchen, den, family room, or work area. You can tack snapshots or enlargements of the kids—either mounted or unmounted—anywhere on a cork wall and change the arrangement often without leaving a mark.

Building-supply stores sell this cork in 12-inch (30 cm) squares with or without adhesive backing; and in 18 x 36-inch (46 x 86 cm) sheets without adhesive. You can cut it with a serrated knife or a fine saw and attach it to the wall with the adhesive usually used for putting down floor tile.

Frame Your Favorites

Frames, like mounts, help separate a picture from its surroundings. Select a frame that adds to the impact of the picture, and avoid frames that draw so much attention to themselves that they detract from the child's image. Frames come in many sizes and styles. A frame can be as simple as four aluminum strips that finish off the edges of your mount—similar to the frames used in some modern-art museums—or it can be as ornate as Victorian furniture with many carved designs. Department stores and some specialty shops usually have a good selection of frames, and many of these stores offer a framing service (for a fee, of course).

If you like to do it yourself, you might prefer to buy an unfinished frame and do your own finishing. You can also buy a framing kit or choose from a variety of wood framing materials available in 8-foot (2.4-meter) lengths from hardware and lumber dealers and custom picture framing shops. This allows you to frame a print in any square or rectangular format.

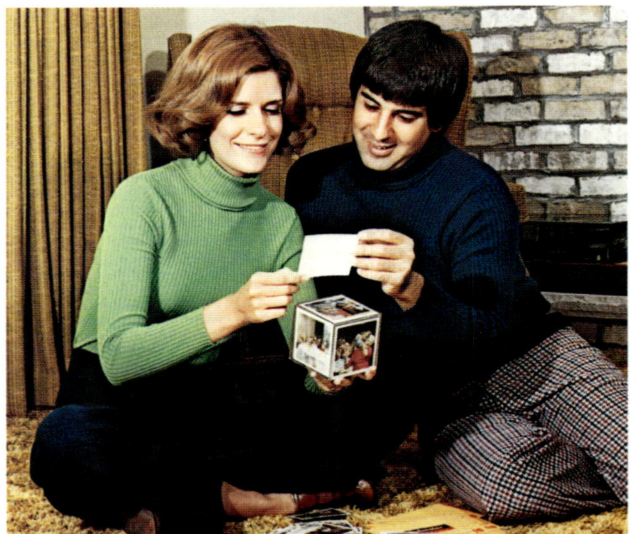

Pictures on Unusual Mounts

An unusual mount can help you group small prints of children and other family members together and can make them draw as much attention as larger pictures. For example, you can mount small prints onto a colorful window shade to create a wall hanging. Or cover a piece of mounting board with colored burlap. You can staple or cement the pictures to the burlap and use a ribbon edging in a contrasting color to finish off the edges of the prints.

For an unusual paperweight, make a cube from a milk carton and cover it with pictures of the kids. Put a rock inside the cube to give it weight, and attach the pictures with double-sided tape. Finish off the edges with yarn held in place with a few dabs of white glue.

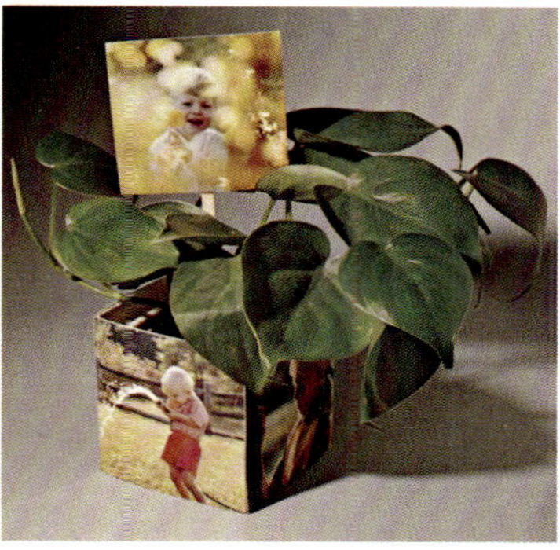

Photo Gardens

Family pictures and plants make a good combination for home decoration. You can tape four snapshots to a plain square planter or cut down a milk carton and make your own planter in the same manner as described for the paperweight above. A picture planter makes a good centerpiece for a table.

You can grow a photo garden by planting pictures! Mount some snapshots on pieces of light cardboard and glue the mounted prints back to back with a flat stick (such as a Popsicle stick) between them. Plant the sticks in a planter along with some house plants and you'll have a photo garden.

Mobiles

Close-ups of children are ideal for mobiles because their images are large even though the prints might be small. You can easily make a mobile by trimming prints to various sizes, mounting them back-to-back on light cardboard, and darkening the edges with a black felt-tipped marker. Use pieces of a wire coat hanger to support the mobile, and suspend the pictures on clear, nylon fishing line. Because the line is clear, the wires and pictures will seem to be floating in air.

From frames to mobiles, there's no end to the ways you can decorate your environment with the pictures you've taken of your children. We hope some of these ideas have inspired you to both take more pictures and display them to good advantage.

Remember—children don't stay children for very long. But pictures—being the eyes of your memory—will help these moments of youth last.

Index

Your Personal Photo Album

THE album pages that follow are not intended to take the place of the many beautiful albums displayed by your photo dealer or many book and department stores. Rather they are included in the hope that they will be useful to you in specific ways. You might well choose to use them as a means of showing your improved skills as you learn to take better and more meaningful photographs of your child. You might make each page a showing of the same basic subject recorded from different angles or using varied techniques. Or you may choose to mount selected prints with an eye to later passing on the book and album to your child as he or she reaches the beginning photographer stage.

To get you started in the right direction, here are a few basic tips for using these album pages:

1. Think about the ways you can use the album and select the one that appeals to you most. Once you've decided, settle upon a logical plan and sequence.

2. Maintaining this order, attach the prints to *every other* album page. Remove alternating blank pages as your album of pictures grows, to correct for the added thickness produced by the bulk of the snapshots. This will make the book close better and not put a strain on the binding.

3. To attach the photos, use tape, like Scotch brand double-coated tape, that is sticky on both sides. Just apply the tape to the back of each snapshot near the corners, turn the print over, and press it into place on the page. Or you can use a cement specially designed for photo albums, such as KODAK Rapid Mounting Cement. Don't use rubber cement or pastes that contain water or penetrating solvents.